KNOW ABOUT YOUR CAR

AA

Produced by the Publications Division of the Automobile Association

Technical Advisers:
   M A I Jacobson, DipAM(Sheff), CEng, FIMechE,
   MSAE(USA), MIProdE, FIMI: AA Chief Engineer
   A W Sims, TEng, (CEI), MIRTE, MBIM, ACI, ARB:
   Manager, AA Technical Services
   Charles Surridge, MSAET, AMIRTE: Head of AA Mechanical
   and Electrical Research

Editors: Roland Weisz (managing), Barry Francis (technical)
   Copy Editors: Chris Webb, David Rowlands
   Index: Neil Davis

Art Editors: David Austin, Neil Roebuck, MA, RCA
   Weekend Workshop design: Michael Preedy, MSIAD
   Creative photographs: Martyn Adelman
   Technical photographs: John Couzins
   Technical illustrations: Industrial Art Studio
   Cartoons: Noel Ford

Contributors:
   M A I Jacobson: (Engine, Transmission, Suspension, Steering, Bodywork, Tyres)
   Charles Surridge: (Heating and Ventilation, Music on the Move, Accessories)
   Peter DeNayer, AA Chief Car Tester: (Second-hand Buying)
   Lawrence Pearce, AA Research Engineer: (Brakes)
   David Rowlands: (Electrics)
   Richard Feast: (Cooling)

Phototypeset, printed and bound by Purnell & Sons Ltd, Paulton, Bristol BS18 5LQ

Published by The Automobile Association, Fanum House, Basingstoke, Hampshire, RG21 2EA

A WORD OF CAUTION

All too often spare-time mechanics do not bother to take safety precautions when working on their vehicles. They think painful cuts and bruises (not to mention serious injury) cannot happen to them – but they do.
SO IT REALLY IS NOT WORTH TAKING CHANCES.
When you are working under the car it should be held up on axle stands on firm, level ground and with the grounded wheels chocked. Never trust the jack alone, or block the car up on house bricks. Drive-up ramps are a useful alternative, except that they cannot be used when working on the wheels and suspension.
And two further points . . . do not smoke when working on or near the fuel system or battery, and keep ties and scarves well away from moving parts.

INTRODUCTION

Know About Your Car explains how
the modern motor car works, how to service it, and
how to diagnose faults and put them right.

The advice in this book comes direct from
the AA's top experts. In each of the 16 sections,
concise practical instructions, together with clear
step-by-step photographs and illustrations,
many in colour, will help to keep
your car in tip-top condition.

And when you know all about your car,
put your new-found knowledge to the test in
Weekend Workshop – 30 pages packed with jobs
designed specifically for the do-it-yourselfer
to tackle from Friday to Sunday evening.

This book takes the mystery out of motor car
engineering. It can save pounds, as well as give the
satisfaction of a job well done.

ENGINE
PAGES 6-35

Know about

engine construction	8-9, 14
four- and two-stroke	10-11
diesel	12
Wankel	13
valve gear	14-15
tappet adjustment	16-17
spark plugs	18-21
fuel system	22-29
lubrication	30-33
fault symptoms	34-35

TRANSMISSION
PAGES 36-65

Know about

gearbox types	38-41
clutch	42-43
lubrication	44-45
clutch adjustment	45-46
hydraulics	47
overdrives	48-49
automatic transmission	50-54, 59
propeller and drive shafts	55-56
constant-velocity joints	57-58
final drive, how it works	60-61
wheel bearings	62-63
fault finding	64-65

COOLING
PAGES 66-85

Know about

air and water cooling	68-69
radiator	70
sealed systems	71
hoses	72-73
flushing, air locks	74-75
pump and thermostat	76-77, 80-81
fans	78-79, 84
anti-freeze	82-83
fault symptoms	85

ELECTRICS
PAGES 86-115

Know about

the battery	88-89
topping up	90
charging	91
ignition	92-93
automatic advance, electronic and ballast resistor ignition	94-95
fitting contacts	96-97
dwell angle and timing	98-100
dynamo and alternator	101-102
drive belt	103-105
generator control	106
starter motors	107-108
instruments	108-110
wipers and washers	111-112
wiring, fuses and horn	112-113
lights	114-115

SUSPENSION
PAGES 116-139

Know about

springs	119-120
dampers	120-122
independent suspension	122
front suspension	123-125
rear suspension	126-129
linked and self-levelling	129-131
servicing	132-135
changing dampers	134-137
fault symptoms	137-139

STEERING
PAGES 140-157

Know about

principles	142-143
columns and wheels	144-145
steering boxes	145-147
checks and lubrication	147-149
power assistance	150-153
steering geometry	154-155
fault finding	156-157

BRAKES
PAGES 158-175

Know about

how brakes work	160-163
renewing disc pads	164-167
adjustment	168
hydraulic systems	168-171
power brakes and servos	172-173
handbrakes	174-175

TYRES
PAGES 176-189

Know about

ply rating	178
cross ply and radials	179
remoulded, tubed and tubeless	180
pressure, markings and tread patterns	182-184
aspect ratio	185
faults	186-188
wheel changing	189

CONTENTS

BODYWORK PAGES 190-209
Know about

how the car is built	192-193
safety and glass	194-195
paintwork	196-199
corrosion	200-202
patching rust holes	202-203
removing dents	204-205
washers and wipers	206-207
adjustments and lubrication	208-209

HEATING AND VENTILATION PAGES 210-221
Know about

heating systems	212-214, 220
controls and performance	215-216
air locks and faults	217-219, 221
air conditioning	221

THE MOT TEST PAGES 222-233
Know about

why	224
where and how much	225
checking lights	226-227
steering	228
suspension	229
brakes	230-231
tyres	231
seat belts, wipers and exhaust	232-233

SECOND-HAND BUYING PAGES 234-243
Know about

what to buy	236-237
where to buy and what to pay	238-239
checking its condition	240-241
how to pay, who to buy from	242-243

ACCESSORIES PAGES 244-259
Know about

what to choose	246-247
making holes	248-249
electrical principles and wiring	250-252
relays	253
rear fog lights	254-255
tow bar electrics	256
reversing polarity	257
fitting an ammeter	258-259

MUSIC ON THE MOVE PAGES 260-269
Know about

what to buy	262
fitting the equipment	263
aerial	264-265
speakers and stereo	266-267
interference and cures	268-269

CURING FAULTS PAGES 270-285

WEEKEND WORKSHOP PAGES 286-315
How to renew:

steady-bar rubbers	288
air filter	291
manifold gasket	292
fuel pump	293, 312
starter motor brushes	294
screenwash motor, headlamp bulb or unit, ignition capacitor, steering rack gaiter	299-302
engine mounting, bolt-on front wing, oil filter element	307-309
steering ball joint	313

How to fit:

electronic ignition	303
child safety seat	310
rear window heater, mudflaps	314-315

How to clean:

crankcase ventilating system	289
mechanical fuel pump	295

How to service, repair or remove:

door trim	290
OHC tappet clearances	291
starter pinion	296, 298
front seat	296-297
solenoid	293
paintwork	304-305

How to cure water leaks 306-307

INDEX PAGES 316-319

Adjust the valves
Remove the rocker cover   16
Adjust: rockers   16
       direct OHC valves   16
       indirect OHC valves   17
Service spark plugs   20-21
Check the carburettor   26
Check the float chamber   26
Adjust a fixed-jet carburettor   26
Adjust a variable-choke carburettor   27
Change engine oil and filter   32
Patch an exhaust hole   33

Despite 100 years of research by scientists and engineers seeking alternative means of motive power, almost all today's cars are powered by the same kind of energy-converting device as the early cars of Gottlieb Daimler and Carl Benz which first ran in the 1880s.
Today, as then, cars are propelled by internal combustion engines. So far no external combustion engine (such as the steam engine) that is compact, economical, safe and reliable has been produced; and the quest for a means of electrical power has turned out vehicles with limited speed and range and little appeal for general personal mobility.

Harnessing the power

The reason the internal combustion engine reigns supreme is because of its versatility, its comparatively low manufacturing costs and the relatively simple way that it converts liquid fuels into usable power. Up to now the fuels suitable for internal combustion engines —hydrocarbons like petrol, diesel and liquified petroleum gas—have been available world wide and are likely to be so for many decades.

Whatever its type, an internal combustion engine is a unit in which the expansion of gas caused by the ignition of a mixture of fuel and air, is harnessed directly to move a piston within a cylinder. By mechanical means the piston is linked to rotate a shaft. As this process determines the engine's design, it is worth looking at the basic components of a car engine before delving into the major variations engineers have played on this theme. The core of the average engine is a block of cast iron or aluminium alloy with cylindrical bores which acts as the rigid frame within which the energy conversion process takes place. A separate, equally rigid, cylinder head is bolted to the block where it seals one end of each cylinder.

In the lower end of the block is the large

chamber which houses the crankshaft, free to rotate in the engine's main bearings. The shaft is a series of crankpins joined by webs; these stiffen the crankshaft balance weights which would otherwise be too flexible. Pistons fitted with hardened metal sealing rings to help prevent the leakage of gas and lubricant, operate in

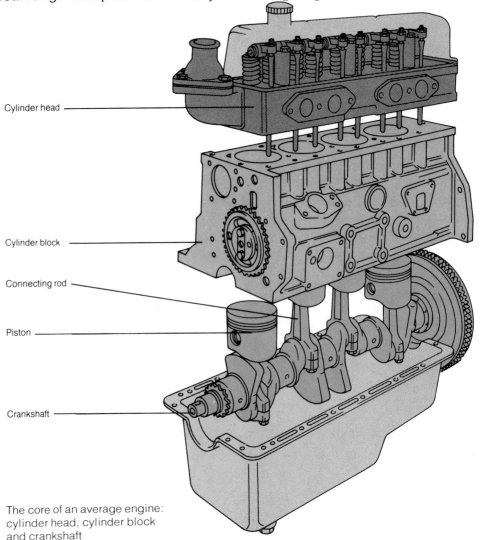

Cylinder head

Cylinder block

Connecting rod

Piston

Crankshaft

The core of an average engine: cylinder head, cylinder block and crankshaft

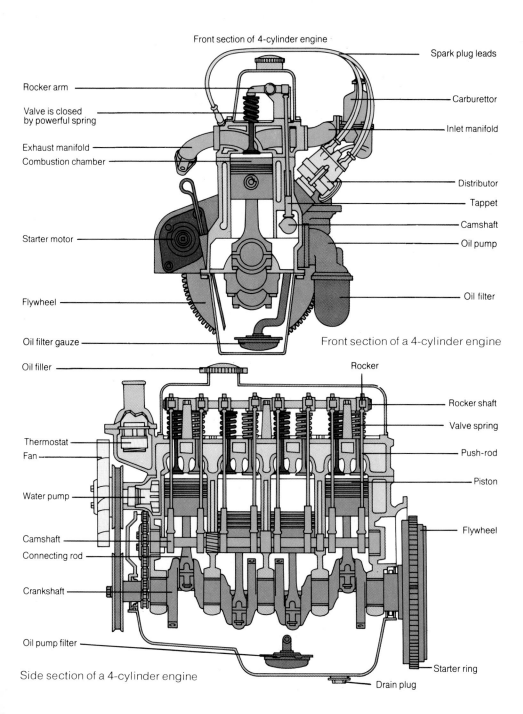

Front section of 4-cylinder engine

Spark plug leads
Rocker arm
Valve is closed by powerful spring
Carburettor
Inlet manifold
Exhaust manifold
Combustion chamber
Distributor
Tappet
Camshaft
Oil pump
Starter motor
Flywheel
Oil filter
Oil filter gauze

Front section of a 4-cylinder engine

Oil filler
Rocker
Rocker shaft
Valve spring
Thermostat
Fan
Push-rod
Piston
Water pump
Flywheel
Camshaft
Connecting rod
Crankshaft
Oil pump filter
Starter ring
Drain plug

Side section of a 4-cylinder engine

the cylinder bores. Each piston is linked by a connecting rod to a crankshaft crankpin.

Sealing the bottom of the crankcase is the deep tray of the sump into which all the engine oil drains after its passage over the moving parts of the engine. The sump acts as a form of heat exchanger. The oil becomes heated by the working of the engine and passes this on to the sump, where air flows over it to cool the oil in circulation. Cast or cut into the block are the tubes and galleries which carry lubricating oil. There is also provision for the efficient circulation of cooling air (by external fins) or water (by an internal jacket) to disperse waste heat.

Like the block, the cylinder head is riddled with holes. It has carefully designed passages to take the flow of fuel/air mixture to the cylinders and extract the exhaust gases. As in the block, galleries are provided for the passage of oil and water. The head face carries the inlet and exhaust valves which admit fuel/air mixture to the cylinders and let out burned gases. On the reverse side are the mountings for the cam or rocker levers which operate the valves.

On these key components, engineers have wrought all the variations in engine design that can be seen in today's cars. Engines can have 2, 3, 4, 5, 6, 8 or 12 cylinders, the volumes of which, added together, give a figure known as the engine's cubic capacity. This can range from as little as 500cc (0.5 litre) to over 7 litres.

Added to this are the variations which can be made in the engine's tuning, flexibility, power output and reliability.

Four-stroke engines

The majority of today's cars are powered by four-stroke engines, so called because there are four phases to each combustion pulse within a single cylinder.

The phases are induction, compression, power and exhaust. During the induction (downward) stroke of the piston a charge of fuel/air mixture is drawn in through the inlet valve(s). The piston, moved by the rotating crankshaft, then moves upward on the compression stroke, compressing the mixture above it, which is then ignited at, or near to, the top of the piston's travel. Forced downward on the power stroke by the expansion of the gases produced by combustion, the piston drives the crankshaft round. At the bottom of the piston travel the gases are spent in force and as the piston travels upward again they are expelled through the exhaust valve. The cycle then starts all over again.

In an engine with several cylinders the sequence of events is staggered from cylinder to cylinder so that the all-important power strokes occur evenly spaced one after the other. The order of the cylinders firing in relation to their position along the crankshaft is also staggered to minimise stress on the shaft and its bearing mountings. On a four-cylinder engine with its cylinders numbered 1 to 4 from the front (or fan) end, the firing order is 1,2,4,3 or 1,3,4,2. There are two revolutions of the crankshaft to every complete four-stroke cycle.

Two-stroke engines

The two-stroke engine is no longer used on cars made for Western markets—mainly because its exhaust gases cannot satisfy the stringent exhaust emission regulations.

The engine does not have any separate valves to admit the mixture and expel burned gases. Instead this is done by the movement of the piston which uncovers ports cut into the cylinder wall. Using the piston as a valve has disadvantages. The main one is that on the induction stroke fuel/air mixture passes through the crankcase, which means that the engine cannot have oil in the sump to lubricate the crankshaft bearings. This lubrication is provided by adding oil to the fuel, which pollutes the exhaust and creates blue smoke.

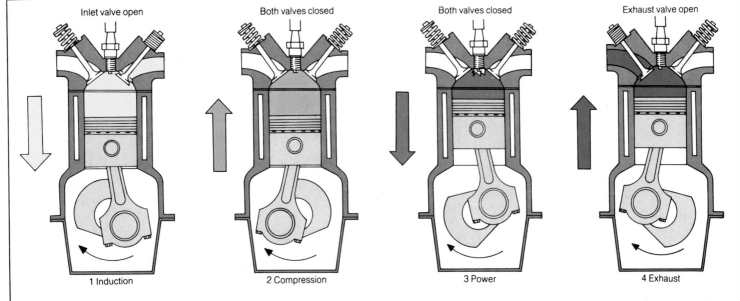

| Inlet valve open | Both valves closed | Both valves closed | Exhaust valve open |

1 Induction | 2 Compression | 3 Power | 4 Exhaust

Induction: fuel/air mixture is drawn into the cylinder through the open inlet valve

Compression: both valves are shut and the rising piston compresses the mixture

Power: both valves are shut, the mixture is ignited and the piston is forced down

Exhaust: the rising piston forces spent gases out past the open exhaust valve

Firing order of the cylinders

There are two revolutions of the crankshaft to every complete four-stroke cycle.

Crankshaft webs give the best balance as well as ensuring that the firing strokes occur regularly. An engine with a firing order of 1, 2, 3, 4 would subject the mountings to considerable stress and vibration. This stress is minimised by a normal firing order of either 1, 2, 4, 3 or 1, 3, 4, 2.

Engines are rubber-mounted in order to reduce the amount of noise and vibration which would otherwise be transmitted throughout the body.

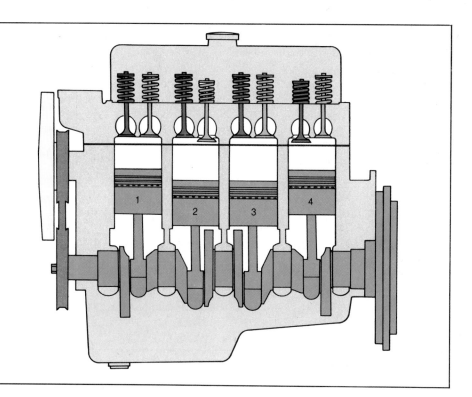

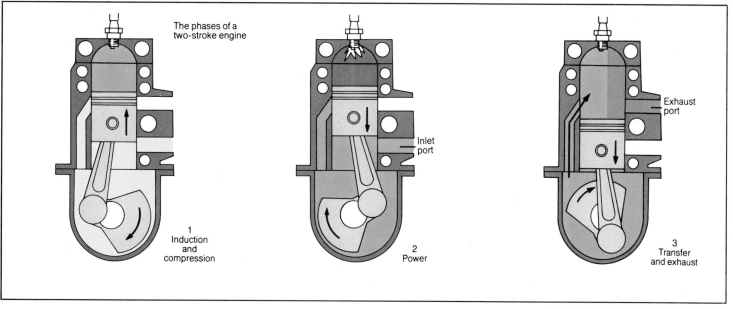

The phases of a two-stroke engine

1 Induction and compression

2 Power

Inlet port

3 Transfer and exhaust

Exhaust port

Diesel engines

Modern car diesel engines operate on the four-stroke principle but the engine design is modified to cope with the higher stresses and the different burning characteristics of diesel fuel.

In a petrol engine the ratio between the whole volume of the cylinder when the piston is at the bottom of its stroke and the volume of the combustion chamber rarely exceeds 9:1. This figure is the engine's compression ratio.

A diesel engine requires a much higher compression ratio because it relies on the heat generated by compression to vaporise and finally ignite this much less volatile fuel. Consequently, diesel engine compression ratios are in the range of 18:1 to 22:1.

Fuel is introduced by an injector. The inlet valve admits air throughout the induction stroke. The injector is supplied by a pump which delivers a quantity appropriate to the demands on the engine and injects it at the correct instant—just before the piston reaches top dead centre on compression. Higher compression plus the much

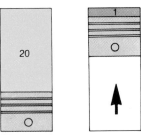

The engine compression ratio

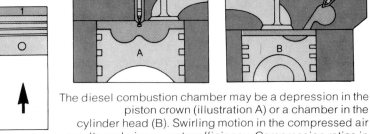

The diesel combustion chamber may be a depression in the piston crown (illustration A) or a chamber in the cylinder head (B). Swirling motion in the compressed air results and gives greater efficiency. Compression ratios in diesels are in the region of 20:1

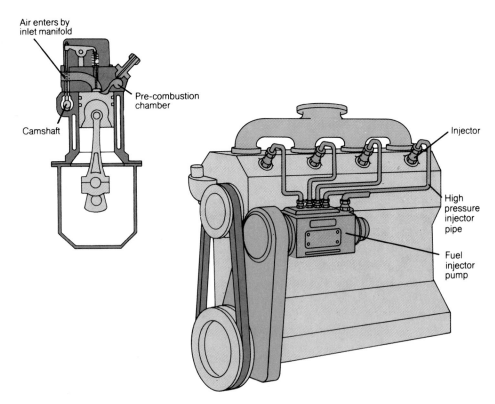

In a typical diesel engine, fuel is introduced into the combustion chamber by an injector, while the inlet valve admits air. The injector is supplied by a high pressure pump which delivers fuel just before the piston reaches top dead centre

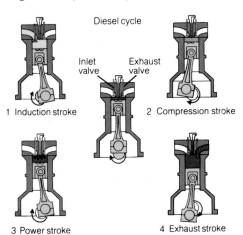

Diesel cycle

Inlet valve   Exhaust valve

1 Induction stroke

2 Compression stroke

3 Power stroke

4 Exhaust stroke

more severe nature of burning diesel fuel put a greater stress on the main engine components and so these have to be made much stronger than in an equivalent-sized petrol engine. Designers also have to pay greater attention to reducing vibration and noise. The result is that both the engines and the cars are more expensive than their petrol-powered counterparts. The benefits are that a diesel engine converts the energy in the fuel with greater efficiency. This means better mpg, longer life and higher mileages between major services.

Wankel engines

A completely new type of four-stroke engine was invented by Felix Wankel and was first used to power cars in the late fifties. The Wankel engine has a 'piston' but it is in the form of a three-sided rotor and its 'cylinder' is a chamber with an outline like a fat figure of eight (technically known as toroidal). The rotor turns eccentrically within the chamber and is geared to a central power-output shaft. Effectively, the shape of the rotor within the chamber forms three combustion spaces, and the rotor movement causes the spaces to vary in volume in the same way as the movement of a piston within a normal cylinder.

The advantages of the Wankel design are compactness, a reduction in moving parts and, as most of the movement is rotary instead of reciprocating, greatly reduced vibration. Its principal disadvantages are high fuel consumption and, until recently, the key parts of the engine, the seals at the rotor tips, have not been sufficiently durable.

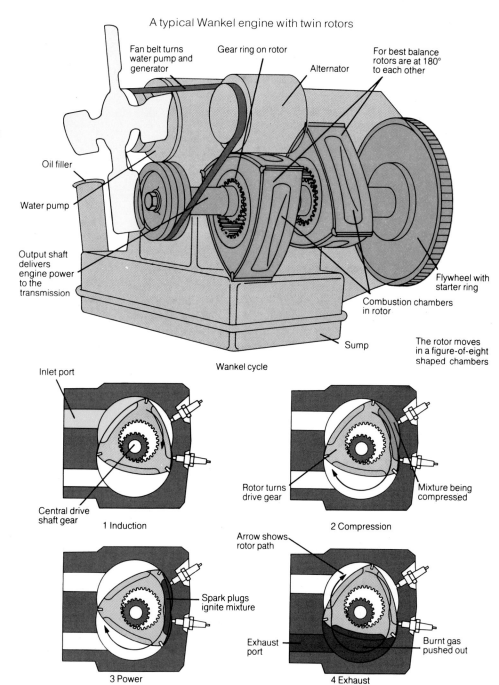

A typical Wankel engine with twin rotors

Fan belt turns water pump and generator

Gear ring on rotor

Alternator

For best balance rotors are at 180° to each other

Oil filler

Water pump

Output shaft delivers engine power to the transmission

Flywheel with starter ring

Combustion chambers in rotor

Sump

The rotor moves in a figure-of-eight shaped chambers

Wankel cycle

Inlet port

Central drive shaft gear

1 Induction

Rotor turns drive gear

Mixture being compressed

2 Compression

Arrow shows rotor path

Spark plugs ignite mixture

3 Power

Exhaust port

Burnt gas pushed out

4 Exhaust

Engine configurations

On multi-cylinder engines, the designer has several options in positioning each cylinder in relation to the others. Most engines have four cylinders alongside each other in a line—known as an in-line engine. Up to six cylinders can be arranged in line, but above six the crankshaft becomes unacceptably long, resulting in torsional vibrations.

The main alternative design for an engine of six or more cylinders is to have a V-shaped block with half the cylinders lined up on one side of the V, and the other half contained in the second bank. In a V6 engine the angle between the two arms of the V is generally 60°, while the angle between the two sets of four cylinders in an eight cylinder V engine (a V8) is usually 90°. This angling improves the mechanical balance of forces acting on the crankshaft. V engines are shorter than in-line engines because it is possible for the connecting rod bearings of two opposite pistons to share a single crank on the crankshaft.

The third main configuration is the flat engine, in which the pistons are horizontally opposed to each side of the crankshaft. This benefits mechanical balance and means that the engine can be made shorter. It is also well suited to air cooling as the two sets of cylinder heads are lower in the car, so it is easy to provide a ducted supply of air.

Valves and valve gear

The combustion cycle is dependent on the synchronised operation of the valve gear. Each valve has a finely ground taper at the edge of its mushroom-shaped head which seats on the

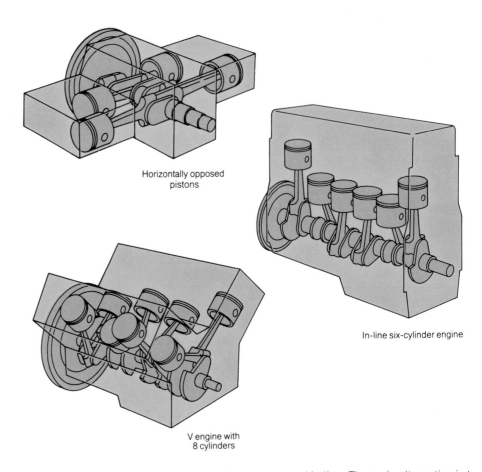

Horizontally opposed pistons

In-line six-cylinder engine

V engine with 8 cylinders

The majority of European engines have cylinders arranged in line. The main alternative is to have the cylinders arranged in a V formation. Less common are engines with horizontally-opposed cylinders, which are well suited to air cooling

similarly tapered edge of each inlet and exhaust port in the cylinder head.

The valve head is on a stem which is pushed and pulled by the valve gear to open and shut each port. The stem slides in a guide which has an oil seal to prevent lubricant entering the cylinder. There are three main ways of positioning and operating valves.

Early engines had side valves in which the ports were cut in the top of the engine block and the valves were upright alongside the appropriate cylinder. The valve stems were operated directly by a cam running in bearings in the block or via pushrods. The cam was rotated by a chain, driven off the crankshaft. Although they are simple to

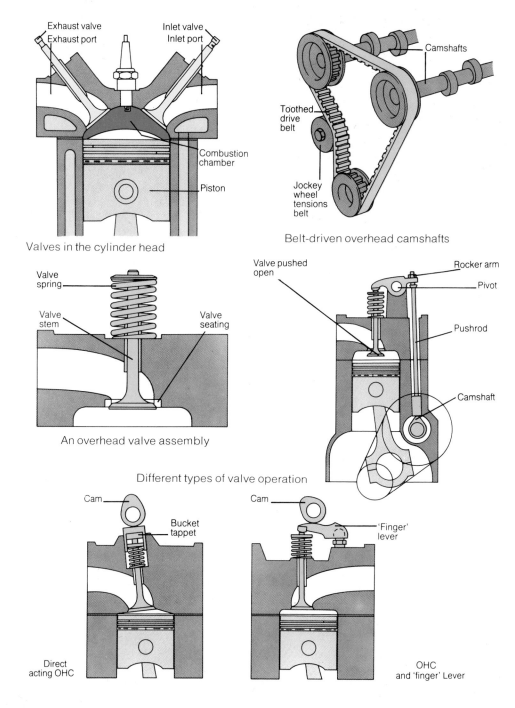

Valves in the cylinder head

Belt-driven overhead camshafts

An overhead valve assembly

Different types of valve operation

make, side-valve engines are not used on current cars. The gas-flow is poor—to get into the combustion chamber the fuel/air mixture must negotiate almost an S-bend. This seriously limits efficiency. Also, valve clearance adjustment can be awkward.

Current engines all have their valves in the cylinder head. They may be operated by a camshaft in the lower half of the engine which transmits the cam's motion through pushrods to rocker arms pivoted in the cylinder head. Or the valve stems may be operated directly (or by rockers or 'fingers') by a camshaft mounted in the cylinder head itself—an overhead camshaft.

Some high-performance engines have twin overhead camshafts, one operating the inlet valves, the other the exhaust valves, which allow the inlet and exhaust valves to face each other at an angle in the combustion chamber—a system that aids gas-flow and engine efficiency.

Camshaft

The camshaft is driven at half crankshaft speed by gears, a chain or a toothed rubber belt. The drive system keeps the valve timing in a constant relationship to the movement of the pistons, and ensures that the exhaust and inlet valves operate at the correct moment in the combustion cycle.

The shape of each cam lobe ensures that each valve stays open for the correct length of time and determines how wide it opens.

To assist gas-flow there is a slight overlap between the opening of the inlet valve and the closing of the exhaust valve at the top of the exhaust stroke.

Valve adjustment

As the engine warms up, the valve-operating gear expands and if it were not for the clearances or gaps designed into the mechanism—which is adjustable to take up wear—the valves could be held partially open all the time. Adjustment involves measuring and, if necessary, altering the gap between the tip of the rocker arm and the valve stem tip or between the valve and the cam lobe. There are many different types of adjustment mechanism—the main ones are shown here.

Removing the rocker cover

Access to the valve gear is by removal of the rocker or camshaft cover (1). Before disturbing it, buy a new gasket and any necessary oil seals so that the cover will make an airtight seal. When refitting it, thoroughly clean off all remains of the old gasket and give the seating faces a light smear of heavy grease before positioning the new gasket. A mis-shapen cork gasket will revert to its correct shape if immersed in water for 30 minutes.

Pushrod and rocker adjustment

Tools required are a ring spanner or a box-spanner (and perhaps a screwdriver to fit the adjuster) and a set of feeler gauges. The car's workshop manual or handbook will indicate the correct clearances for inlet and exhaust valves, and state whether the gaps should be adjusted with the engine hot or cold. For adjustment purposes, a cold engine is one that has been left overnight, while a hot one is at the correct temperature after the car has been driven for about five miles.

Remove rocker cover to expose valve gear

Turning the engine

Each clearance must be checked while the valve is fully closed. To do this it is necessary to turn the engine—use a spanner on the crankshaft pulley nut, if possible.

On pushrod engines it is not obvious when a valve is fully closed, but the valve to be adjusted can be identified if valves are 'paired' on in-line four cylinders, using the 'rule of nine' or similarly, the 'rule of thirteen' on in-line six cylinder power units. With V or horizontally-opposed engines, the manufacturer usually indicates his own pairing system for valve adjustment. To use the 'rule of nine', number the valves 1 to 8 from one end. Rotate the crankshaft until one valve is fully open (with its spring compressed) and subtract the number of this valve from 9; check the valve in the answer. For instance, if valve no. 3 is open, 9-3=6, so the clearance of valve no. 6 should be checked.

Checking the gaps

First identify the inlet and exhaust valves. This is done by checking the position of the manifolds—inlet valves are in line with inlet manifold branches and exhausts align with exhaust manifold pipes.

Turn the engine until the valve to be checked is fully closed. Insert a feeler of the correct thickness into the gap. If it is a firm sliding fit, the gap is correct. But if it fits loosely or cannot be inserted, adjustment is needed.

If the adjuster has a locknut, loosen it with a ring spanner and turn the adjusting screw with a screwdriver (2), clockwise to reduce the clearance or anti-clockwise to increase it. When the gauge is a firm sliding fit, hold the screw with the screwdriver while the locknut is tightened (3). Check that the tightening process has not altered the gap.

Some rockers do not have a locknut. Instead, a screw with a stiff thread is used. Other rockers have a locknut at the centre pivot. On both types the procedure is the same—they are turned anti-clockwise to increase the clearance and clockwise to make it smaller.

Direct-acting overhead camshaft

On engines where the camshaft bears directly on the valves, adjustment is made by changing the thickness of shims above or below the tappets which cover the valve stems. This job needs special equipment and is best left to a garage, but there is nothing to stop the home mechanic from checking the clearances with a feeler gauge to assess if adjustment is needed.

Remove the camshaft cover, identify the inlet and exhaust valves, and turn the

Turn the adjusting screw with a screwdriver

Hold the adjuster and tighten the locknut

Check the gap between 'finger' and valve

Loosen the locknut holding the 'finger'-mounting bolt

engine crankshaft until the camshaft lobe points directly away from the valve. Measure the gap between the heel of the cam and the tappet with the feeler and note the reading. Repeat the operation for the remainder of the valves.

On many overhead camshaft engines, two valve clearances, a maximum and a minimum, are given. Provided the readings fall between these, no adjustment is needed.

Indirect overhead camshaft

Some cars use an overhead camshaft to operate the valves indirectly through 'fingers' or rockers.

Where rockers have an adjuster at the end, adjustment is made in the same way as for a pushrod and rocker system. Make sure that the cam lobe points away from the rocker rubbing-pad when the gap is checked.

Where 'fingers' under the camshaft

operate the valves, one end of each 'finger' pivots on a threaded stud. Check each gap when the cam lobe points away from the 'finger' (4). If adjustment is needed, loosen the locknut at the base of the stud (5). Unscrew the stud (turn it anti-clockwise) to reduce the gap, turn it clockwise to increase it. Tighten the locknut afterwards. Some engines have a stiff bolt adjuster which does not use a locknut.

Igniting the mixture

Just as important to the smooth operation of the combustion cycle as the valve timing, is the correct timing of the ignition spark and its introduction into the combustion chamber.

The timing is performed by the distributor. This is a mechanical component that acts as a dual electrical switch, operating contact-breaker points to activate the ignition coil and routing the high tension electrical energy produced by the coil to the correct spark plug at the right moment in the four-stroke cycle. At the plug the high-tension current jumps the spark gap to ignite the compressed fuel/air mixture.

The way that the electrical spark is produced and distributed is detailed in the chapter on electrics, starting on page 86.

On a four-stroke engine, a spark is needed in each combustion chamber once every two revolutions of the crankshaft. To achieve this, the distributor is driven, like the camshaft, at half engine speed, and it is usual to take the drive for the distributor shaft from the camshaft.

The distributor body is rigidly mounted but has a means to unclamp it so that the body can be turned to make adjustments to the timing.

The spark plug

Though simple in appearance, the spark plugs used in today's cars are sophisticated components ensuring efficient combustion of the mixture and withstanding arduous conditions of rapid pressure and temperature variation in the combustion chamber.

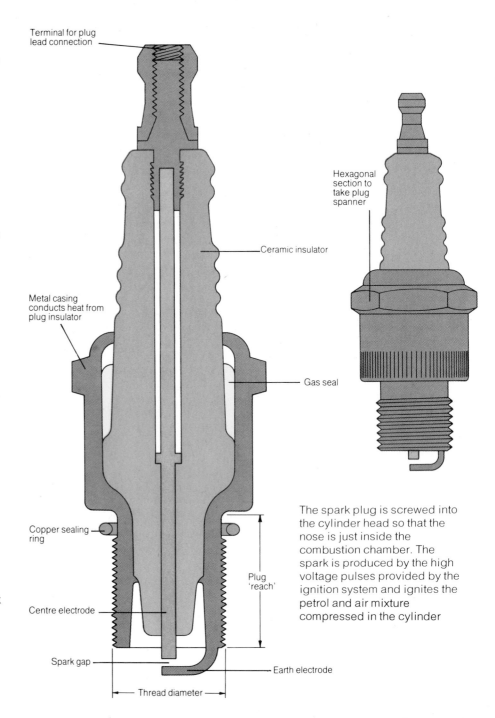

Terminal for plug lead connection

Hexagonal section to take plug spanner

Ceramic insulator

Metal casing conducts heat from plug insulator

Gas seal

Copper sealing ring

Plug 'reach'

Centre electrode

Spark gap

Earth electrode

Thread diameter

The spark plug is screwed into the cylinder head so that the nose is just inside the combustion chamber. The spark is produced by the high voltage pulses provided by the ignition system and ignites the petrol and air mixture compressed in the cylinder

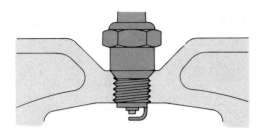

A gasket is not needed for a tapered seat plug since its conical shape provides a very good gas seal

The plug is screwed into the cylinder head so that the nose is just inside the combustion chamber. To prevent the escape of combustion gases, the plug has either a compressible metal gasket or a taper seat in which an angled shoulder on the plug shank mates with a similarly angled recess in the head.

At the tip of the plug are the two electrodes. A side (or earth) electrode is fixed to the plug body, and in the hollow nose a central electrode protrudes from the middle of a ceramic insulator. The gap between the two electrodes is the vital spark gap.

The rest of the plug consists of a ceramic insulator body. Through the insulator is the electrical connection to the centre electrode which terminates in the HT-lead terminal on the plug top. Always fit the manufacturer's recommended type of plug for your car or its strict equivalent in another brand. This is because whatever the outward similarity, plugs differ considerably in performance from type to type.

A major variation is the length of the threaded shank—the 'reach' of the plug—which determines how far the tip projects into the combustion chamber. Another variable is the plug's ability to conduct away waste heat. If the centre electrode is encased in a long, thin ceramic insulator it has poor heat-conduction properties and is specifically designed to run 'hot' so that it burns off any oil or carbon deposited on the tip. This type of plug is used in lower performance, cool-running and two-stroke engines.

A shorter insulator around the centre electrode conducts heat away more quickly. It is designed for high-performance engines in which there is a risk that excess heat could ignite the fuel before the spark. Most cars have plugs designed to cope with conditions between these two extremes.

Because the plug tip is in contact with the burning mixture and is easily removed and replaced in the cylinder head, the visible condition of the electrodes and the colour of the rim are guides to the engine's state of tune.

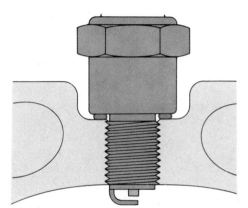

If the cylinder-head section is very deep, a long-reach plug is needed to reach the combustion chamber

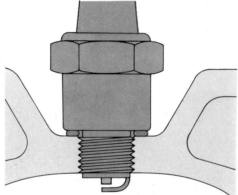

If the cylinder-head section is very thin, a short-reach plug is used to avoid hitting the piston

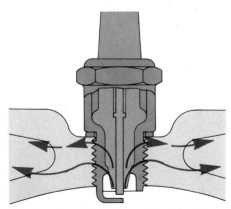

The short insulator of the cold plug allows easy heat loss—suitable for hot-running engines to prevent pre-ignition

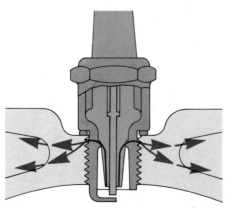

The long insulator of the hot plug allows slow heat loss—suitable for cold-running engines. The heat burns off deposits

Spark plug servicing

Number the HT leads with sticky tape before removing the plug caps (1) and use the box spanner to loosen the plugs. Undo each plug about six turns, and use an old paintbrush (2) to clean out any dirt around it. Fully unscrew the plug and inspect its condition.

Plugs should be discarded after about 10,000 miles but if the two electrode tips are relatively flat they can be re-gapped and the plug re-fitted. Use a special gapping tool (3) to set the distance between the side and centre electrodes according to the figures in your owner's handbook or workshop manual.

Measure the gap with a feeler gauge (4).

Identify each of the spark plug leads and number it with sticky tape

Before removing the plugs, brush away any dirt with an old paint brush

Adjust the side electrode with a special tool

Measure the gap between the electrodes with a feeler gauge

Dark body with light brown electrodes and insulator indicates engine tune is correct

Oil on the plug indicates excessive cylinder bore, valve or ring wear

A sooty plug indicates that the engine is running rich or the choke is in use

A white powdery appearance indicates overheating. Check mixture and timing

When making adjustments, bend only the side electrode. Heavy deposits of carbon can be removed by a garage with a sand-blasting machine, but make sure that the plugs are washed in petrol afterwards to flush away all traces of sand.

Heavily fouled plug has not been given the necessary periodic maintenance

Take care to thread the plug into the hole correctly, especially on alloy heads—it should be possible to turn it by hand. Spark plugs with gaskets should be spanner-tightened a $\frac{1}{4}$ turn past finger tight; those with taper seats are tightened only $\frac{1}{16}$ of a turn past finger

tight. Use a clean cloth to clean and dry the ceramic insulator.

What the plugs can tell you

Spark plugs can provide vital clues if you suspect an engine fault. Remove them and check the colour of the tip that protrudes into the combustion chamber; the main indications are as follows:
Light biscuit-brown colouration (5). Engine is in good tune.
Oily plug top (6). Bore wear or worn or broken piston ring; valve and guide faults. Check first that the correct type of plug is fitted.
Dry sooted-black plug tip (7). Fuel mixture over-rich or choke is in use.
White powdery appearance (8). Fuel mixture too weak (may also have small brown spots on centre insulator due to incorrect timing causing pre-ignition).
Fouled plug (9). Lack of maintenance. For optimum spark plug life ensure that the engine tune—carburettor and ignition timing—is correct.

Carburettors

Most cars use a carburettor to meter the fuel into the air entering the engine. In response to movement of the throttle pedal, a carburettor dispenses fuel through a small jet or orifice (or several jets) into a throated section of the air inlet called a venturi.

The design of the jet and the venturi introduces a mixture of petrol and air into the engine cylinders in droplet and vapour form. The carburettor meters the fuel and air ratio so that it corresponds to the engine's demands. The control of air is by the movement of a throttle butterfly in response to the accelerator pedal. A number of jet orifices meter the petrol supply.

Fixed-jet carburettors

In the fixed-jet carburettor the air flows past a choke butterfly, through the venturi and on past a throttle butterfly into the induction manifold. Petrol is fed by a fuel pump into a float chamber—a device that ensures there is always a constant head of fuel.

From the float chamber, fuel is metered into the discharge points in the airstream through one of at least two jets of differing size. At engine tick-over speed a small idling jet discharges petrol through internal fuel galleries into the air at the throttle butterfly. As the butterfly is opened, a larger main jet feeds fuel through a system which compensates for the pressure and volume of airflow, and then emerges directly into the venturi.

The compensation, designed to weaken the mixture when the induction pressure drops below part-throttle conditions, is usually performed by an emulsion tube.

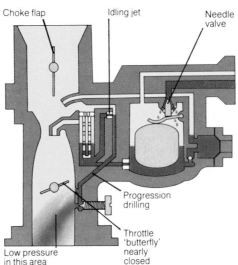

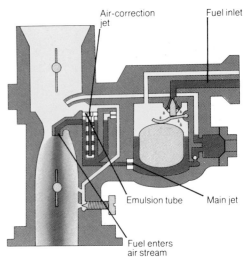

The high vacuum below the throttle valve draws fuel through a separate circuit when the engine is idling

As the vacuum around the main outlet increases, fuel is drawn from it directly into the venturi

This device mixes air with the petrol flowing from the main jet and so reduces the fuel drawn into the venturi. An alternative type has a compensating jet, again to mix air into the fuel.

There are times when it is necessary to enrich the mixture momentarily—particularly immediately after the throttle is fully depressed. Almost instant enrichment is performed by the accelerator pump connected to the throttle linkage, which squirts an extra dose of fuel directly into the venturi.

An extra-rich mixture is also required for starting a cold engine. This is provided by the main jet delivering its full fuel volume when the choke butterfly is closed—this can be by either automatic or manual means.

The closing of the choke flap applies full engine vacuum to the fuel outlet, which draws out the fuel. In order to prevent

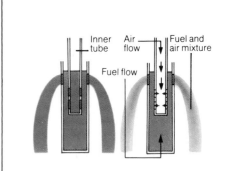

In fixed-jet carburettors, an emulsion tube discharges petrol into the carburettor barrel. Air is drawn through the air correction jet into the cross-drilled inner tube as the engine speeds up and mixes with the petrol, automatically weakening the mixture. Other types have a compensating jet, which again mixes air with fuel

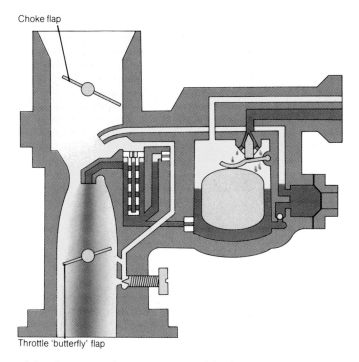

A flap increases the vacuum around the fuel outlet so more fuel is drawn in, providing a rich mixture for cold starts.

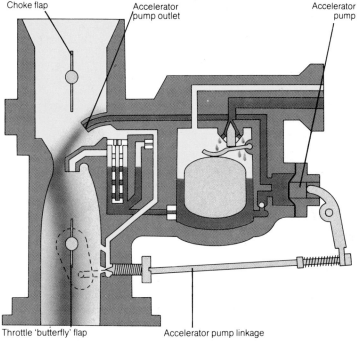

When the throttle is opened quickly, the accelerator pump squirts an enriching shot of fuel down the barrel

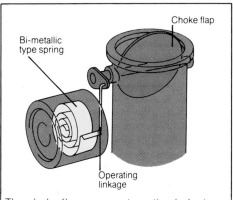

The choke flap on an automatic choke is operated by a temperature-sensitive spring which is expanded by the warming-up of the exhaust or cooling system

over-richness, the choke flap is spring-loaded. This will allow it to open a little to admit air as soon as the engine fires.

Automatic chokes

An automatic system of choke operation is built into many carburettors. Connected to exhaust-warmed air or the water-cooling system, it holds the choke flap closed until the engine reaches a pre-set temperature. The device may be of the diaphragm-type, similar in operation to the thermostat, or it may have a bi-metallic spring which bends as the engine heats up and operates a lever to open the choke flap.

Anti-dieselling valves

For the sake of economy and lower exhaust emissions, modern engines run on very weak fuel/air mixtures. This has the effect of making the engine run hot.

Sometimes, even when the ignition is switched off, a hot engine will run on as the mixture is ignited by compression inside the hot cylinder, in the same way as in a diesel engine. To prevent this from happening, an electric valve is used on some carburettors. It ensures a complete cut-off by admitting extra air at the instant the ignition is switched off. The mixture is then so weak that the engine cannot run.

Variable-choke carburettors

The variable-choke carburettor supplies the ideal mixture for all engine speeds by simultaneously varying the cross-section of the air intake and metering an appropriate quantity of fuel to suit. This is done by a piston which almost blocks the air intake when the engine is at rest, but once the engine is running the piston is lifted against spring pressure by the vacuum in the inlet manifold. Attached to the base of the piston is a tapered needle working in a single jet mounted in the venturi. As the piston rises, admitting more air, the needle is raised with it, leaving a narrower section in the jet and allowing more fuel to flow.

The wider the throttle is opened, the higher the piston rises and the greater the quantity of mixture supplied. To provide progressive enrichment when the throttle is snapped open, an oil-controlled damper prevents the piston from lifting rapidly.

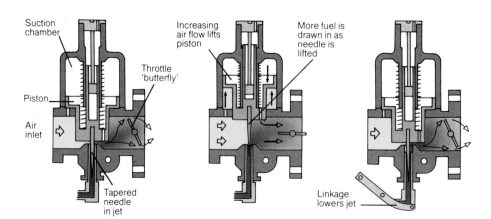

Mixture flow is restricted as the piston falls due to lack of vacuum with the throttle closed

With the throttle open, vacuum lifts the piston, thus providing an increased flow of mixture

Operating the choke lowers the jet so more fuel is drawn into the barrel for cold starting

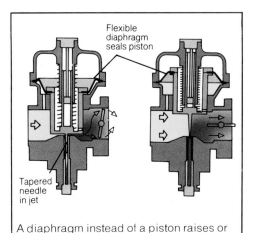

A diaphragm instead of a piston raises or lowers the air valve to adjust air flow in the Zenith-Stromberg carburettor

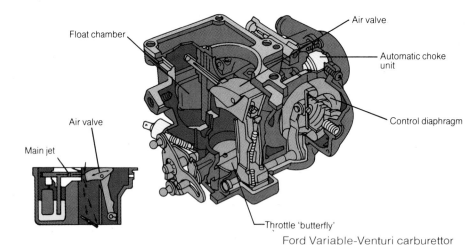

Ford Variable-Venturi carburettor

The slight delay concentrates extra engine vacuum at the jet, drawing in extra fuel. This means that no accelerator pump is needed. Until recently, variable-choke carburettors have been made by Zenith-Stromberg and SU. The main difference between these two carburettors has been the operation of the piston—Zenith uses a flexible diaphragm to raise it, whereas SU uses a close-fitting metal piston operating in a vacuum chamber. Depending on the type of carburettor, cold-starting is allowed for by lowering the jet, which increases the fuel flow by putting it next to a narrower needle section, or by supplying fuel through a separate circuit.

Ford Variable-Venturi (VV) carburettor

A new type of variable-choke carburettor, incorporating many features from fixed-jet designs, made its debut on certain 1980 Ford Cortinas. In this design the size of the venturi is varied by an air valve pivoted on a lever, and controlled by the movement of a large diaphragm subjected to inlet vacuum. A tapered needle is attached to the air valve and meters the fuel.

This VV carburettor has a built-in automatic choke (a small auxiliary carburettor) and a subsidiary idle jet to provide fuel at small throttle openings. This fuel is discharged immediately under the throttle butterfly at high speed, thus aiding dispersal.

Tamper-proof carburettors

Under European exhaust emission laws, all carburettor adjustment points must now be sealed with plugs or caps. This means that all new cars built since about 1977 are equipped with non-adjustable carburettors. If adjustment on these is needed it should be performed by a garage skilled in the particular make of car and having the appropriate exhaust gas-analysing equipment. You can still make DIY adjustments to most cars made prior to 1977, however.

Multiple- and twin-choke carburettors

Engine efficiency improves if the fuel/air mixture is distributed more evenly to the cylinders. Two carburettors feeding two cylinders each, for instance, give better distribution than a single carburettor feeding four cylinders.

Variable-choke carburettors are usually

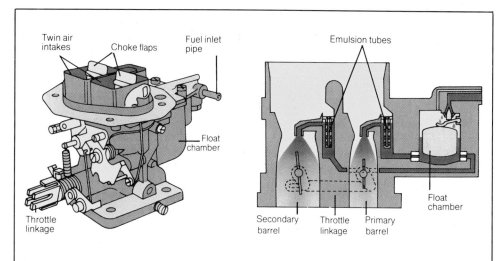

A compound twin-choke carburettor (above left) has linked throttle valves for economy and performance. The secondary barrel comes into operation (above right) only when full power is needed

fitted in pairs, side by side, and coupled by linkages which synchronise throttle and choke operation. Increasing the mixture flow through engines with fixed-jet carburettors is done by fitting a twin-barrelled (or twin-choke) carburettor. Each barrel, fed from a common float chamber, has the appropriate jets and the operating mechanisms of the single-barrel type already described. The barrels may operate in unison, but more usually the barrels are linked so that one opens slightly ahead of the other, or the second choke operates only when the first throttle butterfly is past its half-open stage. This progressive twin-choke action gives the fuel-saving advantages of a single carburettor at small throttle openings, and the performance boost of a twin-choke unit nearer full throttle. A few high-performance engines have multiple twin-choke carburettors.

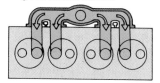

The multi-branched manifold with a single carburettor has a number of sharp bends

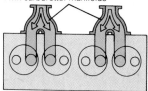

With multiple carburettors, simpler manifolding allows smooth mixture flow

Carburettor checks

For good economy it is essential that all the carburettor linkages operate smoothly. Regular cleaning and light oiling of all the pivots will ensure that problems cannot develop (1). A throttle cable can stick if it is bent or twisted out of the ideal, smoothly curved path or if any part of it becomes kinked. Clean or renew the air filter at recommended intervals (2), and check for water collection or sediment in any fuel filter in the petrol line.

Float chamber checks

Many carburettor faults develop as a result of sediment in the float chamber or blockage of the float chamber needle-valve. The top of the float chamber or the upper section of the carburettor must be removed to gain access to the chamber (3). If this involves disconnecting linkages, make a sketch of their position before dismantling so that they can be refitted correctly.

Check the operation of the needle-valve by sucking the fuel pipe with the valve closed and blocking it with your tongue. The valve should hold a vacuum for 15 seconds. If it does not, it is faulty and should be renewed. Shake the float itself to see if there is any petrol in it. If there is, it is leaking—fit a new one. Clean any sediment from the chamber with a lint-free cloth and tissues.

Adjusting a fixed-jet carburettor

On older cars, two adjusting screws are provided, one for the idle speed and the other for the idling mixture. On carburettors made within the last two or three years the idling mixture screw is

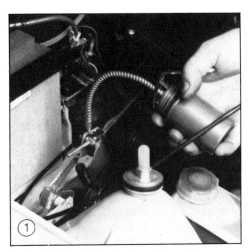

Periodically oil the pivot points on the throttle pedal control linkage and carburettor to help prevent sticking

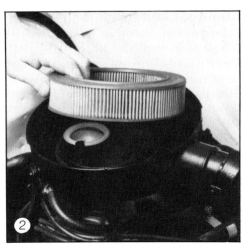

Clean or renew the air filter element at regular intervals, as specified in the car handbook or workshop manual

no longer provided. The hole it once occupied is blanked off (4).

Before making any adjustment, ensure that the spark plugs are clean and correctly gapped, the air filter is in good condition, the valves are properly adjusted and the ignition is correctly set. Warm up the engine and set the throttle-stop screw to give a fast idle of about 1,000rpm (5). Unscrew the mixture screw until the engine begins to run unevenly. From this point, counting the number of turns, rotate the screw clockwise until the engine begins to slow down. Set the screw half way between these points. The engine should now idle with a regular beat. Re-set the throttle-stop screw to the correct idling speed. It may be necessary to make a very small final adjustment to the mixture screw to achieve a completely smooth idle. Twin-choke or compound fixed-jet carburettors can be adjusted in this way

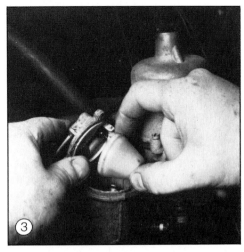

Gain access to the float and needle valve by removing the float chamber or the upper section of the carburettor

if the two chokes share a mixture screw. If there are separate mixture screws take the car to an expert. Do not attempt to make adjustments to tamper-proofed carburettors.

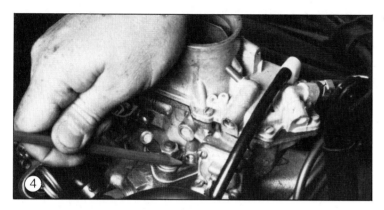

On this type of carburettor the hole once used for the idling mixture-adjusting screw has been blanked off

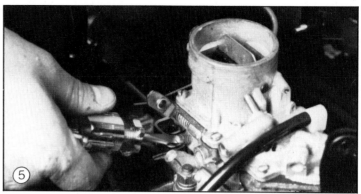

The idle-adjusting (or throttle-stop) screw is usually part of the throttle linkage. Turn it to regulate the tickover speed

With an SU carburettor, screw the mixture-adjusting nut in to weaken the mixture, and out to enrich it

Make a rough check to see if a variable-jet carburettor is adjusted correctly by lifting the piston slightly

Adjusting a variable-choke carburettor

Remove the air cleaner housing and identify the throttle-stop screw, the piston-lifting pin (if fitted) and the jet-adjusting nut or screw which raises or lowers the main jet (6). Check that all other engine adjustments are correct, then warm-up the engine.

With the engine stopped, use a screwdriver to lift the piston to the top of its travel. Allow it to drop back. It should do so smoothly and hit the top of the jet with a distinct click. If it does not, take the car to an expert.

Undo the throttle-stop screw until it just clears the throttle stop—then turn it clockwise $1\frac{1}{2}$ turns and start the engine. Use the piston-lifting pin, or a small screwdriver under the piston itself (7) to lift the piston by $\frac{1}{16}$ in. If the engine speed rises and then settles back immediately to normal, the mixture is correct.

If the engine speed rises and stays high, the mixture is too rich. To weaken it, screw the jet-adjusting nut or screw in a little at a time to raise the jet. Repeat the test. If the engine falters, and possibly stalls, the mixture is too weak. In this case, lower the adjuster to enrich the mixture by unscrewing it, and repeat the test.

After satisfactorily setting the mixture, adjust the throttle-stop screw to normal idle speed.

Ensure that the carburettor dashpot is topped up with engine oil to the level recommended in the handbook.

Air filters

Air entering the carburettor is filtered to remove particles of dirt which would damage the engine. Early cars used a wire mesh coated with oil to trap dirt. This type can be cleaned with paraffin, re-oiled and re-used. Most of today's cars use resin-impregnated, pleated paper filters which must be renewed at the maker's recommended intervals.

Air intake valves

Engine warm-up in cold weather is assisted by taking warm air to the carburettor from near the exhaust system. In summer this is not necessary and most cars have a summer/winter changeover flap which should be re-set annually to take warm or cool air. A later development is to use an automatic valve in the air intake system which picks up heated air during engine warm-up, switching to normal air when operating temperature is reached. The changeover may be made by a temperature-sensitive bi-metallic strip or a wax-type thermostat. The valve regulates the amount of pre-warming of the air to the cylinders—a cool air charge giving greater engine output.

Fuel pumps

As the carburettor is invariably above the level of fuel in the tank, a pump is used to feed fuel to the float chamber. There are mechanical and electric types of fuel pump. Both have a valved pump chamber and use a spring-loaded, synthetic rubber diaphragm to pump the fuel. In the mechanical type the diaphragm is moved by a lever arm worked off the camshaft or crankshaft. An electric fuel pump has a solenoid

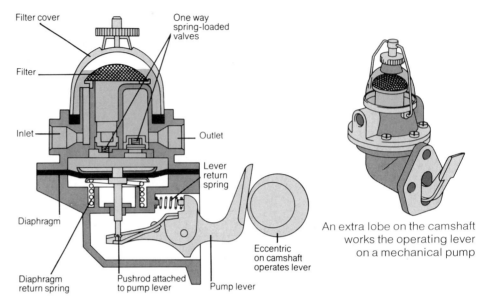

Filter cover
One way spring-loaded valves
Filter
Inlet
Outlet
Lever return spring
Diaphragm
Eccentric on camshaft operates lever
Diaphragm return spring
Pushrod attached to pump lever
Pump lever

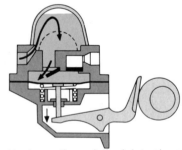

An extra lobe on the camshaft works the operating lever on a mechanical pump

drive coupled to a contact-breaker point. When the ignition is switched on, the solenoid pulls the diaphragm (and draws fuel in), so parting the points. A spring then pushes the diaphragm back to its original position and expels the petrol. The cycle is repeated for as long as the carburettor needs fuel.

Petrol tanks

The fuel tank is of welded steel, and for safety's sake has a recessed filler cap. To prevent a partial vacuum forming as fuel is used, the tank is vented —either through a hole in the filler cap or through vent pipes which rise from the tank into the rear of the boot and then take a U-turn down through the floor pan again and out to free air. Additional pipes may be fitted to aid filling—these run from the tank top into the filler neck to allow foaming fuel to escape. Without a vent, powerful suction could cause the tank to collapse inwards.

Fuel is drawn through the inlet valve as the pump arm pulls the diaphragm down

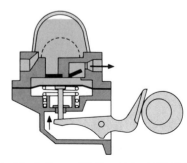

Fuel is delivered to the carburettor as the spring pushes the diaphragm up

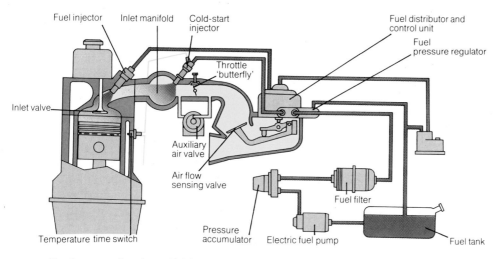

Engine speed and manifold vacuum trigger mechanical fuel injection systems

Labels: Fuel injector, Inlet manifold, Cold-start injector, Fuel distributor and control unit, Fuel pressure regulator, Throttle 'butterfly', Inlet valve, Auxiliary air valve, Air flow sensing valve, Fuel filter, Temperature time switch, Pressure accumulator, Electric fuel pump, Fuel tank

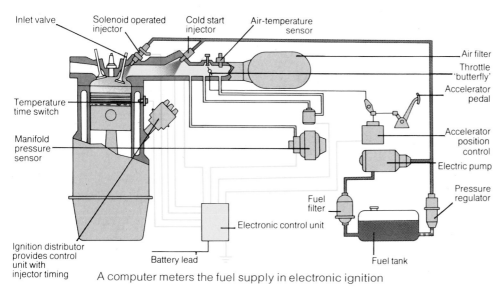

A computer meters the fuel supply in electronic ignition

Labels: Inlet valve, Solenoid operated injector, Cold start injector, Air-temperature sensor, Air filter, Throttle 'butterfly', Accelerator pedal, Accelerator position control, Electric pump, Pressure regulator, Temperature time switch, Manifold pressure sensor, Fuel filter, Ignition distributor provides control unit with injector timing, Battery lead, Electronic control unit, Fuel tank

Fuel pipes and filters

To prevent dirt from reaching the carburettor, a fuel filter is usually fitted. It may be a wire gauze inside the fuel pump or carburettor, although recent cars have a small paper cartridge-type in the fuel line. Fuel lines are mostly of steel tubing but short flexible sections are included to accommodate engine movement. Some carburettors have a fuel-return pipe which feeds any excess fuel, pumped but not required by the carburettor, back to the tank.

Fuel injection offers an alternative to using a carburettor to mix fuel and air and was originally developed for diesel engines. The system may be wholly mechanical or electronically controlled.

Mechanical fuel injection

The heart of this system is a fuel-metering distributor driven at half engine speed. Inside, a rotating cylinder drilled with fuel tubes admits petrol supplied by a pump at up to 100psi (pounds per square inch). The amount of fuel delivered is varied by the position of the accelerator pedal and a lever mechanism which is controlled by the engine's airflow. The injectors are simple, sprung valves which open under the pressure of fuel delivered. For cold-starting there is an additional injector which provides extra fuel until the engine reaches a predetermined temperature.

Electronic fuel injection

In an electronic injection system fuel is delivered at a constant pressure of 25-30psi to solenoid-operated injectors. It is the length of time during which the injector is held open that determines the volume of fuel delivered—a function which is controlled, along with the timing of the spray, by a complex electronic control box.

Sensors which measure air temperature and pressure, throttle depression, engine temperature and ignition timing feed data to the control box. As on the mechanical system, extra fuel for cold starts is provided by a second electrical injector. The major advantage of an electronic system is its instantaneous reaction to any change in demand made on the engine.

Lubrication system

All the engine's moving parts are supplied with oil from a central reservoir or sump—without lubrication they would overheat and break up. High speed and highly stressed components are supplied with oil under pressure from a pump driven by the crankshaft or camshaft. The pressure varies from a modest 15-20psi at idle to 50-60psi when the engine is at speed. The oil's other valuable function is as a coolant of those parts under most stress in areas far from the water jacket.

Engine oil

Modern engine oils are a sophisticated blend of mineral oil with additives. The major additive is a viscosity improver

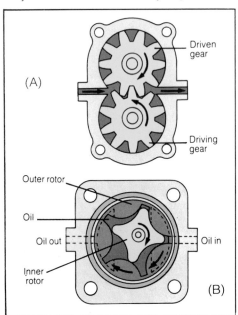

(A)

Driven gear

Driving gear

Outer rotor

Oil

Oil out

Oil in

Inner rotor

(B)

In a gear pump (A), oil is carried by the spaces between gear teeth. Oil is forced out of the rotor-type pump (B) as the space between the rotors decreases

which prevents the oil from becoming too thin at high temperatures while maintaining its 'thinness' in winter conditions.

To prevent combustion by-products such as carbon and water from sludging-up the oil galleries, good quality engine oil now incorporates detergent/dispersant additives which carry these particles, most of which are deposited in the oil filter. A good oil also has a high-pressure additive which prevents 'cracking' of the oil film under the severe conditions which occur on cams and rockers.

These additives are used up or destroyed in lubricating an engine during the normal cycle between oil changes. It is, therefore, essential to change engine oil at the manufacturer's recommended intervals.

Oil pumps

Car engines have one of two main types of oil pump. In the gear-pump, two pinions mesh together inside a sealed housing. Oil drawn from the sump is carried around the housing's periphery between the gear teeth and expelled into the main engine oil galleries as the two wheels mesh. In the second type a star-shaped rotor revolves off-centre in a star-shaped housing. The housing, with one more point to its star than the rotor, also revolves and the result is a series of chambers of expanding and contracting volume which eject oil under pressure.

Oil filters

While oil additives can absorb small particles, when these join together to form larger pieces, they could damage moving parts. These are removed from

the oil, usually by a resin-impregnated paper filter. The filter may be self-contained in a disposable metal cartridge screwed directly to the filter mounting, or the element itself may have to be inserted into a bolt-on filter bowl. In a full-flow filter system all the engine oil passes through the filter before beginning its passage through to the moving parts. In a by-pass system only a proportion of the oil flow from the pump is forced through the filter and this clean oil drains back into the sump.

The oil pressure system

The main parts of the engine requiring pressure lubrication are the bearings of the crankshaft, connecting rods and pistons. Narrow holes are drilled through these so that oil can be force-fed to where it is required. Typically, oil will flow from the pump to the main oil gallery in the block and from there to lubrication points in the crankshaft main bearings. From here it flows through the crankshaft to the big-end bearings of the connecting rods. Having splash-fed the small end bearings, it is finally expelled inside the piston skirt to fall back, lubricating the cylinder walls, into the sump.

Other oilways pass up through the block and cylinder head to the camshaft bearings, through the camshaft and out through the rocker arms. From the top of the cylinder head it may drain down through any pushrod wells to oil the cams and followers or fall through outlets in the head and block direct to the sump.

The minute clearances between the main bearing and the rotating shaft are an integral part of the system, allowing

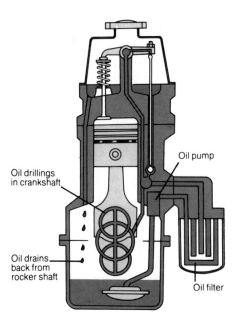

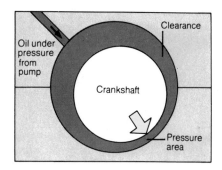

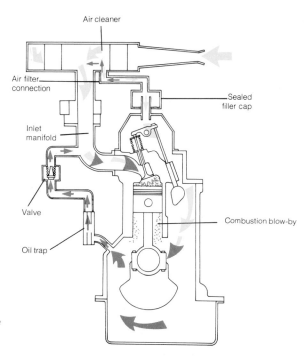

Oil picked up from the sump is forced by the pump through the filter to the engine's oilways. It spills from the various bearings back into the sump

the creation of an oil film or 'wedge' which holds the rotating part out of contact with the stationary surface, so preventing overheating and seizure.

Pressure-relief valves

When oil is cold and difficult to pump, damage can occur to the pump rotors unless the internal pressure is relieved. Pressures may also rise to a critical level at high speeds, so an oil-pressure relief valve is fitted to drain oil from the main pressure system back into the sump at a fixed pressure limit. Another type of valve is fitted in a full-flow filter system. This operates when the filter is clogging or when the oil is cold and difficult to filter. When this happens, oil simply by-passes the filter.

Plain bearings such as used with the crankshaft are provided with oil under pressure. The shaft floats on the oil film —no metal to metal contact occurs

Crankcase ventilation

The escape of exhaust gases past the pistons causes a pressure rise in the crankcase. This gas mixture, laden with oil fumes, was vented to the atmosphere on older engines. Now the crankcase fumes are treated as pollutants, and the manufacturer provides a system— positive crankcase ventilation—which extracts the gases and feeds them into the engine. Usually the fumes are extracted from the rocker cover and pass into the carburettor air intake. A non-return valve in the system prevents an engine backfire causing damage. Fuel/air mixture must not get into the crankcase where it could be a fire risk.

Exhaust system

At the end of each four-stroke cycle a large volume of waste gas is expelled. The gas is very hot and because it leaves the engine at high speed and pressure it also has considerable sound energy. So an exhaust system is provided to cool and quieten the gas without unduly impeding its progress.

Because of combustion gases getting past the pistons, and the pumping action of the engine components, a crankcase breathing system is needed in order to reduce pollution. In the closed system shown, the sump is connected through an oil trap and a one-way valve to the inlet manifold. In addition, the rocker cover is connected to the air cleaner

The system begins at the exhaust manifold, a heat-resistant cast iron 'tree' of tubes bolted on to the exhaust valve side of the cylinder head. The tubes usually join to make a single outlet. From the manifold flange, a wide-bore, mild steel tube carries the gas to a silencer which contains perforated tubes or baffles. These absorb much of the sound energy while allowing the gas to escape.

Engine oil and filter change

Check the engine's sump capacity in your vehicle handbook before starting an oil change and ensure that you have enough of the right grade of lubricant and the correct type of filter.

Warm up the engine so that the oil flows easily. Place a shallow container under the sump drain plug and slowly undo it—some cars require a special square or hexagon key spanner for this job. Never force the drain plug as this can damage the sump and its mountings. Allow the oil to drain out completely (1). Undo the filter housing or cartridge. A stubborn cartridge may have to be removed with a special chain or strap wrench (2). In the very last resort pierce the cartridge with a sharp bar and use this as a lever to unscrew it.

With a new bowl-type element will come a new sealing ring for the filter housing. Remove the old ring from its groove with a compass-point or big needle. Insert the new one with a smear of grease, making sure that it is not twisted. Cartridges have a built-in seal and a

②

①

smear of engine oil is all that is required (3). Put in the new filter and carefully bolt up the housing to the engine. Do not overtighten the fixing bolt. Tighten cartridge types by firm hand pressure only.

Thoroughly clean the sump drain plug and its copper sealing washer and replace it with firm spanner pressure. Refill the sump gradually with fresh oil

The drain plug is usually at the lowest point on the sump. Allow all the oil to drain before re-fitting the plug

If necessary, use a strap wrench to loosen the filter. Time and temperature changes cause it to tighten on to its seat

until the Full mark on the dipstick is reached. Run the engine briefly and check for leaks at the oil filter. Allow the oil to settle and re-check the dipstick. Dispose of old sump oil at a garage or, provided it is in a proper container (the can in which you bought the new oil will do), your local authority may accept the oil for reclamation. It is an offence to pour oil down street or house drains.

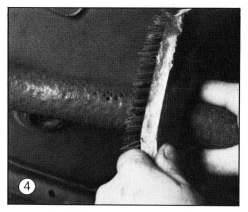

Before applying an exhaust bandage, clean off loose rust from the pipe

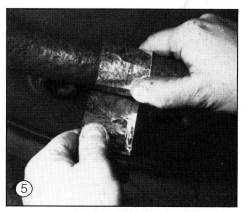

Wrap the damaged area with the metal foil provided in the bandage kit

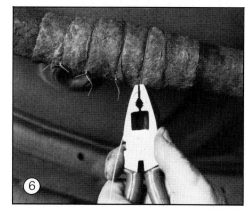

Patching an exhaust hole

A leaking exhaust is not only anti-social and illegal, it can also be lethal. Faulty exhaust systems should be renewed as soon as possible, but a small hole can be repaired with an exhaust bandage kit. This is not intended as a permanent measure, however, and it will be considered acceptable so far as the MOT test is concerned only if the exhaust system is not weakened.

Clean the area to be patched with a wire brush (4). Apply metal foil so that it covers the hole (5), then wind on the

Before fitting a new oil filter element, smear it lightly with engine oil

bandage according to the instructions on the packet. Use pieces of soft iron wire wound round the bandage and with their ends twisted together to hold the repair (6).

Run the engine at tick-over speed for several minutes. This will help to harden the bandage.

Having applied the foil, carefully tape it into position with the heat-resistant bandage. Smooth the bandage into place and secure it with twisted wire

The sight and sound of trouble

Even if a faulty part is buried deep in the engine there will be a number of audible or visual clues that could help you to pin-point the problem. It does not matter that a repair is beyond your capabilities—some knowledge of the problem can often save further damage and expensive repair bills.

Warning lights:

Never ignore the flash of the oil warning light. The problem could be as simple as low oil in the sump, a clogged oil filter or a faulty oil sender. Do not drive on with an oil light glowing. Stop and investigate the cause.

Gauges:

If your car has an oil pressure gauge, memorise the correct readings for various engine conditions from the car's handbook and watch out for abnormal readings. The same applies to the water temperature gauge. Further information on this is given in the chapter on cooling (page 85).

Excessive exhaust smoke:

Blue or blue-black smoke from the exhaust pipe often means that some oil is entering the combustion chambers. This may be from a worn valve guide, a worn piston or a cracked oil-control ring. Inspect the condition of the spark plugs to see if they indicate heavy oiling (see page 21).

Black smoke from the tailpipe (1) suggests that the carburettor may be set too rich—all plug tips will be sooty and so will the inside of the exhaust tailpipe. Check that the choke works correctly and that the air filter is not clogged.

Continuous black exhaust smoke indicates that the engine is too rich. The accelerator pump will produce a burst of black smoke when the throttle pedal is pressed

Oil in water/water in oil:

If the engine stops with a high temperature reading and there are no apparent engine or cooling system water leaks, check for oil in the radiator header tank (take care when removing the radiator cap) or droplets of water on the dipstick. Both conditions can mean a damaged head gasket or a cracked cylinder wall.

Coolant in the exhaust tailpipe when the engine is hot also indicates a blown gasket. If the engine still runs and there appears to be coolant in the reservoir, see if bubbles of exhaust gas rise in the header tank when the engine idles—another clue to a blown gasket.

Fuel supply:

If the engine stops with no overheating symptoms, suspect an ignition fault or fuel starvation. To check the fuel, disconnect the fuel line at the carburettor and insert the end into a container. Have a helper operate the starter and check that fuel flows from the pipe (2). For electric pumps simply turn on the ignition. Take off the tank filler cap (listen for an inrush of air) and re-check pump operation. If fuel now flows, the problem is likely to be a blocked fuel vent—or the wrong type of filler cap. Other fuel supply problems are a blocked filter; blocked pipe; leaking pipe; pump failure and, of course, an empty tank (perhaps you have a faulty fuel gauge). If the fuel supply system is operating, the carburettor jet(s) may be blocked.

Fuel flooding from carburettor:

Partially blocked needle valve in the float chamber or a leaking float.

Using your ears:

Above the normal clatter of an engine it may be difficult to single out a particular sound. A handy stethoscope is a long screwdriver. Hold the blade tip against the engine block or the part to be

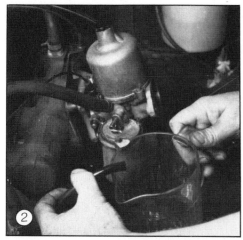

investigated and listen at the handle (3). Be careful of moving parts—remove your tie or scarf before listening.

Light tapping:
Usually worn or out-of-adjustment valve gear—especially if it diminishes or disappears when the engine is warm. If, after adjustment, the noise persists suspect wear in the rockers, the camshaft or in the cam followers.

Check that fuel flows from the pipe

Use a long screwdriver as a stethoscope to help identify obscure engine noises

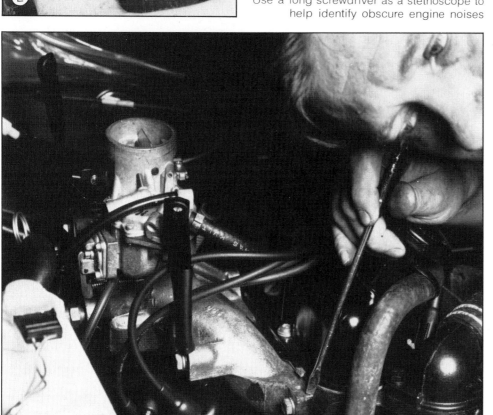

Piston slap:
A light rattle varying with engine speed and load, indicating a worn cylinder bore or a broken piston ring. Some engines suffer from piston slap when cold. It is not detrimental if the noise goes away as the engine warms up and the pistons expand.

Dry rustling sound and/or small popping noise as throttle is opened:
Exhaust leak at manifold flange point—or pin-hole leak in the silencer or front pipe.

Heavy knocking sound or low rumble:
Probably big-end bearings wear (possibly accompanied by low oil pressure).

Rattle at tickover:
Listen with a screwdriver on the timing chain cover—this is often the symptom of a worn chain or a broken or out-of-adjustment tensioner.

Squeals and whines:
Usually a loose fan belt or damaged water pump seals or bearings.

Pinking:
(A dry tinny rattle heard when the engine is under load—when climbing a hill in top gear, for example). The ignition system may need adjustment or you might be using too low a grade of fuel (check the car handbook for specified octane rating).

Continuous running of electric fuel pump (ignition on, engine stationary):
Empty fuel tank, leak in fuel line, ruptured pump diaphragm.

TRANSMISSION

What you can do: Pages

Check mountings and seals 44
Change and top-up gearbox oil 44
Service the clutch 45
Adjust the clutch pedal 45
Adjust clutch clearance 46
Bleed a hydraulic clutch mechanism 47
Service universal joints 58
Check doughnut joints 58
Check constant-velocity joints 58
Top-up an automatic gearbox 59
Clean torque converter grilles 59
Service the differential 62-63
Service wheel bearings 63

The primary purpose of the transmission system is to transmit the power developed by the engine to the car's driving wheels. But it is at least as important to match the engine's power output to the conditions of load and road that the driver encounters.

Under some conditions—such as starting off, when the car's inertia has to be overcome—a great deal of turning effort (torque) is required at the driving wheels. Consequently, the power produced by the engine has, in effect, to be multiplied by lowering the number of revolutions made by the wheels in relation to the number of revolutions made by the crankshaft. This is achieved by the gearbox, which contains a set of gear combinations selected to match the engine's power output to a wide range of motoring conditions.

For a gearchange to be made, the engine must be temporarily disconnected from the transmission system. This is the function of the clutch. Other parts of the transmission cope with transmitting the power to where it is required—at the road wheels—and also allow for the movement of the car's suspension.

The gearbox

A typical four-speed gearbox consists of two sets of gear wheels of various sizes mounted along two main axes. The input and output shafts, separated by a short gap, are on the principal axis. The layshaft is on the second axis, while the reverse idler is on a third.

Gears on the layshaft are fixed, and gears on the output shaft, which are constantly in mesh with the layshaft gears, are connected to it only when in engagement with a dog-clutch splined to the shaft. In direct top-gear drive, the gap between the input and output shafts is bridged by a dog-clutch so that the shafts rotate together.

To provide the required ratios, each gear wheel on the output shaft is locked into mesh with its opposite number on the layshaft. The dog-clutches which bring each gear into engagement are moved by the selector mechanism. This consists of selector forks which operate in response to gear lever movements. There are usually three selector rods—for first and second gears, third and fourth gears, and for the selection of reverse. To provide a guide to the driver, and to ensure that each rod is returned to the neutral position before the next rod is selected, a slotted plate or gate restricts gear lever movements.

Reverse gear is provided by a small idler gear rotating in mesh with a small gear on the layshaft. To engage reverse, either a large gear on the output shaft is moved to mesh with the idler, or the idler gear itself is moved.

Inserting the idler gear between the small layshaft gear and the large output gear reverses the direction of rotation of the output shaft.

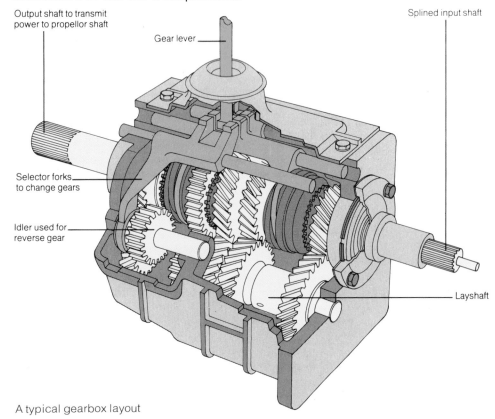

Output shaft to transmit power to propellor shaft

Gear lever

Splined input shaft

Selector forks to change gears

Idler used for reverse gear

Layshaft

A typical gearbox layout

Manual gearboxes

On a front-engined, rear-wheel-drive car, the gearbox is usually sited immediately behind the engine, which puts the gear lever in an almost ideal position close to the driver's seat for direct control. In front-wheel-drive and rear-engined cars this is rarely possible, so a remote-control mechanism is provided to transmit the gear lever movements to the gearbox itself. On a few cars the engine is at the front and, in order to achieve better weight distribution, the gearbox is mounted immediately ahead of the final-drive unit near the rear axle.

All modern manual gearboxes share certain features. They gear down the engine revolutions to increase torque output to cope with differing conditions of engine load. The provision of three forward gear ratios was once thought sufficient, but now the majority of cars have four gears, and five-speed gearboxes are becoming common. The fifth gear may be for economy (an 'overdrive' gear) or to increase the performance of sportier cars.

Synchromesh and baulking mechanisms

In old-fashioned 'crash' gearboxes it was left to the skill (or force) of the driver to get the gears to mesh cleanly and quietly when changing gear.

One technique when changing down was to 'double de-clutch'. In neutral, a blip of the throttle made the gear spin at about the same speed as the output shaft. Double de-clutching is no longer necessary on current gearboxes, which have what is known as a synchromesh mechanism to aid selection of at least three of the gears. The synchromesh is part of the dog-clutch and consists of a conical projection which contacts the gear to be engaged slightly ahead of the dog-clutch teeth. This prior frictional contact spins the gear at the same speed as the dog-clutch teeth, which can then slide into mesh to be locked by a collar. This type of synchromesh is improved still further by the introduction of a baulking ring which will not allow the locking collar to move into complete engagement until all the parts are rotating at exactly the same speed.

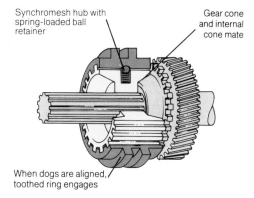

When dogs are aligned, toothed ring engages

A simple synchromesh unit

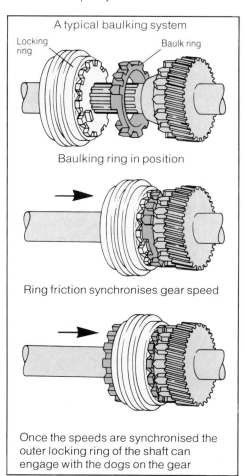

A typical baulking system

Baulking ring in position

Ring friction synchronises gear speed

Once the speeds are synchronised the outer locking ring of the shaft can engage with the dogs on the gear

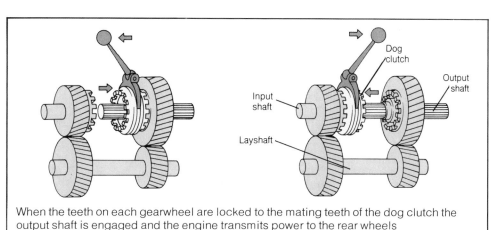

When the teeth on each gearwheel are locked to the mating teeth of the dog clutch the output shaft is engaged and the engine transmits power to the rear wheels

Gear ratios and gear engagement

The gear ratios—in conjunction with the ratio of the final drive and the rolling radius of the driven wheels—are chosen to make the best use of the performance characteristics of the engine and to match the purpose of the vehicle.
For instance, cars with large engines will have higher first-gear ratios than smaller-engined vehicles, as they have more power available for moving off. If the car is designed for high performance, and provides more acceleration, the gears can be designed to be much nearer each other in ratio, and are known as close-ratio.

The ratio of first gear, designed to get the car rolling and move it heavily-laden up steep slopes, is usually between 2.8 and 3.5:1. The figures indicate the number of engine revolutions for one revolution of the output shaft. Second gear (from 1.8-2.1:1) maintains acceleration and is also a hill-climbing gear, while third gear (about 1.4:1) gives additional overtaking acceleration and a low speed (around 20-30mph) crawling capacity as well as the flexibility to deal with minor slopes. Fourth gear is usually 1:1, in which the gearbox output shaft turns at the same speed as the engine.

Direct and indirect-drive gearboxes

In the direct-drive gearbox the output shaft is at the opposite end of the box to the input shaft. To make a more compact gearbox suited to front-wheel-drive and rear-engined car designs it is often more convenient to lower the final-drive assembly between the engine and the gearbox, and have the gear output at the same end of the transmission as the input. This kind of gearbox, in which the output is taken from what would conventionally be the layshaft, is known as indirect drive. Gear selection, however, is conventional.

INDIRECT GEARBOX

Second gear: Power is transmitted from the input to the output shafts. Speed reduction is obtained because the upper gear is smaller than the lower gear

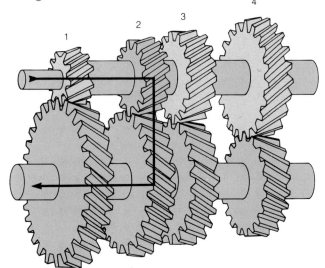

Top gear: The two gears involved here are the same size. No reduction takes place and both input and output shafts turn at the same speed

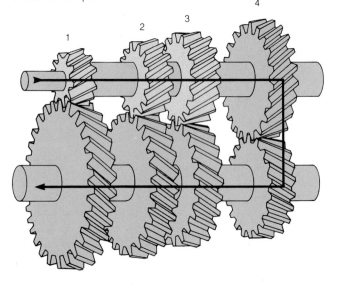

DIRECT GEARBOX

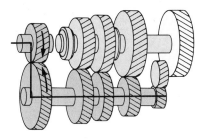

Neutral: A front-engine rear-wheel drive gearbox has a single fixed gear on the input shaft in mesh with the layshaft. The output shaft above has gears that free-wheel. No drive is transmitted

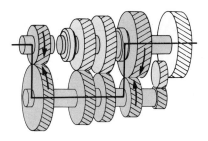

First gear: On the output shaft the large gear is locked by moving the sliding collar against it until the dogs lock on the gearwheel, making it rotate with the shaft, turning it slowly

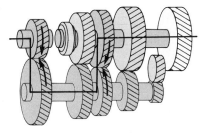

Second gear: The collar disengages from the first gear and slides along the output shaft until its dogs lock the second gear to the shaft. The output shaft turns a little faster

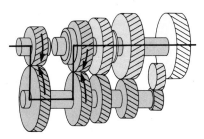

Third gear: The second gear collar disengages and the dog clutch on the leading collar engages with the third gear. Two gears cannot be selected at once due to a selector mechanism with interlock

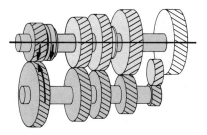

Top gear: The leading collar slides forward, joining the input and output shafts and providing a straight-through drive from the engine to the propeller shaft. No reduction takes place

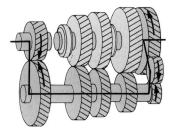

Reverse: An idler engaged between the layshaft and the reverse gear reverses the direction of the output shaft. The gear ratio is similar to that provided in first gear

The clutch

The clutch is a means of uncoupling the engine from the transmission during gearchanges. Fitted between the flywheel and the gearbox, it occupies a large chamber known as the bell-housing. It is a friction device and the principal component, the driven (or centre) plate, wears with use and can need adjustment during its normal life of about 40,000 miles.

How it works

The driven plate is a disc to which pads of a friction material (similar to that used in brake linings) are riveted on both sides. At its centre the plate has a splined collar, matching the splines on the input shaft of the gearbox to which it is mated. With the clutch pedal released, the friction-lined plate is clamped by spring pressure between a machined face on the engine flywheel and a similar face on the clutch pressure plate. The flywheel is bolted to the crankshaft and the pressure plate is held within the clutch assembly which is, in turn, bolted to the flywheel. When the clutch is engaged, the whole set of components revolves at engine speed as the friction material is gripped between the flywheel and the pressure plate. In this way, engine rotation is transmitted direct to the gearbox input shaft.

Depressing the clutch pedal—connected by a hydraulic or cable mechanism to the clutch—moves a release (or thrust) bearing towards the clutch assembly. This, by lever or diaphragm action, moves the pressure plate away from the driven plate, thereby breaking frictional contact.

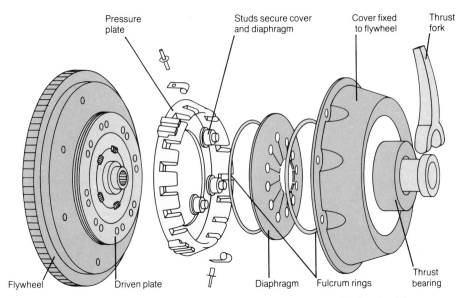

A diaphragm spring clamps the friction-lined driven plate between the flywheel face and the pressure plate in the clutch unit

As the driven plate is free to move along the splines of the driven shaft it comes out of contact with the flywheel too, and the drive is completely disengaged.

Diaphragm clutch

In a diaphragm clutch the spring pressure to hold together the three elements of the clutch is provided by a steel sheet cut with radial lines which, in effect, make it a ring of spring fingers. This diaphragm is also slightly conical and is clamped between two fulcrum rings and held inside the pressure plate and clutch housing. When the clutch is depressed, the release bearing presses on the tips of the spring fingers at the diaphragm centre. This causes the edge of the diaphragm to move in the opposite direction and release its hold on the pressure plate and break the frictional contact.

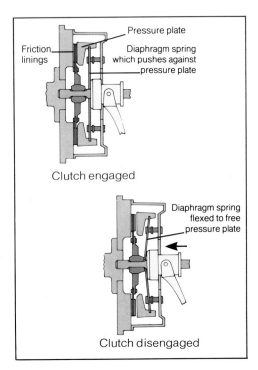

Clutch engaged

Clutch disengaged

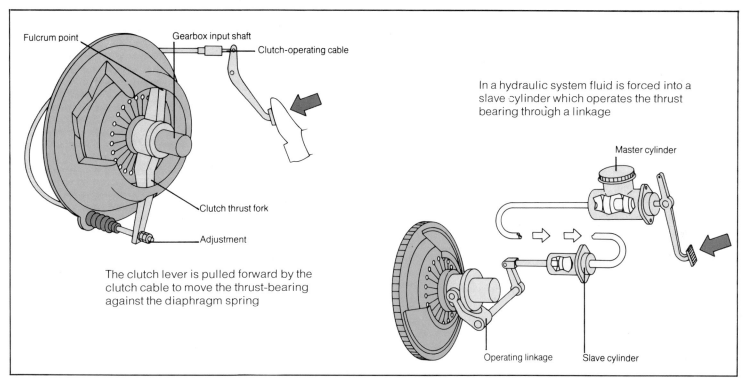

Fulcrum point

Gearbox input shaft

Clutch-operating cable

Clutch thrust fork

Adjustment

In a hydraulic system fluid is forced into a slave cylinder which operates the thrust bearing through a linkage

Master cylinder

The clutch lever is pulled forward by the clutch cable to move the thrust-bearing against the diaphragm spring

Operating linkage

Slave cylinder

Coil-spring clutch

Coil springs can also be used to provide the pressure to lock the clutch elements together. In this type a number of pivoting levers in the pressure plate assembly are operated by the release, or thrust, bearing when the clutch pedal is depressed. Movement of the levers draws the pressure plate away from the driven plate, thereby disengaging the gearbox from the engine.

Clutch design variations

Much research has gone into the composition of the friction materials on the driven plate to improve its resistance to heat and wear. The clutch centre plate is made up of a number of components to allow a slight rotational movement about the centre splined box. This movement is controlled by a set of small coil springs mounted in the plate. The springiness softens the vibration and harshness that would be experienced as the clutch begins to grip, protecting the gearbox from shock loading.

Clutch-operating mechanisms

The spring pressure holding together the clutch components is quite substantial, so it is usual to provide some mechanical or hydraulic assistance to reduce the effort required when operating the clutch to change gear or pull away from rest. The linkage between the pedal and the clutch must also be flexible enough to allow for engine and transmission movement. Three common types of operating mechanism have been developed. Cable or rod operation are the simplest. Assistance is provided by the leverage of the pedal and the clutch thrust fork.

The operation can also be performed hydraulically. In this design the clutch pedal operates the piston of a master cylinder. A flexible hydraulic pipe connects it to a slave cylinder operating the clutch fork. The assistance is provided by making the size of the slave cylinder piston different from that of the master cylinder. The smaller the slave piston diameter is in relation to the master cylinder piston the greater the hydraulic assistance.

Gearbox care

Servicing the gearbox is restricted to checks for oil leaks and mounting security, and, if specified by the manufacturer's schedule, top-ups and refills of lubricant.

Checking mountings and seals

Although the gearbox is rigidly mounted to the engine, at some point on the gearbox casing there will be a rubber or other flexible mounting to take up engine movement.

Rubber mountings can become softened by leaking oil and may also perish. They should be inspected closely with a torch to ensure that they are in good condition. Have a garage renew squashy or split mountings. Inspect the tightness of the bolts mounting the gearbox (or clutch bell-housing) to the engine and look for weeps of lubricant around any gaskets and joints between gearbox casing components. Drips from the clutch bell-housing most likely indicate failure of the crankshaft rear oil seal—or leakage of gearbox lubricant. Curing these leaks is a garage job.

Checking and topping up gearbox lubricant

Carefully check the type of lubricant specified for your gearbox in the owner's manual.

Very few gearboxes on modern cars have oil drain plugs, but unless it is an integral part of the engine (as on Leyland transverse-engined cars) the gearbox will have its own top-up plug. It can be of the level type which needs filling only to the level of the top-up hole, or the plug may have a dipstick attached to it to show the correct lubricant level.

Raise the car on axle-stands or drive it over an inspection pit to clean and remove the oil level plug (1). On some cars it is possible to insert a funnel in the filler hole and pour fresh oil in, but most gearboxes must be filled with an oil syringe type of oil-can or a plastic squeeze bottle dispenser (2). If a gearbox with a level-type filler plug is overfilled, let the surplus drain out before refitting the plug (3). The car should, of course, be level while this work is being carried out.

Most gearboxes should be topped up to the correct level at recommended intervals with a syringe-type dispenser of oil or a plastic squeeze bottle

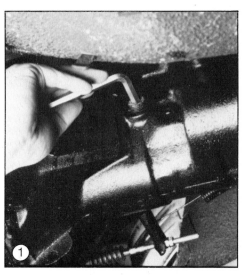

Locate the oil-level plug and remove it with a spanner or an Allen key

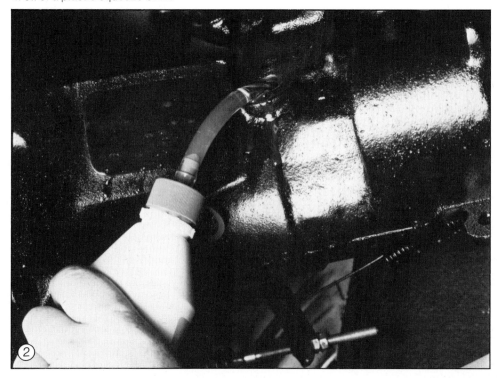

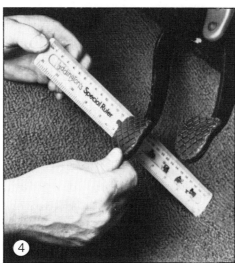

Drain surplus oil before refitting the plug

Measure pedal travel with a ruler

Tighten pedal free play with the adjuster nut

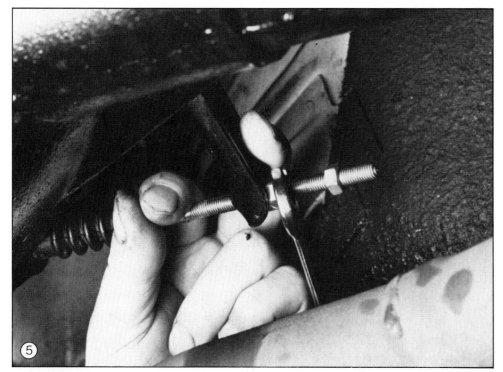

Clutch servicing

Under the car, oil drips from the clutch bell-housing can point to a crankshaft oil seal leak and may result in a slipping clutch (for fault finding, see pages 64-65).

Measure the clutch pedal free travel by holding a ruler at right-angles to the pedal swing. Make sure the ruler is firm against the floor-pan or bulkhead, and press the pedal by hand, noting the travel of the pedal from rest to the point at which resistance to movement can be felt (4).

Check this measurement against that given in the owners' handbook or workshop manual.

Pedal adjustment

On cable- or rod-operated clutch mechanisms an adjuster is usually provided to vary the clutch pedal free travel to allow for cable stretch and wear in the mechanism.

The adjuster will usually be at the cable or rod linkage's attachment to the clutch fork on the side of the bell-housing under the car (5).

When making any adjustment the car must be securely positioned on drive-up ramps, supported by axle stands, or over an inspection pit.

Occasionally the adjuster, often a combination of a nut and locknut on a threaded adjuster screw, is at the pedal end of the linkage. Identify the adjuster and loosen the locknut. Tightening the adjuster nut will reduce the clutch pedal travel and loosening it will lengthen the travel. After adjustment, carefully check the pedal travel with a ruler.

When it is correct, tighten the locknut on to the adjuster nut.

Clutch throw-out stop clearance (BL models)

Hydraulically-operated clutches on BL transverse-engined cars have an adjustment for clutch wear called the throw-out stop. This is a short adjuster screw on the clutch housing, with its top in contact with the clutch-operating lever.

To check the clearance between the lever and the stop (which should be 0.020in), release the return spring from the top of the arm. Pull back the arm by hand (1) and measure the clearance between arm and stop with a feeler gauge (2). If adjustment is required, loosen the locknut and turn the adjuster screw until the correct clearance is obtained. Retighten the locknut.

Release the return spring from the top of the arm and pull the arm back by hand

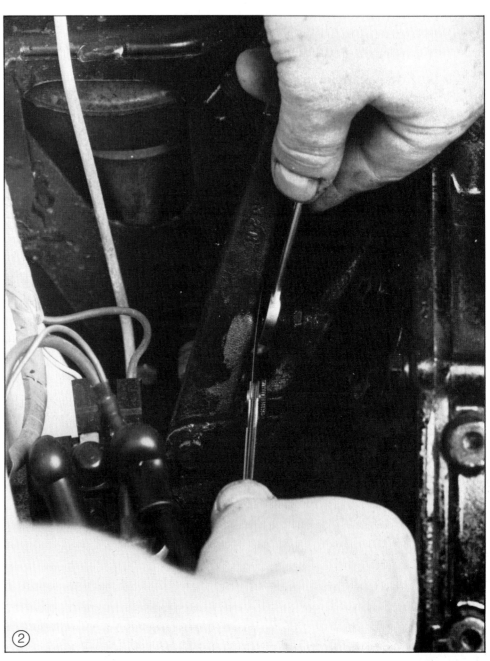

Measure the clearance between the arm and the stop with a feeler gauge. To adjust, loosen the locknut and turn the screw to obtain the right gap

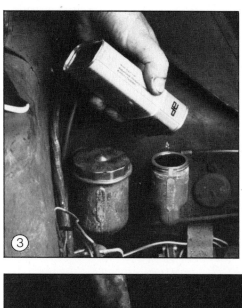

Top up the clutch reservoir fully with the correct fluid

Having attached the tube, slacken the bleed screw. Place the free end of the tube into the fluid and ask a helper to depress the clutch pedal slowly

Servicing and bleeding a hydraulic clutch mechanism

The clutch hydraulic fluid reservoir is often next to the brake master cylinder reservoir on the engine compartment bulkhead. The fluid level should be checked regularly and topped up if necessary with the specified grade of hydraulic fluid. After 18 months or so (at the same interval as the brake fluid) the hydraulic fluid should be completely replaced. Use the following procedure for fluid replacement and also as a step to cure a spongy pedal or loss of clutch action (see fault-finding, page 64). Have ready a supply of brake hydraulic fluid (the universal types are suitable for both brake- and clutch-operating systems), locate the bleed screw on the slave cylinder and clean it. You will also need a length of bleed tubing and a helper. Pour about 1 in of the fluid into a small glass jar and fully top-up the clutch reservoir (3). Connect the tube to the bleed screw and, using a ring spanner, loosen the screw slightly.

Put the free end of the tube under the surface of the fluid in the jar and, while a helper slowly depresses the clutch pedal, undo the screw until fluid flows (4). Before your helper releases the pedal, tighten the bleed screw—a repeat stroke can then be made.

Bleeding is completed when all small air bubbles cease coming from the tube. In the case of complete replacement of fluid, top-up the reservoir between each pedal stroke and stop when clean fluid is flowing from the bleed tube. Finally, tighten the bleed screw while the pedal is held down. Do not drip fluid on the car as it will damage the paintwork.

Overdrives

In designing a car for economy, many manufacturers arrange for the transmission to give a higher top gear than the normal 1:1—such as 0.83:1. This is a condition called overdrive. There are two ways to achieve overdrive—a fifth gear added to the normal four-speed gearbox, or a subsidiary overdrive unit. Not all five-speed gearboxes provide overdrive; it is an economy gear only if the top or fifth gear provides a lower ratio than 1:1. Whereas in a 5-speed gearbox de-clutching is necessary to change up or down, in an overdrive it is possible to change gear without de-clutching. It employs an epicyclic gear arrangement. An overdrive unit is a small subsidiary gearbox fitted between the main gearbox and propeller shaft Most overdrives consist of a clutch mechanism and a sun and planet gear train. In direct drive the clutch locks together the sun and planet gears so that motion is transmitted direct to the output shaft. In overdrive the sun gear is locked by the clutch and drive is transmitted at a slightly higher speed than that of the input shaft by the rotation of the planet gears. Overdrive may be electrically controlled by a switch on the steering column or gear lever, or hydraulically operated. It usually operates on top and third gears.

Four-wheel-drive

Four-wheel-drive greatly increases the capability of cars to travel over poor surfaces which would not offer sufficient grip for forward propulsion with conventional two-wheel-drive. If one wheel begins to spin, forward motion may be lost.

To drive all four wheels of a vehicle requires two propeller shafts and two drive axles. The usual arrangement is that power is taken from the rear of the normal gearbox into a splitting or transfer gearbox (this may have a simple dog-clutch for selection of two- or four-wheel operation) which feeds it to the front and rear differentials. More refined four-wheel-drive systems (the range Rover's, for instance) have an additional front to rear differential. Many four-wheel-drive vehicles have limited-slip or locking differentials (see pages 60-61) to ensure mobility under the most severe conditions.

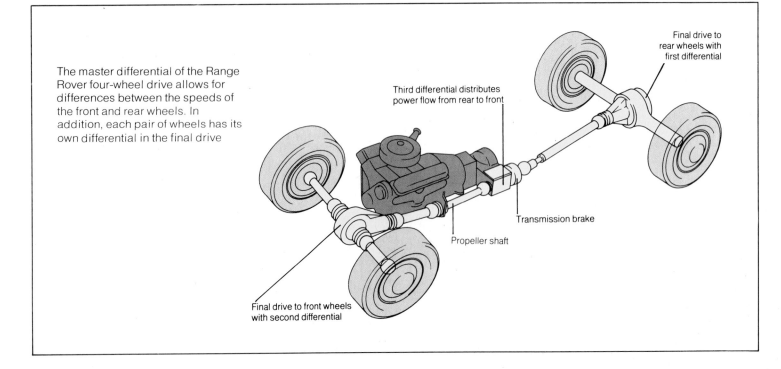

The master differential of the Range Rover four-wheel drive allows for differences between the speeds of the front and rear wheels. In addition, each pair of wheels has its own differential in the final drive

Final drive to rear wheels with first differential

Third differential distributes power flow from rear to front

Transmission brake

Propeller shaft

Final drive to front wheels with second differential

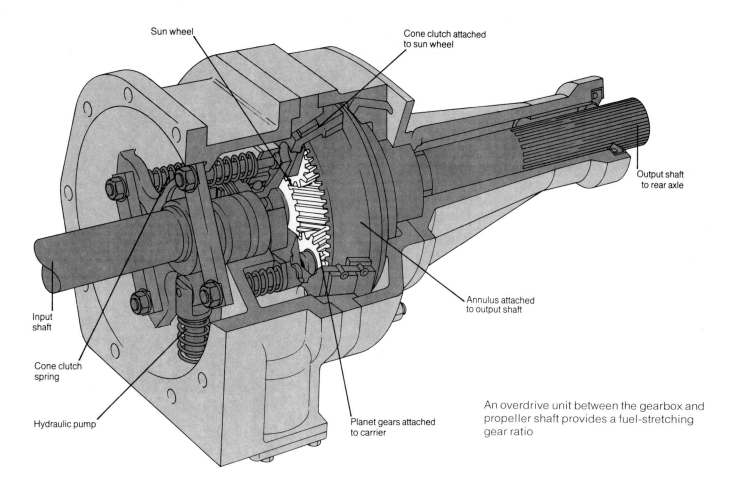

Sun wheel

Cone clutch attached
to sun wheel

Output shaft
to rear axle

Annulus attached
to output shaft

Input
shaft

Cone clutch
spring

Hydraulic pump

Planet gears attached
to carrier

An overdrive unit between the gearbox and
propeller shaft provides a fuel-stretching
gear ratio

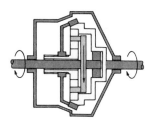

Direct drive: cone clutch
attached to sun wheel grips
annulus. Planet carrier on
input shaft drives unit and
output shaft at same speed

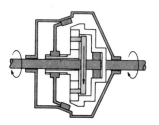

Overdrive: cone clutch grips
casing and stops sun wheel.
Input shaft rotates planet
carrier to drive annulus and
turn output shaft faster

Automatic transmission

Many cars are available with completely automatic transmission, in which there is no clutch and the gearbox selects for itself one of three or four ratios according to road speed and throttle opening.

Two-pedal driving is relaxing, but the penalty for the convenience is usually an increase in fuel consumption of up to 10% compared with a similar car with manual transmission.

Torque converters

Although automatic transmission is clutchless there must still be a means of disconnecting the engine drive from the gearbox when the car is stationary. This is the purpose of the torque converter, which has two other important uses in the transmission system.

Firstly it is of sufficient weight to replace the conventional flywheel. Secondly it is able to multiply the torque (turning effort) of the engine at low speeds, and is effectively a variable-ratio gear diminishing to about 1:1 drive at higher engine speeds.

The central components of the torque converter are encased in an oil-filled converter housing, and consist of vaned impeller and turbine bowls encircling a multi-vaned propeller-like central reactor element. The impeller is engine driven and throws the oil in the casing by centrifugal force at the vanes of the turbine. This turbine is splined to the input shaft of the automatic gearbox.

At engine idle speeds the force of the oil impinging on the turbine is insufficient to rotate it, but as the engine speeds up, the oil begins to drag the turbine round with it.

The central reactor piece is designed to remain stationary between the rotating elements. Its vanes direct the flow between impeller and turbine in such a way that the reaction between the two is considerably increased.

At higher engine speeds a freewheel clutch holding the reactor frees, allowing it to rotate. Thus its beneficial torque multiplying effect decreases. When it travels at the same speed as the impeller and turbine, there is virtually direct drive between the two with as little as 2% slippage.

Turbine shaft to gearbox

Impeller

Outer casing

Reactor

Free-wheel clutch

Turbine

Flywheel

Cross-section of torque converter showing turbine, impeller and reactor

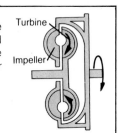

Idling: the impeller is attached to the engine and faces the turbine from which it is separated by a small gap. At idling speed centrifugal force is insufficient for the oil to turn the turbine and so move the car

Turbine

Impeller

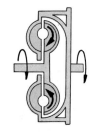

Low to medium revs: centrifugal force pushes the oil into the turbine as the engine speeds up, transmitting some turning effect. There is still 'slip', so the output shaft rotates more slowly than the input shaft

Medium to high revs: when the engine reaches a pre-set speed the force of the oil is sufficient to transmit full power. Direct drive results, with the output shaft rotating nearly as fast as the input shaft

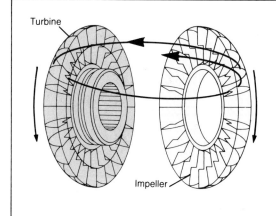

The fluid flywheel takes up the drive progressively. The turbine is driven by oil flung out from the impeller

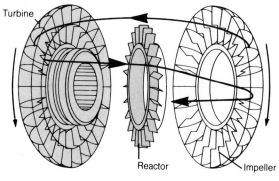

The torque converter has a central reactor which redirects the oil flow to increase torque at low engine-speeds

Epicyclic gears

The majority of automatic gearboxes in use in modern cars today offer three forward gear ratios and one reverse by means of an epicyclic gear train. Epicyclic gears consist of an assembly of a sun gear meshing with carrier-connected planet gears running in an annulus. An automatic gearbox has a number of such epicyclic gear trains. Each assembly can operate in three modes. In the first the central sun wheel can be locked to the gearbox casing by means of clutch elements, and drive applied to the planet gear carrier—the annulus then rotates at a slightly different speed in the same direction. In the second mode, the sun and annulus are locked, the planets cannot turn and the carrier is rotated at the same speed as the sun and annulus. In the third mode, the planet carrier is locked.

Drive applied to the sun wheel will then turn the annulus in the opposite direction of rotation.

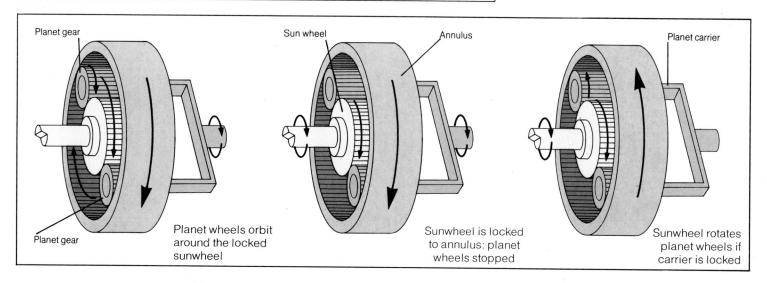

Planet wheels orbit around the locked sunwheel

Sunwheel is locked to annulus: planet wheels stopped

Sunwheel rotates planet wheels if carrier is locked

Inside an automatic gearbox

All three modes of operation are used in providing the output gear ratios of an automatic box. The different elements are held stationary or allowed to turn, and transmit drive to a second or third epicyclic gear set by hydraulically-operated brake bands (encircling the annulus) and clutches acting on the sun and planet carrier elements.

Hydraulic pressure to operate the gearbox is provided by one or two integral pumps drawing an oil supply from the gearbox sump.

Normally the oil is of a special type formulated for good hydraulic *and* lubricating properties, although there are automatic gearboxes designed to operate on engine oil.

If an automatic car is to be used to tow a caravan or trailer, most manufacturers strongly recommend the fitting of a cooler for the automatic transmission fluid, to prevent overheating on hilly or mountainous routes.

Automatic gear selection

By selectively linking elements of the successive epicyclic gear sets, an automatic transmission can provide three or four ratio steps similar to those of a manual box. But transition from one to the next occurs without de-clutching. The driver has the option of fully automatic selection of gears according to road speed and throttle position and, on most boxes, a hold-down to bottom gear only or a restriction to lower gears only. On some gearboxes used on smaller cars, the options are for fully automatic selection or a hold in one of four gears so that the car can be driven as a clutchless manual model. In fully automatic drive (D on the selector) and at medium throttle, the gearbox will change up to the next gear at preset speeds, sensing them by a centrifugal hydraulic valve.

Typically on a three-speed gearbox there is change from first to second at about 12mph and a change to top at round 28mph. Full throttle will deliver more power and delay each upward change until higher road speeds are reached. Sudden down-pressure to the limit of throttle travel in the higher gears will operate a kickdown switch which causes a change-down to the next lower gear.

Normally this will be from top to second for overtaking. The kickdown will not, however, operate if engine revolutions would rise above the safety limit in the lower gear. The top gear to second gear kickdown limit occurs at around 65mph on many cars. Change up will occur when the foot is eased off the throttle pedal.

The inhibitor switch and the Park position

For safety, a car with an automatic gearbox can be started only when the gear selector is in the Neutral or Park position (Neutral only on a few gearboxes). This vital function is performed by an inhibitor switch which senses gear selector position and interrupts the ignition switch to the starter solenoid circuit.

In the Park position the gearbox output shaft is mechanically locked so that the car cannot creep forward during starting and it is normal to leave the lever in this position when parking the car. The Neutral position is used in normal driving to provide a shift out of Drive that avoids any possibility of engaging reverse. Accidental selection of both Reverse and Park while in forward motion is discouraged by a large step in the gate through which the selector lever must deliberately be moved, or by other mechanical interference means.

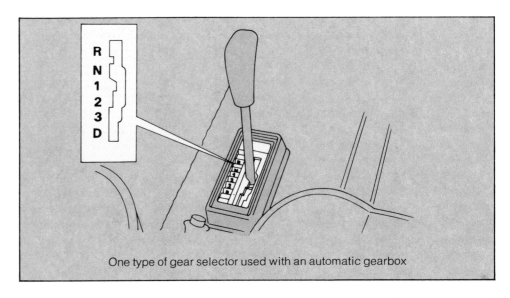

One type of gear selector used with an automatic gearbox

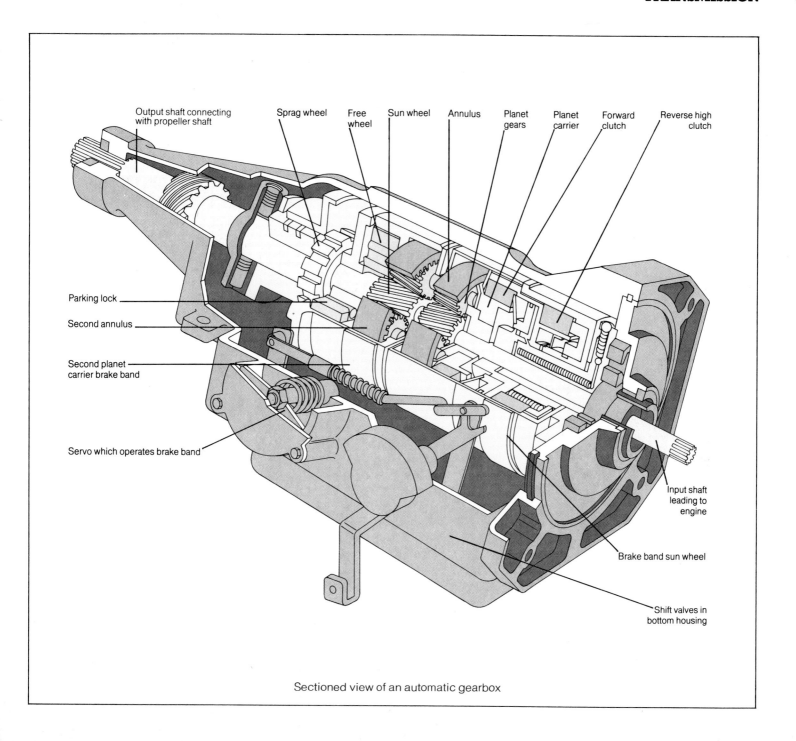

Output shaft connecting with propeller shaft

Sprag wheel

Free wheel

Sun wheel

Annulus

Planet gears

Planet carrier

Forward clutch

Reverse high clutch

Parking lock

Second annulus

Second planet carrier brake band

Servo which operates brake band

Input shaft leading to engine

Brake band sun wheel

Shift valves in bottom housing

Sectioned view of an automatic gearbox

Daf cars (and after Volvo's takeover, the Volvo 66 and 343), however, have a fully automatic, continuously variable-ratio transmission system (known as CVT) which uses belts to take the drive to the rear wheels. The system demands of the driver only the selection of either forward or reverse. There is an engine-driven automatic clutch to take up the drive as the throttle pedal is depressed and the engine speeds up. Allowing the engine speed to drop disengages the drive. The transmission of early Daf vehicles had two V-belts, but modern models use a system in which only one belt is provided. In this system the drive output from the gearbox goes to a large driving pulley formed by two shallow cone-shaped plates.

One plate is fixed and the other moves along the pulley axis under the influence of centrifugal weights and a vacuum chamber which sense throttle position and engine load. The effect of moving the pulley plates together is to make a shallower V and thus force a drive belt to describe a larger circumference.

The drive belt runs between this pulley and a second variable-depth V-pulley consisting of two plates held together by spring pressure.

At rest, the drive pulley plates are wide apart and the driven pulley plates are forced together.

As speed builds up, the centrifugal mechanism forces the drive pulley plates together. The belt consequently pulls apart the plates of the driven pulley. This gives a continuously-variable ratio stepless drive. Two belts and two sets of pulleys are used on some Daf/Volvo models.

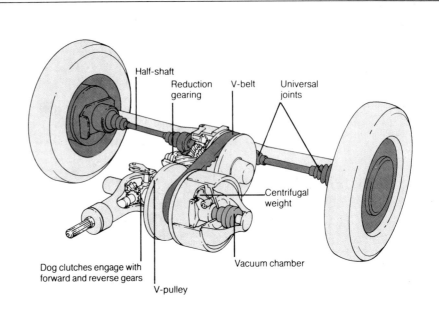

Half-shaft
Reduction gearing
V-belt
Universal joints
Centrifugal weight
Dog clutches engage with forward and reverse gears
Vacuum chamber
V-pulley

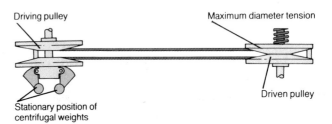

Driving pulley
Maximum diameter tension
Driven pulley
Stationary position of centrifugal weights

At low speed, centrifugal weights do not alter the driving pulley diameter and the driven pulley remains at maximum diameter for lowest possible gear ratio

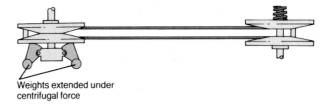

Weights extended under centrifugal force

At high speed, the centrifugal weights increase effective diameter of the driving pulleys so the driven pulley expands against its spring to give a high gearing

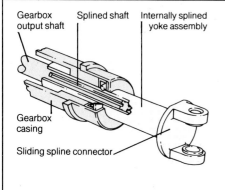

Gearbox output shaft
Splined shaft
Internally splined yoke assembly
Gearbox casing
Sliding spline connector

Propeller shaft and drive shafts

Drive is transmitted from the rear of the gearbox to the final drive unit by a propeller shaft (propshaft) on all front-engined, rear-wheel-drive cars. The propeller shaft takes into account the small length variations and changes of shaft angle caused by the movement of the rear axle in response to road bumps. The slight changes in length are accommodated by connecting the shaft to the gearbox by using a sliding splined joint. Changes in the angle of drive are absorbed by two universal joints, one at each end of the shaft.

Hooke universal joints

On the majority of cars the type of universal joint used on the propeller shaft is the Hooke design. At the gearbox splined joint, a yoke is flexibly linked to a similar yoke on the propeller shaft by a cross-shaped spider. The spider connects the two yokes at right angles to each other. Needle roller bearings, often lubricated and sealed for life, are fitted in caps which locate the spider arms in the yoke mountings and smooth the joint's operation. A similar joint is used at the final drive end of the propeller shaft.

One problem of the Hooke design is that the speed of the driven shaft fluctuates, the greater the angle of the drive the larger the fluctuations. In a modern design, the propeller shaft angle is normally relatively small. Also the gearbox tailshaft and the final drive input shaft are parallel to each other. This means the angle of drive of the first Hooke joint is matched by an equal and opposite one at the rear joint, and the speed fluctuations are largely cancelled out. Where angular changes are large, as in front-wheel-drive cars, and where steering movements have to be taken into account, a constant-velocity joint has to be used.

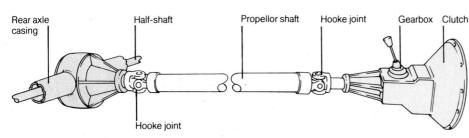

There are two or three universal joints on a propeller shaft. To allow for axle movement a splined sliding connector is provided at the gearbox

Rear axle casing
Half-shaft
Propellor shaft
Hooke joint
Gearbox
Clutch
Hooke joint

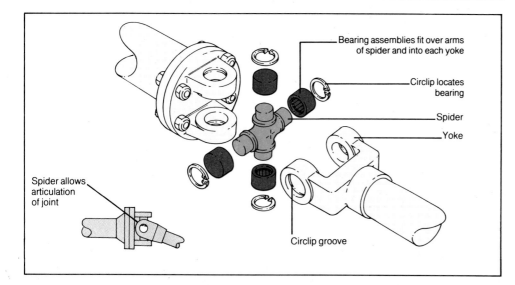

Spider allows articulation of joint

Bearing assemblies fit over arms of spider and into each yoke

Circlip locates bearing

Spider

Yoke

Circlip groove

A cross-shaped spider links two yokes on each shaft in a Hooke-type universal joint. This allows the two shafts to rotate and articulate at the same time

Propeller shaft vibration

As the propeller shaft is a rotating component, it must be well balanced or it will vibrate. Other vibrations can be caused by poor alignment, and the whipping of the shaft out of line is a problem on longer cars. A common cause of vibration on current cars is deposits of underbody sealant accidentally sprayed on the shaft. On cars with a relatively long space between the gearbox tailshaft and the final drive, some manufacturers use a split propeller shaft. The front section rotates in line with the gearbox and terminates in an intermediate bearing. The rear half is a shorter propeller shaft with universal joints at each end.

Drive shaft joints

Two problems arise in the design of front-wheel-drive and rear-engined cars in which there are no propeller shafts—drive transmission is usually direct from the final drive to the wheels by the equivalent of half-shafts.

The first, affecting front-wheel-drive cars only, is that the driving wheels are the steered wheels and a conventional universal joint cannot cope with the wide angle of wheel movement without causing aggravated speed fluctuations. The second problem is that in a conventional drive, the propeller shaft is long enough to act as a torsional spring, smoothing out torque variations. The very short drive shafts necessary on front-wheel-drive and rear-engined cars cannot work in this way.

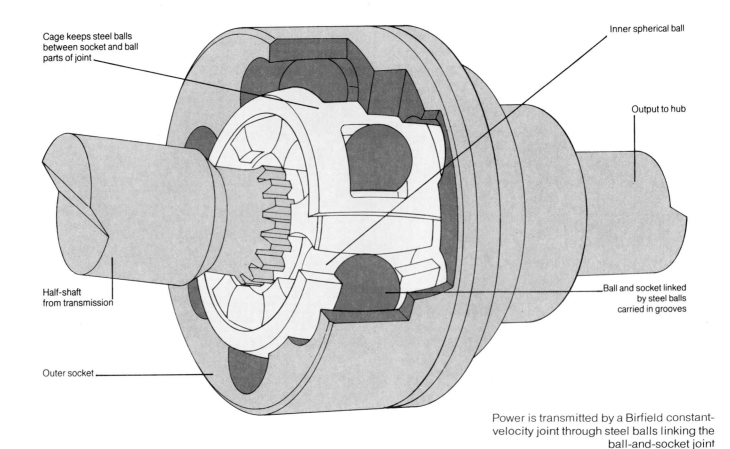

Cage keeps steel balls between socket and ball parts of joint

Inner spherical ball

Output to hub

Half-shaft from transmission

Ball and socket linked by steel balls carried in grooves

Outer socket

Power is transmitted by a Birfield constant-velocity joint through steel balls linking the ball-and-socket joint

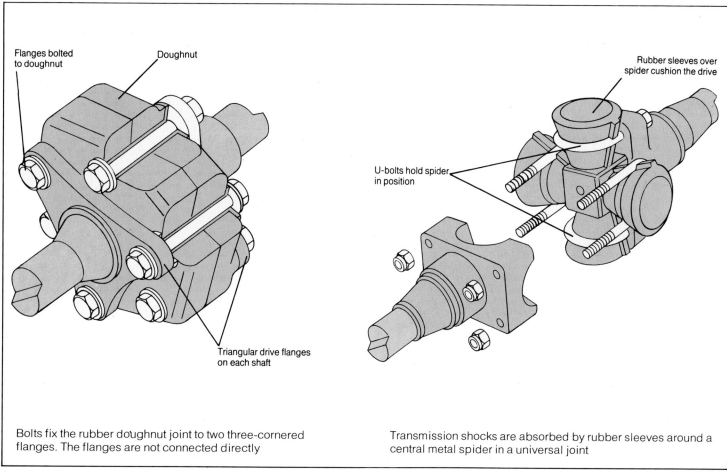

Flanges bolted to doughnut

Doughnut

Rubber sleeves over spider cushion the drive

U-bolts hold spider in position

Triangular drive flanges on each shaft

Bolts fix the rubber doughnut joint to two three-cornered flanges. The flanges are not connected directly

Transmission shocks are absorbed by rubber sleeves around a central metal spider in a universal joint

Constant-velocity joints

A typical joint designed to cope with the steering of driven wheels without speed fluctuation is the Birfield constant-velocity joint. This joint, which can be mounted in the wheel hub or inboard at the output shafts from the final drive, consists of a radially-grooved sphere in a spherical socket with matching grooves. The sphere is connected to the drive shaft by a sliding splined joint which allows movement for length variations. It can move through a considerable angle inside the cage by means of ball-bearings running in the grooves. It is the ball-bearings themselves that transmit the drive from the sphere to the cage. The whole joint is protected from dirt ingress by a rubber gaiter which also seals in lubricant.

Shock-absorbing joints

To take up the shock load of overcoming the car's inertia (resistance to start rolling) in cars with short drive transmissions, some compliance has to be introduced into the drive shafts. This may be arranged by simply making the bearing parts of a conventional Hooke joint in rubber. But much more compliance, as well as a universal joint action, is achieved by using a rubber doughnut joint.

The doughnut is a thick ring of rubber bolted between two triangular flanges. One flange is secured to one side of the doughnut by three bolts and the other flange is attached to the other side.

Servicing universal joints

On many modern cars the propeller shaft Hooke joints are sealed components which require no lubrication or servicing.

Check for universal joint wear by gripping the joint flange in one hand and trying to move the propeller shaft from side to side (1). There should be no movement at all. Establish whether any movement is at the yoke bearings or on the flange. If it is the flange, it may only be necessary to tighten the flange bolts.

Rubber spider universal joints

Thoroughly inspect the condition of the rubber components of the spider. There should be no visible damage or swelling and the components should be free of oil. If there is oil contamination it is likely to come from a leak in the engine or gearbox, in which case early garage attention is advisable. Check joint wear by the same means as the propshaft. Ensure that the U-clamp bolts are tight. A contaminated or loose spider joint may hit the gearbox.

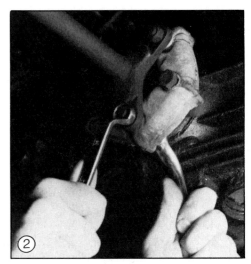

Check for tightness of the six flange-fastening bolts on the doughnut joint

Doughnut joints

The most important point to check on the doughnut joint is the tightness of the six flange-fastening bolts (2). Also inspect for oil contamination and signs of deterioration of the rubber doughnut itself.

Constant-velocity joints

Outboard (and some inboard) constant-velocity joints are generally shrouded by a rubber boot which keeps out dirt and seals in lubricant. This must be closely inspected for cuts, wear or splits (3). Any small hole can allow in dirt and cause premature joint wear. Replacing this simple but vital component is a garage job.

To check for wear in the universal joint, grip the flange with one hand and the propeller shaft with the other. If any movement in the joint is felt when it is pulled and twisted it is worn, and the joint should be replaced before further wear develops

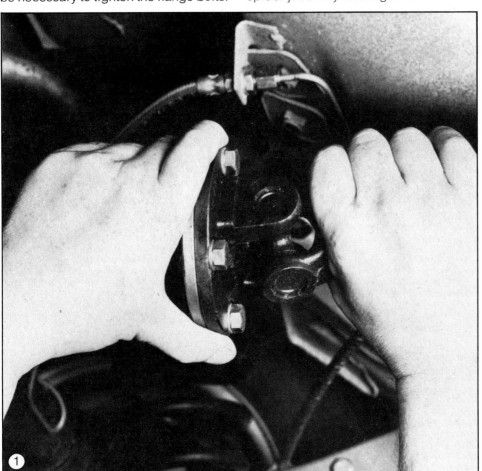

Check the rubber boot on the constant-velocity joint for cuts, wear or splits, which will allow dirt and water to enter

Topping-up an automatic gearbox

DIY servicing of an automatic gearbox is restricted to checks for oil tightness and top-ups of fluid at the manufacturer's specified intervals. It is important to use the recommended fluid. Besides a supply of clean transmission fluid, you need a clean cloth and a small funnel. The torque converter and automatic gearbox are lubricated as one unit. As the fluid for operating the torque converter is fed from the transmission casing, it is essential when checking the level or topping-up the automatic gearbox that the engine is run at idling speed to transfer fluid from transmission casing to torque converter, otherwise a false level reading will be obtained. Anti-friction additives must not be used in automatic transmissions. Always use only the recommended fluid.

Before removing the dipstick, thoroughly wipe the area round the dipstick tube to prevent dirt from entering (4). Make sure that the car is level, with the engine idling and the selector in the Park position. Allow the engine to idle for about two minutes, then remove the dipstick, wipe it quickly, dip again and check the level. If necessary, put the funnel in the dipstick tube and add the required amount of oil (5).

Torque convertor

Some cars have air-cooling grilles on the torque converter bell-housing. These should be cleaned periodically to ensure that road dirt does not block the metal or nylon mesh.

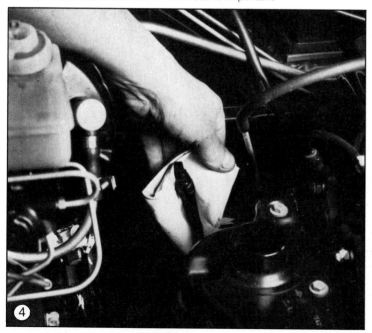

Remove the dipstick, wipe it clean, dip again and check the level. On automatic transmission cleanliness is important

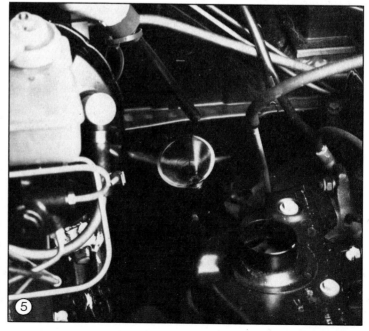

Replace the dipstick and recheck the level. Place a funnel in the dipstick tube and add the right amount of oil

Final drives and differentials

The last link in the transmission system, coupling the engine to the driven wheels, is the final drive unit, a device which splits the single drive from the propeller shaft (or gearbox output shaft) in two and feeds it to each wheel.

It has two other functions. It provides the final gear ratio step of the system, reducing the revolutions of the wheels relative to the engine by a factor of 3 to 4. And it employs a device which allows the wheels to turn at differing speeds—the differential.

This is necessary because when turning a corner the outer wheel travels further than the inner wheel.

Limited-slip differential

Because the differential applies equal turning effort to each half-shaft, if one road wheel loses traction on ice or mud the turning effort falls near to zero and that same effort will be transmitted to the other half-shaft. The result is that one road wheel spins and the other remains stationary. To overcome this and to give more traction for off-road vehicles, a limited-slip differential is used.

In this device, friction clutch cones surround and rotate with the half-shaft pinions and are lightly sprung against the crown-wheel cage. With the car travelling straight, the clutch cones have little effect on differential operation.

However, when more driving torque is applied, say in low gear at high power input, the two half-shaft gears are forced further apart and the clutch cones increase their grip, effectively locking the differential and preventing a single wheel from spinning.

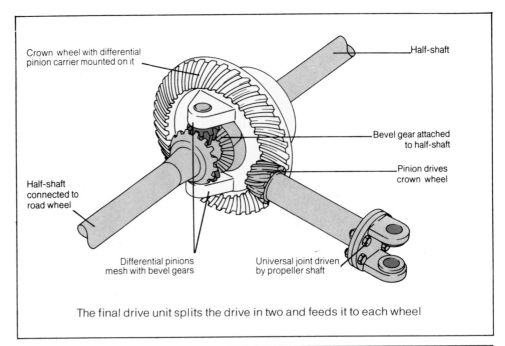

Crown wheel with differential pinion carrier mounted on it

Half-shaft

Bevel gear attached to half-shaft

Pinion drives crown wheel

Half-shaft connected to road wheel

Differential pinions mesh with bevel gears

Universal joint driven by propeller shaft

The final drive unit splits the drive in two and feeds it to each wheel

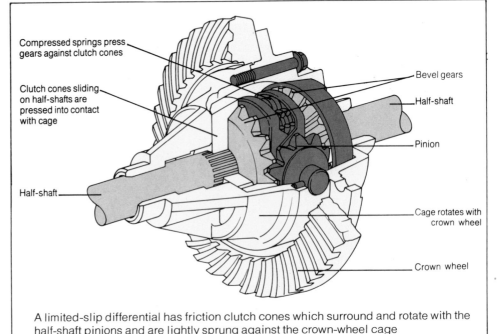

Compressed springs press gears against clutch cones

Clutch cones sliding on half-shafts are pressed into contact with cage

Half-shaft

Bevel gears

Half-shaft

Pinion

Cage rotates with crown wheel

Crown wheel

A limited-slip differential has friction clutch cones which surround and rotate with the half-shaft pinions and are lightly sprung against the crown-wheel cage

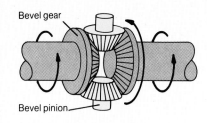

Bevel gear

Bevel pinion

Both drive shafts travelling at the same speed make the bevel pinions orbit with the gears without rotating on their axles

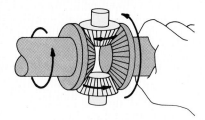

The bevel gears turn on their axles if one shaft is stopped, orbiting the stationary gear and driving the other shaft

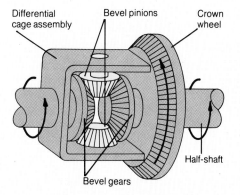

Differential cage assembly

Bevel pinions

Crown wheel

Half-shaft

Bevel gears

The differential is in a cage driven by the crown-wheel. The bevel pinions orbit, but do not spin on their axles when the car is travelling in a straight line. The unit drives both half-shafts equally

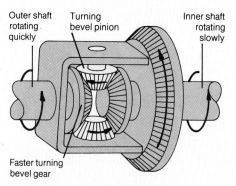

Outer shaft rotating quickly

Turning bevel pinion

Inner shaft rotating slowly

Faster turning bevel gear

The bevel gear on the inner half-shaft turn more slowly than the crown-wheel when taking a bend and the outer half-shaft, driven by the bevel pinion, turns faster. The crown-wheel turns at the average of the half-shaft speeds

How a final drive works

Drive from the propeller shaft turns a small pinion meshing with a large crown-wheel. It is the ratio of the number of teeth on the crown-wheel to those on the pinion that gives the gear reduction. For instance, a pinion with 10 teeth meshing with a 37-toothed crown-wheel would have a gear ratio of 3.7:1.

The crown-wheel also forms a cage which carries two small bevel pinions on short radial axles. These mesh on each side with bevel gears which form part of, or are spline-jointed to, the half-shafts which drive the road wheels. On the straight, the crown-wheel cage rotates and turns the two halfshafts without any movement of the two small differential bevel gears. But on a corner, when one half shaft tends to go faster than the other, the different rates of movement are accommodated by rotation of the bevel pinions.

The action of the differential is to provide a variable-speed drive output to each driven wheel without loss of engine power.

The outside wheel will cover more ground than the inside wheel and therefore travel faster than the inside wheel. The crown-wheel provides continuous power to the differential cage, inside of which the half-shaft's bevel gears and the pinions provide the drive required by each driven wheel. The crown wheel always turns at the average speed of both the driven wheels. The differential housing usually forms part of a rigid rear axle, but it may be a separate unit (on cars with rear independent suspension) or it can form an integral part of the gearbox on front-wheel-drive and rear-engine cars.

Wheel bearings

Two basic types of bearing are used to support and allow the rotation of the car's road wheels whether or not they are driven wheels.

Bearings which are not required to locate the hub, brake and wheel assembly against side forces are the roller bearing or the plain ball-type, mounted in pairs. If the bearing is required to hold part of the system securely in place against side forces as well as allow rotation, it is usual to fit a type called a taper-roller bearing. Bearings are designed to fit very tightly on to the axle and are often fitted by a heavy-duty press and removed with a puller. Ball-bearing types are frequently tightened into place with great force. The clearance between the balls and the grooved part of the bearing races is provided in their manufacture and not by the amount of axle pre-load during assembly.

Taper roller bearings are never tightened to such a high level as it is the small amount of play between the taper of the rollers and the bearing surface on the rotating component that gives the system its inherent stability. Normally the hub-securing nut used with tapered bearings is of the castellated kind or of a type locked by a tab washer. The nut is tightened on to the bearing with a minimal specified pressure. It may be backed off to the nearest position in which it is possible to lock the nut with a split pin or by turning up the tabs on a lock washer. This system gives acceptable play in the bearing.

Rear-wheel bearings used with a beam axle are not usually of the tapered type.

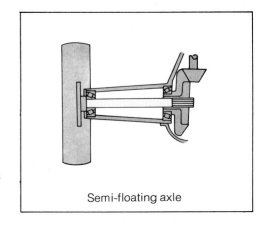

Semi-floating axle

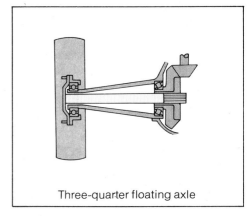

Three-quarter floating axle

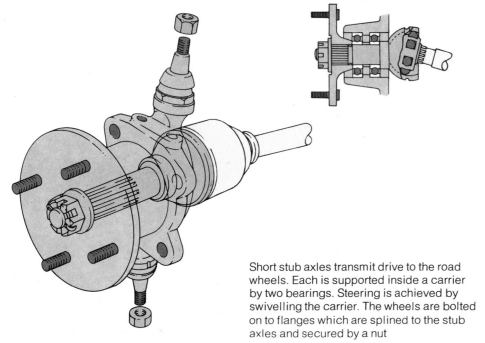

Short stub axles transmit drive to the road wheels. Each is supported inside a carrier by two bearings. Steering is achieved by swivelling the carrier. The wheels are bolted on to flanges which are splined to the stub axles and secured by a nut

In what is known as a semi-floating axle the bearing is fitted between the half-shaft and the axle casing. The half-shaft carries the weight of the vehicle. In a three-quarter floating axle the bearing is mounted on the axle casing and the half-shaft provides drive.

Differential servicing

The final drive is a unit built to very close tolerances, and it is not recommended that DIY mechanics should attempt repairs. It is worthwhile, however, making regular checks for

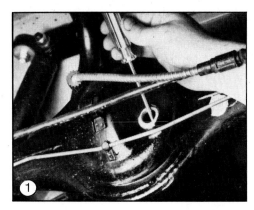

To establish the oil level in the axle dip a screwdriver into the level hole

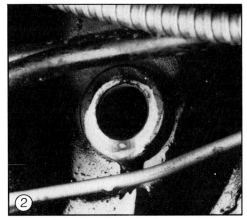

Fill the axle with transmission oil until it drips from the hole

The bearing is covered by a metal cap visible after removing the wheel trim

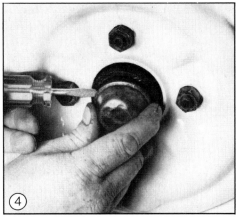

Remove cap with an old screwdriver. Tap lightly all round using a hammer

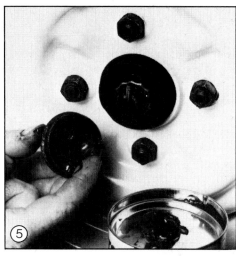

Pack grease into wheel hub. Deposit some in the cap before replacing it

leaks, particularly at the input or pinion seal. Early detection of loss of lubricant may mean a repair rather than replacement of the unit. The lubricant usually specified is hypoid gear oil, specially formulated to cope with the high contact stresses and local temperatures encountered in the meshing of the hypoid pinion and crown-wheel. To top-up the lubricant, locate the filler plug which is at the correct lubricant level and thoroughly clean the area before removing it. The level plug will indicate the correct oil level only when the car is level. Ideally, the car should be raised on four axle stands or driven over an inspection pit for topping-up. Establish the fluid level inside by dipping in a screwdriver blade (1), then, if necessary, top-up until a dribble of fluid comes from the hole (2). It is usually necessary to use a squeezy type of dispenser bottle and a length of plastic tube to inject the fluid.

Servicing wheel bearings

On the majority of cars, the servicing of wheel bearings is restricted to repacking with grease. The bearing is covered by a metal cap usually accessible after removing the wheel trim (3), although it is sometimes necessary to take off the wheel (and in a few cases remove the brake drum). The cap is best removed by using an old screwdriver inserted under the raised seat and lightly tapped with a hammer—tap all round the cap moving it a little at a time (4). Scrape out all hard grease from inside the cap and ensure that any breather hole is cleared. Wipe as much old grease off the bearing as possible. Refill the cap with fresh grease of a grade recommended by the manufacturer to within $\frac{1}{8}$in of the rim (5). Liberally smear the bearing with grease and lightly tap home the cap (use a soft mallet or a block of wood between the hammer and cap).

FAULT FINDING
Manual gearbox
Difficult gear selection: Ensure that you are depressing the clutch fully. If the fault persists, check the pedal free travel (throw-out stop adjustment on BL models). If this is correct the fault is likely to be found in the synchromesh/baulking mechanism.

Jumping out of gear: Ensure that you are depressing the clutch fully. This can be caused by wear or poor adjustment of remote control mechanism, excessive gearbox movement (check engine and gearbox mountings), selector fork wear or synchromesh wear.

Gearbox noise: Harsh noises in one or more gears may indicate damaged gear teeth. A general increase in noise may indicate loss of oil—check that the level is correct and top-up if necessary.

Lubricate gear lever ball pivot

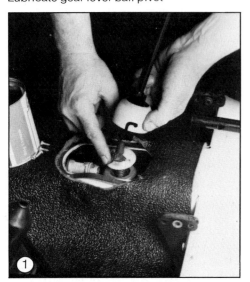

Stiff gear lever: Lubricate gear lever ball pivot (1) and any rod guides in remote-control mechanism. Check for wear or poor adjustment of remote-control mechanism.

Clutch
Not disengaging: (no pedal feel) Check cable/rod linkage or hydraulic fluid level (bleed hydraulic system if fluid level appears correct).

Not fully disengaging: Check the pedal free travel (BL models—check throw-out stop adjustment).

Slipping: Worn clutch or pedal free travel out of adjustment. May also be an oil leak from crankshaft oil seal or gearbox—look for drips at bell-housing (2).

Judder: Softened engine or gearbox mountings. Clutch friction material has been incorrectly riveted to new plate. Check for oil leaks (as above) or incorrect pedal free travel.

Clutch slip may be due to an oil-leak from the engine or gearbox. Look for drips at the bell-housing.

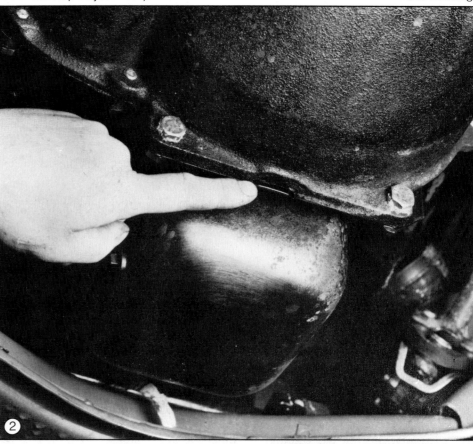

Whirring noise or squeaky rattle
(heard when pedal is depressed with engine running): Worn clutch release—or carbon thrust bearing.

Automatic gearbox problems
Engine will not start in Neutral or Park: Faulty inhibitor switch.

Engine starts but car will not move when in gear: Check the fluid level in the gearbox (3).

Excessive slip: This shows up on the move, when the car fails to accelerate as the throttle is opened, but the engine revolutions rise. Usually this is caused by overheated transmission fluid or an air or vapour lock in the hydraulic mechanism. Allow the fluid to cool and re-start. If the problem persists, expert attention will be required. Overheating may also be the cause of erratic gear selection.

Propeller shaft and drive shafts
Unusual vibration at speed: Almost any fault in the drive train and running gear can give this symptom, but if the tyres are in good condition, there is no wheel damage and there is no engine vibration (eliminate the engine by selecting neutral), suspect the propshaft. The cause is most likely to be worn universal joints. Propshaft vibration differs from unbalanced wheel vibrations because out-of-balance road wheels usually vibrate over a limited speed range. Worn universal joints vibrate over a wide range of speeds.

Rear axle
Grinding harshness: Worn crown gear in differential housing. Immediate repair is not normally necessary.

Clunk from rear on moving off: Excessive play in final drive input or output to half-shafts.

Propeller shaft turns but car does not move: Broken half-shaft or drive shaft—the differential will not transmit power to the unaffected half-shaft.

Constant-velocity joints
Knocks or clicks when steering on full lock in either direction: Worn joint—have it renewed as soon as possible.

Wheel bearings
Rumbling noise: The rumble of a worn wheel bearing increases as the car is steered on one lock, and diminishes on the opposite lock as the bearing is loaded and unloaded. Check by raising the suspect road wheel and rotating it slowly by hand (4). Tight spots as it is turned could indicate that the bearing needs renewing. A badly adjusted or worn bearing will result in a lot of play when the top of the raised wheel is rocked to and from the car (5).

Check the fluid level in the gearbox

Raise the suspect wheel and rotate

Rock the wheel to assess free play

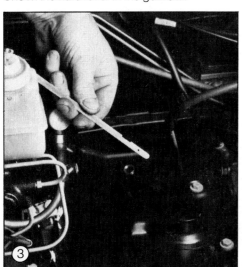

COOLING

What you can do: Pages

Look after radiator and hoses   72
Repair hose leaks   72
Fit a new hose   73
Clean the cooling system   74
Check the pressure cap   75
Cure air locks   75
Fit a new water pump   80
Check the thermostat   81
Replenish anti-freeze   83
Operate Renault bleed valves   84
Check the cooling fan   84

Of the many causes of car breakdown which result in calls to the AA, cooling system problems account for almost as many as electrical faults. But whereas the temporary interruption of an electrical supply rarely causes extensive damage, faults in the cooling system can rapidly destroy an engine.

Less than 25% of the total energy developed by the engine by burning the fuel is converted into motive force, the rest is waste heat energy. Over 35% of this heat is dissipated by the exhaust gases, and about 20% of it is handled by the car's air- or water-cooling system, which protects parts deep inside the engine from damage.

Getting rid of the heat

There are two main methods of removing the excess heat from an engine. In the early days of the internal combustion engine it was common to use air-cooling. This system is still used on some cars and the majority of motor cycles. The alternative is water-cooling, in which a complex system of waterways conducts heat away from the engine's innermost parts to a radiator which transfers it to the airflow around the car.

Air-cooling

As mentioned in the Engine section, the hottest parts of an engine are the combustion chambers and cylinders, and when these areas are being air-cooled, it is important that they receive an unobstructed airflow. This is difficult on an in-line engine with a lot of cylinders, and for air-cooling, flat two- and four-cylinder types and some two- and four-cylinder V designs have proved the most successful. There were, however, many air-cooled in-line engines in the early days of motoring. Besides getting air to each cylinder, it is important to increase the surface area of the engine block around the cylinders and combustion chamber. For this reason, cylinders and cylinder heads

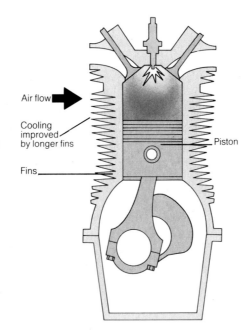

Air flow

Cooling improved by longer fins

Fins

Piston

The large fins on air-cooled engines dissipate heat by increasing the surface area of the hot sections

are cast with fins which protrude from the metal surface into the airflow. The fins conduct heat away from the parts under the most stress and radiate it into the cool air.

Even though the engine may be mounted low down in the car, where it can take advantage of the natural

airflow, it is always necessary to increase the volume of air flowing over the engine—particularly when the car is crawling or stationary. Most modern air-cooled cars do this by using a larger-than-normal fan, usually belt-driven from the crankshaft pulley.

How oil helps to cool the engine

The cooling system, be it air or water, cannot be considered in isolation from the lubrication system. In addition to lubricating sliding components, the engine oil also relieves them of a considerable amount of heat which is transferred through the metal of the engine cylinder block to the air- or water-cooling system.

On most engines the lubricating oil runs hotter than the coolant.

Water-cooling

The principal component is the radiator. In this, hot coolant from the water jacket around the engine passes through a series of narrow-bore, finned pipes. Air flowing past the outside of the pipes and through the fins, draws off excess heat. The airflow is assisted by a cooling fan which is engine- or electrically-driven. Sometimes the radiator can be too efficient. For instance, when starting from cold, the radiator would provide too much cooling and would delay the warm-up, involving prolonged use of the choke and wastage of fuel.

To enable the engine to reach operating temperature quickly, a thermostat is fitted. This is a temperature-sensitive valve which prevents any substantial water circulation through the radiator until the block has reached a sufficiently high temperature.

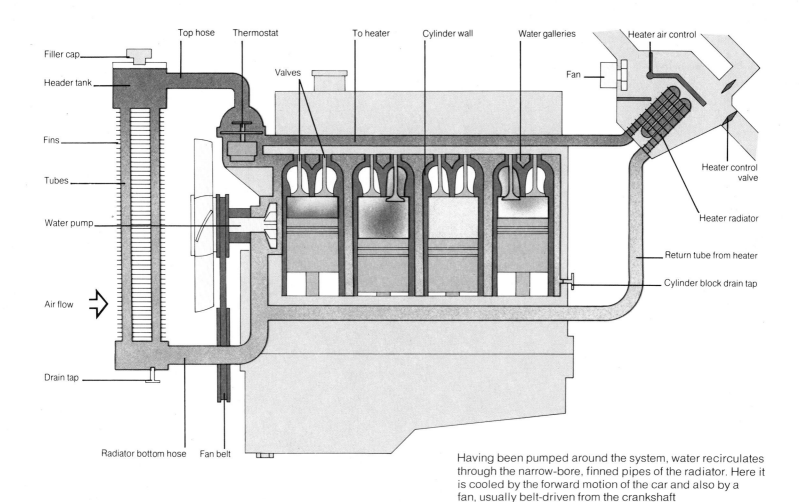

Filler cap

Header tank

Top hose   Thermostat

Valves

To heater   Cylinder wall   Water galleries

Heater air control

Fan

Fins

Tubes

Water pump

Air flow

Drain tap

Radiator bottom hose   Fan belt

Heater control valve

Heater radiator

Return tube from heater

Cylinder block drain tap

Having been pumped around the system, water recirculates through the narrow-bore, finned pipes of the radiator. Here it is cooled by the forward motion of the car and also by a fan, usually belt-driven from the crankshaft

Water will not circulate very efficiently between the block and the radiator without some mechanical help. On older cars with low-efficiency engines, it was considered sufficient to allow the water to circulate by means of natural convection and gravity. The hot water from the engine water jacket was piped upwards to the top of the radiator and, as the airflow past the radiator pipes cooled it, it fell to the bottom to return to the engine solely by the means of this natural thermosyphon. The radiator had to be tall and this, plus the general inefficiency of the system, placed considerable restraints on car design. Nowadays, all water-cooled engines use a water pump to assist circulation. Most manufacturers still retain a top hose which feeds hot coolant into the radiator, with extraction of the cooled water from the bottom. But the radiator can work equally efficiently if the water is pumped through it from side to side, and some cars use this design. To protect the cooling system from icing damage and corrosion, anti-freeze additive containing corrosion-inhibiting chemicals must be used in the coolant all year round, not just in winter.

The radiator

The heart of a water-cooling system is the radiator. This is designed to transfer heat from the coolant to the airstream which flows through the matrix of fine fins and tubes forming the radiator core. The fins provide an enlarged surface area from which the heat can radiate, and they are made, like the water passage tubes, from a good heat-conducting metal like copper or aluminium.

The radiator core is sandwiched between two tanks. In the conventional upright radiator the top tank (or header tank) receives hot coolant from the engine. A bottom tank provides the connection to the bottom hose through which cooled water is drawn by the water pump for recirculation around the engine. The tanks are usually made of metal, but some are of a heat- and pressure-resistant plastic.

Some cars have a variation of this design in which the radiator is mounted sideways, and the coolant flows from top to bottom diagonally. A further variation is the type in which water flows across the top half of the core into the end tank and then back across the core in the opposite direction through the bottom half of the core. Thus the top and bottom hose connections are at the same end of the radiator.

Other radiator fittings may include a drain tap in the bottom tank and threaded fitting holes for a temperature gauge or warning light (these are, however, usually on the block) or a switch for an electric cooling fan.

Hot water is carried through the many fine copper or aluminium tubes of the radiator core. Air passing around these finned tubes disperses the heat

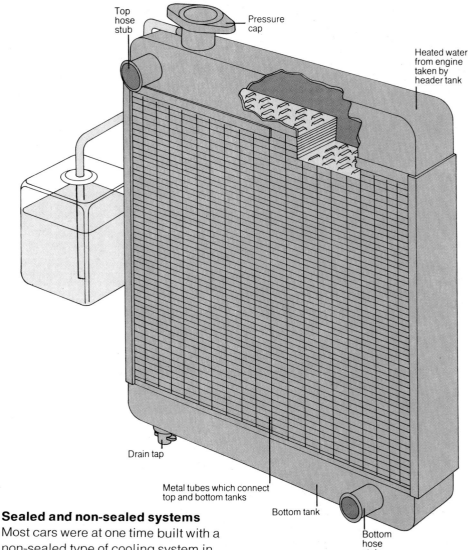

Top hose stub

Pressure cap

Heated water from engine taken by header tank

Drain tap

Metal tubes which connect top and bottom tanks

Bottom tank

Bottom hose stub

Any excess coolant expelled into the expansion tank while the engine warms up is drawn back as the system cools

On this type of sealed system the pressure cap is mounted in the filler neck of the expansion tank and will vent coolant only when a fault develops which causes the liquid to boil. Some cars have a hybrid system in which any normal expansion is taken up by a head-space in the radiator. The system is, however, effectively sealed as the pressure cap used on the radiator filler vents at such a high pressure that vapour will escape only if a boil-up occurs.

Hoses
As the radiator is usually mounted rigidly to the car body and the engine has to be free to move on its mountings, the connecting pipes from block to radiator must be flexible.
The two major hoses of the cooling system, called the top and bottom hoses, are specially constructed of reinforced rubber so that they can flex and withstand high internal temperature and pressure. Each hose is shaped to suit the particular relative positions of the radiator and block connections, and may also have heating system connections ready moulded to it.
Hose connections are secured by hose clips. The worm-drive type is one of the best fixings. More common are those having a double coil of steel wire. Some engines have a small-bore by-pass hose which enables the pump to circulate a restricted amount of water through the block while the thermostat is closed during engine warm-up.

Sealed and non-sealed systems
Most cars were at one time built with a non-sealed type of cooling system in which the radiator filler neck was fitted with a pressure cap. By means of a sprung seating under a pre-set tension, steam pressure (or, in an emergency, boiling coolant) could escape through a small outlet tube which drained it to the ground.
In a sealed system the radiator pressure cap is replaced by a sealed fitting and the overflow outlet is connected to an expansion tank—usually of see-through plastic or glass, enabling the level to be checked easily. The outlet tube is below the surface of the excess coolant in the tank so that any liquid expelled from the radiator while the engine warms up is drawn back as the system cools down.

Looking after the radiator and hoses

There are two important regular service tasks on the cooling system: checks on the coolant level and, at the same time, a visual inspection to check the condition of hoses and look for leaks. Hoses deteriorate in three ways: they crack, de-laminate (when the rubber and reinforcing fabric split apart) or swell. If any of these symptoms is found, a new hose should be fitted.

Some very fine cracking is normal after a few months of service, but more serious are wider and deeper cracks (1) which can cause leaks.

Try to feel the quality of the rubber surface on any unseen sides of the hose. Old age or overheating can cause de-lamination. This often shows first around the hose clips. A de-laminated

Do not ignore deep, wide cracks. They will soon cause leaks

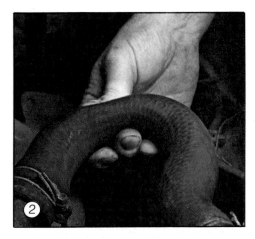

hose feels lifeless and squashy when squeezed between fingers and thumb (2). A bulging hose is seriously weakened. Bulging can be seen at the hose clips, when the engine is fully

Make a careful check around hose clips. Most leaks occur here

Squeeze hoses between fingers and thumb. They should not feel squashy

warmed up. It is sometimes caused by oil on the surface, which weakens it. Keep any oil off the hoses.

Hose leaks

Colouration of the dye used in anti-freeze is a good sign of a leak. Most leaks occur around the hose clips (3), at the joints with the heating system, at the gasket under the thermostat housing and in the radiator core itself. Because anti-freeze has a 'searching action' and can penetrate gaps that will not allow water through, leaks often appear after the addition of anti-freeze solution. Leaks at hose joints are cured simply by tightening the clip. Small leaks in the radiator core, caused by corrosion or small stone penetration, can often be sealed by proprietary sealing fluids.

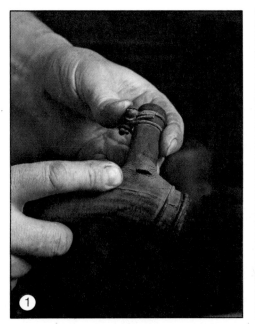

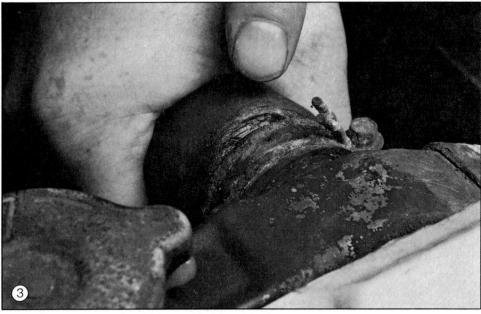

These solidify on contact with the air and block small holes.

A radiator specialist may consider making a soldered repair to a more seriously damaged core, but he will more often offer a new or reconditioned radiator, giving part exchange on the old unit.

Although it is possible to make a soldered repair to holes in the radiator tanks, the heat dissipation of the metal means that a powerful soldering iron or gas torch is needed, and this work is best left to a specialist.

Fitting a new hose

First make sure that you have the correct replacement hose—often a visual comparison is necessary to ensure that the right one is bought.

Drain the coolant into a bowl and, if it contains anti-freeze, retain it for re-use. Draining may have to be through the

Smear on a little washing-up liquid
If necessary, remove the bottom hose

disconnected bottom hose as many manufacturers no longer fit radiator drain taps. If a drain tap is tightly held by sediment and corrosion, do not force it. Instead, remove the bottom radiator hose to drain the coolant (4).

If, after loosening and moving away the clip, the hose to be renewed will not budge from the connection point, cut it free with a sharp knife. Any difficulty inserting the new hose on to the connector can be overcome after immersing the hose in a bowl of warm water and using a smear of washing-up liquid on the connector and the end of the hose to act as a lubricant (5).

Ensure that the new hose is free from kinking, and tighten the clips.

Refill the system with coolant, then run the engine to distribute it thoroughly and top-up as necessary. With the engine hot, check for leaks.

Cleaning and flushing the cooling system

If the engine is unaccountably overheating and the thermostat is operating correctly, the radiator may be blocked externally by dirt (so that air cannot flow) or internally by sediment.

Cleaning the fins

To clean dirt and grease out of the core fins thoroughly, it may be necessary to remove the radiator completely. Drain the system and disconnect hoses and any sensor wires. Remove any shroud, undo the fixings and take out the radiator (1).

Using a soft brush or an aerosol, apply a grease solvent, such as engine cleaner, to the core. With a pressure nozzle on a garden hose, flush the dirt out from the fins in both directions (2).

Thoroughly flush away any debris from the airways in the radiator core

Disconnect the hoses and accessories and carefully lift out the radiator

Flushing out sediment

To clean the inside, the radiator and block should be back-flushed. With the radiator fitted, drain the system, disconnect the bottom and top hoses and take off the filler cap; unbolt the thermostat housing and remove the housing and thermostat. Wrap a piece of cloth round a garden hose so that it is a firm fit in the radiator's bottom hose connection. Run the water for a few minutes, allowing it to overflow from the filler neck (3).

Wait for a minute or two and then apply the hose to the filler neck or top hose connection and flush in the opposite direction. Repeat the process until there is no sign of dirt or scale in the water. Flush the block by inserting the hose in the thermostat bowl and allowing water to run from the bottom hose connection on the block. Repeat this in the opposite direction. When replacing the thermostat it is wise to use a new gasket. Connect the hoses and refill the system with an anti-freeze solution.

Back-flush for a few minutes, allowing water to gush out of the filler neck

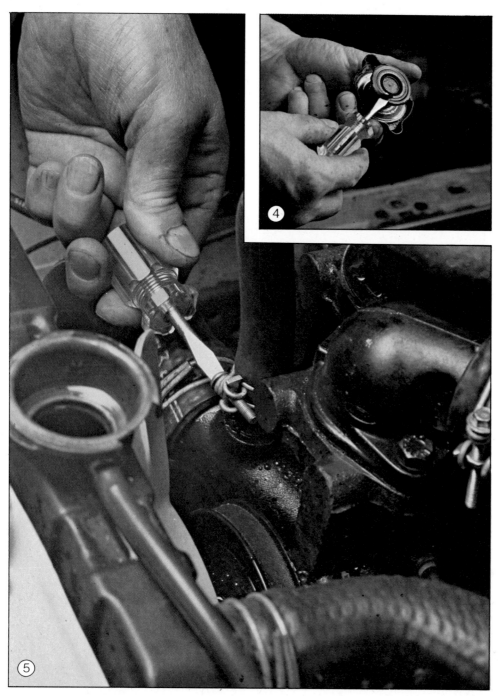

Check the condition of the radiator cap seal. If the rubber or fibre seating is damaged, the cap should be renewed

Checking the pressure cap

Inspect the pressure cap whenever topping up the radiator. Renew it if the rubber or fibre seating appears cracked or damaged (4). If you are losing a lot of coolant and there are no obvious leaks, have the cap pressure-tested by a garage. Most garages have the special equipment needed to do the job.
When buying a replacement, it is a good idea to take the old cap with you as a pattern; this will ensure that you get a cap with the right fitting and pressure marking (the pressure is usually stamped on the top of the cap).

Curing air locks

Pockets of air in the radiator, block or hoses can restrict water-flow through the system and reduce the efficiency of the heater. This can be cured by bleeding a little water out as follows:
Run the engine until the top radiator hose is warm to the touch, indicating that the thermostat is open. Stop the engine and loosen the heater hose at its joint with the bottom radiator hose or water pump (5), so that the hose can be removed. Leave it in place for the moment.
Start the engine and, taking care to keep clear of the fan, remove the hose from the joint until water flows, then immediately reconnect it. Turn off the engine, retighten the joint and top up the radiator.

When bleeding the system, loosen the heater hose where it joins the bottom radiator hose or water pump

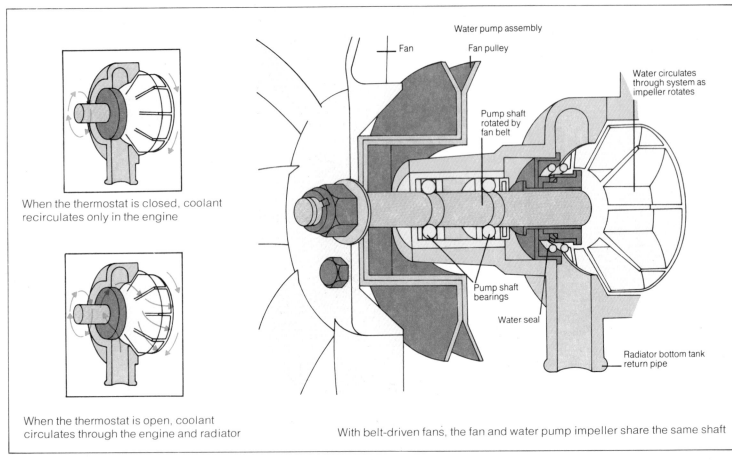

When the thermostat is closed, coolant recirculates only in the engine

When the thermostat is open, coolant circulates through the engine and radiator

Fan

Water pump assembly

Fan pulley

Water circulates through system as impeller rotates

Pump shaft rotated by fan belt

Pump shaft bearings

Water seal

Radiator bottom tank return pipe

With belt-driven fans, the fan and water pump impeller share the same shaft

Water pump

To drive coolant around the engine a water pump is fitted which, on engines with mechanically-driven fans, forms part of the fan mounting to the block. Thus the fan and the pump share the drive from the fan belt. On cars with electric fans, the water pump can be mounted at any point on the front of the engine where it is convenient to pick up the drive, usually with a V belt.

The pump is a relatively simple device consisting of a vaned impeller rotating with the short drive shaft which runs in waterproof bearings. The pump housing is designed with two inlets. One is the bottom hose connection allowing a flow of cooled water from the radiator. The other is a narrower by-pass gallery allowing some circulation of water from the area immediately in front of the thermostat while it is shut. The pump outlet is into the water galleries of the cylinder block.

Most water pumps are sealed units requiring no maintenance, although it is sometimes possible to cure squeaking noises from the bearings by adding a proprietary water-soluble pump lubricant to the coolant. On a few cars a grease nipple is provided to lubricate the pump bearing at intervals specified in the owner's handbook or service manual.

Leaks around the end of the shaft, or a squealing noise, generally indicate failure of the water seal or bearings. Although many pumps are repairable using special equipment such as bearing and seal presses, it is usually cheaper and more convenient to fit a new or reconditioned unit.

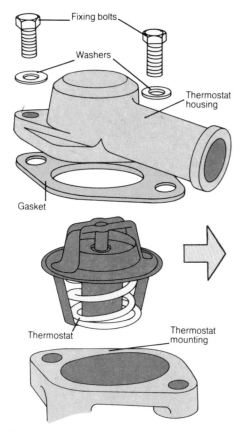

The thermostat unit incorporates a capsule of wax which expands under heat

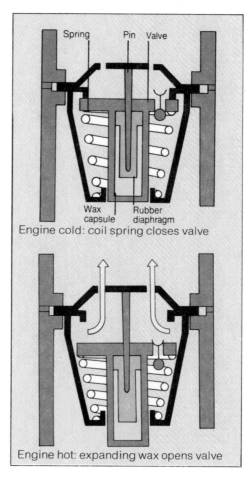

Engine cold: coil spring closes valve

Engine hot: expanding wax opens valve

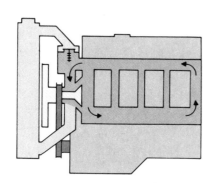

Thermostat shut: water is trapped in block

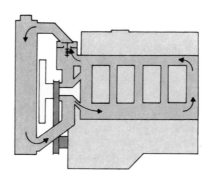

Thermostat open: water flows to radiator

The thermostat

To enable the engine to reach an efficient working temperature as quickly as possible, a thermostat is fitted in the cooling system. This is a temperature-sensitive valve in a housing which, on most cars, forms the outlet from the block to the radiator top hose.

While the coolant remains below the thermostat's operating temperature, the device blocks off the flow to the radiator so that the pump can circulate water only around the cylinder block. But when the operating temperature of the thermostat is reached, the device opens and water circulates freely through the radiator.

There are two types of thermostat. In the bellows type, a concertina-like bellows made of thin copper foil contains a volatile fluid. As engine temperature rises, the volatile fluid boils and the bellows expands to open the thermostat valve. Because it can be adversely affected by pressure in the cooling system, the bellows thermostat is rarely used in modern engines.

The wax type of thermostat is better able to cope with pressure, and is in almost universal use. In this, as the temperature rises, the valve is opened by the expansion of a wax capsule acting on a small piston rod. When the system cools down sufficiently, the valve is automatically returned to the closed position by a coiled return spring.

If a bellows-type thermostat fails, it is likely to revert to the open position as the cause of failure is usually perforation of the bellows. Wax-type thermostats may fail in either the closed or open position depending on the piston and wax-capsule design.

Cooling fans

The airstream passing through the radiator core, forced by the car's movement, is not always sufficient to remove all the waste heat that the engine produces. This is particularly so when the car is stationary or crawling in traffic and on hot days when the airstream has less capacity to absorb radiated heat.

To overcome these problems, additional air is drawn or, in the case of certain transverse-engine designs, blown through the radiator by a cooling fan, provided specifically to supplement the natural airflow.

The fan may be as simple as two blades attached to the water-pump pulley which is turned by a drive belt from the crankshaft pulley. However, vibration and noise are reduced by increasing the number of blades, and most current cars have fans with at least four and, in the case of certain lighter plastic designs, up to 16 blades.

In the search for greater fuel economy, car makers have identified the engine-driven fan as a source of fuel wastage. This is because it needs energy to turn, and at higher road speeds (and in cold weather) it is not needed. In fact, under certain conditions, the engine can be overcooled to below its most efficient temperature. An engine's optimum working temperature, regardless of speed, is about 80°-85°C. Below this, it is not running efficiently and fuel consumption suffers.

The answer has been the development of several different types of fan: viscous-coupled, electromagnetically-coupled or electrically operated.

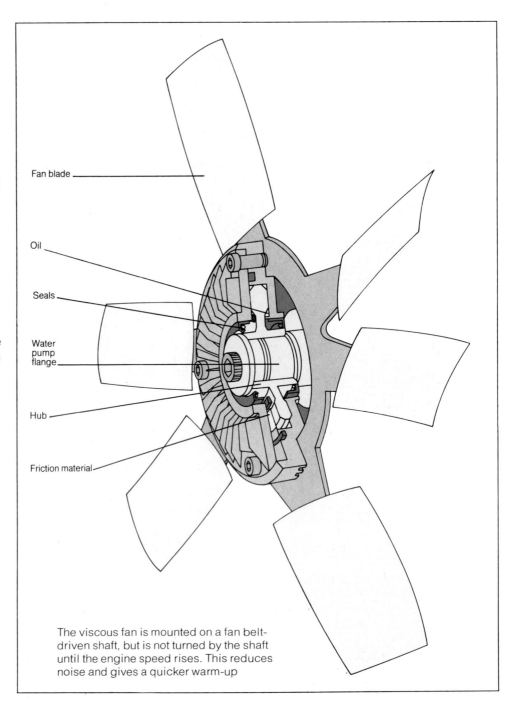

Fan blade

Oil

Seals

Water pump flange

Hub

Friction material

The viscous fan is mounted on a fan belt-driven shaft, but is not turned by the shaft until the engine speed rises. This reduces noise and gives a quicker warm-up

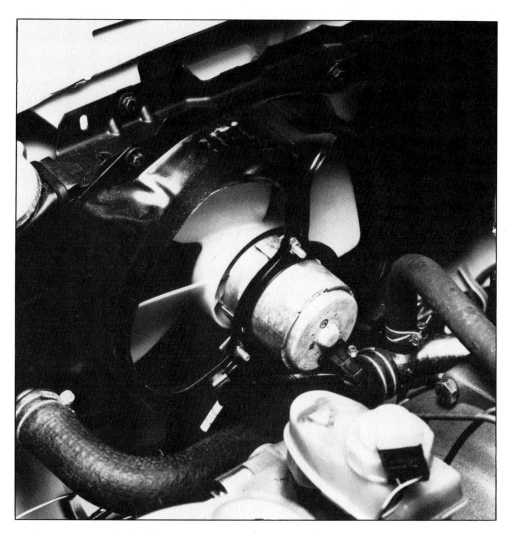

An all-electric cooling fan is an electric motor driving a light fan. It operates automatically when the coolant reaches a pre-determined temperature

Electromagnetically-coupled fans

On some cars the coupling between the fan and its belt-driven drive-shaft is by electromagnets. These are switched on automatically by sensors in the cooling system and operate the fan if the engine nears its maximum safe temperature limit (about 85°C) and are switched off again at a slightly lower temperature (about 75°C).

Electric fans

Some car makers dispense with the conventionally-mounted fan altogether and use all-electric cooling fans. These are usually mounted on a radiator shroud and are placed in front of, or behind, the radiator core.

The unit, which can be bought as an accessory to replace a conventional, mechanically-driven cooling fan, is a simple electric motor driving a light plastic, multi-bladed fan. Control is by a temperature-sensitive switch in the cooling system. The current supply is sometimes taken from a point in the circuit which is independent of ignition switch control. Where this is done, the cooling fan can operate after the engine has been switched off, thus cooling an engine to a safe level should it have reached overheating conditions.

The advantages of the electric fan are that it is in operation only when required (thus the energy required to turn it is minimised), the engine can be made shorter, and under-bonnet vibration and noise are reduced.

Viscous-coupled fans

A viscous-coupled fan is conventionally mounted on the water pump pulley and driven by the fan belt. The hub of the fan consists of an impeller inside a chamber which contains a thick silicone-based fluid. The impeller is driven by the pulley, and the fan, fitted to the chamber, is free to rotate about the impeller. It is driven only by the viscous nature of the fluid and the centrifugal forces set up by the impeller's churning of the chamber contents.

The device is designed so that at high engine speeds the coupling slips and the fan rotates at less than the speed of the drive shaft, thus providing sufficient airflow without absorbing as much power as a fixed-drive fan.

Fitting a new water pump

A persistent water leak that cannot be traced to the hoses or radiator may be caused by a defective water pump. A defective pump invariably leaks at the point where the pulley spindle emerges from the pump casing, and the leak is not always obvious because the rotating pulley sprays leaking coolant across the front of the engine, where it evaporates. Because escaping hot water washes lubricant from the spindle bearings, making them wear out fast, a quick test for a leaking pump is to check the bearing condition.

Loosen the fan belt, grip the pump pulley (or the fan if it is fixed to the pulley) and try to rock the spindle up and down (1). If there is more than the smallest trace of movement, the pump is likely to be leaking.

Reconditioned pumps are available in exchange for your old one. At the same time you should get a new gasket, some non-hardening sealing compound and, where applicable, a new by-pass hose which some engines have to link the pump to the cylinder head.

First drain the cooling system, remove the top hose and hoses attached to the old pump. Loosen the generator and remove the drive belt. If the fan is fixed to the pump pulley, remove it. On some cars the radiator must be disconnected and moved to reach the fan fixings. Remove the pulley. Undo the attachment bolts round the edge of the pump using a socket and short extension. As the bolts are of different lengths, make a note of their position to ensure correct re-assembly.

If the pump has a small by-pass hose linking it to the cylinder head, loosen its hose clips, then remove the pump—if necessary lightly tapping it free.

Remove the old gasket remains from the front of the engine with a knife blade, then fit a new gasket to the replacement pump, holding it in place with non-setting sealant (2). Smear sealant on the joint on the front of the engine. If the pump has a by-pass hose, fit a new one. Clip it lightly to the stub on the pump and slip a clip on its upper end. Fit the pump to the engine, where necessary guiding the by-pass hose on to its fitting stub on the cylinder head. Tighten the pump fixings evenly (3) and fully tighten the by-pass hose clips, if applicable.

Refit the radiator, hoses and fan, then retension the fan belt before refilling the system with coolant.

With the fan belt slack, feel for play by trying to move the spindle up and down

Fit a new pump gasket, holding it in place with a non-setting sealing compound

Fit the pump to the engine, tightening all the fixings evenly to avoid distortion

Checking the thermostat

If the engine overheats rapidly from a cold start and there is no apparent sedimentation in the radiator, or if it takes longer than normal to reach operating temperature, there may be a thermostat problem.

To check the thermostat you will need spanners to fit the housing nuts or bolts, a thermometer reading to over 100°C, a new thermostat housing gasket and some gasket sealant or high-melting-point grease.

Drain about a quarter of the coolant from the radiator (retain it if it contains anti-freeze) and undo the housing bolts. Lift off the housing (4), if necessary tapping it gently with a soft-headed mallet. Never prise the housing off—this can damage the gasket seating on what is usually a soft alloy component.

When the engine is cold, the thermostat should be closed—remove it and fit a new one if it is open.

The opening point of a thermostat can be checked by heating it up in a pan of water (5). Use pliers to hold the unit away from the saucepan base and note the temperature on the thermometer at which the thermostat opens. This should open within 3°C of the temperature stamped on the thermostat body. Renew the unit if it is faulty.

When fitting a thermostat, use a knife to scrape all traces of old gasket off the housing and the block or cylinder head. Fit the thermostat into its seating (6). If it has an arrow on it or the word 'rad', this goes nearest the radiator. Lightly smear the gasket with sealant or grease on both sides and place it in position (7). Bolt up the housing, refit the top hose and refill the cooling system.

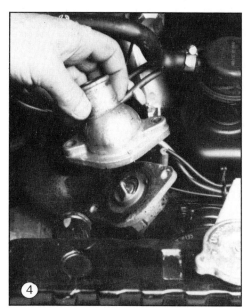

Lift off the thermostat housing, gently tapping it free if necessary

Check the operation of the thermostat by heating it in a pan of water

Check the marking to ensure the thermostat is fitted the right way round

Smear the housing gasket lightly with grease before positioning it

Anti-freeze

If the water in the cooling system freezes, the expanding ice can seriously damage the engine and cooling system. To prevent this happening, it is essential to add a concentration of anti-freeze chemicals to the water.

The anti-freeze consists of a liquid organic chemical which, when dissolved in water in sufficient concentration, depresses the freezing point below the temperatures normally encountered during the winter months. In the majority of anti-freezes the chemical used is ethylene glycol, although there are some cheaper brands that contain methanol (methyl alcohol, the main constituent of methylated spirit).

Methanol is an effective anti-freeze agent, but for use in cars it has one disadvantage. Unlike ethylene glycol it can evaporate out of the coolant solution. Thus it is impossible to predict what strength of anti-freeze remains in the coolant at any stage after it is mixed with the water.

Ethylene glycol does not evaporate to any significant extent, so its concentration in the coolant remains fairly stable and subject only to the dilution caused by topping up the radiator with water.

Inhibitors

Good anti-freeze brands also contain inhibitors which largely prevent corrosion of the many metal parts through which the water passes.

It has been usual, in the past, for anti-freeze makers to use different corrosion inhibitors for engines with iron blocks from those with alloy cylinder

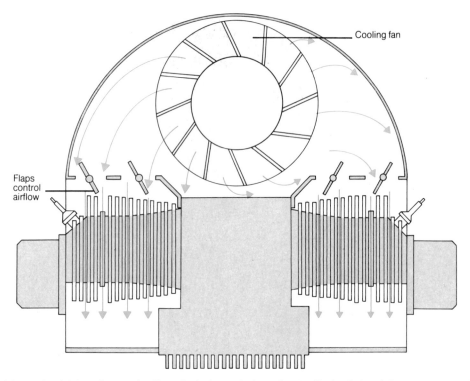

A large fan blows air over the fins of an air-cooled engine to dissipate heat. In some cases, thermostatically-controlled flaps regulate the temperature

blocks. But the advent of engines with iron blocks and alloy cylinder heads made it necessary to develop an anti-freeze suitable for both metals. The majority of brands now available are of a universal type.

New cars generally leave the factory with a mixture of 1 part anti-freeze to 2 parts water, a $33\frac{1}{3}\%$ solution that will protect the engine down to -20°C. This will not normally require renewal or topping up until the car is two years old. It is, however, wise to have a garage check the anti-freeze strength if at any time cooling system faults have been experienced or if regular top-ups have been made using water only.

Anti-freeze not only lowers the coolant's freezing point—its additives also raise its boiling point. This has become a significant factor on modern engines designed to operate at higher temperatures and pressures in the cooling system.

At one time it was usual to drain anti-freeze from the system during the summer months, but now it is accepted practice to keep the required concentration of anti-freeze in the coolant all year round for both its corrosion-inhibiting and temperature advantages. But if the heater loses its efficiency, you may need to bleed the system of air. On cars with bleed valves this job is easy (see page 84). Otherwise you may have to remove a heater hose as is described on page 75.

Air-cooled engines

These radiate heat from fins cast on the outside of the cylinders and cylinder head components. These fins provide a large heat transfer surface, and the longest fins are sited around the areas where most heat is developed.

All air-cooled engines have large fans which blow air over the fins. Generally the fan impels air into a ducting or shroud which fits closely over the engine and ensures that the air is evenly distributed.

Some engines have thermostatically-controlled flaps which direct more air over the engine as its temperature rises. The flaps may be controlled by a temperature-sensitive bellows and lever, or by a bi-metallic strip bending due to heat.

Replenishing the anti-freeze

Anti-freeze should be renewed at the interval recommended by the car manufacturer. At the same time it is wise to flush out any sediment and change any suspect hoses (see pages 73 and 74). As this operation involves removing the thermostat make sure that you have a new gasket.

When the system is clean and empty, reconnect all the hoses, tightening the clips firmly, refit the thermostat, close any drain taps and either set the heater control to 'hot', or ensure that the water valve is open.

Car makers state the capacity of the cooling system in the handbook. Mix the required quantity of anti-freeze and water (clean rain water is best if you have any) in a watering-can. The proportion of anti-freeze to water that you use depends on the protection required—details will be given on the anti-freeze containers.

Where there is an expansion reservoir, first fill this one-third full or to the level marked on the side.

On cars without bleed valves in the cooling system, fill the radiator slowly (1). When the level reaches the filler neck, start the engine and run it at a fast tick-over, leaving the filler cap off. As air bleeds from the cooling system into the radiator, the level will drop. Keep it topped up, and after five minutes stop the engine. Replace the cap, run the engine until it reaches normal operating temperature, then check the system thoroughly for leaks.

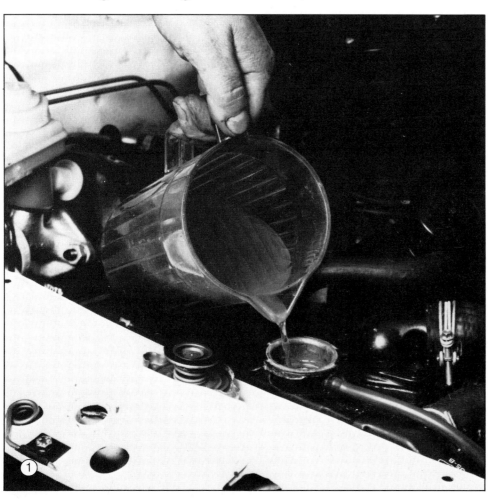

Fill the radiator until coolant reaches the filler neck, then run the engine at a fast tick-over with the cap off

Cars with bleed valves

A few cars have bleed valves to relieve air locks as the system is filled. On these, the hoses with bleed valves are usually blocked off during filling by squeezing them with clamps. Self-grip wrenches with their jaws covered with strips of hardboard, to prevent damaging the hoses, will do.
Renault—which fits bleed valves to its 5 and 12 models—recommends the following system: Fill the radiator, then clamp the heater return hose and the manifold heater hose as near the water pump as possible (1).
With the bleed valves open, run the engine at a fast idling speed. The level in the radiator will drop as air is expelled from each valve. Keep the radiator topped up, and close each of the bleed valves in turn as coolant, without any trace of air in it, flows from each valve. Remove the clamps or wrenches, then refit the radiator cap, run the engine to operating temperature and look for leaks. Also check the condition of the expansion hose.

Checking the cooling fan

The only service operation on an engine-driven fan is a regular check on fan belt condition and tension (see pages 104-105).
Electrically-operated fans are usually reliable but if you suspect that the unit or the control switch is faulty, carry out the following check: Locate the switch on the radiator header tank. If the fan works only with the ignition on, turn it on and, using a test light, determine whether or not one terminal has a current supply (2) (if one does not, the fault is in the wiring).

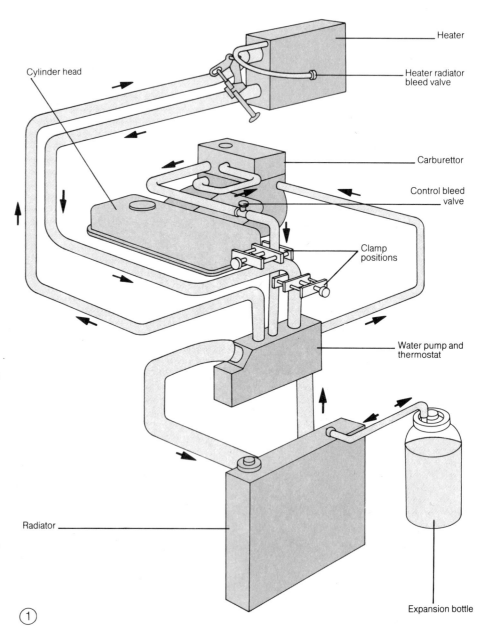

Heater

Heater radiator bleed valve

Cylinder head

Carburettor

Control bleed valve

Clamp positions

Water pump and thermostat

Radiator

Expansion bottle

(1)

Bleed the cooling system on certain Renaults by using clamps (a pair of self-grip wrenches will do) to block off the two pipes as shown. The engine should be run at a fast tick-over while the bleed valves are open

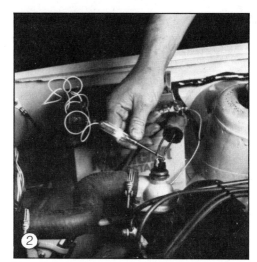

Use a test light to check that one of the control switch wires is live

Remove the leads and hold them together; the fan should work

Take the two leads off the switch and short the ends together (3). The fan should operate—this indicates a fault in the switch.

If the fan does not operate, check the wiring to it with a test light and tighten all connections. Only then should you consider that the fan itself may be faulty.

FAULT FINDING

Most cooling system problems result in overheating; the chart shows the most common causes and cures.

When examining a hot cooling system, leave it at least 15 minutes before taking the filler cap off, to allow the coolant temperature to drop below boiling point, then loosen the cap with a thick wad of rag wrapped round the hand so that it shrouds the filler neck. Turn the cap to the pressure-release position (usually a quarter turn) to allow steam to escape before removing it completely. When refilling, allow the engine to cool until it is hand-hot before adding cold water to the cooling system. Pour the fresh water in slowly so that it mixes thoroughly with any existing coolant.

Condition	Cause	Cure
High temperature gauge reading, ignition warning light on	Fan belt loose or broken	Stop immediately. Tighten belt or fit a new one (pages 104-105)
Loss of coolant (1)	Hose leaking	Tighten hose clips. Renew damaged hose (pages 72-73)
Loss of coolant (2)	Pressure cap faulty	Have cap tested by a garage – fit a new one if it is faulty
Loss of coolant (3)	Leaking radiator	Have radiator pressure-tested. Renew if faulty
Loss of coolant (4)	Water pump failure	Check and renew if necessary (page 80)
Loss of coolant – water on carpets	Leaking heater	Renew damaged hoses (page 73) or heater radiator
Overheating (1)	Blocked radiator matrix	Remove radiator. Clean dirt from matrix (page 74)
Overheating (2)	Radiator blocked internally	Back-flush to remove sediment (page 74). If no improvement, fit a new radiator
Overheating (3)	Thermostat jammed shut	Remove and test thermostat (page 81). Renew if faulty
Overheating (4)	Cooling fan ineffective	Check belt tension. Ensure viscous fans rotate with engine, test electric fans (page 84)
Heater stays cool	Thermostat jammed open	Test thermostat (page 81). Renew if faulty

ELECTRICS

What you can do:

	Pages		Pages
Care for the battery	90	Set the contact-breaker gap	97
Check electrolyte level	90	Use a dwell meter	98
Test electrolyte strength	90	Set ignition timing statically	98-99
Charge the battery	91	Set timing stroboscopically	100
Remove corrosion	91	Check the high-tension	
Check the case	91	components	100
Service the ignition system	96	Service the generator	104
Renew contact-breaker points	96	Tension the drive belt	104
		Reset an adjustable pulley	104
		Lubricate the generator	105

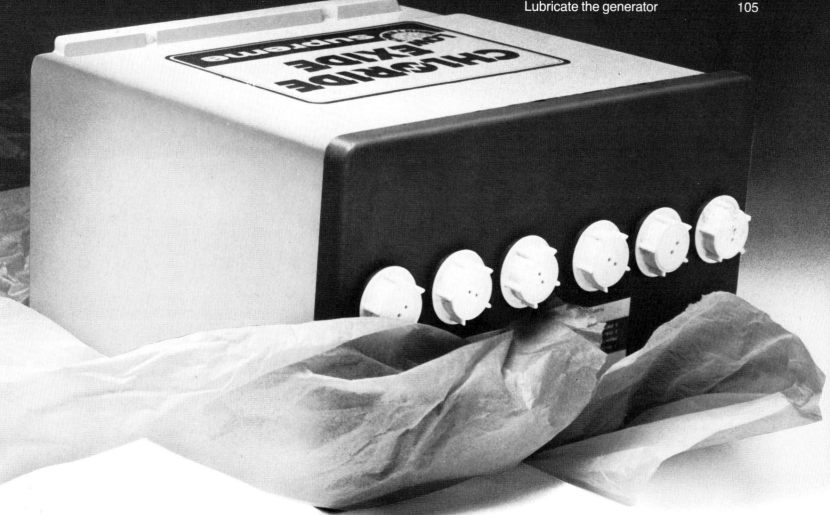

Since the early days of motoring it is the car's electrical system that has undergone the most drastic changes in design.

The advent of materials such as plastics for insulation and alloys for the manufacture of lightweight generators, plus the continuing advances made in semi-conductor technology have meant that, as each year goes by, car electrical systems become more sophisticated and complex yet, ultimately, more reliable.

It is progress that is urgently needed, because electrical faults still account for most roadside breakdowns and are responsible for the majority of calls to the emergency services.

The electrical circuitry of modern cars is becoming very advanced, with many sealed units serviceable only by specialists, and some that are simply discarded as uneconomical to repair once a fault is found in them. Nevertheless an understanding of how each circuit works can still prevent breakdowns or save hours of kerbside delay and worry. Except when it is impossible to carry out checks and tests without doing so, always disconnect the battery from the car when carrying out electrical work.

Battery

All cars have a lead-acid battery—a means of storing and recovering generated electrical energy. A 12-volt car battery has six separate cells containing an electrolyte solution of diluted sulphuric acid. Suspended in the acid are plates made from two different forms of lead. Plates of lead peroxide are inter-leaved with plates of a chemically active form of pure lead. Within each cell the lead peroxide plates are connected electrically to the battery positive terminal, and the active lead plates are joined to the negative terminal.

When the battery is connected into an electrical circuit, a chemical action starts in which the acid in the electrolyte changes the lead compounds into lead sulphate. As the battery power is used, acid enters the plate, progressively diluting the electrolyte's acid strength. Recharging the battery reverses the process. When a power source (the car's generator or a battery charger) is connected to the battery, the lead compounds change back to their original state.

Electrical power is produced by the flow of minute atomic components called electrons. The force or pressure with which they flow, often called the potential, is measured in volts. All modern cars have batteries with a potential of 12 volts, although there are a few old European cars still running with 6-volt batteries.

Battery capacities

Voltage is not the only way in which a battery is rated. The actual amount of electricity which the battery can provide is dependent on the number of plates in each cell, and is measured in ampere/hours.

Simply, this indicates the number of hours during which the battery will supply useful current. Known as the battery capacity, it is measured over 10 or 20 hours (quoted as the 10- or 20-hour rate) to provide accurate performance comparisons between different batteries.

Batteries installed by car manufacturers are usually rated in the 30-40 ampere/hour range. Batteries with larger capacities can be fitted. These have more reserves of power to cope with accessories that may be switched on when the engine is not running (perhaps powering a caravan's lights), or greater capacity to deal with frequent starting or the problems of very cold weather.

Polarity

Every battery has a positive (+) and a negative (−) terminal denoting the direction in which current flows when a circuit is connected between the two. The way the battery is connected determines the polarity of the system. Most modern cars have negative polarity, or negative earth, where the negative battery terminal is connected by a thick wire or strap to the car's bodywork, while the positive terminal is connected to the main charging and power supply leads.

Up to ten years ago, most British cars had a positive-earth system, where the main earthing strap went from the positive battery terminal to the car body. Polarity has little effect on the day-to-day working of the electrical system, but it is important to know the polarity when reconnecting a battery into a car, when charging the battery, when selecting electrical accessories, and when using jump-leads.

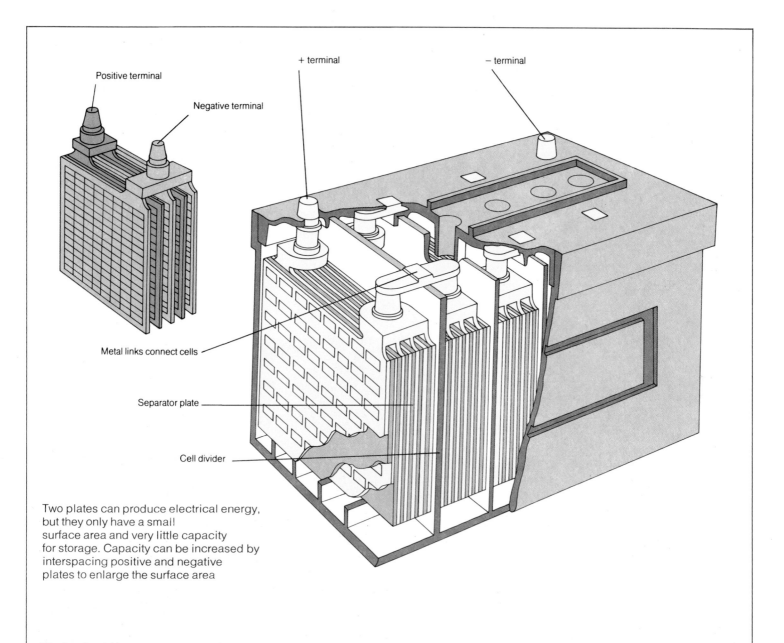

Positive terminal

Negative terminal

+ terminal

− terminal

Metal links connect cells

Separator plate

Cell divider

Two plates can produce electrical energy, but they only have a small surface area and very little capacity for storage. Capacity can be increased by interspacing positive and negative plates to enlarge the surface area

The lead-acid battery stores electrical power to start the car and operate the lights when the engine is not running. Its capacity is measured in ampere/hours. A 48-hour battery should deliver a current at 1 amp for 48 hours, 2 amps for 24 hours. Greatest demand on the battery is when the engine is started—300 to 400 amps may be needed to get the engine moving on a cold morning

BATTERY CARE
Checking electrolyte level

The level of the electrolyte should always be maintained high enough to cover the plates in each cell. As some water is used up in operating the battery, this must be replenished occasionally. To top up a battery *use only de-ionised or distilled water.*

On modern, translucent plastic-cased batteries it is possible to see the electrolyte level (a torch held behind the case often helps), but on older units with black casings the only way to see the level is to remove the caps and peer through the cell filler holes. Dispensers of top-up water sold by garages have spouts that enable topping-up to be done a few drops at a time (1).

Testing electrolyte strength

A measure of electrolyte strength provides a guide to the state of battery charge. Measurements are taken with a battery hydrometer.

The hydrometer can be a simple glass tube containing three coloured plastic balls. They float in electrolyte, which is withdrawn from a cell by a rubber bulb. More accurate hydrometers have a calibrated float inside the stem of a pipette.

Before using a hydrometer, top up each electrolyte cell to the proper level and charge the battery for at least one hour. From one cell, draw sufficient electrolyte into the instrument to support the float or the plastic balls fully, and note the reading (2). Return the liquid to the correct cell before proceeding to the next one.

After use, wash out the hydrometer with tap water. Battery acid is corrosive and destroys clothes, irritates skin and attacks car bodywork. If a drop is spilled, wipe it up immediately and wash the affected area with tap water.

If the hydrometer has a calibrated float, this is what the readings mean:
1.270-1.290 fully charged
1.190-1.210 about half discharged (below this level a battery must be charged immediately to prolong its active life)
1.110-1.130 fully discharged

These figures apply at an air temperature of 13°C-18°C

Top-up a battery with a dispenser which has a spout that enables the correct amount of water to be added

Draw sufficient electrolyte into the hydrometer to support the float fully, then note the reading

Battery charging

Battery chargers often have a high and low charging range, a meter to give a rough indication of the current being restored to the battery, and fuse protection of both the mains input (in the mains plug) and the low voltage output leads. The high charging rate corresponds to a maximum output of approximately 4amps and the low rate to about 1amp. Take care when using a charger to connect it correctly, clipping the positive charger lead to the positive battery terminal and the negative to negative. Incorrect connection may blow a fuse or damage the charger.

Wire-brush off powdery corrosion on the battery posts and connectors

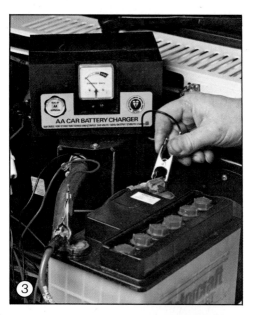

Connect the charger leads to the battery before switching on the charger

It is not necessary to disconnect the battery leads, but if the battery is removed from the car, always put it in a well-ventilated area—the gases liberated during charging are inflammable.
Connect the charger leads to the battery before switching the charger on at the mains (3). When switching off, be careful to disconnect the charger at the mains before unclipping the leads.
It is not advisable to use the high charging rate all the time—a battery responds better to a lengthy period of charging at a lower rate. Check and if necessary top-up electrolyte levels with distilled water before charging begins, for if a charger is left on inadvertently, a considerable amount of electrolyte can disappear.

Getting rid of corrosion

Powdery corrosion on the battery posts and connectors should be wire-brushed off (4) and any residue washed away with a solution of household soda. Thoroughly dry the components and smear the surfaces with petroleum jelly after making the reconnection (5).

Checking the case

Examine the case for any signs of leakage or cracking—battery acid seriously corrodes car bodywork. Check the security of the battery clamps—vibration and loose movement of the battery cause rapid deterioration of the plate materials.

Smear the surfaces with petroleum jelly after reconnection

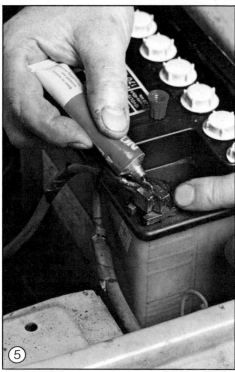

Ignition system

A key part of the electrical circuitry, and the part most prone to breakdown, is the engine ignition system. On most cars this consists of a group of three components—the ignition coil, spark plugs and distributor.

The ignition coil is designed to raise the car's battery or generator voltage (12-14 volts) to the high voltage (4,000 to 12,000 volts) needed to create an electrical spark at the gap between the centre and side electrodes of a spark plug. The link between the coil and the plug is made by the distributor which performs two vital functions.

Contact-breaker points

Inside the distributor, a cam (rotating at half engine speed) opens and closes a set of contact-breaker points. This action switches on and off the battery voltage supplied to the coil, and produces a high voltage from the coil's secondary windings which fires each spark plug at the correct moment in the engine's firing cycle.

Capacitor

Each time the contact-breaker points open, a current of about 300 volts is generated in the coil primary windings. This would arc across the contacts, burning them if the contacts were not protected by a capacitor.

The capacitor, which is connected between the moving contact point and earth, absorbs the high voltage generated as the contacts open. This then discharges it back through the primary windings in the coil, thus assisting it to produce the high voltage in its secondary winding.

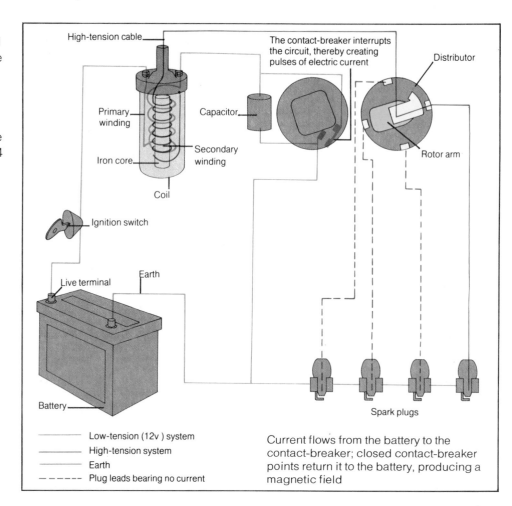

High-tension cable

The contact-breaker interrupts the circuit, thereby creating pulses of electric current

Distributor

Primary winding

Capacitor

Secondary winding

Rotor arm

Iron core

Coil

Ignition switch

Earth

Live terminal

Battery

Spark plugs

Low-tension (12v) system
High-tension system
Earth
Plug leads bearing no current

Current flows from the battery to the contact-breaker; closed contact-breaker points return it to the battery, producing a magnetic field

Ignition timing

Distributor adjustments can be made to alter the timing of the spark at the plug in relation to the position of the piston within a cylinder at the time of firing. Ignition timing is always related to this position and is quoted as the number of degrees turned by the crankshaft before the piston reaches the top of its stroke (top dead centre) on the firing stroke—for instance, 3°BTDC (before top dead centre).

Adjustments can also be made to the distance between the two contact-breaker points (the contact gap) when they are held fully open by the distributor cam—this gap affects both their performance and the timing of the spark.

Another ignition measurement is the dwell angle, which is the number of degrees rotated by the distributor cam while the points are closed. This can be measured using a dwell angle meter.

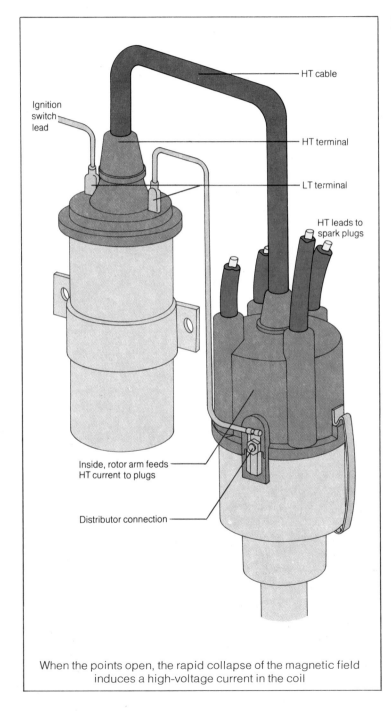

Ignition switch lead

HT cable

HT terminal

LT terminal

HT leads to spark plugs

Inside, rotor arm feeds HT current to plugs

Distributor connection

When the points open, the rapid collapse of the magnetic field induces a high-voltage current in the coil

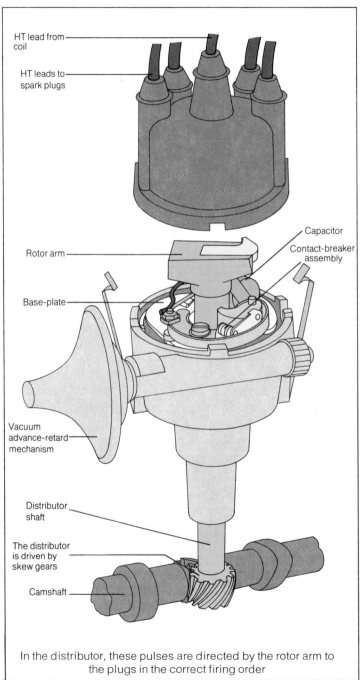

HT lead from coil

HT leads to spark plugs

Rotor arm

Base-plate

Capacitor

Contact-breaker assembly

Vacuum advance-retard mechanism

Distributor shaft

The distributor is driven by skew gears

Camshaft

In the distributor, these pulses are directed by the rotor arm to the plugs in the correct firing order

Automatic ignition timing

To enable the engine to perform efficiently at all speeds, the ignition timing needs to be varied automatically. The fuel/air mixture in the combustion chamber takes time to burn and produce power, so as engine speed increases, it is necessary to start burning the mixture sooner—later if the engine speed is reduced. This is done automatically by a mechanical, and sometimes also by a vacuum-assisted, ignition-advance mechanism.

With a mechanical advance system, the distributor cam which opens the contact-breaker points is connected to the distributor shaft through a pair of spring-loaded flyweights. As the engine speed increases, centrifugal force throws the flyweights outwards, and this action twists the distributor cam in advance of the drive shaft, so that the contacts are opened sooner, igniting the mixture earlier.

A vacuum-advance system adjusts the ignition timing in response to engine load, and is operated by inlet manifold vacuum. When, for instance, the throttle is only partly open, and inlet manifold vacuum is high, only a small quantity of air is drawn into the combustion chamber, and the mixture burns relatively slowly. It is therefore desirable to start the mixture burning earlier.

The adjustment is made by a vacuum capsule connected to the inlet manifold which moves the contact-breaker assembly in relation to the distributor cam. Moving the assembly in the opposite direction to cam rotation advances the ignition. Vacuum advance works in addition to centrifugal advance.

Distributing HT current

The distributor's other function is to distribute each burst of spark energy from the coil to the correct spark plug in the sequence of the engine's firing order. This is done by a rotary switch under the distributor cap which is fed by a single HT or high tension lead (the king lead) running from the coil to the centre of the distributor cap.

Inside the cap this HT lead makes contact through a small spring-loaded brush, or leaf spring, with the centre of a rotor arm which is keyed to, and turns with, the distributor cam.

As the rotor arm rotates, its tip passes close to a series of metal segments moulded into the cap. Each segment is connected by a high tension lead to a spark plug.

Spark energy which is released by the coil travels along the king lead, down through the brush, along the rotor arm, and jumps the tiny gap to the metal segment from where it is sent on to the corresponding spark plug.

Electronic ignition

Electronic ignition is being used increasingly on new models. The systems vary considerably, but all have one important feature: the mechanical contact breakers, which wear and alter the ignition timing over a period, are replaced by an electrical means of switching—a sealed, non-serviceable semi-conductor component that cannot wear out.

This means that electronic systems can be adjusted to give correct ignition timing and then forgotten—service adjustments should never normally be necessary.

Ballast resistors

A ballast resistor may be a length of resistive wire in the car's wiring loom, or it can take the form of a ceramic-bodied component, which is mounted next to the ignition coil.

It is used in conjunction with a 7-8 volt coil, and its purpose is to reduce battery voltage to that required by the coil. When the engine is started, battery

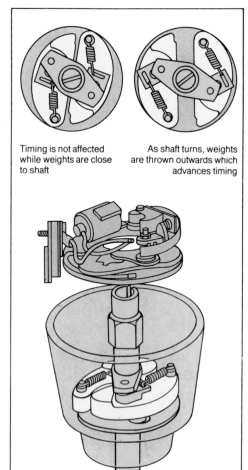

Timing is not affected while weights are close to shaft

As shaft turns, weights are thrown outwards which advances timing

The centrifugal advance mechanism is located in the bottom of the distributor

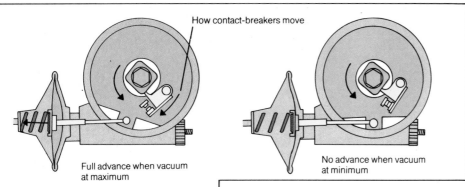

How contact-breakers move

Full advance when vacuum at maximum

No advance when vacuum at minimum

voltage can be reduced significantly by the starter motor load. To compensate for this, the ballast resistor is switched out of the circuit and the coil is supplied directly with the full available battery voltage (perhaps as low as 9 volts with the starter working).

Even this lower voltage is higher than the coil's normal potential and the result is bigger sparks at the plugs, which assist starting.

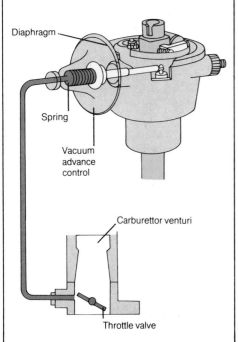

Diaphragm

Spring

Vacuum advance control

Carburettor venturi

Throttle valve

The amount of throttle used alters the vacuum in the inlet manifold and controls the degree of ignition advance. A closing throttle will increase suction on the diaphragm. But as it is opened suction is reduced. Spark timing is advanced and retarded by the movement of the contact-breakers in relaton to the cam

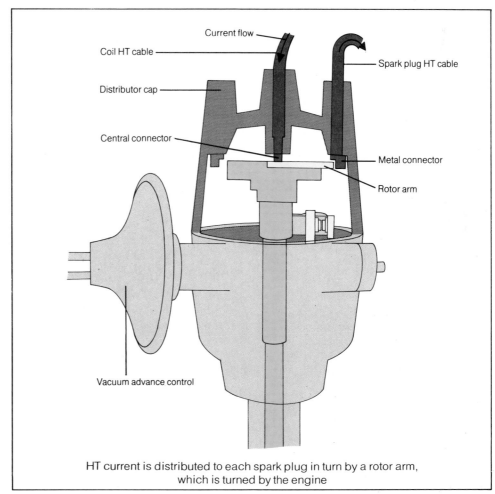

Current flow

Coil HT cable

Distributor cap

Central connector

Spark plug HT cable

Metal connector

Rotor arm

Vacuum advance control

HT current is distributed to each spark plug in turn by a rotor arm, which is turned by the engine

Servicing the ignition system

Ignition servicing calls for a small set of special tools and instruments. You will need feeler gauges—thin metal blades varying in thickness from 1½-15 thousandths of an inch (0.04-0.4mm) and a 12-volt test light. If you have a hand-held tachometer/dwell meter, it will determine both engine speed and the dwell angle of the contact-breaker points.

Ignition timing is best checked with a stroboscopic timing light, which is used while the engine is running. Where static timing information is given in the car handbook, the 12-volt test light can be used.

Renewing contact-breaker points

Lift off the distributor cap after prising off the two spring securing clips. Underneath you will find one of three different designs. In Lucas, Motorcraft, some AC Delco, some Bosch and some Ducellier distributors, the base plate on which the contact breakers are mounted is revealed, with relatively easy access to the points (1).

On some AC Delco and Marelli distributors a shield bearing the rotor arm is exposed (2), and to get at the contact-breakers this must be taken off (underneath are the centrifugal advance weights) by undoing two further screws (3). In some Bosch distributors, an upper bearing plate must be removed to reach the points.

On all types, the contact-breaker sets are removed by undoing the fixing screw(s) (4), and disconnecting a single wire connection (5). Make a note of the position of all components so that the new contacts can be assembled correctly.

Replacement contact-breaker sets are supplied as single or two-piece units depending on the type of distributor. Modern sets can usually be assembled only one way, but on earlier contacts it is possible to create a short circuit by assembling them incorrectly. If the engine will not start afterwards, make sure that the points are opening and closing and that the spring blade is connected to the feed wire. Also ensure that the feed wire is insulated from the distributor body.

The points are easily accessible

The shield bearing the rotor arm exposed

Undo two screws to remove the shield

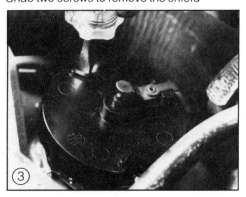

Unscrew the contact-breaker set

Disconnect the wire connection

Setting the gap

Stand the car on flat ground, engage top gear and release the handbrake. Remove the distributor cap and push or pull the car backwards and forwards until the plastic heel of the contact-breaker is resting on the highest point of the cam lobe.

Select the correct feeler gauge (the right setting of the points gap will be given in the car handbook) and place the metal strip into the gap between the two contact points (6).

Loosen the securing screw(s) slightly and use a slim screwdriver blade to lever the fixed part of the contact-breaker (7) until the gap is the same as the thickness of the feeler gauge—signalled by a small resistance to the blade as it is inserted between the two points.

Retighten the fixings and recheck the gap to ensure that tightening up has not disturbed the adjustment.

Check that the points are fully open before sliding the feeler gauge into the gap. If the points are pushed apart or the feeler is loose, the points need adjusting

Slacken the securing screw and with the screwdriver, lever the fixed contact to adjust the gap to the correct setting. Tighten the locking screw and recheck

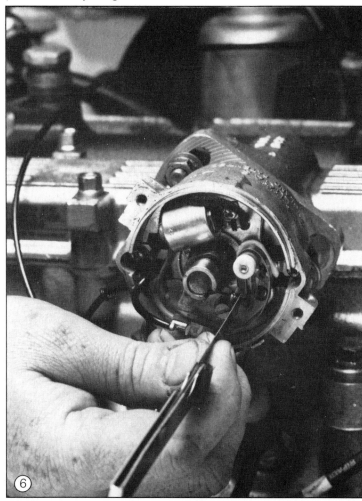

(6)

(7)

Gap setting by dwell angle

In use, a small pile builds up on one contact and a corresponding pit forms on the other. This makes accurate feeler gauge measurement impossible, but worn contacts can be adjusted if an electronic dwell meter is used. The meter also takes into account any wear in the distributor.

If fitting new points, set them to approximately the right gap using feeler gauges, and reassemble the distributor. Connect up the dwell angle meter (usually the leads are connected to the distributor side terminal and to earth). Start the engine and allow the idle speed to settle. Check the dwell angle reading on the scale of the meter (1). It will probably be in the range 42°-56° for four-cylinder engines, but the exact figure, within a small tolerance range, will be given in the car handbook. If not, try the workshop manual.

If the dwell angle is incorrect, stop the engine, remove the distributor cap, and set the moving contact so that it is fully propped open by one lobe of the cam (see page 97). Loosen the fixings and reduce the gap slightly to increase the dwell angle, or enlarge the gap to reduce the angle. Retighten the fixings, refit the cap and check again with the meter.

Static ignition timing

The ignition timing is one of the most important settings on the car as it affects engine performance and fuel economy. The static method of setting the timing is fairly accurate, and the only special equipment required is a 12-volt test lamp. Connect the lamp between the small terminal on the coil to which the

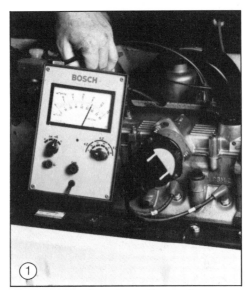

(1)

Check the dwell angle reading on the scale of the meter. The manufacturers can supply exact figures

Examples of how the timing marks are displayed on different cars

distributor wire is connected, and earth (the car body or engine block). Loosen the distributor clamp bolt so that you can just turn the body of the distributor by hand. Do not turn it at this stage. Locate the engine timing marks—these are usually in the form of a scale or pointer on the engine block adjacent to the crankshaft pulley, which lines up with a reference notch on the pulley itself. On many front-wheel-drive cars the timing marks are under a small plug or cover plate on the flywheel— refer to a workshop manual.

Lift off the distributor cap and use a spanner on the crankshaft pulley nut, or push the car forward in top gear, to turn the engine until the distributor rotor arm points towards the plug lead connected

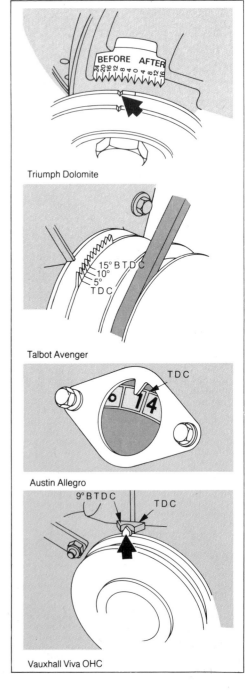

Triumph Dolomite

Talbot Avenger

Austin Allegro

Vauxhall Viva OHC

Use a spanner on the crankshaft pulley nut until the rotor arm points towards the lead connected to the timing cylinder

Turn the distributor a little until, at the moment the contact-breaker points open, the test light comes on

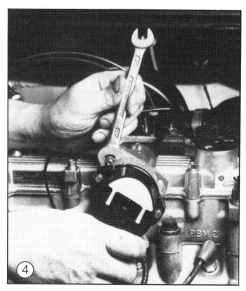

When you are sure you have found the exact point, clamp the distributor firmly in this position

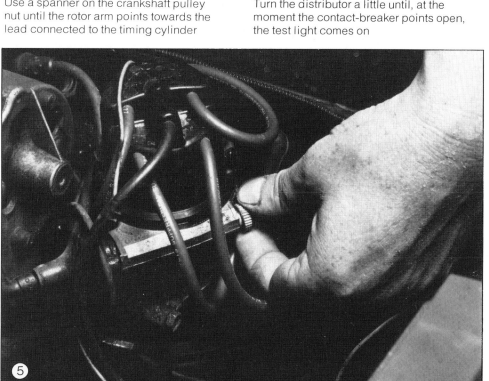

to the timing (usually no. 1) cylinder (2). This will bring the timing mark close to the pointer or scale. Check with a workshop manual that the mark is lined up with the correct point and finely adjust them into line.

Switch on the ignition and turn the distributor a little in the same direction as the rotor arm, then turn it in the opposite direction until, at the instant the contact-breaker points open, the test light comes on (3). Try this a few times until you are confident about the exact point, and clamp the distributor down firmly in this position (4). Some distributors have a knurled nut for fine adjustment which can be used after the clamp is tightened (5).

Some distributors have a knurled nut for fine adjustment which can be used after the clamp is tightened

Stroboscopic timing

Timing data in workshop manuals usually gives a setting for stroboscopic timing, which differs from the static setting. Other data is also given, the most important being the engine speed at which the setting should be performed—usually idling speed. It will also indicate whether or not the vacuum mechanism should be disconnected for the setting. If it should be disconnected, pull the rubber connector off the distributor diaphragm housing.

Connect up the stroboscope (timing light) and tachometer, following the maker's instructions. Start the engine and check that it is running at the correct speed—use the throttle-stop screw adjuster or idling screw to get the speed right (1). Loosen the distributor clamp bolt only just sufficiently to turn it. Point the light at the timing marks (2). The flashing light will 'freeze' the marks so that they appear stationary in relation to each other.

If necessary turn the distributor until the correct marks line up, then tighten the clamp. Reconnect the vacuum pipe.

The stroboscopic light flashes will 'freeze' the marks so that they appear stationary in relation to each other

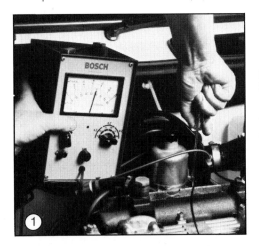

Use the throttle-stop screw adjuster or idling screw to get the speed right

Checking the high-tension components

Make sure that the insulation on the plug leads is free from dirt, moisture and fine surface cracks. High-tension cables (3) are sold in sets by garages—fit a new set if the old cables are damaged. Examine the distributor cap inside and out for signs of hairline cracking. A cap in this condition must be replaced. The same kind of cracking may also affect the insulator around the coil's terminals. If so, fit a new coil.

Examine the spark plugs about every 5,000 miles. If you have the plug electrodes sand-blasted clean by a garage, make sure that you wash the plugs thoroughly in petrol afterwards. To set the gap, use a gapping tool to bend the side electrode until the correct size feeler gauge fits snugly between the side and centre electrodes. On most

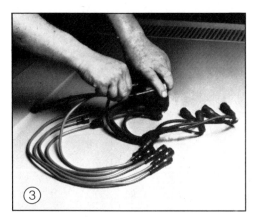

High-tension cables

Waterproof the electrics twice a year

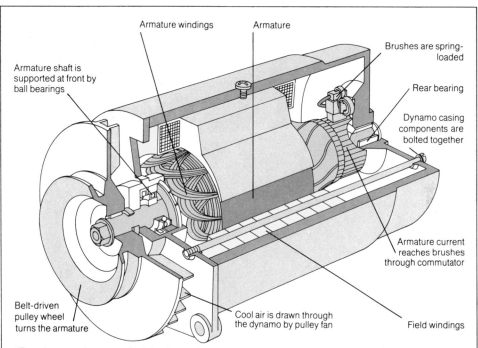

The dynamo has a cylindrical metal case and two pole pieces wound with coils of wire. The armature is turned between them when the dynamo is running

When an opposite magnetic pole passes the stator and winding (A) produces negative current, it passes through diode (2) but not diodes (1) or (1a). The other two windings will be producing negative current while stator winding (A) is at its maximum positive

cars the plug gap is .025-.040in—the exact dimension will be given in the handbook. On cars with conventional ignition systems, plugs should be replaced every 12,000 miles.
Check that all HT connections on the coil and at the plug and distributor caps are secure. Loose-fitting terminals cause sparking and burning. Use pliers or a screwdriver blade to re-shape loose terminals until they fit tightly. Damp start problems can be prevented by spraying low and high tension areas with a proprietary damp-proofing sealant (4).

Generators

When the car is on the road, the generator creates enough energy to supply the whole electrical needs and charge the battery, quickly replacing the current consumed in starting the car. Generators produce electricity by the principle that the movement of either a conducting wire or a magnetic field causes a current to flow in the wire. Two different types of generator are used. Many older cars have a dynamo in which it is the rotation of many coils of wire inside a magnetic field that produces the current. The most recent alternator does exactly the opposite—

the magnetic field is rotated at high speed inside stationary coils which provide the output.

The dynamo

A car dynamo has a heavy cylindrical metal case, inside which are clamped two metal pole pieces wound with coils of wire so that they become electro-magnets when the dynamo is running. Plates at each end of the body have bearings to support the armature shaft which is turned by a pulley. The pulley is connected to the engine through a drive belt—usually the same belt that turns the cooling fan.

Mounted on the armature shaft are the wire windings in which the current is generated, and a segmented commutator from which carbon brushes collect the generated current.

Without the commutator a dynamo, like all simple magnetic generators, would produce alternating current (ac), a form of electricity incompatible with the car's direct current (dc) system. So besides passing current generated in the rotating armature to the brushes, the commutator also, in effect, rectifies the alternating current to give an output in direct current. As we shall see, alternators need electronic help to do this job.

The alternator

Although it is belt-driven like the dynamo, the alternator pulley is smaller and runs fast enough to produce a significant current output even at engine idling speed.

The three-piece body has two end sections which clamp together over the stator, a metal former interlaced with the coils of wire in which a current is made. On the rotor shaft is mounted a large single coil of wire clamped between two magnetic pole pieces, which have interlocking toothed segments designed to produce a number of magnetic field changes per revolution. Also on the rotor are two slip rings wiped by stationary carbon brushes; these supply current to the rotating coil, which produces the field.

An alternator can be damaged by connecting or disconnecting it while the engine is running. Reversing battery connections, or a loose battery connection, will also damage it.

Rotating magnet

Stationary windings

In the basic dynamo, current flows through two stationary brushes

Field magnet shoe
Coil rotates in magnetic field
AC to DC commutator
Brushes
Windings for field magnets

AC current is converted to DC by diodes
Stator windings
Stator
Pulley
Rotor windings
Brushes
Slip rings
Slip rings
Rotor windings
Stator assembly houses rotor

Slip rings
Rotor windings

Stator windings

Iron stator

In the basic alternator, current is generated in a stationary winding by a rotating magnet. Current in the winding or stator is continually reversed as the magnet or rotor rotates

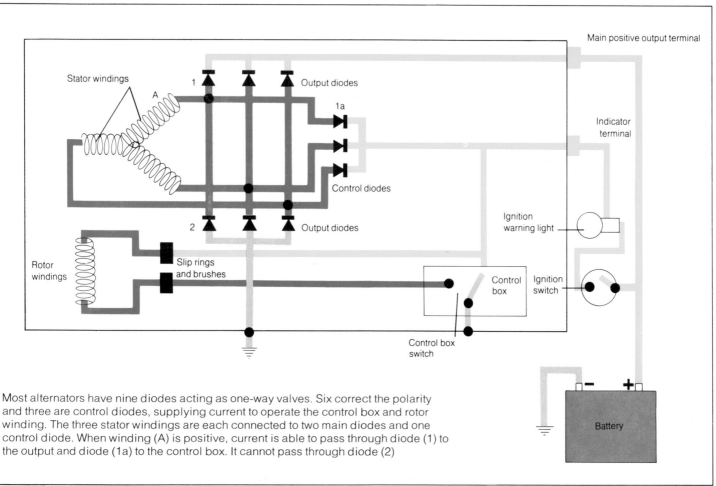

Stator windings

1   Output diodes

A

1a

Control diodes

2   Output diodes

Rotor windings

Slip rings and brushes

Control box

Control box switch

Main positive output terminal

Indicator terminal

Ignition warning light

Ignition switch

Battery

Most alternators have nine diodes acting as one-way valves. Six correct the polarity and three are control diodes, supplying current to operate the control box and rotor winding. The three stator windings are each connected to two main diodes and one control diode. When winding (A) is positive, current is able to pass through diode (1) to the output and diode (1a) to the control box. It cannot pass through diode (2)

Electronic rectifier

As its name suggests, an alternator produces alternating current which has to be modified (rectified) to the direct current required by the car's system. This is performed electronically by a diode rectifier pack.

There are six or nine of these small semi-conductor devices in the rectifier. Each one will allow an electrical current to pass in only one direction between its two connections. The diodes are arranged so that they produce an electronic maze into which alternating current passes to emerge flowing as direct current.

Drive belts

The whole electrical system relies on the condition and the correct adjustment of the V-belt which drives the generator, and often the fan and water pump too. If the belt—which is made from a strong combination of rubber and reinforcing fibres—is too tight there is a risk of over-stressing the generator and water pump bearings. If it is too loose it will not fully transmit the drive to the generator from the crankshaft pulley. The resultant slipping will quickly wear out the belt and also reduce the current generated. Always carry a spare fan belt of the correct size for your car, as emergency or temporary belts are not very efficient and can sometimes be rather difficult to fit.

Servicing generators

Most dynamos and alternators are bolted to the engine block in such a way that loosening the fixings allows the generator to be swung outwards to tension the drive belt.

Tensioning the drive belt

Belt tension should be checked once a week. The correct tension is gauged by the amount of free play in the middle of the longest stretch of the belt between two pulleys—for cars with alternators and short belt runs, ½in free play is correct. Up to ¾in free play is acceptable for longer belt runs and cars with dynamos. To adjust the belt tension, loosen the two pivot bolts of the generator (some models may have just one long bolt).

Loosen the adjusting-bracket bolt (if the generator has to be moved a long way the bolt securing this bracket to the cylinder block may also have to be loosened) until the generator is just free to move (1).

Pull the generator away from the block until the fan belt tension is correct, if necessary using a wooden lever. When tension is correct, tighten the adjusting bolt to secure it. Tighten the remaining fixings. Having fitted a new fan belt, recheck its tension after 100 miles.

Adjustable pulleys

A few cars, including the VW Beetle and Fiat 126, have generators with non-adjustable mountings. On these the fan belt is adjusted by removing spacer washers (or shims) from between the two halves of the generator pulley. Removing shims narrows the pulley, restricting its V-profile, and taking up

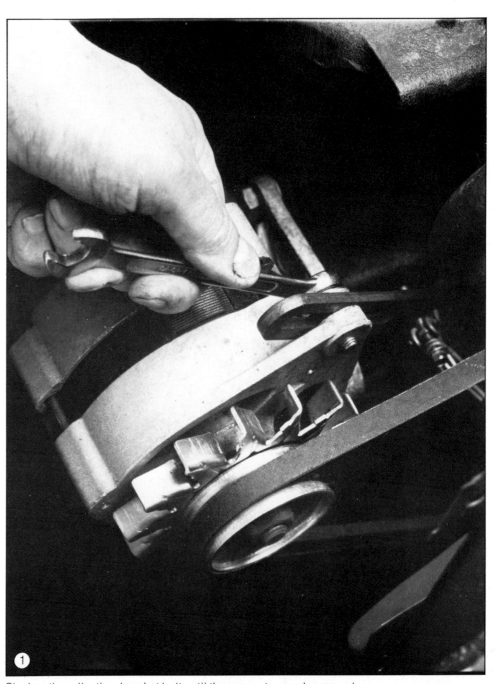

① Slacken the adjusting-bracket bolt until the generator can be moved

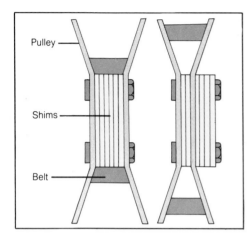

Pulley

Shims

Belt

With a split-pulley system, removing shims from between the two halves of the pulley makes the belt run wider and so increases its tension

slack by forcing the belt to ride higher in the groove.

Fiat uses a three-stud pulley mounting and normally up to five spacers are inserted between the pulley halves. A central bolt secures the VW pulley and up to eight washers are provided.

To tighten a slack belt it is usually necessary to separate the pulley halves and remove only one washer.

Do not discard washers as they are removed—they should be retained for future use by placing them between the fixings and the pulley.

Lubrication

Most dynamos have felt oiling pads to lubricate the bearing at the opposite end to the pulley. A few drops of oil in the oiling hole every 10,000-12,000 miles will extend bearing life (2). Alternators do not normally have a lubrication hole. Their bearings are packed with high melting point grease.

Apply a few drops of oil in the oiling hole every 10,000 – 12,000 miles to extend bearing life

GENERATOR CONTROLS
Dynamo control box

More sophisticated electrically than the dynamo itself is the dynamo control box, which acts as a guardian to the charging and electrical supply system. It is a semi-sealed unit, serviceable only by experts. It performs three jobs:

a it disconnects the dynamo from the electrical system so that the battery does not discharge through the generator while the engine is idling;

b it senses when dynamo output voltage is sufficient to supply the car's electrical needs and charge the battery, and regulates the output voltage to around 13 volts;

c it prevents current demand on the dynamo reaching the point at which the armature windings and commutator segments could be damaged by overheating.

There are two types of control box, both operating in similar ways: one has two electrical relays (two-bobbin type) and the other has three relays.

In the two-bobbin type, one relay is a cut-out which connects the dynamo in circuit when the output current reaches about 13 volts, and cuts out the dynamo if output falls to a point at which battery current starts feeding back through the generator.

The other relay is the combined current and voltage regulator and is normally switched on, allowing current to flow from the brushes to the dynamo field windings. When dynamo output is around 15 volts the magnetic field generated in the relay winding switches off the relay. The dynamo field weakens (although it is still fed a small current through a resistor) and voltage output

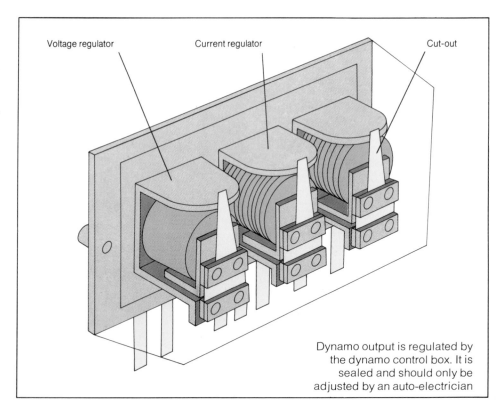

Voltage regulator   Current regulator   Cut-out

Dynamo output is regulated by the dynamo control box. It is sealed and should only be adjusted by an auto-electrician

falls until a spring closes the regulator contacts again. This cycle is repeated many times a second in normal operation, in this way controlling the dynamo's maximum output voltage. To control current, this relay is wound with an extra thick wire carrying the dynamo's total current output. If demand reaches a critical level the magnetic field produced by current in this wire delays the closure of the regulator points, adding to the restriction on output imposed by the voltage regulator. In this way the dynamo armature is protected from overheating. In the three-bobbin type, the voltage and current regulating functions are provided by separate relays.

Alternator voltage control

The one-way diodes used in a rectifier mean that the alternator does not need a cut-out, so the only regulation needed is of voltage. The voltage regulator unit is usually built-in and consists of a small sealed pack.

This contains an integrated circuit which electronically reproduces the on-off switching action of the voltage-control relay in the dynamo control box. Its effect is exactly the same—to switch off the field current supply at the correct voltage output and restore it as the voltage falls slightly below the acceptable level. Alternator output voltage is slightly lower than dynamo voltage—about 14–14.4 volts.

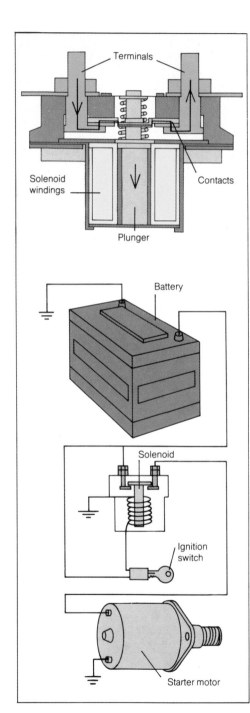

Terminals

Solenoid windings

Contacts

Plunger

Battery

Solenoid

Ignition switch

Starter motor

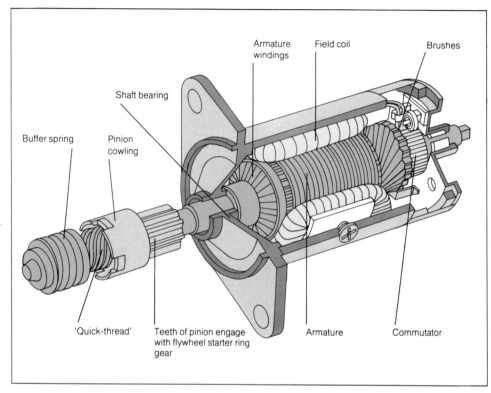

Armature windings

Field coil

Brushes

Shaft bearing

Buffer spring

Pinion cowling

'Quick-thread'

Teeth of pinion engage with flywheel starter ring gear

Armature

Commutator

Starter motors

To stir an engine to life and crank it at over 50rpm against the compression of the pistons and the resistance of cold oil demands a powerful motor.

The current demand during starting is very high—up to 360amps sets the motor turning, settling down to about 100amps while cranking, and so a circuit is provided almost exclusively to power the starter.

In its sturdy cylindrical body the starter has four magnetic pole pieces surrounded by aluminium or copper windings.

The solenoid is a magnetically-operated switch which is connected between the starter motor and the battery

The inertia starter has an extended armature shaft which carries a toothed pinion mounted on a 'quick-thread'

The armature rotates inside these field magnets. It is wound with coils of thick wire which provide minimal resistance to current flow. Large stationary brushes pass current to the armature windings through a commutator.

Power comes to the motor through a thick insulated cable leading from the battery to the starter solenoid—a heavy-duty remote switch that is triggered by the key-operated starter switch. From the solenoid, the feed is passed to the brushes from where it passes through the armature windings and the field coils to earth.

STARTER DRIVES
Inertia drive
This is used on starters operated by a separate solenoid mounted in the engine bay. As the motor is kicked into life by the initial burst of current through the armature and field windings, a small pinion gear, sliding on a spiral splined section of the rotor shaft, is thrown into engagement with the flywheel ring gear, and the starter begins to crank the engine.

Immediately the engine starts and picks up speed, the ring gear turns the pinion faster than the starter, so screwing the pinion back down the spiral rotor shaft, out of engagement. A buffer spring is fitted to the end of the shaft to reduce the shock which occurs when the pinion engages with the engine flywheel.

Pre-engaged pinion
This type of starter has its solenoid mounted to the motor body, where it performs the dual functions of pushing the pinion into engagement and switching on the motor. It is arranged so that the pinion engages with the ring gear just as the motor begins to turn. The pinion stays engaged with the flywheel until the ignition key is released.

INSTRUMENTS
Speedometer
Although it is driven by a cable, a speedometer works on electro-magnetic principles. Inside, a magnet rotates close to a drum of non-magnetic alloy which is fixed to a spindle carrying the speedometer needle. The movement of the instrument's needle pivot is restricted by a spiral clock-spring.

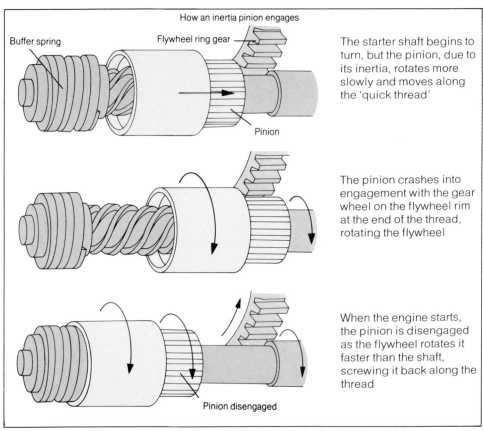

How an inertia pinion engages

Buffer spring — Flywheel ring gear — Pinion

The starter shaft begins to turn, but the pinion, due to its inertia, rotates more slowly and moves along the 'quick thread'

The pinion crashes into engagement with the gear wheel on the flywheel rim at the end of the thread, rotating the flywheel

When the engine starts, the pinion is disengaged as the flywheel rotates it faster than the shaft, screwing it back along the thread

Pinion disengaged

As the car speeds up, the rotating magnet creates electrical (eddy) currents in the adjacent drum. These currents form an electro-magnetic coupling that rotates the drum and speedometer needle in the same direction as the magnet. Since the needle is restrained by the spring the distance it can move is in direct proportion to the forces generated by the magnet. So the faster it goes, as the car speeds up, the more the drum moves the speedometer needle across a calibrated scale. The cable also mechanically drives the odometer or mileage recorder.

Tachometer
Commonly referred to as a rev-counter, a tachometer indicates engine speed. Early instruments were cable-driven but current models are electronic and are connected into the engine ignition, producing a reading based on the number of high-tension impulses supplied to the spark plugs.

The tachometer circuits produce a voltage pulse each time a spark occurs and by averaging it against time, a current proportional to engine speed is produced. The tachometer provides an rpm reading which varies according to the current produced.

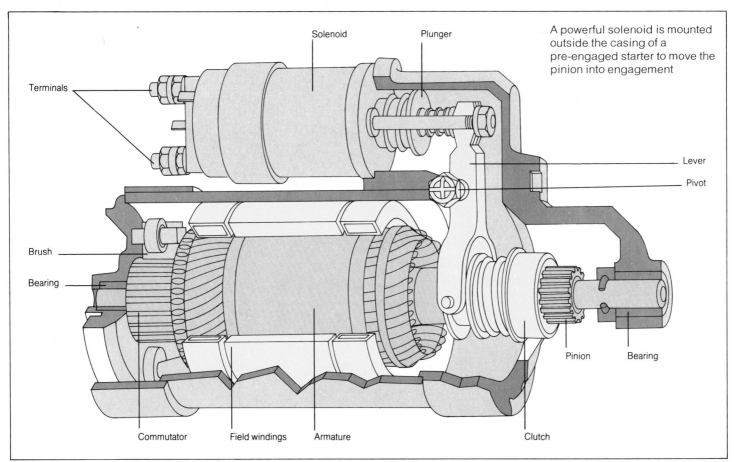

Terminals

Solenoid

Plunger

A powerful solenoid is mounted outside the casing of a pre-engaged starter to move the pinion into engagement

Lever

Pivot

Brush

Bearing

Pinion

Bearing

Commutator

Field windings

Armature

Clutch

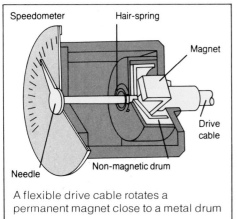

Speedometer

Hair-spring

Magnet

Drive cable

Needle

Non-magnetic drum

A flexible drive cable rotates a permanent magnet close to a metal drum

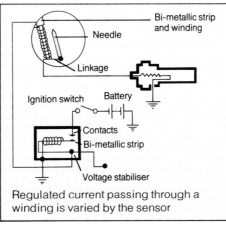

Bi-metallic strip and winding

Needle

Linkage

Ignition switch

Battery

Contacts

Bi-metallic strip

Voltage stabiliser

Regulated current passing through a winding is varied by the sensor

Bi-metallic instruments

Bi-metallic strip instruments work on the principle that a strip laminated from different metals that expand at different rates will bend when heated. Around the strip is wound a thin wire coil which warms up according to the current flowing through it. The strip is mechanically linked to a needle which can be moved across a scale. A sender device, which varies the current in the instrument circuit according to the quantity being measured, operates the gauge.

Fuel gauge

The fuel gauge sender is in the petrol tank and consists of a float on an arm which is connected to a variable resistor. When the tank is full the resistance of the sender is low, and more current passes through the winding on a bi-metallic strip. This bends to its maximum and gives a full-scale reading on the calibrated scale. As petrol is used, the resistance rises, the voltage at the gauge decreases, the strip straightens, and the reading drops.

Temperature gauge

The temperature gauge sender is fitted into the engine water-jacket near the thermostat. It contains a material, the electrical resistance of which decreases as temperature rises. This varies the voltage applied to the coil round the bi-metallic strip, and provides the appropriate reading.

Voltage stabiliser

Bi-metallic instruments are, in essence, voltmeters, and as the voltage can vary from 12 to about 14.5 volts, this difference could give false readings. To prevent inaccuracies, these instruments are fed current at an average of about 7 to 10 volts by a voltage stabiliser.

The voltage stabiliser also works on the bi-metallic-strip principle, but instead of moving a needle, the bending strip separates a pair of contacts carrying the power supply to the instruments. As the strip bends, the contacts separate, cutting the supply of current. The strip then cools and straightens to shut the contacts and make the circuit

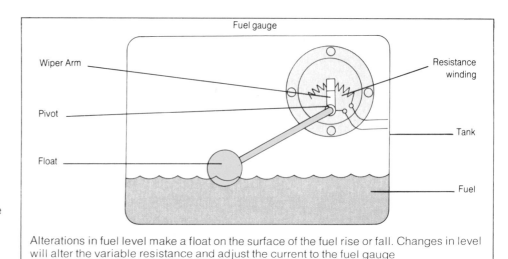

Alterations in fuel level make a float on the surface of the fuel rise or fall. Changes in level will alter the variable resistance and adjust the current to the fuel gauge

again. This takes place relatively slowly—about once a second—although the actual rate varies with the voltage.

The output from the stabiliser varies between zero and peak generator voltage, but since the instruments it feeds are very slow to react, they give a reading based on an average of the time the stabiliser contacts are closed.

Voltmeter and ammeter

Most car voltmeters are of the bi-metallic strip type and differ from fuel and temperature gauges only in their calibration. Because they must indicate the voltage of the system, they are not supplied by the voltage stabiliser. On some cars the voltmeter is called a battery condition indicator. In fact it only performs this function when the generator is not operating. While the engine is running at anything more than idle speed, the voltage shown on the scale is the output of the generator. The moving-coil ammeter contains a

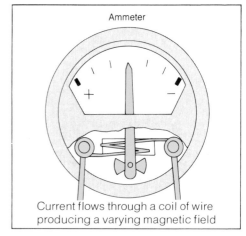

Current flows through a coil of wire producing a varying magnetic field

coil of wire through which current flows. As the flow fluctuates, it produces a varying magnetic field which is sensed by the movement of a small, finely balanced permanent magnet at the pivot of the instrument needle. Ammeter readings—usually on a scale calibrated from −30amps (discharge) to +30amps (charge)—show the amount of current being drawn from, or restored to, the battery.

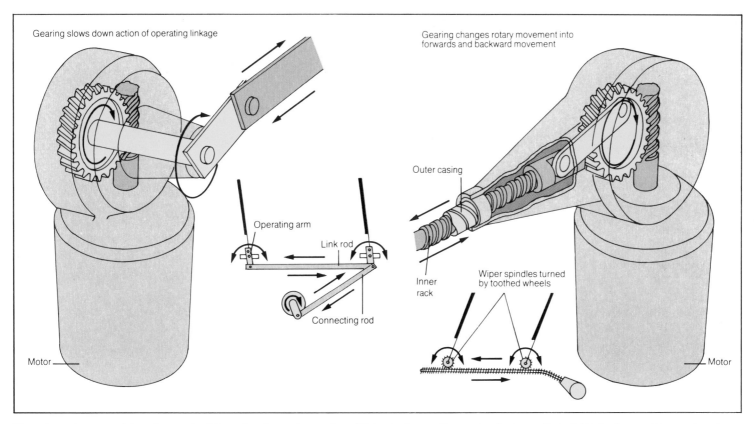

Gearing slows down action of operating linkage

Gearing changes rotary movement into forwards and backward movement

Operating arm

Link rod

Connecting rod

Outer casing

Inner rack

Wiper spindles turned by toothed wheels

Motor

Motor

The wipers here are driven by an electric motor, through a series of links and operating arms. A connecting-rod in a wiper motor gearbox is used on many cars to work a flexible rack (right) which engages with toothed wheels at the wiper arm base and operates the blades

Windscreen wipers

The driving force behind the windscreen wipers is a compact and powerful electric motor which is usually of the permanent-magnet type. Motor rotation is transferred through a worm gear to a large pinion. Near the edge of the pinion is a small pin which is linked to a short connecting rod.

On older cars, the connecting rod is pulled backwards and forwards in a housing as the pinion rotates, and its movement is transferred to a spiral-wire rack running in a metal tube. Attached to the other end of the tube are wheel-boxes, each containing a pinion, engaged with the rack. The pinion spindles are attached to the wiper arms and convert the push-pull action of the rack to the sweeping movement of the wipers. On newer cars, the to and fro motion is transmitted to the wiper spindles by a rod linkage.

Wipers are usually controlled by a stalk switch on the steering column and have up to four positions. These may be arranged from the bottom up, and provide wiper delay action, off, low speed and high speed. On more expensive or better-equipped cars, there may be a connection via the screenwash circuit which gives a wipe action when the washers are in use. Working the windscreen washers may also activate headlamp washers and wipers, if these are fitted.

Wiper-delay mechanisms are small transistorised circuits which rely on the action of a capacitor. This soaks up current until a point is reached at which it trips a transistor switch into operation to give a single wipe. The time delay, which is variable on some cars, is a valuable feature when the wipers are needed only intermittently.

Rear window wipers

Many small saloons with a hatchback or a sharply cut-off tail tend to draw road spray on to the rear window. Often a rear window wiper is fitted to keep the glass clean. As it has only one blade to drive, the motor is usually a little smaller than a normal wiper motor. It usually has a self-contained gearbox to provide reciprocating movement of the arm.

Screenwashers

By law, all cars on Britain's roads must have a working screenwash system. Although a few cars have hand-pumped washers, it is more usual now to have an electrical system powered by a small water pump mounted on, or close to, the screenwash fluid reservoir. This is usually controlled from the same stalk switch as the windscreen wipers, although some cars have a foot-operated bulb which incorporates an instant-wipe switch.

The pump draws water and screenwash additive from the reservoir through a pipe which has a small mesh filter on the end. Water then passes under pressure through a tube to jets which spray the water on to the screen. To prevent water draining back into the reservoir, a non-return valve is fitted in the system. Usually a flap valve is incorporated in the filter assembly. Most cars with rear window wipers have their own rear washer system.

Wiring systems

Each electrical part must have at least two connections—a feed from one battery pole and a return conducting path back to the opposite battery pole. Running two wires to each part in the car

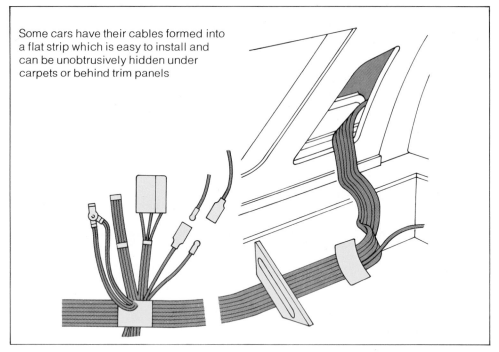

Some cars have their cables formed into a flat strip which is easy to install and can be unobtrusively hidden under carpets or behind trim panels

would result in an enormous tangle of connections and cables. The system is simplified, and the amount of wire almost halved, by using a single feed-wire through a switch to each component and allowing the car body, a good metallic conductor, to act as the return half of the circuit.

In electrical terms the car body, connected by a heavy duty metal strap or cable to one pole of the battery, becomes the earth. On the few cars with non-conductive glass-fibre bodies, each component has two wires and the one carrying the return circuit is joined to the nearest metal chassis member. Even using the bodyshell as a return circuit, there is over 200ft of wiring in the average car, and to simplify assembly, the wires to groups of components near each other are bundled into looms.

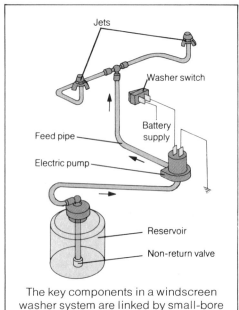

The key components in a windscreen washer system are linked by small-bore plastic pipes

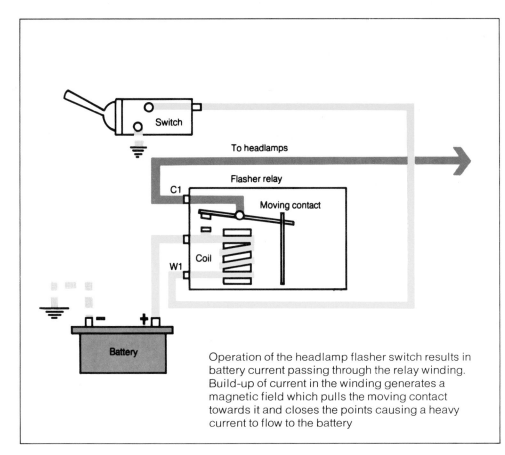

Operation of the headlamp flasher switch results in battery current passing through the relay winding. Build-up of current in the winding generates a magnetic field which pulls the moving contact towards it and closes the points causing a heavy current to flow to the battery

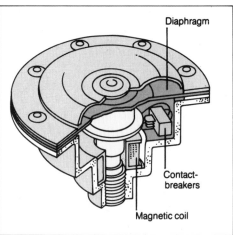

The diaphragm of an electric horn vibrates hundreds of times a second

Some cars have up to six of these separate wire bundles. An alternative to tying the wires together is to combine the cables on a flat strip, secured on one side by backing tape. BL uses this system on the Allegro.

To help identify them, wires in the loom are colour-coded by primary insulation colour and the use of bands or strips of up to two more colours. The colour code of each wire is given in a wiring diagram shown in the car handbook.

Fuses

To prevent a fault overheating the wiring and possibly starting a fire, the electrical system is protected by fuses. Most of these will be in a fusebox under the facia or in the engine compartment, although some are fitted in individual cables as line fuses. Each fuse may be a wire in a glass cartridge, or a solid ceramic cartridge with the fusible wire outside. On both, the wire melts if the circuit is overloaded.

Most cars made after 1975 are fitted with a fusible link. This is a special wire leading from the battery to the car's electrical systems. It is so designed that if a massive short-circuit occurs—say, in an accident—the wire will melt, disconnecting the battery.

Relays

A relay is an electrically-operated switch which prevents a heavy current flowing through the switch operated by the driver. It is used to operate components carrying heavy loads, such as driving lamps, twin horns and air-conditioning systems. When the driver operates his switch, a small current is sent to the relay which magnetically switches on the feed to the component.

Horns

Sound is produced from an electric horn by vibrating a metal diaphragm many hundreds of times each second. The diaphragm carries an armature which, when the horn button is pressed, is attracted towards a magnetic coil. As it moves, it opens a pair of contacts, the magnetic field collapses, and the diaphragm straightens until the contacts close and the cycle starts again.

Headlamps

Most headlamps have a one-piece shell made of glass with a lens and silvered reflector formed together. A standard tungsten or quartz-halogen bulb fits into an aperture in the reflector.

The bulb has two filaments. One, usually at the centre of the reflector, provides a straight-ahead main beam. The other filament is offset or shielded so that the reflector deflects its light downwards to provide the dipped beam. The headlamp lens shapes the spread of the beam.

If they overheat, tungsten bulbs deposit molecules of tungsten from the filaments on the glass, which blackens it. Once this happens, the bulb must be renewed. Quartz-halogen bulbs are intended to run at high temperatures. A trace of halogen gas inside discourages tungsten molecules from blackening the quartz glass.

These bulbs should not be handled directly during fitting. If one is accidentally touched, clean the surface with a tissue moistened in methylated spirit, otherwise oil from the hands will stain the bulb and shorten its life.

Some cars have sealed beam headlamps, which are made completely of glass with a silvered reflector and two built-in filaments. If a filament breaks, the complete unit must be renewed.

Side and tail lights

Small 5-watt tungsten bulbs are used, either behind separate white-lensed side light units or shining through a small hole in the headlamp reflector silvering. At the rear, the 5-watt filament in the tail light usually shares the same bulb as a 21-watt filament which

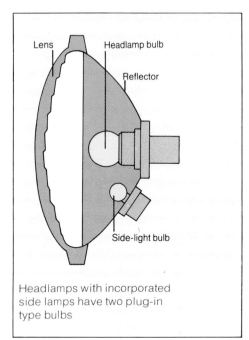

Headlamps with incorporated side lamps have two plug-in type bulbs

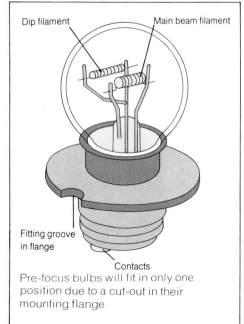

Pre-focus bulbs will fit in only one position due to a cut-out in their mounting flange

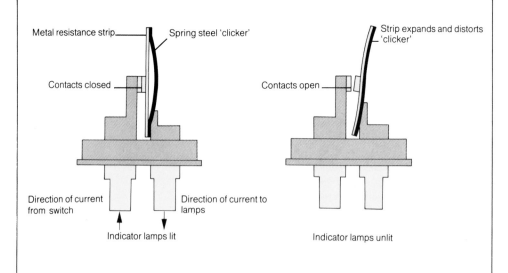

In the flasher unit current passing to the flasher bulbs heats up the resistance strip which expands, allowing the 'clicker' to open the contacts. This turns off the flasher bulbs. The resistance strip contracts and the clicker closes the contacts again, restarting another cycle. This happens 60 to 120 times a minute

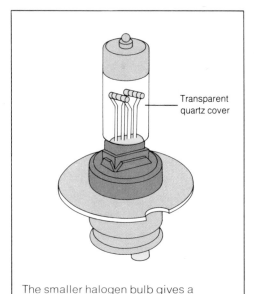

The smaller halogen bulb gives a brighter light than a normal tungsten filament bulb

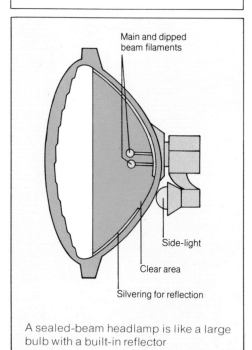

A sealed-beam headlamp is like a large bulb with a built-in reflector

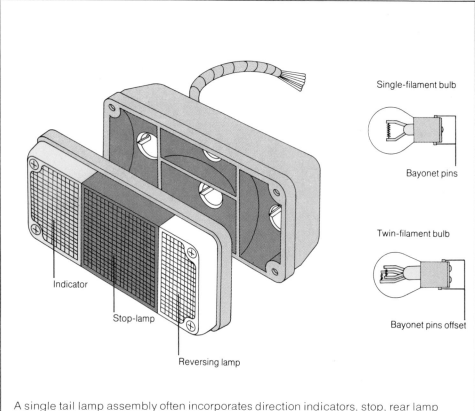

A single tail lamp assembly often incorporates direction indicators, stop, rear lamp and reversing lamp bulbs. Offset bayonet pins prevent incorrect assembly of a twin-filament stop/rear lamp bulb

operates the brake lights.
The brake lights are supplied by a separate circuit triggered by a switch in the brake hydraulic system or near the brake pedal, which operates when the pedal is applied.

Other rear lights
New cars must now have one or two red fog lights. The switch should have a 'tell-tale' to show the driver when the lights are on. Reversing lights, where fitted by the manufacturer, are turned on automatically by a gearbox switch which operates when reverse is selected. If a manual switch is used it must have a 'tell-tale'.

Flashing indicators
Once the direction indicator switch is operated, the amber indicator lights are flashed at the correct rate by a temperature-sensitive switch in a sealed canister.
Most modern flasher units use a spring-steel 'clicker' diaphragm to open and shut the contacts that switch the indicator lamps on and off.

SUSPENSION

What you can do: Pages
Check and service suspension   132
Measure the ride height   132
Make a visual inspection   132-133
Lubricate the system   134
Renew a telescopic damper   134-135
Renew a lever damper   136-137
Cure squeaks   139

Without a means to cushion its bodyshell against the knocks and shocks of road surface irregularities, the average car would be uncontrollable— not to say uncomfortable for the driver and his passengers.

The suspension system has far-reaching effects on steering, braking, roadholding and handling, as well as on the wear and reliability of other car systems. And for the occupants, it makes travelling less fatiguing. Many parts of the car, not in themselves part of the suspension system, affect the way it rides. Flexing of the car body itself is an example—just one of the many factors that the designer considers in selecting the type of suspension system to be used for a new car.

This section highlights the many components on a car suspension and shows how they are combined to make up a complete system.

General principles

The main aim of the suspension designer is to devise a system which enables the wheels and axles to move up and down as they meet bumps and hollows while the body of the car experiences little or no vertical or rocking motion. So the initial requirement of the suspension system is that it should provide damped springing to support the car on its axles.

Springs of various kinds provide this effect but these alone cannot achieve a stable ride. A spring will compress in reaction to an upward movement of the wheels but equally, the energy stored in the spring is released in a rebound movement. This rebound can add a further mode of movement to the car body, removing any benefit gained in the spring's initial reaction. The answer is to combine the action of the spring with that of a damper, which allows the spring to compress but controls the release of energy on the rebound. All cars with metal springs have dampers to absorb some of the rebound energy. The damper is widely known as the shock absorber.

The more of the vehicle's total weight

that can be suspended in this way, the more efficiently the system works, and the designer makes every attempt to

reduce the unsprung weight. Unsprung components are those between the spring and the road, such as the axles and wheel assemblies.

As the system provides the vehicle's link with the noise and vibration caused by ground contact, further compliance— usually in the form of rubber joints and bushes—is introduced where the suspension is joined to the car body. These help to reduce road noise and vibration.

Suspension systems vary but the typical small car layout has leaf springs at the rear and coil springs at the front

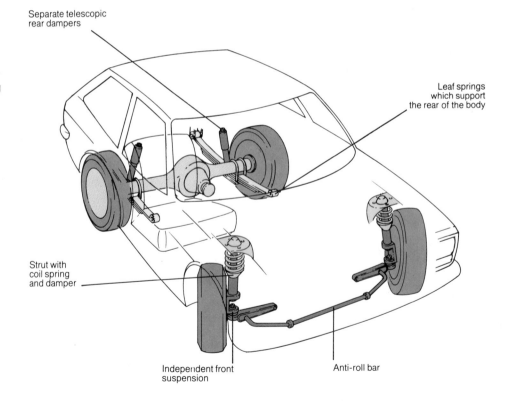

Separate telescopic
rear dampers

Leaf springs
which support
the rear of the body

Strut with
coil spring
and damper

Independent front
suspension

Anti-roll bar

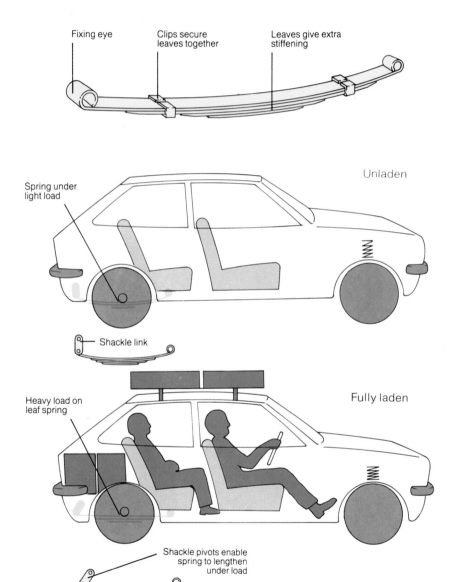

Fixing eye

Clips secure leaves together

Leaves give extra stiffening

Unladen

Spring under light load

Shackle link

Heavy load on leaf spring

Fully laden

Shackle pivots enable spring to lengthen under load

A leaf spring may have one or more leaves, sometimes with interlayers of plastic. It is mounted at the rear on a swinging shackle to accommodate its change in length as it flexes

Leaf springs

Cars evolved from horse-drawn carriages and were fitted with a simple form of suspension made and repaired by the coach-builder. This was the leaf spring—a bent blade of steel attached at both ends to the body with the wheel axle clamped at its centre-point. The mid-point of the spring was stiffened, and its spring action reinforced by the addition of further leaves held in place by the axle clamp and metal clips. On early cars they were often enclosed in a leather jacket fitted with grease or oiling points to reduce the slight friction between the spring leaves.

Leaf springs are still used extensively on cars, although grease lubrication is now dispensed with. It is achieved by oil spray or sheets of PTFE (the 'non-stick' plastic) between the leaves. Advances in metal technology make it possible to make a spring with a single leaf that is thicker at the middle and tapers towards the mounting points or shackles.

Leaf springs are fixed to mounting points on the car body by bolts through rubber bushes. The forward spring mounting is fixed but the rear one has a short moving link which allows for the spring's change in length as it flexes. The chief advantage of the leaf spring is that it is cheap to make and comparatively robust and reliable. Its major disadvantage is that, under the forces of acceleration or braking, it can distort. When this happens it cannot adequately locate the rear axle without the assistance of other braces and supports. With the exception of vans and cross-country vehicles, the leaf spring has vanished from the front suspension on today's cars.

Torsion bars

If a steel bar is twisted it will store the energy applied and spring back when the tension is released. The twisting force applied is called torsion, and the spring action of torsion is used in two car suspension applications. The most common is the anti-roll bar (see page 124) but torsion bars can be used as the primary springing medium, usually for the front suspension only, although certain Renault models use them at the front and rear.

Torsion bar suspension consists of a bar fitted parallel to, or across, the car's longitudinal centre line. It is fixed to the body at one end by a splined joint which will allow some adjustment. To the other end is fixed the suspension arm carrying the wheel. As the wheel moves up and down, a twist is applied to the bar and energy is stored and released just as in the leaf spring.

Coil springs

Torsion also gives the coil spring its springiness. Used extensively in various forms of car suspension, compression of a spiral spring coil is, in effect, the application of a twisting force.

The spring is mounted between a moving suspension member and a fixed point on the car body. Coil springs are used on front and rear suspension systems. Their advantages are compact size, high capacity, comparatively light weight and long life.

Dampers

The problem with the simple spring is that the rebound—after the initial compression to absorb a road jolt—is equal and opposite in force. To control this rebound and the natural tendency of the spring to oscillate up and down, some kind of damper (sometimes called a shock-absorber) has to be fitted. On older cars the dampers consisted of a friction device in which metal plates rubbed against sheets of wood, leather or friction material.

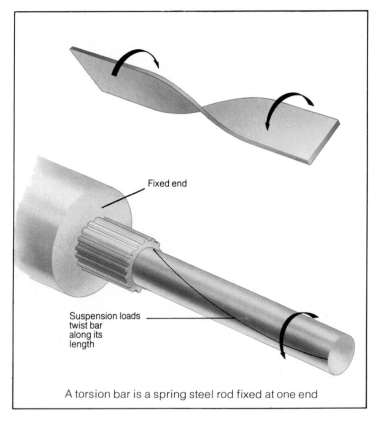

Fixed end

Suspension loads twist bar along its length

A torsion bar is a spring steel rod fixed at one end

The coil spring is a torsion bar formed into a spiral

Telescopic dampers

All current cars are fitted with hydraulic dampers. The widely used telescopic type is, in effect, a small pump containing hydraulic fluid. The bottom section is attached to a moving suspension member and the top section to the car body. The sections consist of a piston, a piston-rod assembly and a cylinder.

As the spring compresses and the road wheel moves upwards, the piston is pushed into the cylinder and some of the sealed-in hydraulic fluid is forced through a valve in the piston face into part of the device called the working cylinder. When the spring rebounds, the piston is moved in the opposite direction, forcing the hydraulic fluid back from the working cylinder. Flow is slowed down by another valve in the piston face. These restrictions control the oscillations of the suspension. If the damper restricts the flow of hydraulic fluid in both directions it is known as a double-acting type. A second mode of control within the damper is that some of the fluid is allowed to escape under pressure into a reservoir or recuperating chamber. This helps to dissipate heat generated in the fluid when it passes through the restricting valves.

On rough roads dampers work hard—faster than once a second at quite moderate road speeds—and are generally expected to last no more than 40,000 miles or about four years of normal motoring in the UK. The rougher the roads, the shorter their life. Worn dampers cause excessive bouncing, which if left unchecked can be dangerous.

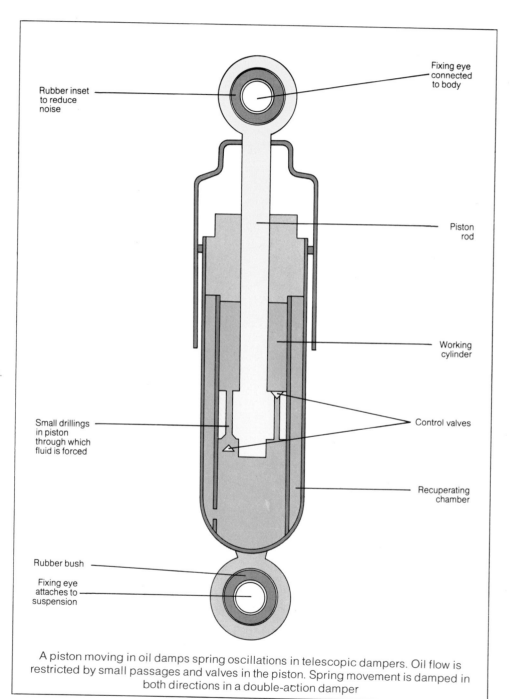

Fixing eye connected to body

Rubber inset to reduce noise

Piston rod

Working cylinder

Control valves

Small drillings in piston through which fluid is forced

Recuperating chamber

Rubber bush

Fixing eye attaches to suspension

A piston moving in oil damps spring oscillations in telescopic dampers. Oil flow is restricted by small passages and valves in the piston. Spring movement is damped in both directions in a double-action damper

Lever dampers

Most people will be familiar with a very simple type of lever damper. It is almost exactly similar in operation to those door-closing devices that allow the door to be opened normally and then slowly, but forcefully, close it again. A link with the moving suspension member is connected to a lever arm which in turn acts on a back-to-back piston sliding in an oil-filled cylinder. Movement of the piston causes fluid to be pumped from one end of the device to the other through passages and restricting valves in the cylinder body.

Both telescopic and lever dampers may be separate units or a fully integrated part of the suspension system. For instance, a telescopic damper is incorporated in the MacPherson strut suspension system (see page 124), while the arm of the lever damper often forms the upper load-bearing link of the suspension system.

Independent suspension

When a wheel has its own system of suspension, allowing it to move vertically without being affected by the movement of the wheel on the opposite side of the car, this is known as independent suspension. Except for a few vans and four-wheel-drive cross-country vehicles, all cars now have independent front suspension. At the rear, the benefits of independent suspension are not as obvious. On front-engined, rear-wheel-drive cars, the inexpensive models do not have independently-sprung rear wheels, although the system is used on higher-priced models. Cars with front-wheel-drive can, however, be

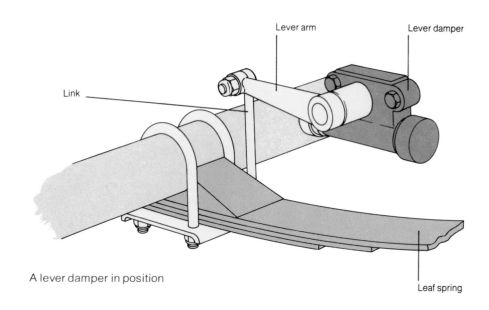

A lever damper in position

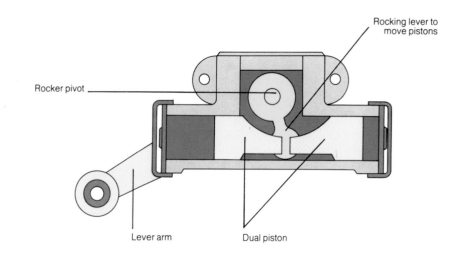

A lever mechanism operates the back-to-back pistons in lever dampers in response to wheel movements. Oil is passed from one end of the casing to the other through restricting valves

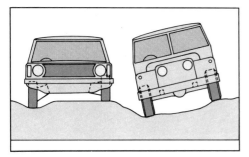

Independent front suspension (left) helps to keep the car body riding level

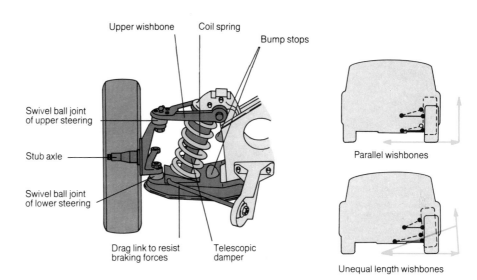

Upper wishbone   Coil spring
Bump stops
Swivel ball joint
of upper steering
Stub axle
Swivel ball joint
of lower steering
Drag link to resist   Telescopic
braking forces   damper

Parallel wishbones

Unequal length wishbones

Double wishbone independent front suspension is designed to withstand the forces of acceleration, braking and cornering. Parallel wishbones create a change in track when the car is laden, wearing out tyres and affecting the handling. Unequal length wishbones keep the track constant and improve cornering by allowing a change in wheel camber

designed with all-round independent suspension at no great cost penalty. The principal advantage of independent suspension is that it enables each wheel to absorb the jolts in its path without having to cope with any additional forces transmitted to it by the reaction of the other wheel. On powerful cars in particular, the interaction between two driven wheels on the same axle can cause skidding on loose, uneven surfaces. Independent suspension can improve traction because wheel-to-road contact changes are kept to a minimum. An independent layout on a rear-wheel-drive car allows the final drive and differential to be rigidly mounted to the body, so reducing unsprung weight.

Front suspension systems

Because the front wheels steer the car and the precision of the steering is directly affected by the attitude of the wheel to the road, an independent front suspension system must, so far as is possible, be designed to prevent anything other than vertical movement. The system must also accommodate the steering movement of the wheel.

Wishbone suspension

In this layout the wheel, on a pivoted stub axle (or short drive-shaft), is held vertical by two wishbone suspension members. The two arms of each wishbone are hinged to the car body and the stub axle is pivoted top and bottom, where it joins the arms, by swivelling ball-joints. The suspension spring—usually of the coil type—is located between the lower wishbone and the car body, frequently with a telescopic damper inside. On cars with torsion bar suspension, the lower wishbone is fixed to the torsion bar. The upper wishbone may be formed by the arm of a lever damper.
A double wishbone suspension linkage is admirably braced against all the forces to which the wheel is subjected, particularly those induced by

acceleration, braking and cornering. If the system was designed with equal-length, parallel wishbones the wheel would always remain vertical, provided the car did not roll. However, movement of the wishbone arms would vary the wheel's track (the distance between the front wheels) which would cause rapid tyre wear. This is overcome if the top wishbone is a little shorter than the bottom one and they are at a narrow angle to each other. The geometry slightly tilts the wheel as the spring is compressed, giving it a small negative camber (the top of the wheel tilts inwards). Although camber changes promote wear on the shoulders of the tyres, the negative camber can be doubly beneficial as the wheel tends to stay vertical to the road surface as the car rolls, thereby improving grip.

MacPherson strut suspension

The MacPherson strut combines the stub axle, coil spring and telescopic damper in one unit. It is easy to fit to a car in production, and is commonly used on the front suspension.

The lower end of the strut has a steering swivel joined to either a wishbone-type link or a single member known as the track-control arm. The shape of the wishbone type means that it can absorb acceleration and braking forces, but a track-control arm requires the assistance of an anti-roll bar (see below) to resist these forces.

The strut, consisting of a telescopic damper mounted inside a coil spring, extends up from the axle to a flexible and swivelling upper mounting in a specially reinforced section of the front wheel-arch, sometimes called the suspension turret.

Anti-roll bars

Although true independent suspension means the absence of a linkage between two wheels on the same 'axle', it often helps to have a connecting member which is able to assist spring action when the car rolls on corners. The anti-roll bar is such a device. It is a torsion bar mounted at its centre to the car body and at each end to the lower linkage of the suspension system.

The spring steel bar comes into play when the suspension on the outer wheel of the cornering car is compressed by body roll.

The opposite suspension unit, being more lightly loaded, is in extension and therefore exerts a twisting force on the anti-roll bar which, in effect, stiffens the spring under compression and so resists the car's roll.

On MacPherson strut systems with a track-control arm, the roll bar also forms the locating link of the lower swivel, stabilising it against acceleration, braking and cornering forces. Anti-roll bars are sometimes also used at the rear of the car.

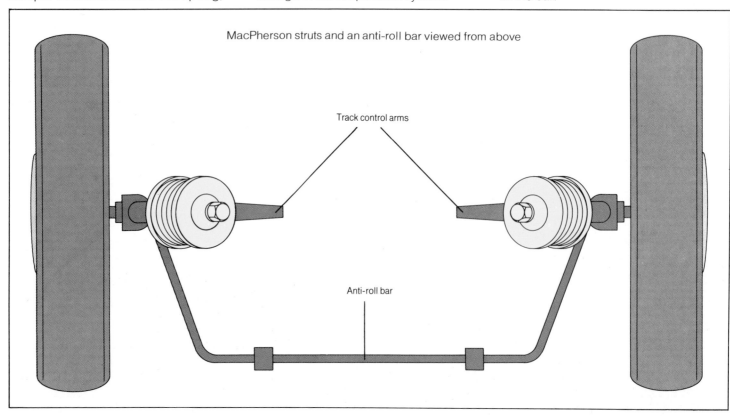

MacPherson struts and an anti-roll bar viewed from above

Track control arms

Anti-roll bar

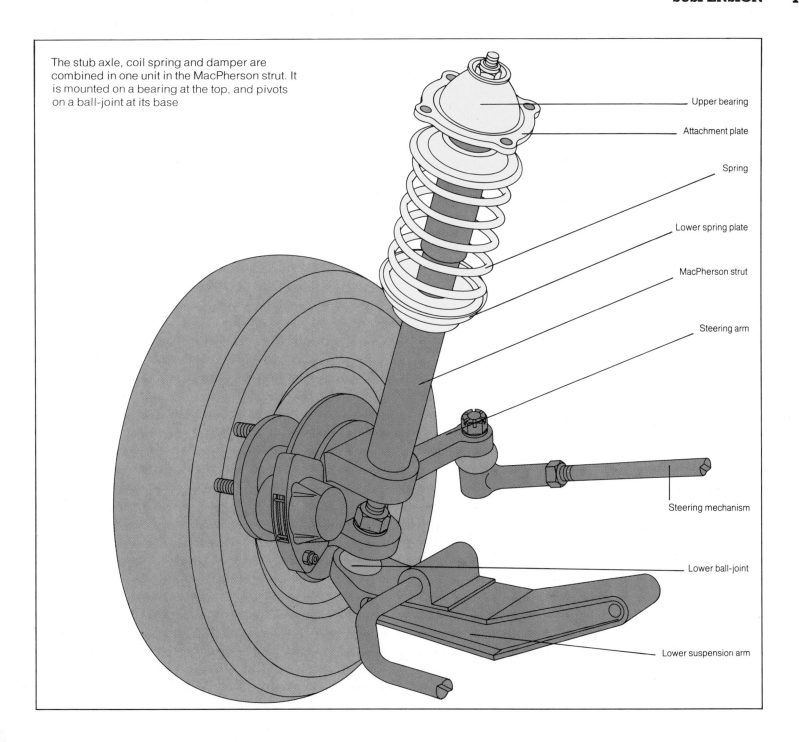

The stub axle, coil spring and damper are combined in one unit in the MacPherson strut. It is mounted on a bearing at the top, and pivots on a ball-joint at its base

Upper bearing

Attachment plate

Spring

Lower spring plate

MacPherson strut

Steering arm

Steering mechanism

Lower ball-joint

Lower suspension arm

Rear suspension systems

The function of the front suspension is to keep the wheels in contact with the road to aid the car's steering and roadholding. On a rear-drive car the rear suspension also has to combat the considerable forces of traction, as well as the unevenness of the road.

The Hotchkiss drive

The simplest form of rear suspension is the combination of a rear axle with leaf springs and telescopic dampers. It is called the Hotchkiss drive and consists of a rear axle and final-drive housing clamped to the leaf springs by U-bolts. The forward ends of the leaf springs are fixed on rubber bushes to the body, and the trailing end is linked to the body, again with rubber bushes through a pivoted shackle, which allows for the slight extension of the curved spring under compression. The dampers are mounted between the spring and a point on the body.

Although the Hotchkiss drive is a cheap and generally adequate form of rear suspension for small to medium-sized cars, it suffers a major disadvantage on heavier and more powerful vehicles. Under acceleration, the forces transmitted from the driven wheels to the leaf springs tilt the U-bolt shackle in such a way that the spring forms a shallow S-shape and the axle is displaced forwards.

This is known as axle wind-up. The axle winds up until the forces stored in the spring are released, perhaps when the wheel momentarily leaves the ground over a bump, and the system springs back into place.

Under rapid acceleration this can happen several times a second and the driver experiences a very violent and noisy juddering from the rear of the car.

With the simple Hotchkiss drive, leaf springs give the live axle lateral location. But the springs can wind up, causing judder on hard acceleration

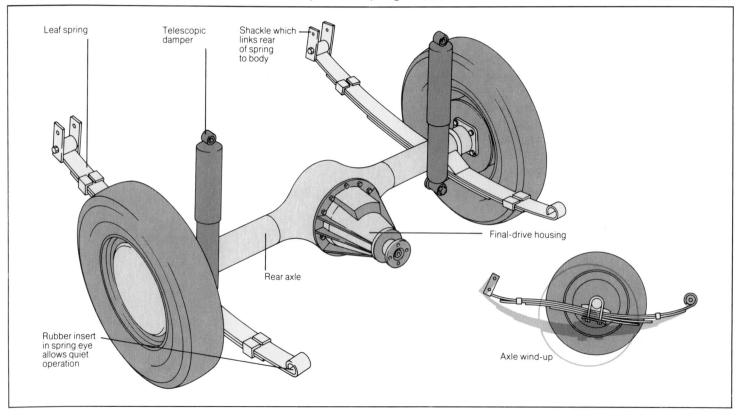

Leaf spring

Telescopic damper

Shackle which links rear of spring to body

Final-drive housing

Rear axle

Rubber insert in spring eye allows quiet operation

Axle wind-up

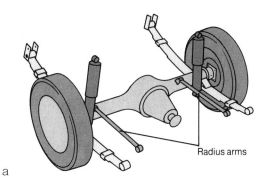

a

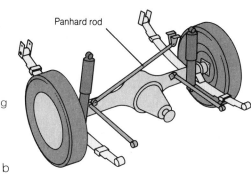

Panhard rod

b

a
By fitting two radius arms from the outer ends of the axle to the car body, the axle is prevented from twisting and causing axle 'wind-up'

Radius arms

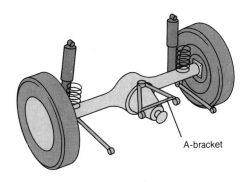

c

A-bracket

c
With coil spring rear suspension, radius arms and a rigid A-bracket prevent forwards, rear or sideways movement of the axle

b
On some medium-sized cars a Panhard rod may be used with leaf springs to help reduce the sideways movement of a one-piece axle assembly

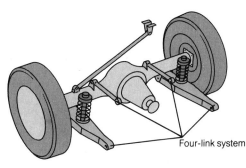

d

Four-link system

d
In a four-link system the axle is prevented from moving forwards or backwards. A Panhard rod helps prevent sideways movement

Rear suspension-location systems
To prevent axle wind-up and sideways movement which would steer the car, there is a variety of devices to brace the rear suspension. The simplest is the fitting of two radius arms from the outer ends of the axle to the car body, which prevent the axle from twisting and so eliminate wind-up. These may be additionally reinforced by a small A-bracket having two pivots on the car's body and a single fixing to the top of the final drive housing.
The A-bracket, or a Panhard rod, prevents any sideways movement of the axle. A Panhard rod is fitted from one end of the axle to a point on the body in line with the axle but on the other side of the car.

Independent rear suspension

Many front-wheel-drive cars have independent rear suspension systems, and it is also possible to have independent suspension on rear-drive cars. This is more complicated than a rigid axle, however, because the final drive must be universally jointed to the driven wheel hubs so that the vertical suspension movement can be provided for. Many such systems use coil springs.

Trailing arm suspension

A trailing arm is a pivoted member hinged at its leading edge to the car body and extending rearwards to a fixing on the axle behind the wheel hub. The arm may have a single bearing, in which case it is usual for there to be other means of axle location such as radius arms, an A-bracket or a Panhard rod. More usually the trailing arm has two bearings on the car body so that it is well braced against the forces of acceleration, braking and cornering. The spring itself is mounted between the trailing arm and the car body, with each end bearing in cup-shaped retaining plates. The final drive and differential housing is mounted rigidly to the car body. Parallel trailing arms keep the rear wheels absolutely vertical in relation to the car body, but as in the case of front independent suspension, the addition of a little negative camber to the wheel as the car rolls, keeps the wheel vertical to the road surface, so giving improved traction. A variation of the trailing arm-type of system that provides this advantage is the semi-trailing arm, in which the hinge axis of the arm is at an angle to the lateral axis of the car.

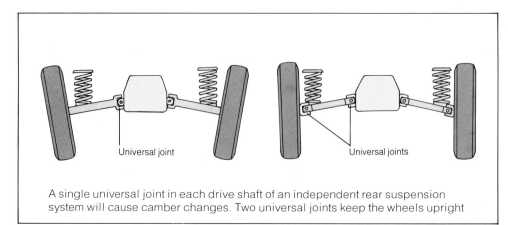

A single universal joint in each drive shaft of an independent rear suspension system will cause camber changes. Two universal joints keep the wheels upright

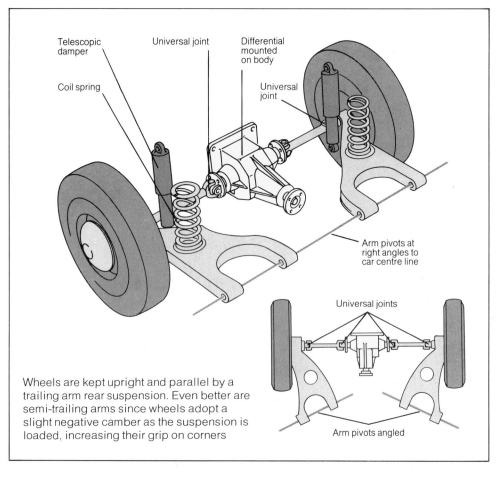

Wheels are kept upright and parallel by a trailing arm rear suspension. Even better are semi-trailing arms since wheels adopt a slight negative camber as the suspension is loaded, increasing their grip on corners

Jaguar independent rear suspension

A unique form of independent rear suspension, similar in operation to the wishbone type of front suspension, is used in Jaguar cars. The lower suspension arm is a wishbone bearing the spring and the bottom mounting of the telescopic dampers. But the upper link of the system is provided by the drive-shaft itself. As on wishbone front suspension, the bearings of the lower suspension member are aligned with the car's centre-line axis and the drive-shaft provides a non-parallel and unequal length top linkage.

Dead beam rear suspension

A number of manufacturers of smaller front-wheel-drive cars have adopted a system of rear suspension which combines the beneficial effects of an anti-roll bar and trailing arms, although it is not an independent system. In this dead beam or dead axle system, the trailing arms, pivot-mounted on the car body, are linked by a tubular, T- or I-beam section and sprung by coil springs.

De Dion rear suspension

In the de Dion suspension system the final drive unit is mounted on the body and drive is transmitted to the wheels by universally-jointed half-shafts to wheels suspended on coil springs. The two sets of suspension are semi-independently linked by a tubular-beam dead axle, pivoted centrally on the car body. It has a sliding joint to allow for the track difference caused by the swing of the wheels through their separate arcs. This type of suspension frees the rear axle from the twisting action of the propeller

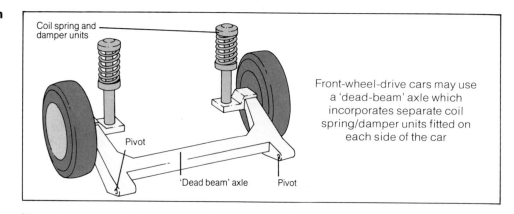

Coil spring and damper units

Pivot

'Dead beam' axle Pivot

Front-wheel-drive cars may use a 'dead-beam' axle which incorporates separate coil spring/damper units fitted on each side of the car

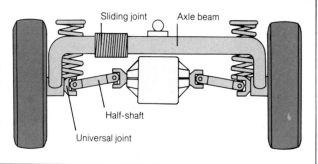

The de Dion system is not a genuine independent suspension because the axle links the wheels, but does not carry the differential. The axle is free of the turning effect of the propeller shaft and wheel drive because of the separate mounting

Sliding joint Axle beam

Half-shaft

Universal joint

shaft while making a beneficial torsion anti-roll link between the two wheels.

Linked suspension systems

A number of car designers have attempted, with varying success, to link the front and rear suspensions on each side of the car with the object of preventing the car from pitching as it meets a bump. Citroen's design, for its small cars, is a mechanical link. It is a rod and spring coupling running from front to rear each side of the car. When the front wheel suspension meets a bump the link spring is extended and some of the energy is transferred to the rear suspension, lifting the car slightly and levelling it.

If the front wheels in Citroen's linked suspension system are pushed up, the springs connecting them to the rear wheels pull them down to keep the car level

BL Hydrolastic and Hydragas suspension systems

BL's Hydrolastic and Hydrogas designs hydraulically link front and rear suspension. Early Minis were produced with a system of rubber cone-sprung suspension, invented by Dr Alex Moulton. This invention proved to be difficult to use on larger cars so the principle of the hollow rubber spring was taken a stage further to make a fully front to rear-linked system, unique to Leyland, called Hydrolastic.

A Hydrolastic suspension unit consists of a hollow rubber spring forming half of a sealed double chamber, interconnected by a damper valve. The unit is connected to a similar one at the rear of the car by small-bore pipe and the whole system is pressure-filled with a fluid consisting of alcohol and water. Mechanical connection to the suspension is by a piston acting on a thick rubber diaphragm.

As the front wheel responds to a bump, fluid is displaced through the damper valve and along the pipe to the rear unit to extend the rear suspension and thus level the car. After the bump has passed, the fluid returns to restore normal ride height. In this way the Hydrolastic unit acts not only as a spring but also as a damper.

Hydragas is a further development of this system in which the rubber spring is replaced by a gas spring. The gas is contained at high pressure in a domed housing separated from the fluid by a thick rubber diaphragm. The damping action and the front to rear fluid displacement are similar to those of the Hydrolastic system.

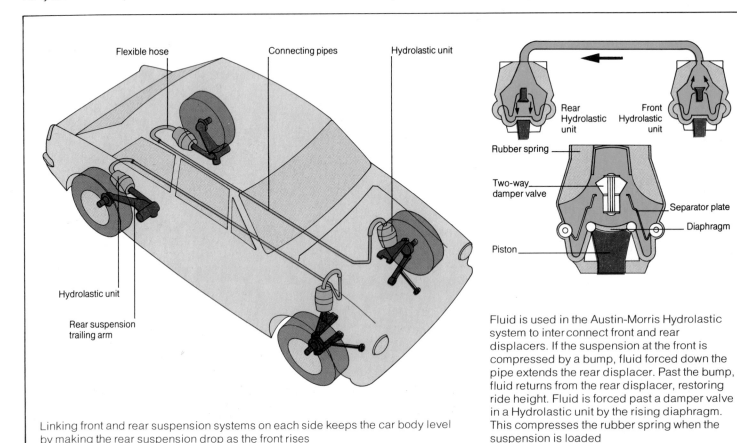

Flexible hose   Connecting pipes   Hydrolastic unit

Hydrolastic unit

Rear suspension trailing arm

Linking front and rear suspension systems on each side keeps the car body level by making the rear suspension drop as the front rises

Rear Hydrolastic unit   Front Hydrolastic unit

Rubber spring

Two-way damper valve

Separator plate

Diaphragm

Piston

Fluid is used in the Austin-Morris Hydrolastic system to inter connect front and rear displacers. If the suspension at the front is compressed by a bump, fluid forced down the pipe extends the rear displacer. Past the bump, fluid returns from the rear displacer, restoring ride height. Fluid is forced past a damper valve in a Hydrolastic unit by the rising diaphragm. This compresses the rubber spring when the suspension is loaded

Citroen Hydropneumatic self-levelling suspension

One major suspension problem is that when the rear of the car is heavily laden, the springs are compressed and the available travel to take up road bumps is greatly reduced. Also the tail-down attitude points the car's headlamps upwards so that they dazzle oncoming drivers unless they are re-adjusted. A system of suspension that automatically takes into account load variations and

Some Austin-Morris cars have Hydragas displacers (shown here) which use an inert gas spring, separated from the fluid by an extra diaphragm. It has the same interlink arrangements as the Hydrolastic system for front and rear displacers

levels the vehicle is used on Citroen medium and large cars.

The Citroen Hydropneumatic system consists of all-round independent suspension units, each linked by a piston arm to its suspension members. The unit is a gas-filled spring (nitrogen is used) contained by a rubber diaphragm which separates the gas from hydraulic fluid. The fluid is supplied under pressure from an engine-driven pump, triggered by a suspension height-sensing valve. At rest, with the engine off, the car is

suspended on the gas springs alone, but as soon as the engine is started, the hydraulic pump supplies fluid to the suspension units and the car rises until the set height is reached and a rod linkage on the suspension member moves the valve to a neutral position. In this way the car is held at a fixed height regardless of the load carried. If the load decreases and the suspension rises, the valve lever switches the valve to a third position, allowing fluid to drain from the suspension units back into a reservoir.

Unladen
Bounce position
Inert gas 'spring'
Fluid at high pressure
Flexible diaphragm between gas and fluid
Damper valve
Hydragas unit connection
Flexible diaphragm
Operating strut connected to suspension

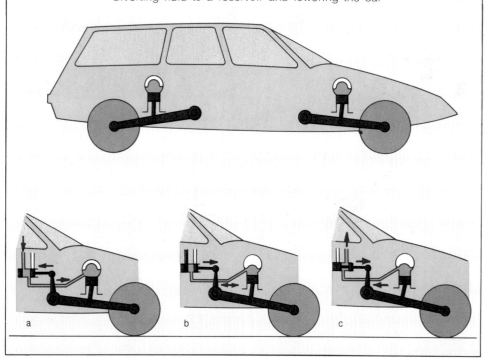

Citroen's self-levelling, Hydropneumatic suspension works by pumping hydraulic fluid under pressure between a piston and a diaphragm below a gas spring. A linkage opens a hydraulic valve when the car is laden (a) and fluid is pumped above the piston to raise the car. The linkage puts the valves into a neutral position (b) as the body rises to the desired level. If the body rises further (c), the valve is moved by the linkage, diverting fluid to a reservoir and lowering the car

Checking and servicing the suspension

The security of the suspension mountings forms part of the annual MOT test (see page 229). So does the operation of the dampers and the state of corrosion at spring mountings. These simple checks will enable you to spot trouble early and save a heavy repair bill or a test failure.

Measuring the ride height

Some manufacturers give the ride height in the owner's handbook, together with the reference points between which they should be measured. If these figures are not available, ask a dealer or refer to a workshop manual at the library.

Make sure that the car is parked on level ground and that the wheels are clear of obstructions such as kerbs and drains. The measurements will be made from either the wheel centre to the point on the wheel arch directly above (1), or from the ground vertically through the wheel centre to the same point on the wheel arch.

Make the measurements all round the car. Compare the two figures from the front wheels—there should be no more than 1in between them. Do the same at the rear, then compare the figures with the manufacturer's. There should be no more than 1in difference from the designed ride height. If you do find any variation over this allowance for settling, take the car to a garage for a full test.

Visual inspections

Suspension systems are best checked with the car on axle stands and the wheels removed. Use a torch to illuminate the darker corners, and with a

① Measure the wheel from the centre to the point directly above on the wheel arch

stiff wire brush, remove dirt from joints. Corrosion is the main problem. Thoroughly check the condition of wishbones and lower suspension members as these are the most exposed to salt and corrosive build-up of water-retaining dirt. On leaf-springs, wire-brush the edges—this enables you to see if any leaves are broken (2). A damaged spring means that both springs on the same axle must be renewed—to change one would have a harmful effect on the car's handling. Examine the condition of the mounting

points—if necessary probing the bodywork with a sharp instrument. Clean up the area around the rubber bushes with a wire brush and look for cracking, splits or distortion, especially if the area is oil- or grease-fouled. Use a lever to prise the joints on the shackle (3). A small amount of play, as the rubber bush compresses, is allowable. If it is more than this, have new bushes fitted. BL's Hydrolastic-suspended cars have sub-frames carrying the main suspension members, and the area around the rear Hydrolastic units is

Wire-brush the edges of leaf-springs to check if any leaves are cracked or broken

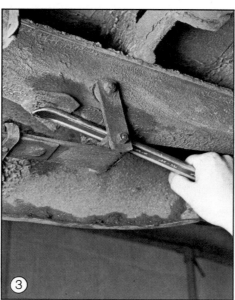

Check for any signs of wear in the shackle pins and bushes by using a sturdy lever

Use an old screwdriver to probe suspect areas of metal for signs of corrosion

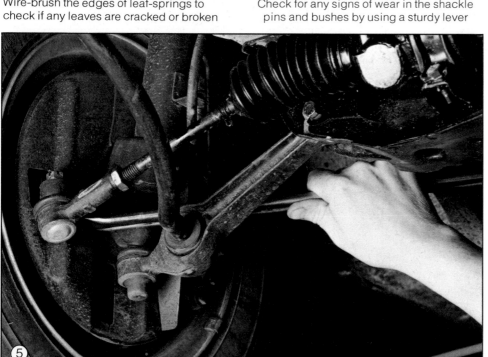

Attempt to prise apart the top and bottom suspension arms and feel for play

likely to corrode. Brush dirt from the frame and use a probe to jab at suspect metal (4). If corrosion has weakened it, a garage can fit a new sub-frame.

Examine the top of suspension turrets where MacPherson struts are mounted— this area traps dirt, and any corrosion here may have to be cured by welding on a strengthening plate. Test for play at bushes and mountings by pulling or levering suspension members at right angles to the normal vertical motion. There should be virtually no play in any mounting pivot or bush in a suspension system. No play is allowed in the steering swivel joints of the front suspension either. This can be tested by attempting to lever apart the top and bottom suspension arms (5).

Lubricating suspension systems

While there are a considerable number of cars on the road that require absolutely no lubrication of the suspension system, some have bushes and pivots that are fitted with nipples for high-pressure greasing. Greasing, using a lithium-based grease (unless the manufacturer specifies otherwise), should be carried out about every three months. Lubricating steering swivels (1) is the most important job, and as the lower swivel is the lowest point of the suspension it is often found that this grease nipple is corroded or blocked by dirt. Unscrew it and fit a new one if you cannot force grease into the joint. Rover de Dion rear suspension needs a periodic top-up with engine oil to lubricate the sliding joint. Use a pressure oil can or a squeeze bottle applicator and fill only to the level of the filler hole. Citroen systems require periodic checks on the level of hydraulic fluid in the reservoir (2). For top-ups use only the fluid recommended by the manufacturer.

Renewing dampers

Worn-out dampers allow the car to bounce erratically on uneven roads. Their weak action is caused by lack of oil and they are easily identified on the car because the damper body will be coated in the oil that has leaked out. By contrast, a sound damper will appear dirty but dry.

If the damper forms part of the coil spring assembly, replacing it is a garage job. Where a telescopic damper is fitted as a separate part of the suspension, renewing it is a straightforward do-it-yourself task.

Regularly lubricate steering swivels with a lithium-based grease

Use only the recommended hydraulic fluid when topping up the reservoir

For balanced suspension, dampers should be renewed in pairs, front or rear.

Changing a telescopic damper

With the suspension supported on axle stands, remove the road wheel and undo the bolt and nut securing the damper to the suspension (3).
A nut on a threaded stud usually fixes the top of the damper to the bodywork. Use a spanner on the flats, which are

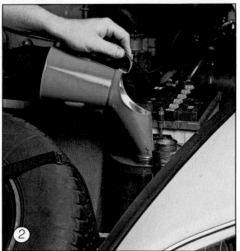

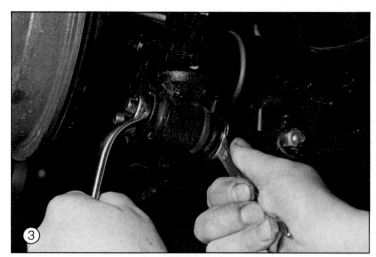

Support the suspension on axle stands, remove the road wheel and dismantle the nut and bolt securing the lower damper fixing

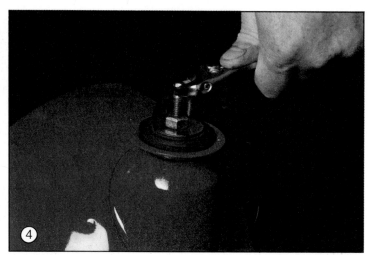

Use a small spanner on the flats, which have been ground in the end of the stud to prevent it from turning when undoing the nut

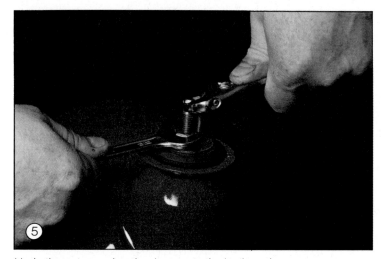

Undo the nut securing the damper to the bodywork

Remove the damper from under the wheel-arch

provided on the stud to prevent it from turning (4) and undo the nut (5). With the nut, washer and rubber mounting removed, take out the damper from under the wheel-arch (6).

Replacement dampers should be held upright, fully extended and then compressed two or three times in order to redistribute the fluid inside, and so eliminate air locks. If this is not done, the damper will probably 'knock'.

The new damper will come complete with rubber mountings. Remove the upper rubber and washer from the stud and have a helper insert the stud through the upper mounting hole from the wheel-arch side. From the other side of the mounting hole, thread the rubber and washer on to the stud and screw on the fixing nut.

At the wheel-arch, compress the damper and fit the bottom bolt and nut. Tighten all fixings securely. Renew the opposite damper in the same way.

Renewing a lever damper

When a lever-type damper forms part of the front suspension, changing it takes longer and involves more equipment than renewing a simple telescopic damper. The pictures show what is involved on the front suspension of a Morris Marina.

Raise the car and support the body on axle stands so that the suspension drops. Remove both front wheels.

Use a jack to raise the suspension to approximately its normal laden position (1). Take care not to lift the body off the axle stand.

Undo the nut locking the damper lever arm to the top steering swivel (2), having first unlocked a tab washer, if necessary.

A special tool is now needed to draw the lever arm off the tapered ball-joint pin (3). Once the joint is separated, lift away the damper arm.

Unbolt the damper body from its mounting on the car and lift it out (4). Before fitting a new one, grip the body lightly in a vice and work the lever arm fully up and down at least ten times to distribute the fluid inside (5). Fitting the new damper is a reversal of the dismantling process, except that no special tools are needed. Tighten all fixings firmly, if necessary using new lock-washers. Turn up the tab of a lock-washer against a hexagon flat to prevent the fixing from rotating.

Renew the damper on the opposite wheel in the same way.

Fault-finding

The suspension system is designed to take the rough and tumble of road conditions, so it is extremely robust and among the more reliable parts of the car.

Remove the wheels and jack up the suspension to its normal laden position

Unscrew the upper swivel retaining nut

Use a taper-breaking tool on the joint

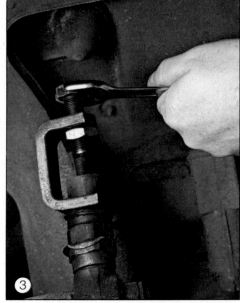

Unbolt the damper from its mounting and remove it from the body

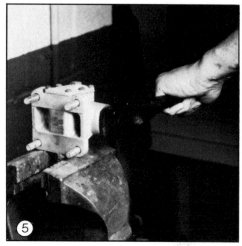

Work the lever up and down ten times

The two major problems that occur are the deterioration of the dampers, which usually need replacing after about 40,000 miles or four years, and corrosion of the suspension-mounting points—a serious condition calling for prompt attention.

The following is a guide to these and other problems:

Suspension is low on one side of the car

On BL cars with Hydrolastic or Hydragas suspension, this condition will generally mean a loss of pressure in the fluid system. This may need repair or simply repressurising to the correct level—BL dealers must do this job. On torsion bar-sprung cars there may be failure of the bar mountings (perhaps due to corrosion) or 'set' of the bar, a term describing the slow settling of the spring under load. A set spring can be readjusted by a garage. On leaf or coil-spring suspensions, a low ride height may be caused by the weakening or breakage of the springs or corrosion of the mountings. Check leaf springs thoroughly for signs of cracks in the leaves.

Excessive roll on corners

Weakened springs can cause this problem but more usually it is a sign of worn dampers (check for oil leakage) or failure of one or more anti-roll bar mountings.

On cars with Hydrolastic suspension, the reason may be loss of fluid pressure on one side of the system. The car will have a permanent lean to one side when this happens. Excessive roll can also be caused by misalignment of suspension parts after an accident, or chassis corrosion. A garage with special equipment can check the alignment of the suspension if the car has been in a collision.

Bouncing and swaying when driving in a straight line

A completely failed damper unit will give this symptom, although it can also be caused by a broken or extremely weak spring. Another possible cause is due to broken anti-roll bar mountings.

Judder from rear axle on acceleration

This happens mainly on leaf-spring rear suspension. Even some new cars will show these symptoms of axle wind-up if the accelerator and clutch are used too harshly, so this fault must be judged in the context of the car's normal behaviour.

If juddering develops, first check the rear suspension mountings— particularly the tightness of the U-bolts holding the axle to the springs (1). Check all other mounting bushes, paying special attention to those at the spring shackle. Weak springs will cause judder but when the spring is to blame, it is often because a leaf has broken. Worn bushes must be rectified as soon as possible before further problems develop. Check bushes by levering against the suspension eye with a large lever and looking for wear.

Ride becomes hard

Apart from over-inflated tyres (check the pressures), weakened springs or worn dampers make the ride uncomfortably harsh, transmitting severe jolts almost without cushioning. Measure the ride

Without suspension, every bump in the road will be transmitted to the car occupants

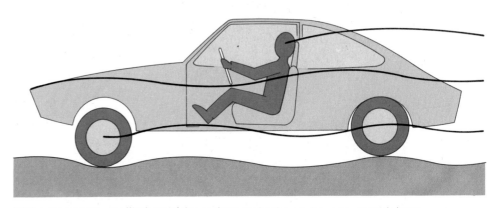

Without dampers, oscillations of the springs make the car bounce up and down

With effective suspension, wheels move up and down easily, but the car remains level

Check the tightness of the U-bolts holding the axle to the springs

Lubricate rubber and plastic parts with an anti-squeak product or washing-up liquid

heights all round the car and if they vary from the manufacturer's specification, have the suspension checked by a garage. Check the dampers for leakage.

Squeaks from springs

Leaf springs and some of the rubber and nylon parts used to add compliance to the suspension mountings can occasionally squeak. Often these are difficult to trace (the squeak may disappear when the road is wet) and it is really a matter of trial and error to find them. Most can be pin-pointed by listening to the suspension at a road wheel, while a helper bounces the car.

Use a lubricant on all visible rubber or plastic parts of the suspension. There are some commercially available anti-squeak preparations on the market but neat washing-up liquid is an excellent substitute (2). Never use oil as this can damage rubber parts.

If the noise is coming from the leaf spring, detergent or anti-squeak preparation can give a temporary cure, but deterioration of any interleaved parts may be the cause of the problem. If this is the case, the squeak will probably soon return. The only permanent cure is a set of new leaf springs.

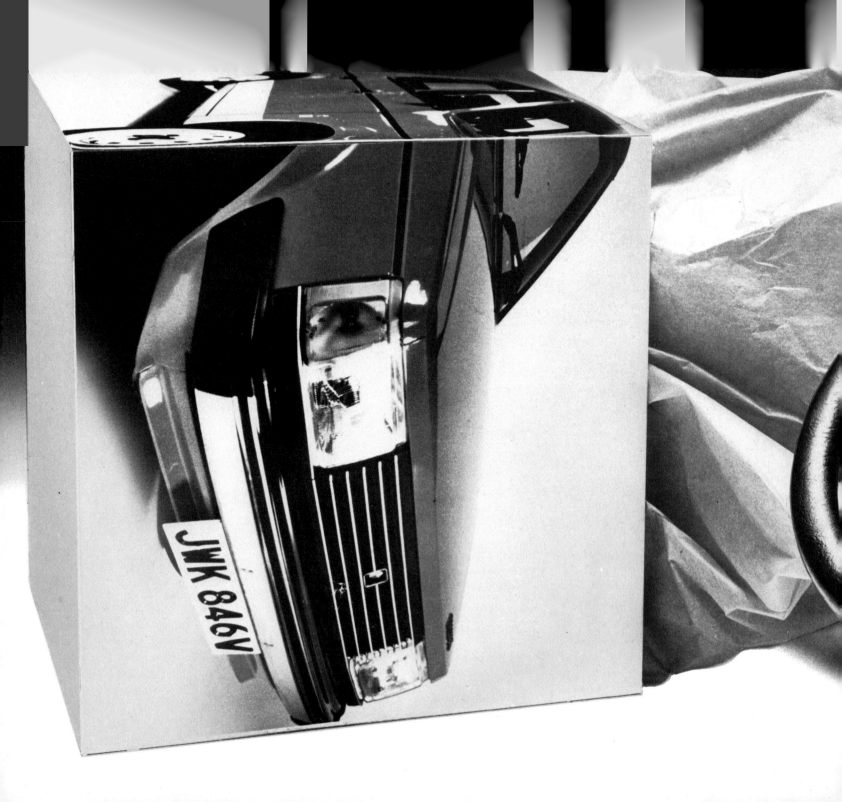

STEERING

What you can do: Pages
Make regular steering checks   147-148
Lubricate the steering system   148-149
Service power steering   152
Check reservoir and top-up   152
Examine drive belts and hoses   152-153

Draymen and stagecoach drivers hardly twitched a muscle to steer their cumbersome vehicles—they just pointed the motive force, the horses, in the right direction. The tremendous force necessary to turn the wheels to a new angle was all part of the animals' lot. A medium car may put half a ton of weight on its front wheels which the driver has to steer. The comparatively large area of friction in contact with the road, combined with the speeds a car can achieve and the cornering forces it generates, mean that only a Mr Universe could cope with a car's steering if it were not for the assistance given to the driver by the steering mechanism.

General principles

To aid control, the steering system should provide the driver with some 'feel' of the road, but should not allow excessive kick-back when a wheel hits a pothole.

It must also have a built-in tendency to return to the straight-ahead position after a turn has been made.

Other major factors to be taken into account in steering design are that when cornering, the inner and outer wheels have different turning circles, and that the smallest compliance in the way that the wheels are mounted allows them to deviate slightly from the intended path. These problems are solved by the design of the steering geometry, the attitude of the wheel to the road and its relationship to the axle mounting and the configuration of the suspension system.

Lastly, the steering wheel and column are the driver's nearest point of contact with any substantial part of the car structure. This closeness has, in the past, caused many deaths in accidents through chest injuries.

Now, steering columns and wheels are engineered to cause the minimum possible injury—one of the major advances in car safety engineering of the last 20 years.

The main components

A universally-jointed steering column connects the steering wheel to a gearbox, which is linked to the road wheels by a transverse linkage. In rack-and-pinion steering the main transverse link is the rack itself, but in other types it is a series of metal rods. The main linkage is made to move from side to side by steering wheel movement and is coupled to a steering arm at each road wheel by ball-jointed track rods. As well as pivoting, the joints allow for the vertical movement of the wheel on its suspension system.

The road wheel was once mounted on a swivelling post called the kingpin. With the introduction of independent front suspension, the kingpin all but disappeared. Its principal disadvantage was that it needed at least one more set of pivot bearings than modern equivalents.

Today, the stub axle (or drive-shaft hub carrier) swivels on upper and lower ball-joints in the front suspension members. Alternatively, the axle is part of a MacPherson coil spring and damper strut which swivels on an upper bearing on the car body and a lower ball-joint on the lower suspension link. The reduction of effort required to turn the steering wheel is achieved by a combination of the size of the wheel and the gearing of the steering box or the rack-and-pinion. Hydraulic power-assistance can also be applied to the steering mechanism.

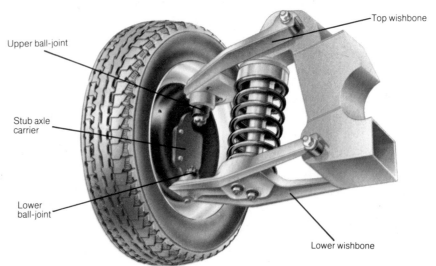

Upper ball-joint

Top wishbone

Stub axle carrier

Lower ball-joint

Lower wishbone

On cars with wishbone front suspension, the stub axle swivels on ball-joints

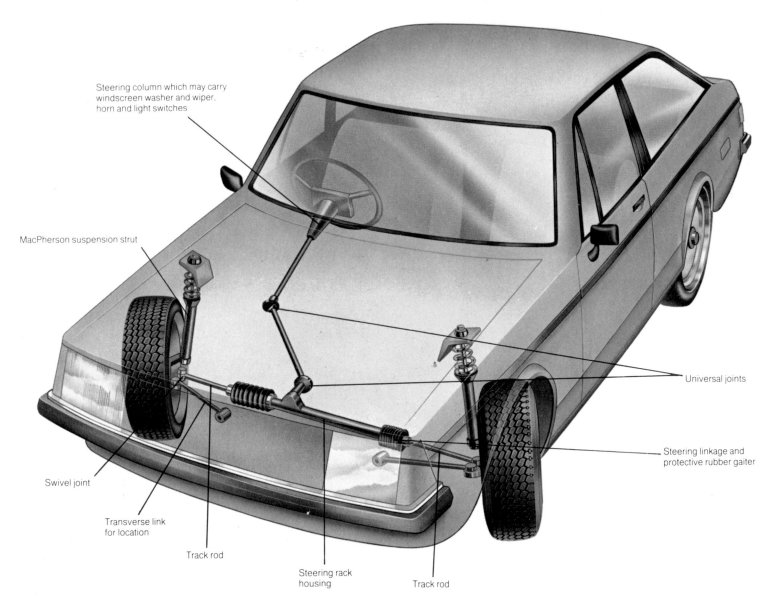

Steering column which may carry
windscreen washer and wiper,
horn and light switches

MacPherson suspension strut

Universal joints

Swivel joint

Transverse link
for location

Track rod

Steering rack
housing

Track rod

Steering linkage and
protective rubber gaiter

Components of a typical steering arrangement

Steering columns and wheels

On most cars there is at least one universal joint in the steering column between the steering box and the steering wheel. This enables the designer to position the wheel in the best position for the driver, regardless of the position of the steering box. The top of the column is mounted in bearings on the front bulkhead.

For safety, the column has a collapsible device, sometimes more, to ensure that in an accident injury to the driver is minimal.

One safety device is the use of a tubular section of steel mesh in the upper half of the column. It is strong enough to accept the twist of the steering action but it will collapse if compressed lengthwise, absorbing much of the force of the impact. A similar effect is gained by using a partially convoluted section of thin steel tube in the column. Another system is the disconnecting joint. For normal driving, two sections of the column are rigidly jointed by an offset pin located in a rubber bush. Any lengthwise compression of either the upper or lower sections will pull out the pin and, in the event of the driver being pitched forward on to the wheel, allow the upper section to collapse progressively on its mountings, so absorbing impact energy.

A third safety method is to angle the steering column on universal joints. If the angle between the sections is sufficient and the wheel mounting has collapsible characteristics, the joint will give little resistance to wheel collapse. This system is most commonly used in cars in which the steering wheel angle can be adjusted.

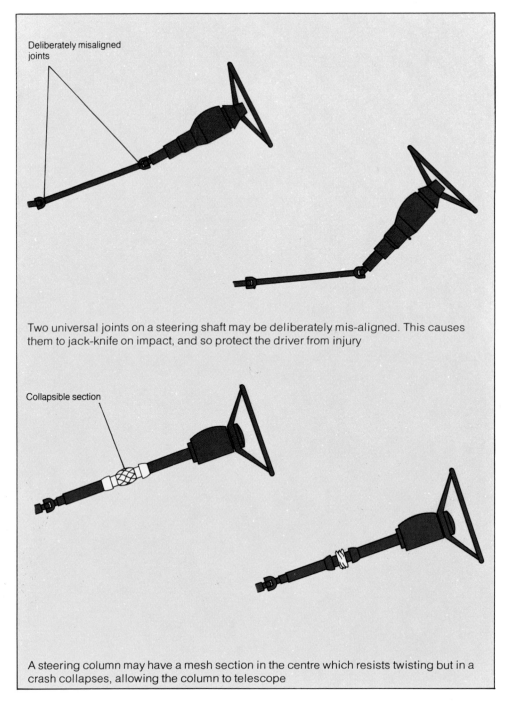

Deliberately misaligned joints

Two universal joints on a steering shaft may be deliberately mis-aligned. This causes them to jack-knife on impact, and so protect the driver from injury

Collapsible section

A steering column may have a mesh section in the centre which resists twisting but in a crash collapses, allowing the column to telescope

To complete the safety system, the wheel is made slightly dish-shaped, and a heavily padded boss is mounted at its centre to spread the impact loads over the driver's chest.

Although there are exceptions, the modern steering wheel generally has fewer spokes than its earlier counterpart. This increases its capacity to deform and absorb impact energy. The steering wheel may not necessarily be circular. Many car designers have used wheels with very slight ovality or a squaring-off of the lower part of the rim when the wheel is in the straight-ahead position, in order to make it easier for the driver to get in and out.

As the steering wheel is the control nearest the driver, a number of minor controls are mounted on the column of most cars. Older automatics, and a few manual cars, have a column-mounted gear selector. It is mainly the indicator and lighting switches, combined with those of the wipers and washers, which are fixed to the column on most cars these days. The steering wheel boss may house the horn button, although today many horns are operated by one of the column-mounted stalks.

Rack-and-pinion steering

One of the simplest ways to connect the steering column to the steering linkage is to use a rack-and-pinion system. At the end of the steering column there is a small pinion gear which meshes with the toothed rack inside a housing. The ends of the rack housing are sealed by rubber gaiters and are connected to the track rods by ball-joints. The sealed rack is filled with lubricant.

The comparatively few joints in a rack-and-pinion system mean that it has very little backlash or free play, and imparts a positive 'feel' to the steering.

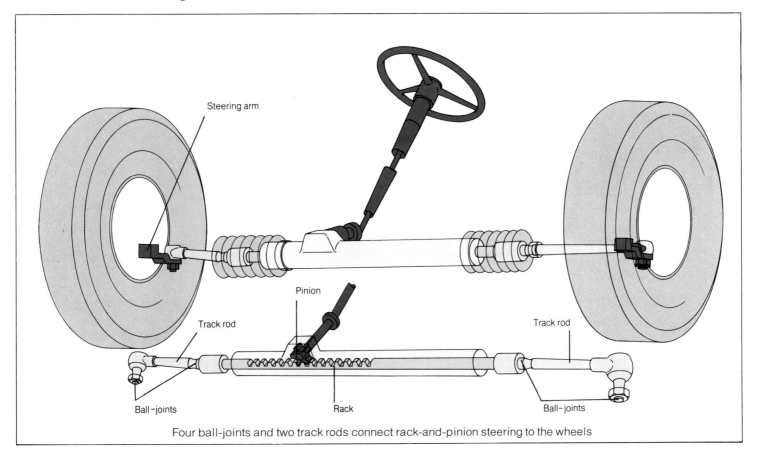

Steering arm

Pinion

Track rod

Track rod

Ball-joints

Rack

Ball-joints

Four ball-joints and two track rods connect rack-and-pinion steering to the wheels

Cam-and-peg steering

An alternative method of transmitting motion from steering column to steering linkage is by using a type of gearbox incorporating a cam which looks like a coarse worm-gear. Running in the groove of the worm is a peg attached to a short operating shaft, which moves a drop-arm connected to the steering linkage. This type of steering box is little used on today's cars.

Worm-and-nut steering

As in the cam-and-peg system the steering column turns a worm-like cam. But in this type of box the operating arm is moved by a large threaded nut which has a peg located in a fork in the operating arm. In effect, the nut is screwed up and down the worm. The action of this type of box is assisted by ball-bearings running in the worm threads. This is known as recirculating-ball steering and is used extensively by Japanese car manufacturers.
The disadvantage of the worm-cam steering boxes is that there is some unavoidable play in the system because it also incorporates a number of ball-jointed links. Compared with the direct-acting rack-and-pinion type, this gives less precise control when manoeuvring, and also can lead to a loss of road 'feel'.

Making the steering easy to turn

Mechanical aids to assist the driver in turning the steered wheels, which on most cars bear at least 50% of the car's weight, start at the steering wheel. The larger the diameter, the greater the leverage that can be applied. But much more assistance is provided by the

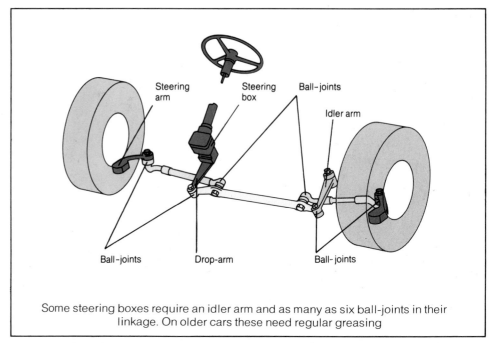

Some steering boxes require an idler arm and as many as six ball-joints in their linkage. On older cars these need regular greasing

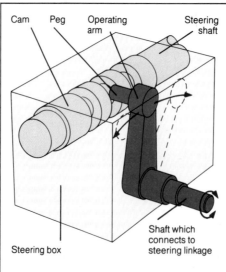

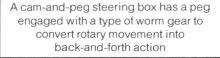

A cam-and-peg steering box has a peg engaged with a type of worm gear to convert rotary movement into back-and-forth action

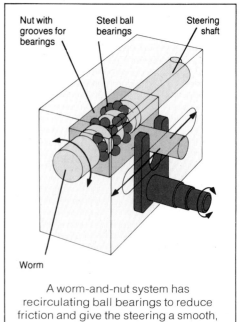

A worm-and-nut system has recirculating ball bearings to reduce friction and give the steering a smooth, easy action

reduction gearing of the rack-and-pinion or the steering box.

Normally about 2½ to 4 turns of the steering wheel will result in a lock-to-lock road wheel turn of around 60°. This can be roughly equated to a mechanical advantage of about 15:1 for smaller cars with 2½ turns, and 24:1 for large cars with 4 turns from lock to lock. On rack-and-pinion systems the gearing is varied by the number of teeth on the pinion (fewer teeth mean greater assistance) and the length of the steering arm from the track-rod end to the axle.

On a steering box the amount of assistance provided is decided by the pitch of the worm cam and the length of the operating and control arms.

Regular steering checks

Examine the free play in the wheel by measuring the movement of the steering wheel rim between the points at which the wheels begin to move in each direction. For rack-and-pinion cars it should be no more than 1in—on cars with a worm-cam steering box it should be no more than 2in (anything over 1in should be adjusted out). Also shake the steering wheel up and down—any discernible play means renewal of the steering column bearings (often easily replaced nylon inserts).

With the front of the car on ramps, carefully examine the condition of the convoluted rubber gaiters which seal lubricant into the rack (1). Any cracks or damage will allow lubricant to leak and let in dirt, leading to premature wear of the mechanism. If there are any signs of leakage or damage have them renewed.

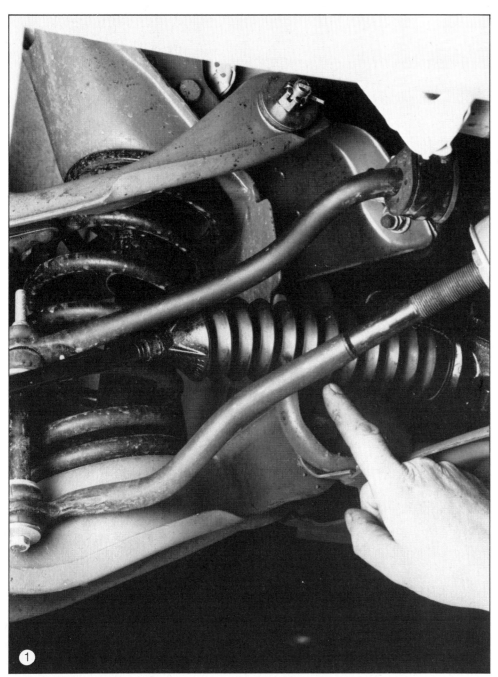

Examine the convoluted rubber gaiters which seal lubricant into the rack

Check each track-rod end joint by grasping it while a helper moves the wheel slightly from lock to lock (1). If there is any play in the joint you will feel it. Have a joint changed if it shows signs of free play.

Identify the steering mounting bolts, and, using a spanner of the correct size, check them for tightness (2). If bolts persistently loosen there may be excessive vibration which could be caused by wheel misalignment or wheel imbalance. Proprietary bolt-locking compounds can be used to ensure that the bolts will not work loose.

Check the universal joints on the column (3). With the wheels on the ground, hold each joint while a helper rocks the wheel to and fro. If any play is felt in the joint, have it renewed by a garage—joint failure can cause complete loss of steering.

Lastly, check for play on the top and bottom steering swivels, as described on page 133.

Lubricating the steering system

Lithium grease in a high-pressure grease gun is used to lubricate the top and bottom steering swivels if the manufacturer has provided grease nipples (see page 134).

The rack of a rack-and-pinion system is oil-filled and it should be topped up only if there has been a leak through a defective gaiter. Gaiter replacement involves resetting the wheel alignment and is best left to a garage with the correct special equipment.

Most modern track-rod ball-joints are pre-packed with grease and do not need lubricating. However, check for a grease nipple. If there is one, use

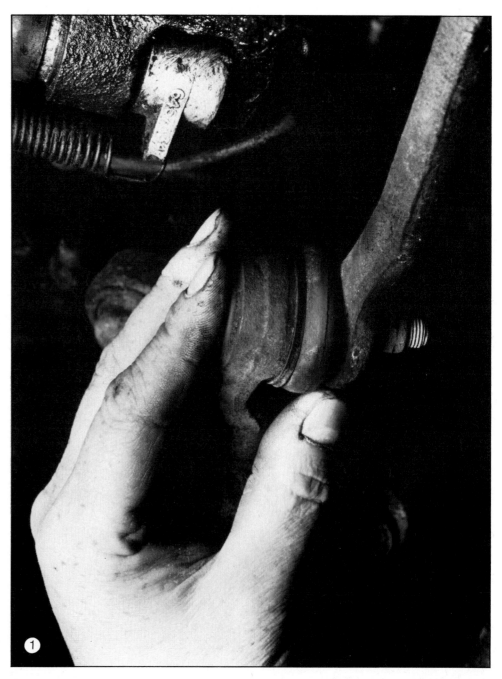

Check each track-rod end joint by grasping it while the wheel is moved

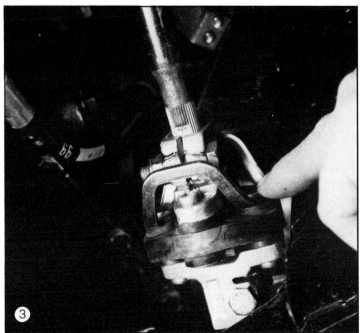

Check the universal joints on the column. If any play can be felt in a joint it should be renewed

Use a spanner to check the steering-box mounting bolts (above, left)

lithium-based grease in a high-pressure grease-gun. Clean the nipple first to prevent dirt from entering the joint. If the nipple is damaged or faulty, unscrew it and fit a new one.
Steering boxes and idler-arm bearings on older cars will need occasional top-ups of oil via the filler/level hole (4). On current cars, however, this is not usually required.

Steering boxes and idler-arm bearings on older cars need occasional top-ups of oil through the filler/level hole

Power-assisted steering

With manual steering, a car's weight may make the steering unduly heavy. For instance, the reduction gearing necessary to obtain a lighter steering wheel effort, particularly when parking, could mean exceeding the ratio of four wheel turns from lock to lock, which is close to being unpleasantly low geared. In this case, the answer is a power-assisted steering system.

Most European power-steering systems are based on a rack-and-pinion layout and consist of a control-valve mechanism fitted in the steering column just before the pinion. Valves direct fluid supplied under pressure from an engine-driven pump to a double-acting piston that considerably assists the action of the rack.

In operation, there is a small amount of free play —the 'sneeze factor'—about the straight-ahead position of the steering wheel which allows for the engagement of a left or right steering valve in the control box.

As the wheel is turned and the valve operates, the hydraulic fluid (or light oil) is directed to the appropriate side of the piston. This then acts to assist the driver's own effort at the wheel, which is transmitted to the rack in the normal manner.

The use of a rack-and-pinion system means that some feel of the road is retained. This can be improved upon in a number of ways. Some power systems use a torsion bar linkage which senses the degree of effort required and correspondingly adjusts the pressure of supply to the system. This means that normal small steering movements to stay on the straight-ahead path receive little assistance and the driver gets a manual steering feel. But when parking, when a considerable effort is needed to turn the wheel, the system gives full assistance. Turning the wheels between full locks when stationary, however, will put excessive strain on the system.

On large Citroen cars the power-assisted steering is designed to give as near normal a feel as possible throughout the whole turn of the wheels by restricting the valves towards the full-lock position. This means that the driver has to apply much more effort at the extremes of lock, just as he would in a manually-steered car.

Fail-safe

Power-assisted steering is designed to fail-safe. It is usually belt-driven, and if there is a pump failure or fluid loss, the car can still be steered by the normal rack-and-pinion system, although it becomes extremely heavy. Another safety advantage is that power steering reduces kick-back to the wheel to a minimum, which should enable a driver to maintain control if a tyre blows-out or when the wheel hits an unexpected obstacle. Not only that, the system also acts as a form of automatic fluid damper to reduce side-to-side wheel vibration, known as 'shimmy'.

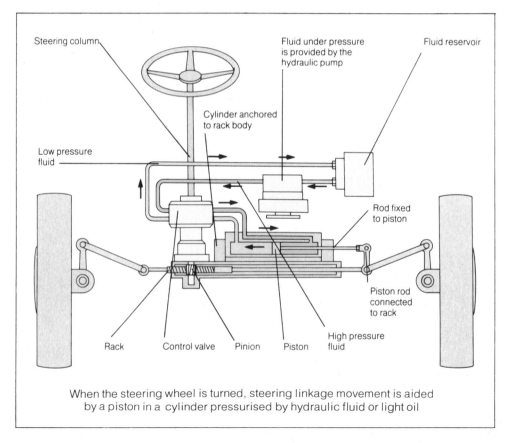

When the steering wheel is turned, steering linkage movement is aided by a piston in a cylinder pressurised by hydraulic fluid or light oil

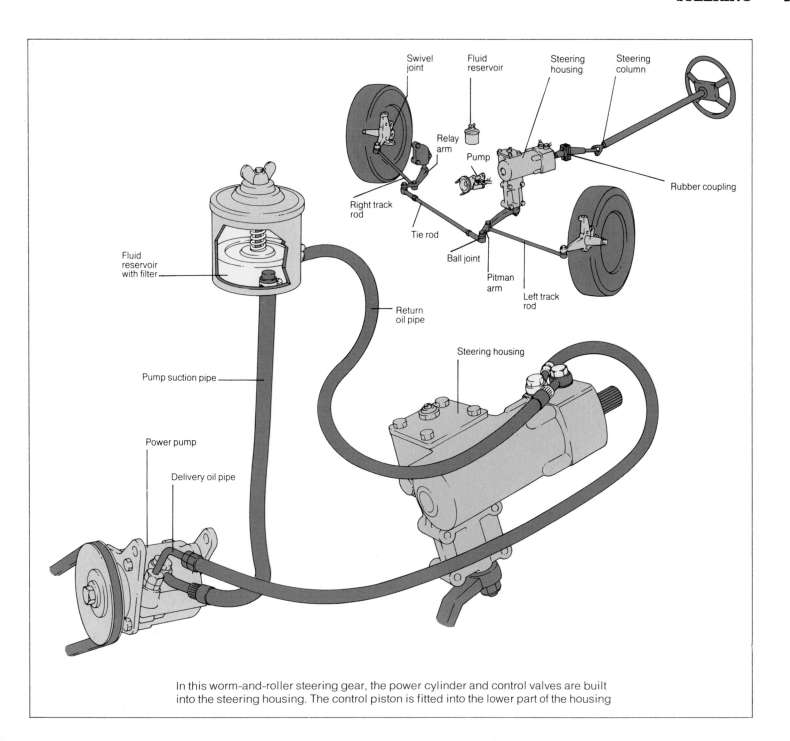

Swivel joint

Fluid reservoir

Steering housing

Steering column

Relay arm

Pump

Rubber coupling

Right track rod

Tie rod

Ball joint

Pitman arm

Left track rod

Fluid reservoir with filter

Return oil pipe

Pump suction pipe

Steering housing

Power pump

Delivery oil pipe

In this worm-and-roller steering gear, the power cylinder and control valves are built into the steering housing. The control piston is fitted into the lower part of the housing

Servicing power steering

First ensure that you have a supply of the correct type of fluid to top-up and service a power-assisted steering system. Some manufacturers use automatic transmission fluid, others specify engine oil. To be certain, check the fluid specification given in the owner's handbook.

Checking and topping-up the reservoir

The reservoir is usually mounted on top of the pump body and may contain a filter. The reservoir cap may also have a short dipstick attached (1) which gives the levels required when the pump is hot or cold. Check the level and top-up the reservoir as required. On other systems, it is necessary to top-up until fluid covers the filter body. Always observe high standards of cleanliness—never use dirty or old fluid. Clean off the area around the filler cap before opening it up, and clean the cap (and any vent hole) thoroughly before refitting it.

Pump drive-belts and hoses

On a few cars the pump is driven by an extension of the generator shaft; normal adjustment of the generator drive belt will ensure that it is driven correctly. On many systems, however, the drive is from a separate belt running in a multiple-grooved pulley on the crankshaft or is itself driven by a belt from the crankshaft pulley. If the pump is driven in this way, the belt adjustments are similar to those for the generator. Slacken the adjustment and adjust the tensioner until the belt deflects no more than ½in on its longest run when subjected to firm thumb pressure (2).

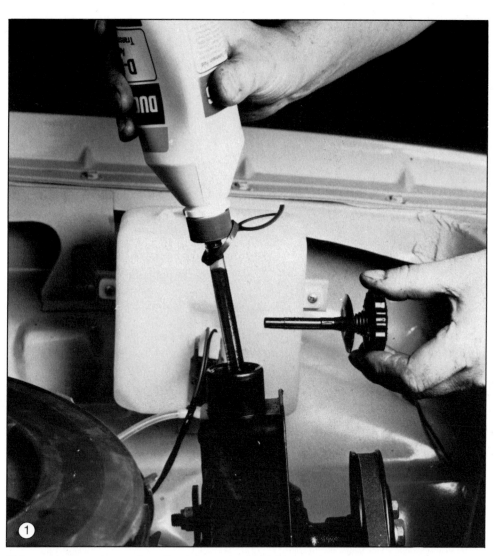

(1)

This reservoir cap has a short dipstick attached which gives the levels required when the pump is hot or cold. Top up the reservoir as required, using the correct fluid

Check hoses and unions thoroughly for signs of leaks and splits or cracks. Power-assisted steering hoses are often exposed to a lot of oil fouling and it helps to preserve their life if this is cleaned off from time to time.

If the system is leaking, a car will fail its MOT test (see page 228). Check the tightness of the hydraulic unions. If this does not stop the leakage, have a garage check through the system thoroughly, and rectify any faults.

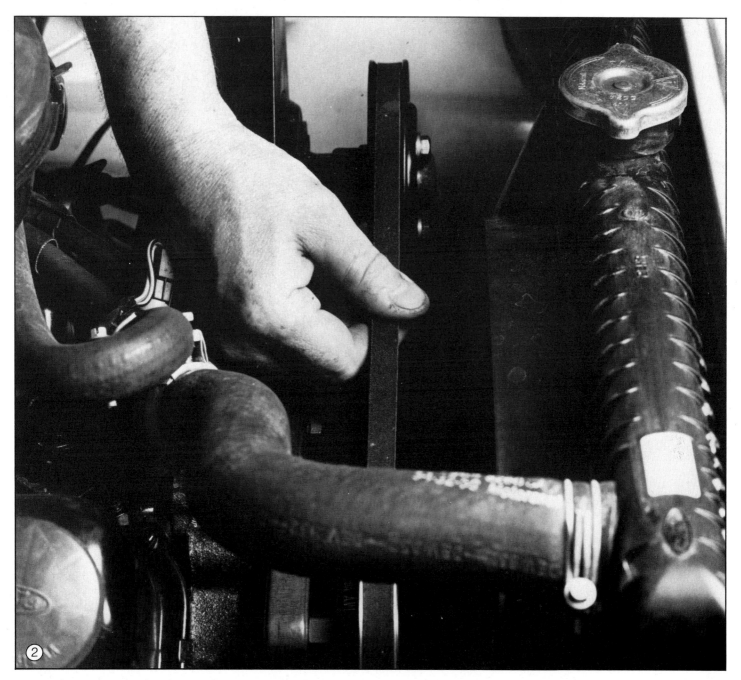

Adjust the tensioner until the belt deflects no more than $\frac{1}{2}$in on its longest run when firm thumb pressure is applied

Steering geometry

While the mechanics of the steering are relatively simple in principle and operation, there are many other factors which affect the car's steering, roadholding, traction and handling. Foremost among these is the steering geometry.

One of the main guidelines was set long before the car was invented. In 1818 Rudolf Ackermann established the fact that, to be geometrically correct, the two steered wheels of a four-wheeled vehicle must be turned at slightly differing angles if they are to make a turn around the same turning circle centre. The outer wheel of the circle has to be turned less than the inner wheel because it is describing a circle of larger radius.

On a car this is easily arranged by making the combination of the rack and track rods (or the steering linkages) slightly shorter than the distance between the steering swivels.

Toe-in and toe-out

No system of steering or suspension is without a certain amount of free-play and built-in compliance. This makes it difficult to keep the two wheels parallel when moving in a straight line. On most cars the wheels tend to diverge, spreading apart at the front as the car's speed increases. To counteract this, and at the same time minimise tyre wear and any adverse effects on the steering, most cars have their front wheels set with a very small amount of convergence, called toe-in. Up to $\frac{3}{16}$in (about 4mm) is the usual allowance. It is a figure which is a compromise between the wheel's toe-in at low speeds and

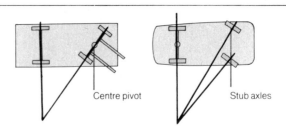

Centre pivot Stub axles

On a cart (above left), the front wheels steer about the same centre, but on a car (above right), the inside wheel swivels more than the outside one

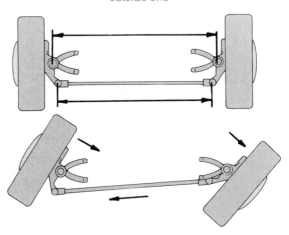

If the steering linkage is shorter than the distance between the pivots, the inside wheel moves through a greater angle than the outside one when lock is applied

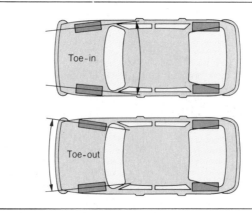

Toe-in

Toe-out

Front wheels are usually set with toe-in or toe-out to compensate for a small amount of compliance in all the steering and suspension joints when the car is on the move. Front-wheel-drive cars normally have toe-out, rear-wheel-drive cars have toe-in

possible toe-out at higher speeds. On a few front-wheel-drive cars the reaction to the wheel's traction tends to make the wheels toe-in, so they are set with a very slight toe-out.

All cars have some means of adjusting front wheel alignment, usually by means of a locknut and screw adjustment of one or other track rods. Tracking, the measurement and adjustment of the alignment, requires special measuring tools. DIY equipment is available for the amateur, but if in doubt have the job done professionally. Alignment should be checked if you spot uneven wear of both front tyres, and after even minor accidents or hitting a kerb very hard.

Camber angle

Because the steering swivels supporting the front wheel axles are slightly to one side of the wheel, considerable strain is exerted on them. The strain is reduced, and the steering lightened, by designing the steering so that an imaginary line extending through the steering swivels to the ground falls at the centre line of the tyre's contact patch with the road. To achieve this the wheel is angled slightly; this angling is called the camber of the wheel.

Cars may be designed with negative camber, where the wheels are wider apart at the bottom than the top, or positive camber, in which the opposite condition applies.

Castor angle

To encourage the steering to return to straight ahead after a turn, the wheel is made to castor. This is achieved by angling the steering pivots so that the imaginary line through them meets the ground very slightly ahead of the centre point of the tyre contact patch.

The angle at which the pivot is inclined to the vertical is the castor angle. A further advantage of castor is that it cuts out the tendency for the tyre to wander at speed. Castor angle, like wheel alignment, can be altered by accident damage, so a garage check should be made if any wheel wobble is experienced after striking a kerb hard. Tyre damage may also have occurred.

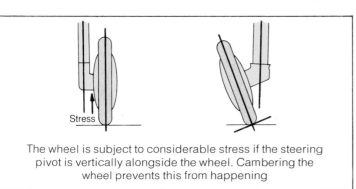

The wheel is subject to considerable stress if the steering pivot is vertically alongside the wheel. Cambering the wheel prevents this from happening

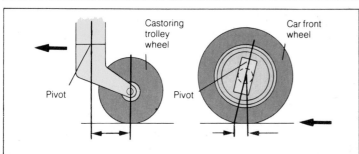

A trolley wheel trails behind its pivot. On a car, a similar effect is achieved by tilting the steering pivot. If a line along its axis falls ahead of the centre of the tyre, the wheel will castor

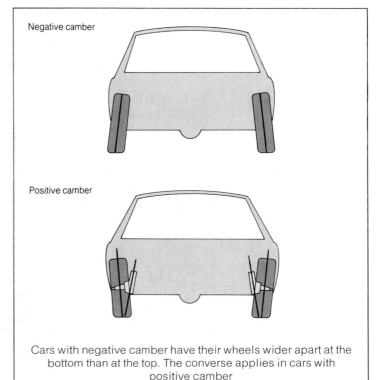

Cars with negative camber have their wheels wider apart at the bottom than at the top. The converse applies in cars with positive camber

Fault-finding

The steering mechanism on most cars is mechanically simple and robust. Complete failure is rare but faults due to wear do develop and it is essential to be able to distinguish from which part of the car's running gear the problem arises. Unfortunately, the very fact that the steering is a sensitive control system makes it possible for many other faults, such as those in the tyres, wheels or suspension, to manifest themselves as steering problems. Here are some clues:

Steering wheel judder:

If this occurs above 40mph and disappears at certain speeds, it is usually caused by a badly fitted tyre or imbalance of the tyres and wheels. Have the wheels dynamically balanced (1); this should eliminate it. If there is no improvement, suspect incorrect wheel alignment or, on front-wheel-drive cars, some drive-shaft imbalance—this can be minimised by balancing the wheel on the car.

A slightly different pattern of judder occurring at higher speeds and growing worse as the car goes faster may be rear wheel misalignment caused by a corroded suspension mounting or accident damage.

Complete loss of steering:

If no effort at all is required to turn the wheel the failure may be at one of the universal joints or safety joints in the column. Check them back through to the steering box. On BL Minis and 1100s, make sure that the pinch-bolt securing the splined joint at the foot of the steering column to the rack pinion is

Dynamic wheel balancing should eliminate steering wheel judder. If it persists it may be cured, or at least minimised, by balancing the wheels on the car

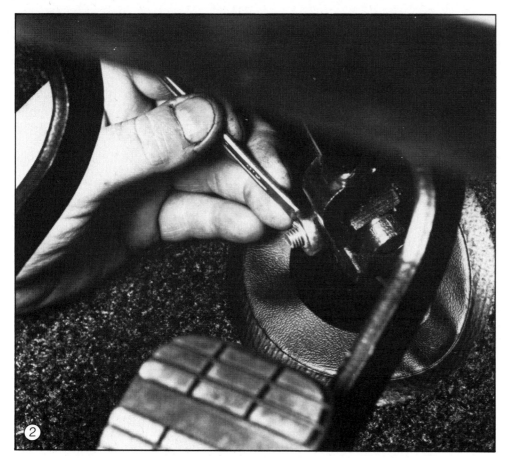

Check that the pinch-bolt clamping the splined·joint at the foot of the steering column to the rack pinion is firmly tightened

firmly tightened (2). If some effort is still required to turn the wheel, suspect track-rod ball-joint failure.

Steering goes very stiff:
On cars with power-assisted steering, check the level of fluid in the pump reservoir. If there is no fluid, search for leaks—usually they are found at the hose unions to the pump, the rack or the valve assembly. On manually-steered cars, stiffness can result from low tyre pressures, accident damage or front wheel misalignment. Bad stiffening is usually a result of loss of steering box or rack lubricant or a need for adjustment of the pinion loading or steering box mechanism—seek professional advice.

Excessive steering play:
On a rack-and-pinion system there should, ideally, be no discernible play in the wheel, although with age and wear, up to 1in is acceptable. This is the point at which you should seek garage attention for adjustment. On cam-type steering boxes, up to 1in of free play is normal and up to 2in is acceptable. Beyond this, you should seek garage advice. Other sources of free play are in the track-rod ball-joints and the pivots of the steering swivel.

Steering wanders:
Tyre pressure differences, uneven loading of the car or roof rack, front wheel bearing wear, steering swivel wear and rear suspension problems are the usual causes of steering wander. It is, however, occasionally the symptom of steering box or track-rod wear. Strong, gusty crosswinds can also cause a car to wander.

Pulling to one side:
Many people complain of the car pulling to one side when the problem is, in fact, the combination of road camber and cross winds. Check on a sheltered section of straight and flat road by driving to about 20mph and taking your hand from the steering wheel momentarily. The car should travel straight on. Any fault found may be due to tyre pressure differences, binding brakes, wheel misalignment or suspension problems.

Steering noises:
Rattles from the rack on bumpy roads may mean that the spring-loaded yoke, which is a vibration damper, needs adjustment—a garage job. Squeaks from the steering column indicate the need for lubrication of the column bearings but, in cars with nylon bearings, replacement is the best cure.

BRAKES

What you can do: Pages
Renew disc pads —
   fixed calipers   164-165
Renew disc pads — fist-type   166-167
Adjust drum brakes   168
Service the servo   173
Adjust the handbrake   174-175

All car brakes work by pressing a piece of friction material into contact with a metal surface attached to, or driven by, the car wheels. The metal surface can be in the form of a disc or drum – which accounts for the two basic types of brake mechanism fitted to cars. In each case, friction slows the car and converts the energy of the moving vehicle into heat. Disc brakes and drum brakes are equally popular – each type has its own advantages. Currently, most manufacturers fit disc brakes to the front wheels and drum brakes to the rear wheels of their popular cars.

How brakes work

The footbrake on all modern cars is operated by hydraulic pressure which is generated whenever the brake pedal is applied. In a disc brake, the pressure clamps friction pads on to opposing sides of the disc in a similar action to the caliper brakes of a bicycle. With a drum brake, hydraulic pressure is applied to the two brake shoes which are lined on the outside with a friction material. Pressure makes them expand away from each other and contact the internal surface of a brake drum. The hydraulic system consists of a master cylinder connected by small-bore pipelines to the four brakes. Flexible rubber hoses allow for suspension movement. The master cylinder is directly linked to the foot-brake pedal and usually incorporates a reservoir so that hydraulic brake fluid can be supplied to the system. Depressing the pedal causes the master cylinder to pressurise the hydraulic system, working all four brakes at once. A handbrake or an emergency brake is a legal requirement. Worked by a cable or mechanical linkage, it usually operates only on the rear wheels. Because disc brakes require more pressure than the drum type, a vacuum servo is often fitted to lessen brake pedal effort. The servo may be of the direct-acting type connected directly to the brake pedal, or of the indirect type, which is linked into the hydraulic line from the master cylinder.

Recent refinements include the use of split-circuit systems to minimise the risk of total brake failure, and the widespread use of pressure-limiting devices acting on the rear brakes to prevent rear wheel lock-up.

Drum brakes in detail

Drum brakes have a pair of mutually-opposed, C-shaped brake shoes, enclosed by a cast iron drum. The drum is usually bolted direct to the wheel hub and its open end faces a backplate which is rigidly attached to the car's axle or suspension member. The brake shoes are lined on their outer surface with a friction material and can be forced apart so that they rub against the inner rim of the brake drum by hydraulic wheel cylinders, pressurised from the master cylinder. When a handbrake is fitted, a mechanical arrangement does the same job. The brake shoes, wheel cylinder (or cylinders) and handbrake mechanism are attached to the backplate which prevents them from rotating with the brake drum. A manual or automatic adjustment system limits excessive travel before the brake shoes contact the drum; and return springs stop the brake shoes from binding against the drum when the brakes are off. Usually the wheel cylinder acts on only one end of the brake shoe.

Leading-and-trailing shoes

If the leading edge of the friction lining is moved against the rotating drum, the arrangement is called a 'leading shoe'. Similarly, if the trailing edge of the lining makes contact first, it is known as a 'trailing shoe'. In practice, a leading shoe provides greater braking effort as it has a self-applying action which generates a high braking force from a moderate pedal pressure. A trailing-shoe arrangement needs higher pedal pressure to achieve a similar result. Most European cars with drum brakes use either a two-leading-shoe or a leading-and-trailing-shoe arrangement. The leading-and-trailing-shoe brake uses a double-acting or a sliding wheel cylinder which operates both brake shoes simultaneously. It is normally used on the rear wheels because it works equally well in both directions – which is desirable when reversing. The two-leading-shoe arrangement is normally used on the front wheels only, where its greater efficiency can be used to full advantage. A two-leading-shoe brake needs two wheel cylinders and is more expensive; it also does not work well in reverse – as the two leading shoes then become two trailing shoes. Self-adjusting rear brakes are now a common fitment, particularly when matched to front disc brakes which are inherently self-adjusting. They provide a specific clearance between the shoes and drum, regardless of wear.

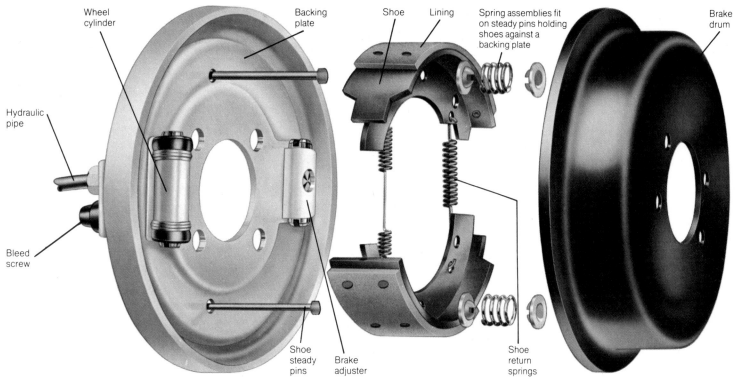

Wheel cylinder

Backing plate

Shoe

Lining

Spring assemblies fit on steady pins holding shoes against a backing plate

Brake drum

Hydraulic pipe

Bleed screw

Shoe steady pins

Brake adjuster

Shoe return springs

The brake shoes, wheel cylinder and steady pins and springs are attached to the fixed backplate. This prevents them from rotating with the brake drum, which turns with the wheel

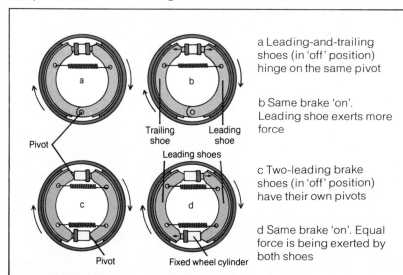

Pivot

Trailing shoe

Leading shoe

Pivot

Leading shoes

Fixed wheel cylinder

a Leading-and-trailing shoes (in 'off' position) hinge on the same pivot

b Same brake 'on'. Leading shoe exerts more force

c Two-leading brake shoes (in 'off' position) have their own pivots

d Same brake 'on'. Equal force is being exerted by both shoes

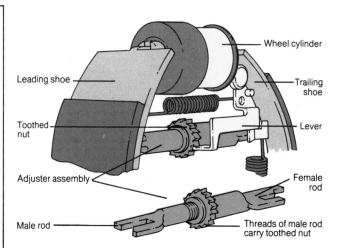

Wheel cylinder

Leading shoe

Trailing shoe

Toothed nut

Lever

Adjuster assembly

Female rod

Male rod

Threads of male rod carry toothed nut

As the linings wear, movement of one shoe operates a lever resting on a toothed nut in this self-adjusting brake

How disc brakes work

The disc brake consists of a cast iron or steel disc rotating with the wheel, but passing through a fixed brake caliper containing friction-lined pads. Depressing the pedal causes hydraulic pressure to act on cylinders and pistons in the caliper and squeeze the two pads together, clamping the disc.

The pads are usually visible through an opening in the caliper, and are held in place by a combination of pins and clips, or by wedges. They are sometimes backed by shim plates to minimise brake squeal.

When the brakes are off, each piston is retracted slightly into the cylinder by the flexible rubber seal surrounding it. This prevents the pads binding, minimises brake pedal travel, and automatically compensates for pad wear as it occurs. The friction lining is based on a tough resin-asbestos mix, moulded and bonded into recesses in a steel backplate. On some designs, an electrical contact is built into the friction pad. When the pad is worn thin, contact with the disc activates a warning light which alerts the driver.

Fixed and moving calipers

There are two basic types of caliper, the fixed type, and the moving caliper—it may be of the floating, swinging or sliding type. Fixed calipers contain two, three, or four pistons bearing on the friction pads. The pistons move or 'float' so that pad loads on either side are equal. The caliper has internal passages to allow brake fluid to pass from one side to another. Calipers with four pistons have a separate hydraulic supply to each pair of opposing

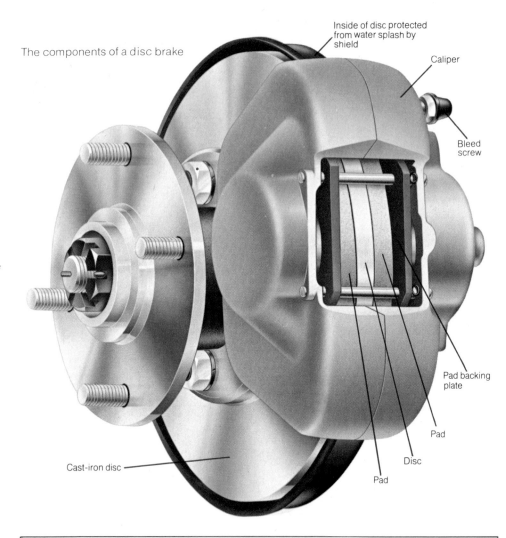

The components of a disc brake

Inside of disc protected from water splash by shield

Caliper

Bleed screw

Pad backing plate

Pad

Disc

Pad

Cast-iron disc

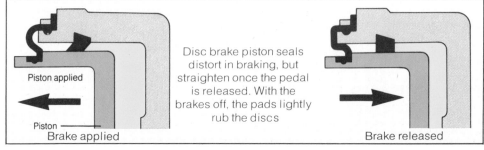

Piston applied

Piston

Brake applied

Disc brake piston seals distort in braking, but straighten once the pedal is released. With the brakes off, the pads lightly rub the discs

Brake released

cylinders. Each pair of cylinders is connected to its own hydraulic circuit in order to provide a 'fail-safe' system. This arrangement also allows much larger pads to be used.

On a floating caliper, only one friction pad is operated by a hydraulic piston – the other pad is actuated by movement of the caliper itself. The caliper is mounted so that it resists braking torque, yet is free to move laterally across the disc.

A swinging caliper pivots about a hinge pin so that the body of the caliper clamps one of the friction pads, the other pad being clamped by a single, direct-acting hydraulic piston.

The sliding caliper has one or two pistons in a single cylinder. Again, one piston acts directly on one pad. If two pistons are used, the other piston causes the whole caliper to slide along a groove and apply the opposite brake pad. On sliding calipers with one piston, hydraulic pressure causes the caliper body to move in the opposite direction to the piston and apply the other pad.

Disc brakes have their working surfaces exposed and therefore operate in conditions that allow them to be more efficiently cooled than drum brakes. For additional cooling, some high performance cars have specially ventilated disc brakes.

These have two adjacent discs linked by a series of vanes, in the form of a single casting. Air passing between the discs increases the cooling effect.

This single-cylinder caliper has one piston acting on a pad. A sliding yoke is moved by the other piston to apply the other pad

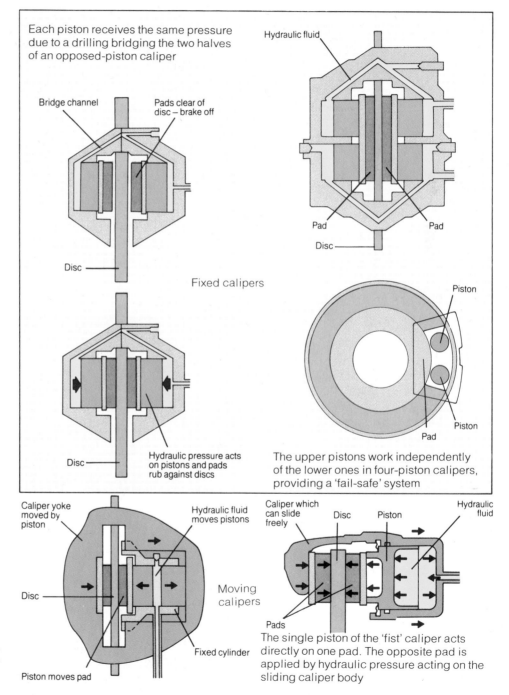

Each piston receives the same pressure due to a drilling bridging the two halves of an opposed-piston caliper

Bridge channel

Pads clear of disc – brake off

Disc

Hydraulic fluid

Pad

Pad

Disc

Fixed calipers

Disc

Hydraulic pressure acts on pistons and pads rub against discs

Piston

Piston

Pad

The upper pistons work independently of the lower ones in four-piston calipers, providing a 'fail-safe' system

Caliper yoke moved by piston

Hydraulic fluid moves pistons

Disc

Moving calipers

Fixed cylinder

Piston moves pad

Caliper which can slide freely

Disc

Piston

Hydraulic fluid

Pads

The single piston of the 'fist' caliper acts directly on one pad. The opposite pad is applied by hydraulic pressure acting on the sliding caliper body

Renewing disc pads

Although disc brakes are self-adjusting, they should be inspected every 5-6,000 miles to check the rate of pad wear. Brake manufacturers advise renewing disc pads when the lining thickness approaches $\frac{1}{8}$in (3mm) (1). Below this figure, excessive heat is transferred to the brake fluid, while if the lining wears away, the steel backing plate will damage the disc.

Disc brake calipers vary in design, but from the pad-changing viewpoint there are two types – the fixed caliper, where the pads are changed by removing them from an aperture, and the moving caliper, which may need to be separated from its mounting in order to change the pads. (See also pages 162-163.)
Examples of both types are shown here. Although the calipers on your car may look different, the pad-changing principle will be similar, but if in doubt, consult an appropriate dealer. If you get into difficulties, remember that the opposite caliper is a mirror image of the one you are working on, and can be used as a reference.

Fixed calipers

Raise the car, support it on axle stands and remove the wheels. Use pliers to pull out any small clips from the pad-retaining pins (2), then withdraw the pins. With an old screwdriver, gently prise each pad away from the disc (3), then grip each backing plate with pliers and pull the pad out (4).
Scrape dirt and rust from the pad aperture with an old screwdriver – then, with an old paintbrush, clean the area with brake-cleaning fluid or methylated spirit. Do not use any other solvent.

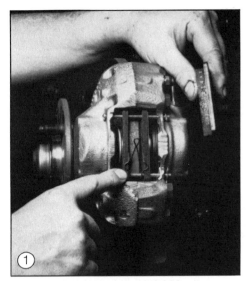

Inspect brake pads every 5-6,000 miles

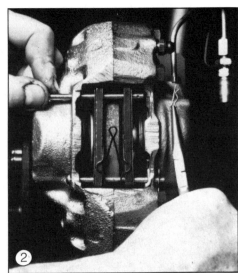

Gently prise each pad away from the disc

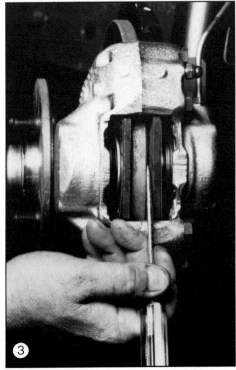

Withdraw the retaining pins

Pull the pads out with pliers

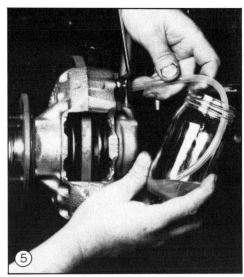

Connect a tube to the bleed valve

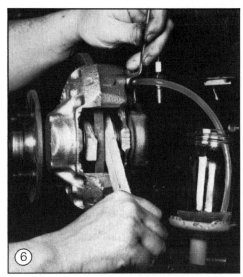

Open the bleed valve half a turn

Fit shims with the arrows vertical

Fit new retaining pins and clips

Any accumulated rust can be removed from the edge of the disc quite easily by resting the old screwdriver blade on the caliper so that it bears on the edge and spinning the disc.

The caliper pistons must now be retracted into their cylinders to make room for the new, thicker pads. If you do not have a special piston-retracting tool, this can be done by using a piece of wood as a lever.

First connect a flexible tube to the bleed valve and insert the free end into a container (5). Using the timber between the disc and piston, lever the piston back into its bore. At the same time, open the bleed valve half a turn (6). Fluid will emerge from the tube as the piston retracts. Close the bleed valve when the piston is fully retracted in the caliper. Repeat the same operation on the opposite piston. Opening the bleed valve prevents fluid being forced back through the hydraulic pipework to the reservoir. If the reservoir has been overfilled, some fluid may spill out. Pack old rags round the reservoir to prevent any fluid from reaching the paintwork. Split-circuit calipers have two bleed valves. In that case, open them both in turn, and carry out the same procedure as already described.

Fit the new pads into the aperture with their linings facing the disc. If there are shims behind the backing plates, these are fitted so that any arrows on them point in the direction of forward wheel rotation (7).

Fit new pins and clips (8) and repeat the operation on the opposite caliper. Refit the wheels, lower the car and before driving it, pump the brake pedal until the new pads contact the disc.

'Fist' (moving) calipers

The single-cylinder 'fist' caliper is one of the moving type increasingly being fitted to small cars because its compact shape enables it to fit easily behind a small-diameter road wheel. The caliper must be removed from its mounting on the hub to change the pads.

Raise the car, support it on axle stands and remove the wheels. Use pliers to straighten and remove the two caliper split pins, top and bottom (1). Tap out the upper and lower wedge-shaped caliper guides (2) and remove the caliper from its carrier. Rest it out of the way on the suspension so that no load is put on the flexible hose.

The pads are in the carrier. Pull them sideways to remove them (3).

Use a wire brush to remove dirt and corrosion from the pad abutments and the guide seatings. Clean rust from the disc edge by rotating it against an old screwdriver blade resting on the bracket.

A 'fist'-type caliper

Use pliers to straighten and remove the two split pins from the caliper, top and bottom

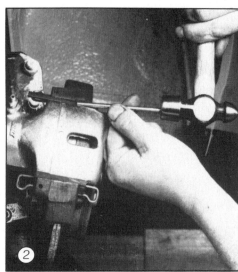

Tap out the upper and lower wedge-shaped caliper guides and remove the caliper

Remove the pads from the caliper by pulling them out sideways

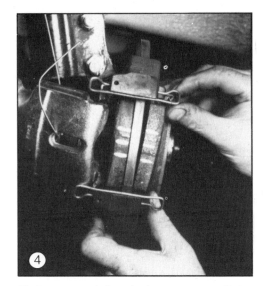

Fit the new pads into the bottom recess first, then locate the clip

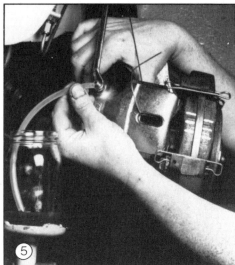

Connect a rubber pipe to the bleed valve and lead the free end into a container

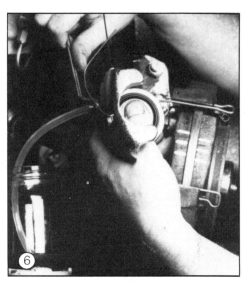

With the bleed valve open half a turn, push the piston into its bore by hand

If the pads are held by spring clips, transfer these to the upper edge of the new pads. Fit the new pads into the bottom recess, then swing in the top of each pad and locate the clip (4).

On the caliper, clean the area around the piston with a cloth dipped in methylated spirit, then connect a rubber pipe to the bleed valve and lead the free end into a container (5). Open the valve half a turn, then press the piston into its bore by hand (6). When it is fully retracted, close the bleed screw.

Refit the caliper into the bracket. If it is spring-loaded, make sure that it sits on top of the springs (7). Refit the guides, pressing the caliper towards the springs. Align the guide holes with the split pin holes and fit new pins.

Repeat the operation on the other caliper. Refit the wheels, lower the car and before driving it, pump the brake pedal to move the piston up to the pads.

If the caliper is spring-loaded, it is important that it sits on the springs

Drum brake adjustment

Some drum brakes need to be adjusted manually to compensate for lining wear. The adjuster is usually a square-ended screw that protrudes through the backplate. Leading-and-trailing shoe brakes have a single adjuster; two adjusters are fitted to two-leading-shoe brakes.

Although brake adjustment does not normally involve getting under the car, it is best to support the vehicle on axle stands. Raise one end of the car, remove both wheels, and chock the wheels that are on the ground. The handbrake must be released.

If you are not familiar with brake adjustment, first identify the adjusters (1) – the handbook may give details. Make sure that you do not mistake a bleed valve for an adjuster. The valve has a nipple on the end and will let air into the hydraulic fluid if it is loosened. If you cannot identify the adjusters, check with a dealer for the make of car – it may have self-adjusting brakes.

Apply the footbrake hard to centralise the shoes within the drums, then rotate, by hand, the drum to be adjusted (2). It should turn freely without binding on the linings. Driven wheels will be stiff to turn because of the dragging effect of the transmission.

As the drum is rotated, turn the adjuster with a brake adjusting spanner (3) until the linings are felt to drag against the drum. If nothing happens, the adjuster is being turned the wrong way – turn it in the opposite direction.

Once the linings have made contact, press the brake pedal to re-centre the shoes, and check again by rotating the drum. If necessary, turn the adjuster

further. From the point of contact, turn the adjuster in the opposite direction until the drum spins freely – a trace of rubbing is acceptable. Most adjusters have a 'notching' action with four distinct tight-spots per revolution. Set it between tight-spots.

Two-leading-shoe systems have two adjusters. Set them one at a time, as above. On a few cars, a star-shaped adjusting nut is fitted inside the brake drum and is turned by a screwdriver through a hole in the drum or backplate. Once the linings make contact, reverse the direction of the adjuster until the drum spins freely. Repeat the adjustment operation on the other drum on the axle.

Master cylinders

The master cylinder is the heart of the hydraulic system. It consists of a single cylinder linked to a fluid reservoir, and a piston joined by a short pushrod to the brake pedal. Depressing the brake pedal pushes the piston into the

Identify the brake adjusters

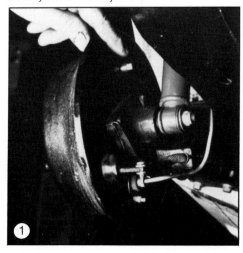

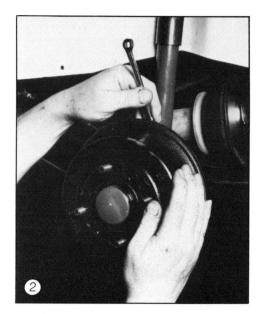

Rotate the drum to be adjusted by hand

Turn the adjuster until the linings drag

cylinder, forcing hydraulic fluid out into the brake pipes. As it moves, the piston shuts off the port supplying fluid to the system from the reservoir.

On drum-braked cars, a check-valve is built into the end of the master cylinder to maintain a small residual pressure in the hydraulic system. This pressure is insufficient to overcome the brake-shoe retaining springs, but lessens the chance of air entering the system. This check-valve is not used with disc brakes as it would result in excessive binding of the friction pads.

The fluid reservoir is generally made from a translucent plastic so that the level can easily be seen. Sometimes an electric switch is built into the cap to operate a warning light should the fluid level fall too low.

All new cars have a tandem master cylinder which operates a divided or split braking system. This has a single cylinder, but two pistons, two fluid reservoirs and two outlets. The rear (primary) piston is connected to the pedal and generates pressure in one hydraulic circuit. The hydraulic pressure is applied to a secondary piston which moves forward to pressurise the other hydraulic circuit. By careful design, it is possible to ensure that if one circuit fails, there is sufficient pedal travel available to operate the other circuit and so provide at least some stopping power.

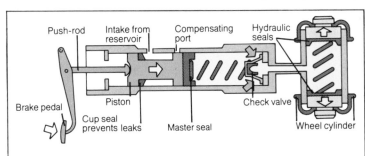

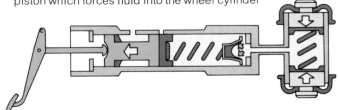

Brakes on: The compensating port is blocked by the moving piston which forces fluid into the wheel cylinder

Pedal released: Fluid re-enters the cylinder past the check-valve which maintains slight pressure in the fluid lines

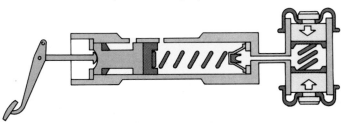

Brakes off: The retracted piston uncovers the reservoir port. Wheel cylinder springs keep the pistons up to the shoes

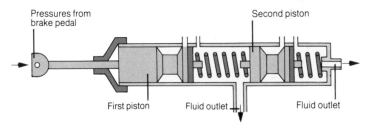

A dual-line master cylinder

Normal condition
When the master cylinder is operating normally, the first piston creates pressure in the first hydraulic line and applies pressure to the second piston. This creates pressure in the other line. Separate reservoirs and hydraulic fluid supplies are provided to each half of the master cylinder

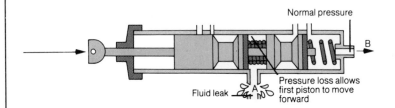

Emergency condition
If a leak occurs in the first hydraulic line (A), the first piston, meeting no resistance, is pushed forward until it contacts the second piston. The latter then creates pressure in the second hydraulic line (B). The driver will notice an increase in pedal travel, but the brakes will still work

Wheel cylinders

Wheel cylinders may be either single- or double-acting, depending on whether they have one or two pistons. The piston extends beyond the cylinder and is slotted to engage with the tip of the brake shoe. Rubber seals prevent hydraulic fluid from escaping past the pistons, and an additional rubber boot prevents dirt getting in. A bleed screw is fitted so that air can be removed from the system.

When the footbrake is depressed, the master cylinder feeds pressurised brake fluid throughout the hydraulic system. This acts on the wheel-cylinder pistons, forcing the brake shoes against the drum. The double-acting wheel cylinder is a convenient means of activating a leading-and-trailing drum brake, although some designs use a floating, single-acting wheel cylinder.

Brake fluid

Hydraulic fluid is the life-blood of the braking system. It is usually a mixture of vegetable oil, alcohol and additives which is harmless to natural rubber seals and chemically stable at the high temperatures attained in modern braking systems. Good lubricating properties and the capability of preventing the formation of gums or sludges are other requirements. Unfortunately, brake fluid is hygroscopic – it absorbs moisture from the atmosphere, which lowers its boiling point. In the car's hydraulic system, moisture is taken in through the flexible rubber hoses, contaminating the fluid. If this process is allowed to continue, the fluid could boil, causing total brake failure. For this reason, it is essential to

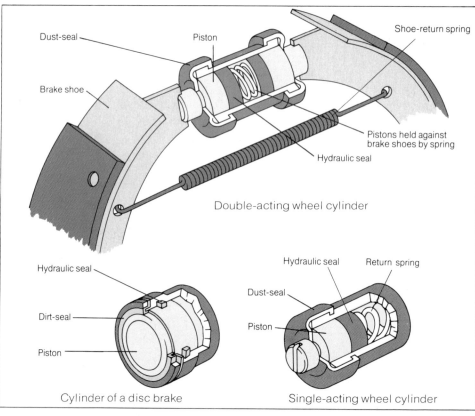

Double-acting wheel cylinder

Cylinder of a disc brake

Single-acting wheel cylinder

have the brake fluid changed at the specified periods. When topping-up, it is important that the correct fluid is used, and that it is *new* and in no way contaminated. Always clean the reservoir cap before removing it.

Split-circuit systems

The disadvantage of a hydraulic circuit is that failure of a single component renders the whole system inoperative. A split system largely overcomes this objection as, in effect, it comprises two independent braking systems linked to a common footbrake. It is unlikely that both will fail at once, and one circuit is sufficient to meet normal braking

requirements. The driver has only to apply more pedal effort in the event of one circuit failing – a natural reaction. Most new cars are sold with split systems as a legal requirement. There are four main types in use.

Front/rear split

The simplest is the front/rear split with independent circuits for both the front and rear brakes. A disadvantage with this system is that very little braking effort is provided by the rear wheels (particularly on front-wheel-drive cars) in the event of a front circuit failure. Stability with only the rear wheels being braked is also poor.

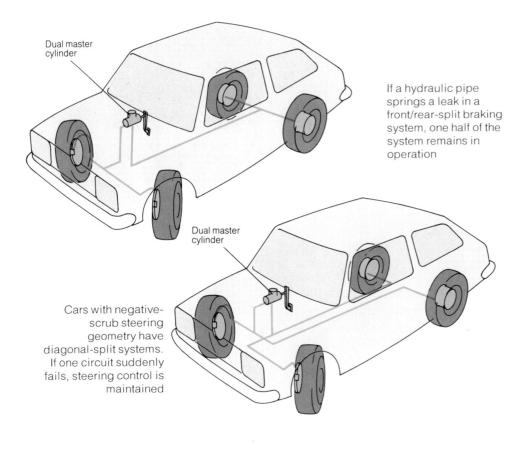

Dual master cylinder

If a hydraulic pipe springs a leak in a front/rear-split braking system, one half of the system remains in operation

Dual master cylinder

Cars with negative-scrub steering geometry have diagonal-split systems. If one circuit suddenly fails, steering control is maintained

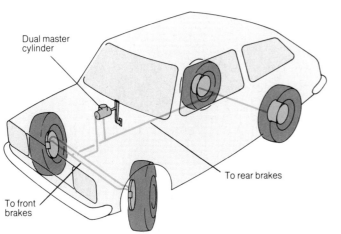

Dual master cylinder

To rear brakes

To front brakes

The L-split system has one outlet to half the four-piston front calipers and the other to all the wheels. The front brakes work if one line fails

Three popular split-circuit systems

Diagonal split

This system has independent circuits for diagonally-opposed wheels. If either circuit fails, one front brake and one rear brake still work. The system requires negative offset wheel geometry to maintain stable braking.

Front/front-rear split

The third system, referred to as a front/front-rear split, has one circuit working on all four brakes with an auxiliary circuit also operating on the front brakes only. Four-piston calipers are required for this arrangement, which ensures that the front brakes will always work should one circuit fail.

L-split

Two independent circuits, each working both front wheel brakes and a single rear brake, are a feature of the L-split system. Otherwise, this system is similar to the previous one.

Preventing rear wheel lock-up

During heavy braking, weight is transferred from the rear to the front wheels. On some vehicles this would cause the rear wheels to lock. To discourage this (locked wheels contribute less to slowing a car than those which are rotating just a little), many vehicles are now fitted with a means of limiting hydraulic pressure to the rear brakes. A limiter system is an almost universal fitment on today's cars, regardless of whether they are front- or rear-wheel drive. There are three types of limiter, which are triggered respectively by hydraulic pressure, vehicle deceleration and the nose-down attitude of the car.

The pressure-limiting valve

This limits the hydraulic pressure to the rear braking system whenever pressure throughout the circuit exceeds a predetermined level. The valve consists of a piston and spring mounted in the hydraulic line between the master cylinder and the rear braking circuit. At a set pressure, the piston overcomes the spring pressure and closes to prevent any increase in hydraulic pressure from reaching the rear wheel cylinders. A refinement of this type is the pressure-reducing valve. This enables the pressure in the rear circuit to increase at a lower rate than the front circuit, once a threshold has been exceeded.

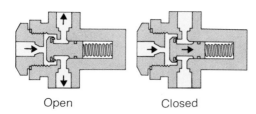

Open   Closed

A pressure-limiting valve stops the rear wheels from locking. Rising pressure in the line makes the valve shut off fluid to the rear brakes. The additional fluid is then fed to the front brakes

Inertia valve

This valve usually cuts off pressure to the rear brakes whenever a given rate of deceleration is exceeded. As the car decelerates, a ball rolls up an inclined ramp, permitting a spring-loaded valve to close, and isolating the rear braking circuit. Alternatively, it may be of the pressure-reducing type which restricts the rate of increase in rear-brake circuit pressure once a certain limit has been reached.

Load-sensing valve

Load-sensing, pressure-limiting or pressure-reducing valves respond to changes in rear suspension height, and are operated by a lever connected to the rear axle, anti-roll bar or other parts of the rear suspension. With this type, the rear circuit hydraulic pressure is governed both by load and deceleration, since both these conditions affect the suspension height.

Power brakes

Power braking systems, as distinct from the common servo-assisted type, are currently fitted to certain Citroens and other cars. A hydraulic fluid is pressurised by an engine-driven pump, and stored under pressure in reservoirs called accumulators. A regulator governs the maximum pressure available. In the case of Citroen, the same fluid is also used for suspension and power steering requirements. The footbrake acts on a slide valve which allows fluid stored in the main accumulator to pressurise the front brake circuit. This pressure is applied to a second slide valve within the same cylinder, which controls the rear brakes. Because the supply of fluid to the rear brakes is taken from the rear suspension, rear brake pressure is automatically limited in relation to load, which minimises the risk of the rear wheels locking when the brakes are applied hard on a lightly laden car.

Servo assistance

Most servos work by making use of the partial vacuum in the engine inlet manifold to provide braking assistance. If a fault occurs, the brakes still work but

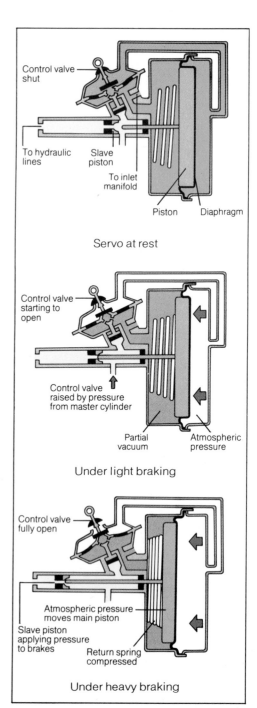

Servo at rest

Under light braking

Under heavy braking

greater driver effort is required. Essentially, the servo consists of a large cylindrical enclosure, containing a piston or diaphragm acting on a small hydraulic slave cylinder. With the engine running and the brakes off, a partial vacuum is applied to both sides of the diaphragm, itself held in position by a return spring. When the brakes are applied, the vacuum acting on one side of the diaphragm is shut off, and filtered air at atmospheric pressure is admitted. The diaphragm moves forward, acting on the slave cylinder and pressurising the fluid in the outlet pipe. In general, the fluid in the outlet pipe is under about twice as much pressure as the fluid in the inlet pipe, due to the assistance provided by the diaphragm. Most servos have a non-return valve so that the vacuum is retained for short periods, irrespective of whether or not the engine is running. All servos have an air filter to protect the control valves from dirt. Each brake application results in a small volume of air being drawn in by the diaphragm, and this is subsequently sucked into the engine inlet manifold.

Servo servicing

All brake servos contain hydraulic components (1) which require servicing whenever the rest of the hydraulic system is overhauled – usually every 40,000 miles or at four-yearly intervals. This work should be carried out by a specialist.

Servo filters can be replaced by the car owner, and should be renewed at the intervals recommended in the handbook. External filters are usually retained by a single screw in the top of the unit. Undoing this and removing the

Ensure that brake servo components are overhauled by a specialist

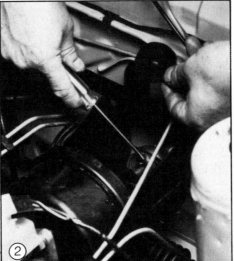

filter cover reveals the filter itself. The filter on a direct-acting servo is usually hidden under a rubber boot behind the brake pedal. It is co-axial with the brake pedal pushrod and is held in place by a retainer (2). To fit a new one, peel back the boot, remove the retainer and the old filter, then cut through one side of the new filter so that it can be slipped round the rod. Refit the retainer and the rubber boot.

Gain access to the servo filter by peeling back the rubber boot behind the pedal

Handbrake

All cars are fitted with a mechanically-operated handbrake working on one pair of wheels through a system of cables, rods and levers. The handbrake itself has a ratchet action so that the brakes may be left on for parking. Drum brakes have the advantage of providing a simple, efficient handbrake operation. Disc brakes are more difficult to work mechanically and sometimes have an auxiliary caliper attached to the main caliper. This contains its own handbrake pads which are mechanically clamped to the disc. Adjustment may be manual or automatic.

Simpler systems are now available on moving-caliper disc brakes – both swinging and sliding types. One system uses a lever-and-cam arrangement to force two hydraulic pistons apart in a sliding brake caliper. These systems operate on the existing brake pads and are self-adjusting. Some cars with disc brakes front and rear use small auxiliary drum brakes, formed within the central part of the disc, for the handbrake.

The simplest handbrake linkage has two cables, one for each wheel. This type of system cannot compensate for uneven wear; better mechanical linkages have a compensator to equalise the braking effect at each wheel.

Adjusting the handbrake

Although handbrake linkages vary considerably, the same rule applies to them all. With the handbrake lever off, there must be a trace of slackness in the linkage. A tight linkage will keep the brakes partially applied, not only wearing out the linings but also causing

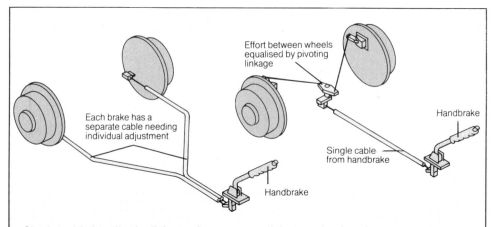

Effort between wheels equalised by pivoting linkage

Each brake has a separate cable needing individual adjustment

Handbrake

Single cable from handbrake

Handbrake

Single-cable handbrake linkages have an equalising mechanism that apportions the effort between the rear wheels. Where two cables are used, the load at each rear wheel must be adjusted individually. The handbrake lever operates with a ratchet and pawl mechanism. Pressing a button in the end of the lever frees the pawl, allowing the handbrake to be released

Using an old rag and a wire brush, clean old grease and dirt off any of the pivots

Apply a generous dose of penetrating oil to ease any stiffness in the mechanism

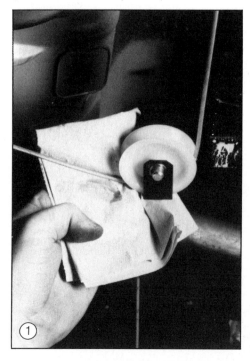

(1)

(2)

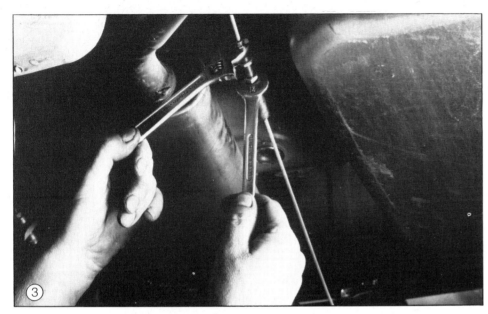

On both the single-cable handbrake (above) and the twin-cable type (below), loosen the locknut and turn the adjusting nut to take up excessive slackness in the cable

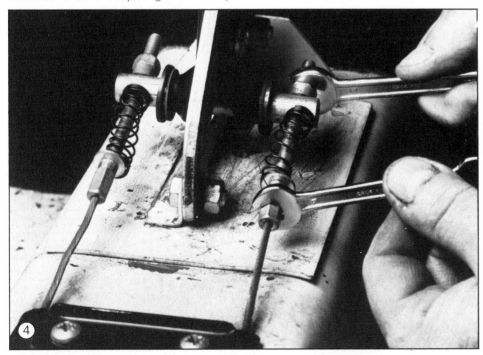

increased fuel consumption.

Raise the car, support it on axle stands, and chock the grounded wheels.

Release the handbrake and, if applicable, adjust the brakes – see page 168 for details.

Using an old rag and a wire brush, clean grease and dirt off any pivots (1) and test them by hand to make sure that they move freely. Apply penetrating oil to ease any stiffness (2), then coat the pivot with fresh grease.

On brakes with a single cable attached to the lever, loosen the adjuster locknuts (usually under the car), then rotate the adjuster nut to take up some of the cable slackness (3). Retighten the locknut and check that there is still some slackness in the cable.

Some handbrakes have two cables, one to each wheel. Each cable has its own adjuster – usually where it connects to the handbrake lever. On these, brake balance must be checked after adjustment to ensure an even pull.

With the car on axle stands, turn each adjusting nut clockwise to take up excessive slackness from each cable (4). A hexagon section on each cable-end can be held with a spanner to prevent the cable ends from turning and trying to wind up the cable.

After adjustment, apply the handbrake lightly and rotate each braked wheel in a forward direction in turn. The brake drag on each wheel should be the same. If it is not, slacken the adjuster on the tighter cable until the handbrake applies an equal effort.

Before lowering the car to the ground, check that the wheels rotate freely with the handbrake off. If they do not, check the cable tension again.

TYRES

What you can do: Pages
Check the tyre pressures   188
Find and cure a leaky valve   188
Change a wheel   189

Tyres provide a car's only contact with the road. Through them the vehicle is steered and stopped and the engine power is transmitted. They also act as pneumatic dampers to smooth out minor irregularities in the road.

Tyres look simple enough from the outside, but under the skin is a complex structure of stiffening cords and wires which ensures that the tyre stays firmly on the wheel and is able to deform without loss of structural strength.

The average life of a tyre is very difficult to define because so much depends on the type of tyre, the sort of car it is fitted to and the owner's driving style. There is no doubt, however, that its life can be considerably extended by sympathetic use and regular attention, both of which are detailed in this section.

What's in a tyre?

In essence, a tyre is a circular vessel containing air under pressure. It is a complex structure made of synthetic rubber and other materials which range from steel to man-made fibre. All tyres have a hoop of tough steel bead wires, in order to hold them securely on to the wheel rim.

The heart of a tyre is the carcass structure made up of nylon, rayon or other man-made fibres, woven into a fabric and embedded in rubber. With the tyre inflated, the carcass provides most of the strength, and is deliberately designed to flex under load as the tyre rolls along the road.

A modern radial tyre has two or more reinforced 'belts' of rubber over the outer periphery of the carcass to provide a strong, virtually inextensible belt. The rubber tread, which makes contact with the road, is placed over the top of this, and forms the final layer.

The type of road grip provided by the tyre in the dry or in the wet, or on mud, snow or slush-covered roads, is dependent on a number of variables: the blend of synthetic and natural rubber,

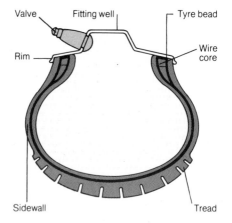

Valve — Fitting well — Tyre bead
Rim — — Wire core
Sidewall — — Tread

the various compounding and hardening agents used and, of course, the tread pattern.

All tyres are built up in layers, on special tyre-building machines. The various parts are bonded together under heat and pressure in a mould which gives the tyre its final shape and tread pattern.

When the heating and moulding processes are completed, the result is a tyre with a permanent shape and with properties suitable for the type of use for which it is intended.

Ply rating

With the exception of a few tyre plants, mainly in India and Egypt, cotton yarn is no longer used in manufacture.

However, you may find marked on the sidewalls of some tyres the symbol PR or ply rating. A 4PR marking does not mean a sidewall made up of four plies of woven textile, each covered with a thin film of rubber. It indicates that the sidewall strength is *equivalent* to one made up of four plies of a standard cotton weave.

Nowadays this may be two plies of rayon or nylon, or even one ply of polyester or similar man-made fibre fabric. Steel wires are not used for the carcass plies of car tyres, but are common on truck tyres which support much greater loads and run at very much greater inflation pressures.

A steel radial car tyre has steel wires embedded in the rubber of the stabiliser or reinforcing belt instead of the usual man-made fabric cords.

A tyre has reinforcing cords to strengthen the carcass, and steel wires to strengthen the bead where it meets the rim

Cross-ply or diagonal-ply tyres

The textile strands or cords in each ply of the carcass run in one direction only. Successive layers of such rubber-covered plies are overlapped so that the cords in one ply cross those of the other at an angle, giving a carcass or casing of considerable stiffness and strength. The ply bias angles are so chosen as to give fairly uniform strength all round, and to avoid unnecessary internal structural stresses when the tyre is rotating and under load.

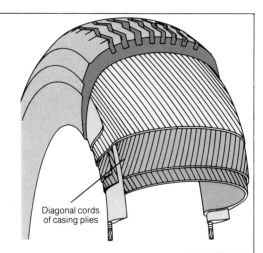

Diagonal cords of casing plies

Radial-ply tyres

The cords in the carcass plies run from bead to bead across the crown at right angles, not diagonally as in the cross-ply tyre. This gives great pliability and comfort, but little or no directional stability. The stability comes from tread-bracing layers, a belt of cords running round the tyre beneath the tread.
The construction of the radial-ply tyre reduces cornering wear and greatly increases its overall life.

Sidewall cords are at right angles to tyre crown

Breaker cords

Bias-belted tyres

Although widely used in North America the bias-belted tyre is rarely seen in this country. It has a cross-ply casing and a radial-ply glass-fibre belt of tread-bracing layers.

Winter tyres

Both cross-ply and radial-ply winter tyres are available. They have a chunkier tread than normal tyres and are designed for use on loose surfaces such as snow, slush and mud.

A winter tyre with stud holes

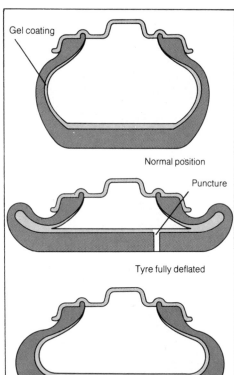

Gel coating

Normal position

Puncture

Tyre fully deflated

Safety tyres

Partial re-inflation

It is not possible to drive on an ordinary tyre when it is punctured, but the Dunlop Denovo run-flat tyre can be driven for up to 100 miles at up to 50mph when fully deflated.
The latest Denovo 2 version has its beads engaged in two shallow grooves in the wheel, which prevent the tyre from being dragged off the rim after deflation. A gel coating on the inside of the casing helps to plug the leak, provides lubrication and prevents overheating if the tyre fully deflates. In this condition, the car can be driven normally without materially affecting its handling.

Remoulded tyres

Remoulds or retreads allow worn-out tyres to be re-used. On a remould, the rubber on the old carcass is completely renewed from bead to bead; on a retread, however, only the tread of the tyre is renewed. Remoulded tyres are considerably cheaper than new ones but they have their limitations. Although they usually give reliable and satisfactory service under normal operating conditions, remoulds are only as good as the carcass on which the new tread is moulded. There is no way of knowing whether this suffered from persistent rough driving by the previous owner—although reputable remould manufacturers discard obviously damaged casings.

Unfortunately, not all remoulders are equally scrupulous when it comes to rejecting a doubtful carcass, so always select a well-known brand. The products of all trustworthy manufacturers, who either make new tyres or specialise in remoulding, are always marked with a brand name. Reputable remoulded tyres are marked with the word 'Retread' or 'Remould'. If they are tubeless they are marked 'Tubeless' and if they are radial-ply they are marked 'R'.

Not all new tyres are perfect, so a certain percentage of the slightly sub-standard tyres are sold by the manufacturers at a reduced price and marked 'Remould Quality.'

Because remoulds and retreads are built on a second-hand carcass, the British Standards Institution recommends that they are not used at speeds over 70mph, regardless of the size of wheel. They are not suitable for prolonged high speed driving, such as on a motorway. The recommendations on the mixing of different tyre types apply equally to remould tyres. Because remoulding does not make a tyre new again, make sure that the tyre carries the designation BSI AU 144b to indicate that it is of a reliable make. If it does not, or you are doubtful as to its quality (some spurious tyres are even remoulded twice), do not buy it.

Tubed or tubeless?

Most new cars are fitted with tubeless tyres in which the tyre casing makes an airtight seal with the wheel. To prevent air leakage, the casing has a special rubber layer on the inside, and the valve is made airtight with the wheel.

Tyres with separate inner tubes are used where the wheel cannot be made airtight—on wire-spoked wheels for instance, and on some aluminium wheels which can be porous.

Of the two types, tubeless tyres are less liable to deflate suddenly, and statistics show that the risk of a puncture with a tubeless tyre is about three and a half times less than with a tubed one. A further advantage is that in an emergency, most tubeless tyres can be temporarily repaired by plugging

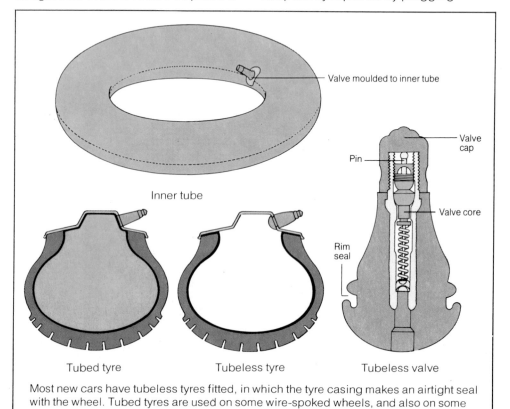

Valve moulded to inner tube

Inner tube

Valve cap

Pin

Valve core

Rim seal

Tubed tyre

Tubeless tyre

Tubeless valve

Most new cars have tubeless tyres fitted, in which the tyre casing makes an airtight seal with the wheel. Tubed tyres are used on some wire-spoked wheels, and also on some aluminium wheels which are porous and cannot be made airtight

without removing the tyre from the wheel. They are also less liable to lose air when pierced by small nails and flints than the tubed type.

Using an old or excessively repaired tube is false economy. It is likely to leak and may deflate suddenly, causing irreparable damage to the tyre. When a new tubed tyre is fitted, it is advisable to fit a new tube. Make sure that it is of the correct size and type recommended by the tyre manufacturer.

Value for money

Radial-ply tyres cannot be made and shaped as easily as cross-ply tyres and call for higher standards of accuracy in manufacture. These factors make them more expensive. But on the other hand, because of their longer life, tyre cost per mile is lower.

Such small undesirable features as a greater resistance to steering at low speeds, which calls for more steering effort when parking, are more than compensated for by the improvements in handling and greater puncture resistance of the tyre.

Slip angle

To steer a car round a corner, the tyre must generate a side force to push it away from the straight-ahead path. This force is produced by the tyre tread in contact with the road (the contact patch) becoming distorted and running at a small angle to the direction of travel of the wheel.

The angle is known as the slip angle. Even with the car travelling straight-ahead, the tyre must produce a similar force to resist the effect of road camber or crosswinds.

Understeer and oversteer

The size of the slip angle on both the front and rear tyres will affect the handling of the car. If the front slip angles are greater than those at the rear, then the car is said to understeer and will tend to run wide on corners; if the rear slip angles are greater than those at the front, the car is said to oversteer, and the tail will try to slide outwards.

Although current cars are designed to have neutral steering so far as possible (with no tendencies to either understeer

or oversteer), this cannot always be achieved under all motoring conditions. It is safer to have a vehicle with a tendency to understeer rather than oversteer, as it is easier to control in an emergency because it is less liable to go into an uncontrollable spin.

The actual slip angle depends on the tyre construction; it is smallest in a steel-braced radial and increases progressively in a fabric-braced radial, radial-ply winter tyre, cross-ply road tyre and cross-ply winter tyre.

In understeer, the front of the car runs wider than the rear

Though hard to achieve on this car, the rear is running wide in oversteer

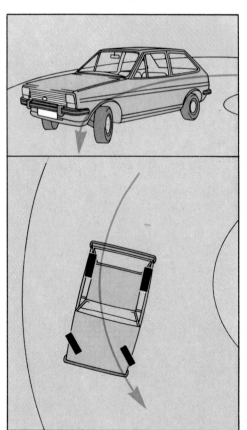

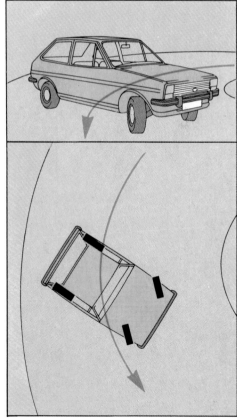

Aquaplaning

If a tyre has insufficient tread depth or inadequate drainage channels, it cannot clear water away quickly enough; a wedge of water then builds up under the tyre and eventually the tyre will literally ride on a cushion of water. In this dangerous condition—known as aquaplaning—front wheels can cease to rotate and all steering control is lost; stopping distance is also increased drastically. For this reason it is best to renew tyres when the tread depth nears 2mm.

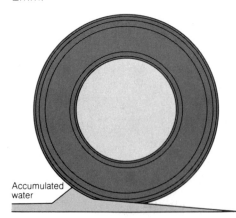

A tyre with a well-worn tread cannot clear water, which builds up causing aquaplaning

Braking in the wet

In shallow pools of surface water, a car travelling at 60mph with only 2mm of tread remaining on the tyres has only about half the road grip that the tyres would exert on a dry road. It is therefore unwise to travel any faster than 50mph under such conditions, especially on a motorway, if tyres are worn to this depth of tread. Most accidents in wet weather happen on damp, traffic-polished roads. The build-up of oil and rubber after a dry spell can also make roads slippery.

Pressure

Incorrect inflation pressure will shorten tyre life. Radial and cross-ply tyres respond differently to incorrect inflation. For cross-ply, too high a pressure makes the tread bulge, causing accelerated wear at the centre; too low a pressure wears the edge of the tread and can cause the tyre to overheat. For radials, too high a pressure stiffens the sidewalls. Too low a pressure causes a damaging build-up of heat where the tread and sidewalls meet. Some radials wear rapidly at the centre when under-inflated.

Always check tyre pressures with a reliable gauge at the start of a journey when the tyre is cold. The correct pressures will be given in the vehicle handbook. Do not rely on the appearance of the tyre as a guide to the pressure. This can be deceptive, especially with radial-ply tyres which, because of their more flexible sidewalls, tend to look under-inflated.

Pressure rise

Tyre pressures increase fairly rapidly with the running of the vehicle; the higher the speed, the more rapid the increase. The amount of pressure rise depends on the surrounding air and road surface temperatures and the method of carcass construction. Cross-ply tyres run hotter than radials. In this country, the increase on a basic pressure of 24psi will be roughly as follows:

On a 1-2 mile trip	2-4psi cross-ply
	1-2psi radial-ply
Over 10 miles in	3-5psi cross-ply
average traffic	1-3psi radial-ply
For high speed	6-10psi cross-ply
motoring	3-5psi radial-ply

Over-inflation produces wear in the centre of the tread

Under-inflation produces wear on the edges of the tread

On the Continent, high speed motoring in summer temperatures would produce an average increase of 6-12psi cross-ply, and 3-5psi in radial-ply. Never reduce pressures during a long journey, when hot tyres will have increased pressure from the cold setting.

Loads and speed

Tyre pressures must be adjusted for load carrying and towing and for high speed driving. Details are usually given in the vehicle handbook, but when this is not available, use the following as a rough guide. For maximum load and when towing, increase rear tyre pressures 2-4psi. For sustained high speed driving, raise all tyre pressures by 2-6psi.

Contrary to popular opinion, lowering the tyre pressure does *not* give a better grip on wet roads or on snow and ice, since it tends to close the tread pattern and reduces the grip. Worst of all, because of excessive flexing and the heat built up in the carcass, it considerably reduces the life expectancy of the tyre.

Tyre life

The two conflicting requirements of providing fairly soft springing for comfort by means of flexible sidewalls, but a relatively stiff structure in the tread area for steering and stability, are difficult to achieve in a cross-ply tyre, because of the way in which it is constructed.

In the radial-ply tyre, the two requirements are met separately by the very flexible sidewalls and the inextensible bracing layer under the tread. The tread bracing enables the radial tyre to provide the necessary side force or cornering power at a much lower slip angle than the cross-ply. There is also less scrubbing of the tread when cornering. The result is a much increased tyre life.

Random checks suggest that the 'average' tyre lasts 25,000 miles, with 85 per cent of drivers achieving between 15,000 and 35,000 miles. Much higher mileages are possible, however. Wear is most rapid when the tyre is new, and at the final stages when the tread depth nears the legal minimum of 1mm. High-speed cornering, fierce braking and violent acceleration increase the rate of wear. Speed will also make tyres wear out more quickly. If the speed of 30mph is assumed to be normal, then the mileage expectancy on urban and rural roads would be as follows: 40mph–98% of normal mileage; 50mph–85%; 60mph–70%; and 70mph–55%.

On motorways, where the road is straighter and less cambered and curves and hills are more gentle, the wear rate is less.

Mixing tyres

It is best not to mix tyres, but if this is done, tyres on the same 'axle' must be of the same size and type of construction; either both cross-ply or both radial. If tyres of mixed construction are fitted, the radials must be on the back and should be of the same make.

Tyre markings

Radial tyres are code-marked to indicate their maximum speed. Tyres marked SR are suitable for speeds up to 113mph, those marked HR are suitable for up to 130mph, while radials marked VR can be used above 130mph.

The safe maximum speed for cross-ply tyres varies according to the size. Details of these speeds are given in the table below.

Rim diameter	Size mark only	S	Speed mark H	V
10in	Up to 75mph 120kph	Up to 95mph 150kph	Up to 110mph 175kph	
12in	Up to 85mph 135kph	Up to 100mph 160kph	Up to 115mph 185kph	
13in and over	Up to 95mph 150kph	Up to 110mph 175kph	Up to 125mph 200kph	Over 125mph 200kph

Tread patterns

The tread should provide a good grip for acceleration, braking and steering on all surfaces over which it is travelling. Although a completely smooth tyre would give the best grip on a dry road because it would provide the biggest contact patch, it would be virtually useless on a wet road or a soft surface. So tyre makers use a complex tread pattern designed to give the best grip under varying weather conditions. On a wet road, zig-zag grooves and channels in the tread allow most of the water to be displaced to the rear, the remainder being mopped up by small knife cuts (known as sipes), leaving a relatively dry contact area for the rest of the tyre tread to grip. To provide an adequate grip at 60mph on a wet road, the tread pattern of an average-sized tyre has to displace more than 1½ gallons of water a second.

Tread patterns incorporate grooves, channels and sipes to displace water

Main drainage grooves

Secondary drainage grooves

Sipes

Complicated tread designs give the best grip under varied weather conditions

The stiff-sidewalled cross-ply tyre is now largely superseded by the radial-ply type

With a symmetrical-tread radial the tread is the same on each side of tread centre line

An asymmetrical tread is different on each side of the centre line

Aspect ratio

A tyre's aspect ratio is a way of expressing its profile: it is the ratio of its cross-sectional height to its cross-sectional width when fitted to the appropriate wheel rim. On early tyres, the sectional height was about the same as the width, giving an aspect ratio of 100%. The current trend is to make tyres wider and shallower, reducing the height from tread to rim while increasing the width across the tyre's section in order to improve grip.

Over the years, the aspect ratio has been greatly reduced—first to 95% in the cushion-type tyre, then to 88% in the medium-profile tyre, and down through 77% to 70%, 65% and 60%. Racing cars, with their extra wide wheels, may use tyres with an aspect ratio as low as 30%.

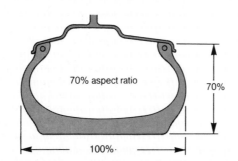

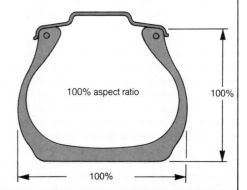

Running-in

The engine is not the only part of a car that needs running-in. Tyres, particularly high speed ones, need a settling-in period. For the first 50-100 miles it is advisable not to exceed 50mph. Speed should be increased gradually over the first 250 miles, and severe cornering should be avoided during the period.

Tyre and wheel balance

A front wheel that is not properly balanced may set up disturbing vibrations that can be felt through the steering wheel, particularly at high speeds, and by the passengers. If not corrected it also leads to excessive tyre wear and wears the wheel bearings and swivel joints.

For smooth running and maximum tyre life, all four wheels should be balanced, preferably while on the car. Special garage equipment is needed for this; balancing is achieved by clipping or sticking small weights at the required points on the wheel rim.

Always have the wheels balanced whenever new tyres are fitted and, if possible, have them re-checked after the first 500 miles—particularly radials. The balance of a wheel can be upset by damage to the rim, and continual high speed cornering causes rapid tread wear which can affect its balance.

Changing round the wheels

Once it was common practice to change the position of all wheels on the car at regular intervals to equalise tread wear between all five tyres. Now, with modern suspension systems and higher vehicle performance, the need for precise wheel balancing has become considerably more important. This means that once wheels are removed and their positions interchanged, re-balancing is often necessary; with rising labour charges, this cost can more than nullify any possible saving in tyre life.

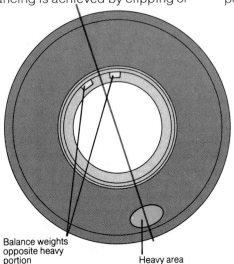

Balance weights opposite heavy portion

Heavy area

A statically-balanced wheel is weighted opposite the heavy area

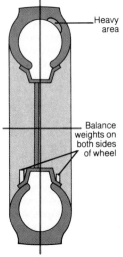

Heavy area

Balance weights on both sides of wheel

Dynamic balancing calls for a weight to be fitted on each side of the rim

Tyre faults and their causes

Provided tyres are correctly inflated, the car is in good mechanical order and all the wheels are properly balanced, the length of time a tyre will last depends entirely on how the car is driven.

Maximum tyre life can be achieved only if the tyres are treated with respect and so long as accidental damage is avoided. But the trouble is that tyres are all too often fitted and then simply forgotten by neglectful owners. Tyres which have plenty of useful tread depth can be written off instantly in an impact that fractures the carcass, such as when the tyre hits the kerb hard, while careless parking will result in sidewalls being rubbed away against the kerb.

Some of the most common types of damage can be seen here. None of the tyres shown is fit for further use.

Severe heat distortion here was caused by the tyre being run flat

Wear caused by faulty steering geometry, usually incorrect toe-in or toe-out

Sidewall damage is often caused by careless kerbside parking

Flat-spots on the tread can be caused by faulty dampers or other suspension defects

A sharp foreign body lodged in a tyre can cause irreparable damage to the carcass

Tread separation is most likely to occur on retreaded tyres

Chunking happens when rubber is thrown off by centrifugal force

Checking pressures

By law, the tyres on your car must be operated at the pressures recommended by the car or tyre manufacturer. Check them once a week, preferably when the tyres are cold. If you do not have a pump, keep the tyres as cool as possible by driving gently at 30mph to the nearest garage and using the airline. After driving to a garage add 2psi to the recommended pressures to allow for the tyres being warmed up. Unscrew the dust cap from the tyre valve and use a hand-held pressure gauge to test air pressure (1). Hand gauges tend to be more accurate than garage forecourt gauges.

If the pressure is low, inflate the tyre, either with a pump (2) or an air-line, checking the pressure at regular intervals. If the tyre becomes over-inflated, press the valve pin with the edge of a finger-nail or the domed end of the valve cap to let out a little air until the pressure is correct.

Unscrew the dust cap and use a hand-held pressure gauge to test air pressure

If pressure is low, inflate the tyre with a foot pump. If no pump is available, take the wheel to a garage air-line

Curing a leaky valve

A trace of dirt on the seat of the tyre valve will allow air to seep out. A valve can be checked easily with washing-up liquid. Remove the valve cap and block the end of the valve with a smear of fluid. If it is leaking it will blow a bubble. The leak can be repaired by fitting a new valve core. This inevitably means the tyre will go flat, so make sure that you have a pump to re-inflate it. The core is unscrewed by using a special notched tool (3) or one that is supplied as part of a pressure gauge. Insert it into the valve, engage it with the end of the core, and turn it anti-clockwise to unscrew the core (4). Use the same tool to screw in the new core. Re-inflate the tyre and check the valve again for leaks.

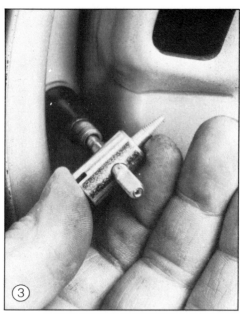

A notched tool unscrews the core. This type can be bought from accessory shops, others come with the gauge

Turn the removing tool anti-clockwise to unscrew the valve core and replace the core using the same tool

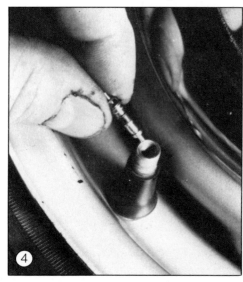

Wheel-changing

Every car comes with a jack and wheelbrace to enable the road wheels to be changed. If you have not changed a wheel before, remember that the wheel fixing nuts or bolts should be slackened a little *before* the car is jacked up.

If the wheel has been put on by a garage mechanic using a long wrench, you may not be able to apply enough leverage with the wheelbrace in the toolkit to loosen the fixings. The leverage of an L-shaped wheelbrace can be increased if a metal pipe is slipped over the end to make it longer. Use the wheelbrace *on its own* when tightening the fixings. Some wheels are secured by a single 'knock-on' centre nut which usually has a left-hand thread and is undone by striking it clockwise with a copper mallet. Knock-on nuts are generally marked with an arrow indicating the direction of rotation to undo them.

Before taking a wheel off, make sure that the spare is in roadworthy condition, apply the handbrake and chock one of the other wheels.

At the road wheel, lever off the nave plate (5) or covers on the wheel bolts, loosen the fixings half a turn, if necessary using an extension on the wheelbrace (6).

Engage the jack with a recommended jacking point and raise it until the wheel is clear of the ground (7). If the wheel has been balanced on the car, mark it and the hub with a pencil or chalk so that it can be refitted in the same position (8). Remove the wheel.

Fit the spare wheel, tightening the fixings as much as possible with the wheelbrace. Lower the car, remove the jack, and fully tighten the wheel fixings.

Lever the nave plate off the wheel and loosen the fixings half a turn

Using the recommended jacking point, raise the wheel clear of the ground

If the nuts are overtight use an extension on the wheelbrace

Mark the wheel and the hub so that the wheel is refitted in the same position

Get rid of paint chips
Spray-paint larger areas   198
Mask off prior to painting   198
Put on the paint   199
Guard against corrosion   202
Patch a rust hole   202-203
Eliminate small dents   204-205
Look after wipers and washers   206
Change wiper blades: push-on   206
   hook-on   206
   pin-mounted   206
Change wiper arms   207
Service the windscreen washers   207
Adjust fittings   208-209
Lubricate the hinges   209

Cars were once built with all their mechanical components bolted to a sturdy chassis frame, and the bodywork that was mounted on top merely had the job of keeping the passengers warm and dry.

Now only a few cars have a separate chassis. It is quicker, cheaper and safer to build a combined body and chassis on the production line from many pieces of sheet steel, wrapping the metal into box-sections in appropriate places to provide mounting points for the heavier mechanical components.

The modern body/chassis unit can be made safer than a car with a rigid chassis because the front and rear can be built to crumple progressively in an accident, absorbing some of the collision force before it reaches the passengers.

Making a bodyshell from a lot of bits of sheet steel is not without its problems. For instance it is difficult to paint inside some of the box sections, and because they are not air and watertight, rust can form. The many stiffening pieces and awkward corners underneath the body can trap mud, causing further rusting.

Car manufacturers are aware of the problems and are tackling them. This section describes what they are doing, and shows what you can do to keep your car's body beautiful.

while a rear sub-frame supports the rear suspension.

In production, the mechanical assemblies are built up on their sub-frames and the frames are then attached to the bodyshell using rubber-insulated mountings. The bodyshell still provides the overall structural strength of the car.

Cars that still use a separate chassis are those which are hand-built in low numbers by specialists. The bodywork may be moulded from glass-fibre-reinforced plastic (GRP) or made from aluminium.

In both instances, the mechanical components are built up on the chassis, and the bodywork is added afterwards. The number of people needed to build these bodies (aluminium ones are

UNDER THE SKIN
What goes into a bodyshell

Although the modern bodyshell is built of metal that may be only 0.028in (0.7mm) thick, it must be strong enough to resist all the loads imposed on it. It needs beam stiffness so that it does not sag in the middle, and torsional stiffness so that it does not twist unduly when travelling over uneven surfaces. On the other hand, it must not be too rigid – a completely rigid body will transmit a lot of road shocks to the passengers and would absorb little impact energy in a collision. With this in mind, the modern bodyshell is designed to flex a little. Although cars with a separate chassis are rare, many mass-produced cars have sub-frames which carry the major mechanical assemblies. On the BL Mini, a front sub-frame carries the engine, transmission and front suspension,

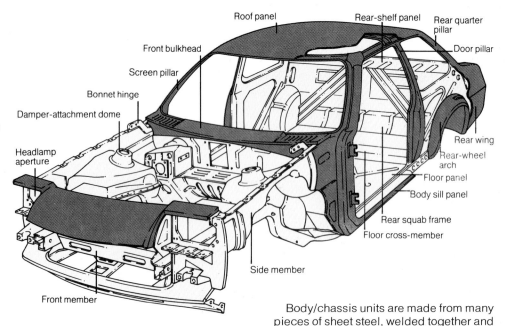

Body/chassis units are made from many pieces of sheet steel, welded together and fabricated into box sections to provide strong points where necessary

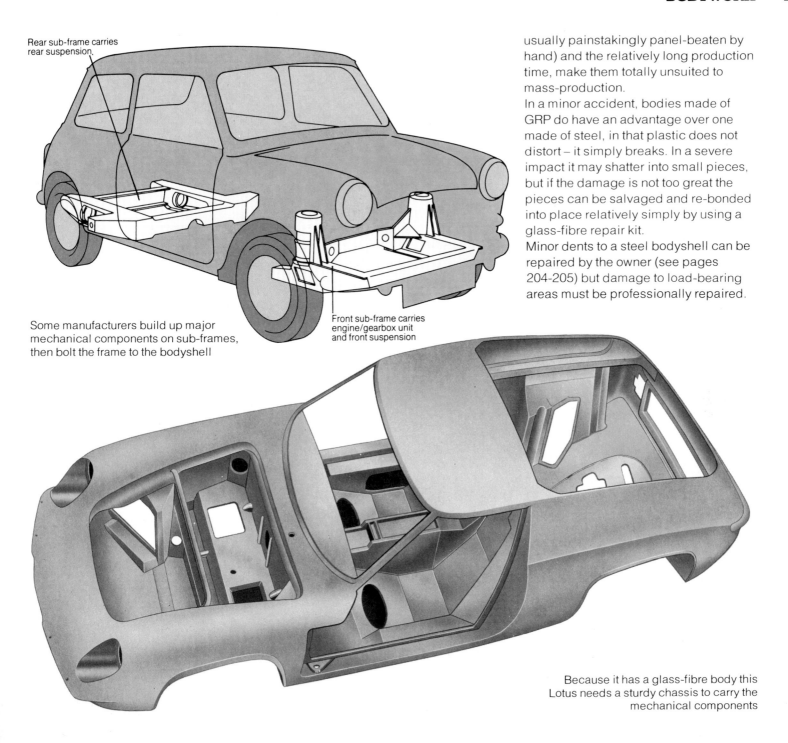

Rear sub-frame carries
rear suspension.

Some manufacturers build up major
mechanical components on sub-frames,
then bolt the frame to the bodyshell

Front sub-frame carries
engine/gearbox unit
and front suspension

usually painstakingly panel-beaten by
hand) and the relatively long production
time, make them totally unsuited to
mass-production.

In a minor accident, bodies made of
GRP do have an advantage over one
made of steel, in that plastic does not
distort – it simply breaks. In a severe
impact it may shatter into small pieces,
but if the damage is not too great the
pieces can be salvaged and re-bonded
into place relatively simply by using a
glass-fibre repair kit.

Minor dents to a steel bodyshell can be
repaired by the owner (see pages
204-205) but damage to load-bearing
areas must be professionally repaired.

Because it has a glass-fibre body this
Lotus needs a sturdy chassis to carry the
mechanical components

SAFETY

One of the bigger problems facing a car body designer is that when he has finished, someone will take one of his new creations and smash it head-on at 30mph (48kph) into a concrete block to make sure that the front acts as a shock-absorber by crumpling progressively, and to check that the doors do not fly open.

The crash test ensures that the car satisfies international safety regulations. After the impact, the strong passenger compartment should be virtually intact, the doors must open and close, the steering column must not have moved backwards more than 12in (300mm), the seats must remain on their runners and supports, and the seat belts must hold their wearers (dummies in the crash test) safely in place.

In addition, the car is then impacted from the rear, and shortly all cars will have to withstand side impact tests to ensure that the doors do not cave in during a side-on collision.

The concrete-block crash test simulates conditions encountered in about 85% of all recorded car accidents. Most adults, properly restrained by a seat belt, should suffer only minor or recoverable injuries in such a collision.

In addition to crumple zones, the modern bodyshell has its interior planned with safety in mind. Control switches and knobs are either recessed into the facia, made of soft material or designed to break off in an accident. The interior mirror, flanked by padded sun visors, is fitted into a frame to prevent splinters of glass breaking off in an impact and, like most window winders, it is fitted so that it will snap from its mounting if struck hard.

On the outside, sharp projections, such as bonnet mascots and protruding door handles which could injure pedestrians, have disappeared.

All volume-produced cars sold in Britain are safety-tested by smashing a production model into a concrete block at 30mph (48kph) and measuring the deformation. There should be no substantial damage to the passenger compartment

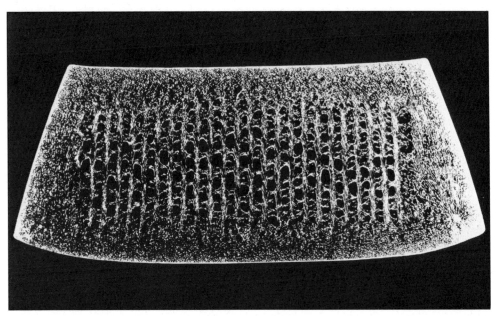

Toughened glass, until recently the most common type of glass used on mass-produced cars, shatters into small fragments when chipped

Spears of glass from a laminated screen may detach and fly into the car

A damaged 'Ten-Twenty' screen gives good vision with less risk of injury

Safety glass

Most popular British cars have toughened glass windscreens which shatter into tiny fragments in a collision or if hit by a stone. The theory is that the small fragments are not big enough to cause injury if a passenger's head should hit them.

The drawback is that a tiny chip from a single stone breaks the whole screen, and because it is difficult to see through the fragments, this means that the screen must be taken out immediately to provide an adequate view of the road ahead.

Until recently the only alternative was a laminated windscreen, in which two relatively thin sheets of plain glass are separated by a transparent plastic interlayer. When hit by a stone, the damage is restricted to the area that the stone hits, and the car can be used until it is convenient to fit a replacement. The worry here is that in a crash, spear-shaped shards of glass can break away from the interlayer and fly into the car, maybe injuring the occupants.

The best of both worlds is the 'Ten-Twenty' Triplex windscreen fitted to BL Rover and Triumph models. This is a lamination of plain glass on the outside and toughened glass on the inside. In this case, a stone chip does not mean that a new screen is needed immediately, but in the event of a serious impact, the toughened inner surface breaks into many harmless fragments.

PAINTWORK

During production, the bare metal bodyshell picks up a coating of oil from the press, as well as lanolin, grease and dirt – all of which must be removed before the shell can be painted. This is done by an alkaline spray, after which the bodyshell is thoroughly washed in hot and cold jets of water.

It is then sprayed, or sprayed and dipped in a hot phosphate solution which etches the surface to form a thin, rust-resistant layer.

Putting on the primer

Some manufacturers treat the hidden areas of the body, such as inaccessible box-sections, by immersing the shell up to at least waist height in a large tank of primer paint.

The paint finds its way through special holes in various panels into all cavities, to coat the inside and outside of every panel.

Another method is to use electricity to attract the pigments in a water-based primer into inaccessible areas. In this process, the whole shell is immersed in a huge tank of heated paint and then electrically charged. The process is called electro-coating or electro-phoresis.

On areas of the bodyshell liable to stone chipping, such as the sills, lower portions of the wings and doors and the front valance, a layer of thicker surfacer paint or a PVC coating is applied over the primer coat. This acts as a semi-resilient barrier.

After priming, the bodyshell gets one or more colour coats. It then goes to an oven where the finish is baked at a high temperature.

Modern car plants have large tanks in which the car bodies are covered in primer. Strategically placed drain holes allow paint to flow inside box sections

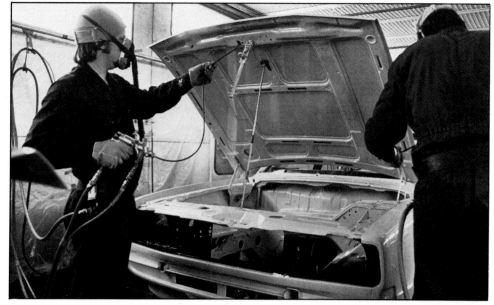

To improve rust resistance, some car makers use special injection equipment to spray rust-preventive fluid into box sections during production

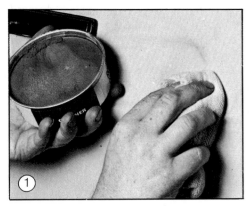

Rub compound along the scratch, or . . .

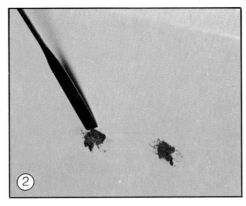

After priming, brush on top-coat, or . . .

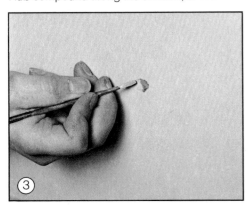

. . . first, scrape away rust with a blade

. . . first, apply stopper with a knife

The car may then receive a rust-preventive treatment at this stage. Since it is difficult to guarantee perfect primer coverage in hollow sections, more manufacturers are now using special lances to inject a waxy, oily rust-preventive compound into these areas, preventing moisture and air from reaching any unpainted metal.

Hiding minor paint blemishes

It is practically impossible to drive a car on public roads without losing a little paint. If you do not scratch it yourself, road chippings thrown up by the car in front will nick small spots of paint from the front. A similar process goes on behind the wheel arches where the paint is chipped by small stones thrown up by the tyres.

Smoothing out a scratch

Light scratches can be polished out with a mild cutting compound. This contains tiny abrasive particles which smooth the rough edges of the scratch so that it merges with the surrounding paint.

First wash the scratched area to remove surface dirt; then, using cutting compound on a soft cloth, work it back and forth along the length of the scratch (1). Because the compound removes a thin film of paint, wipe it off frequently with a clean dry cloth and check the result. Stop polishing as soon as the scratch disappears. On cars with metallic paint, cutting compound will remove only light scratches.

Getting rid of paint chips

If bare metal has been exposed by chipped paint, it should be covered as soon as possible to discourage rust forming. In the absence of brush-on touch-up paint, a dab of nail varnish will provide a temporary rust barrier.

To make a more permanent repair, clean the area to remove dirt and if the bare metal has become rusty, scrape any rust and loose paint away with a blade (2). Treat the metal with a rust-killing fluid, following the maker's directions, and once it has had time to act, apply a coat of primer with a small brush. When the primer is dry, finish by brushing on top-coat (3).

If the paint chip is in a prominent place, you may be disappointed by the result, as the chip will still show up as a depression in the surrounding paint. It can be levelled after priming if it is treated with cellulose stopper. This is applied thinly with a knife (4), and each coat takes about 20 minutes to dry at 15°C.

Once it has hardened, use a small piece of 400-grit wet-or-dry paper dipped in water, to blend it into the surrounding paint. Dry the area and finish by brushing on top-coat. Leave the top-coat for one week to harden, then polish it with mild cutting compound to remove the brush marks.

Spray-painting larger areas

Where a large area of bodywork has to be painted, it should be sprayed. Cans of aerosol paint big enough to cover a car door or a complete wing are sold by accessory shops, who can supply the primer (also in an aerosol), masking tape and wet-or-dry paper that are also needed.

Paint should be applied in a warm (15°C), dry, dust-free atmosphere. Always shake an aerosol for as long as the manufacturer states in his instructions – paint pigments settle during storage and the thick paint at the bottom of an unshaken can will not only be the wrong colour, but will also block the nozzle.

First prepare the surface to be sprayed. Wipe it with a clean cloth dipped in methylated spirit to remove any traces of wax polish, then, using plenty of water and 400-grit wet-or-dry paper, rub down the surface (1).

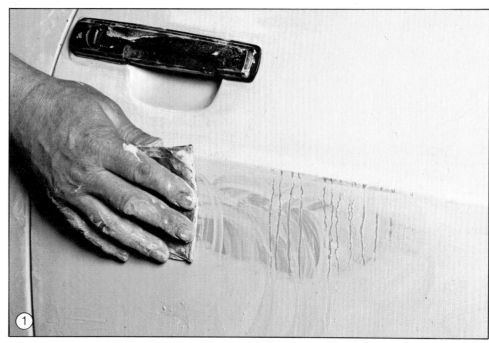

After wiping the surface clean with methylated spirit to remove all traces of polish, rub down with wet-or-dry paper

Masking

Where possible, the new paint should finish at a natural body join, such as the edge of a door or bonnet, or even where a change of angle occurs, since this will disguise any slight mis-match between the new and existing paint.

Lay a sheet of newspaper on the roof of the car and stick masking tape along one edge so that it overlaps and sticks the paper to the roof. Peel off tape and paper and position them where needed (2). Mask off small components such as side lamps and radio aerials with just tape. On components like these that are fixed to the body, make sure that the edge of the tape exactly follows the edge of the component (3), otherwise

Be generous with the newspaper, taping it in place to avoid overspray. Finish at a natural body join if possible

unsightly overspray will have to be carefully removed later on.

Where it is impractical to paint a complete panel, apply masking tape around the area to be sprayed, leaving a 1in (25mm) border of existing paint round the edge. Apply primer, allow it to dry, then remove the tape and feather the edge of the primer with 400-grit wet-or-dry paper, used wet, to blend it into the existing finish. Re-mask the area, sticking the edge of the tape 1in out from the primer edge, before applying top-coat.

Putting on the paint

Paint can sometimes splutter a little at the instant the button is pressed, so start the spray on the masked area, then move the spray steadily on to the work, keeping the can upright about 9in from the surface. Holding it too close will cause the paint to run; too far away and patchiness will result.

Primer is easier to spray than top-coat, because the finish is not so critical. Begin with a very thin coat, moving the can horizontally back and forth across the work, starting at the top and working down so that on each stroke the spray overlaps the paint applied on the previous pass (4). Once the panel has been covered, allow the paint to become touch-dry (test on the overspray on the masking paper) before putting on a second coat.

When the primer is dry, lightly rub any rough spots with 400-grit paper, used dry. If the paint has run, rub down any unevenness with the same grade of paper, used wet.

Reprime the area afterwards.

Top-coat is thinner than primer and more tricky to spray. First, put it on very thinly and do not worry if it appears slightly dull – a gloss will come as the paint thickness builds up.

Apply two or three coats, allowing each to become touch-dry before the next is put on (5). If the final gloss does not match the remainder of the finish, do not apply a thicker coat of paint – it will merely run and you will have to rub the panel down and start again. The gloss can be improved after the paint has been allowed to harden for a week by polishing it with a mild cutting compound.

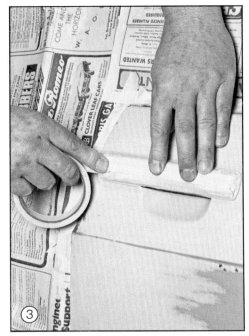

③ Tape carefully all round the component

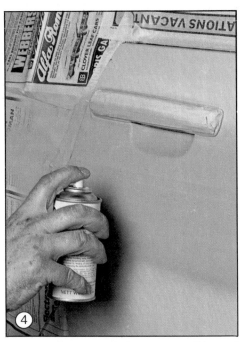

④ Start by spraying on a very thin coat

Spray on two or three coats, allowing drying time between each coat

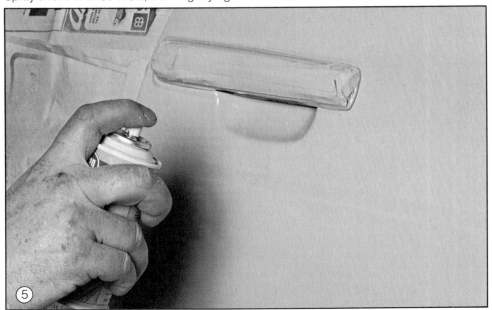

⑤

CORROSION

Corrosion is caused when oxygen in the air reacts with the bare metal surface to form a thin film of oxide.

Once formed, oxide coatings on most types of metal act as a barrier to further corrosion. But on steel it forms rust, which with its soft texture, offers little protection.

Rusting is accelerated by moisture – particularly if it contains airborne acid or alkaline substances – and although, in theory, car bodywork is sealed from the environment by its paintwork, a glance at most cars over four years old will show that they are starting to go rusty. Part of the problem is that no paint is completely impervious to moisture. Most corrosion takes place where it cannot be seen – inside the closed box sections and in double-skinned areas that are meant to stiffen the bodywork. Britain's temperate, humid climate encourages condensation in these places, and if the paint covering has not been effective, rust quickly takes hold.

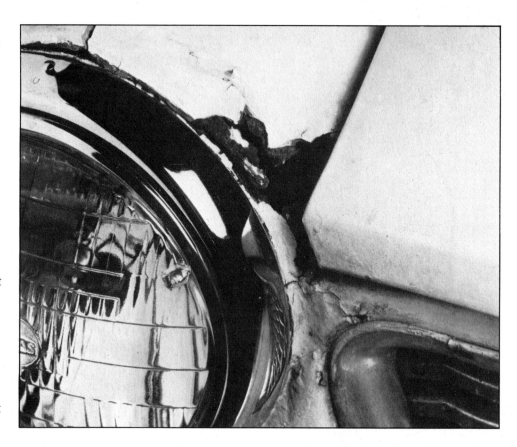

Look for rust, particularly around the headlamps, at the top and bottom of the front wings and along the bottom of doors

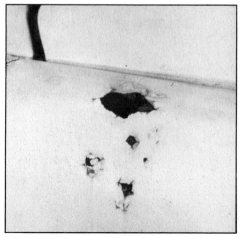

Rust traps

Crevices in the underbody form moisture traps and will pick up and hold road dirt against the metal. In winter, salt used for de-icing the roads is sprayed on the dirt and each time it rains thereafter, this saline poultice is re-activated. A saline solution is so corrosive that it is used in industry as a standard method of inducing corrosion. Common vulnerable areas are around headlamps, in under-wing crevices and the floor pan, which can rust on the inside if water has seeped under the carpets, and on the outside if grit and stones have eroded the paint.

Resisting the rust

Although many car manufacturers take strong measures to discourage their cars from rusting, chains of specialist rustproofing stations have been operating for a number of years, offering long-term rust protection for new or nearly-new cars.

The treatment involves spraying the underside with a sealing compound containing a rust preventive. These compounds usually retain a toffee-like consistency which enables them to 'self heal' if a flying stone breaks the skin. To treat closed box sections, operators drill holes at strategic points and use long lances to spray the inside with a petroleum-based waxy, oily fluid. The oily constituent has a 'creeping' action which takes it into tiny crevices. It will also displace water, laying a film on the surface underneath. When the solvents in the fluid have evaporated, a waxy film which seals out air and moisture coats the treated panel.

It is tempting to assume that once a car

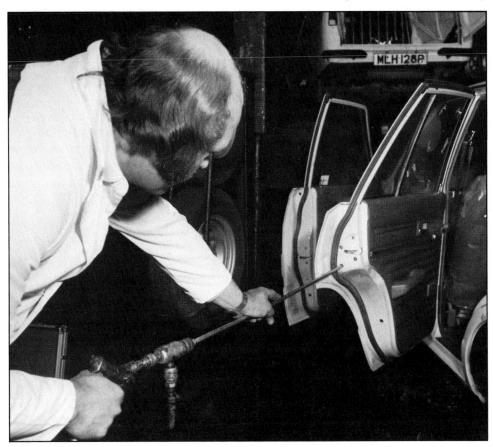

Special lances are used to spray rust-preventive fluid into closed areas

has been treated, it will never go rusty. But experience shows that rust can be kept at bay only if a treated car is inspected at regular intervals and any extra protection added as necessary. The guarantees issued by rust-prevention stations stipulate that regular inspections be made – usually once every two years, and after the underside has been power-cleaned.

Rust prevention kits for do-it-yourself application are available, sometimes with the same fluids as used by the professionals. But it is worth knowing

that your car can actually rust more quickly if rust preventive fluid is incorrectly applied.

Tests have shown that a box section only half painted rusts more slowly than a similar one which may be 85% covered in paint or rust preventive. Rust is not easily sustained over a wide area, but when concentrated in a small spot it works more effectively.

So if you decide to try rustproofing your car, it is important to make sure that the interior of each of the box sections is completely covered.

Guarding against corrosion

Inevitably all cars pick up pockets of road dirt on the underside. The most likely collection points are the sharp corners at the top of the front wings, ledges inside the wheel-arch pressings and any suspension mountings in the wheel arch areas.

Because the dirt can start corrosion, the inside of the wheel-arch cavities should be sprayed with a high-powered hose to remove it at least once every six months. Use a stiff-bristled brush to clean out any dirt that the hose cannot shift.

After the wheel arches have been cleaned and have dried, put the car over an inspection pit or on drive-up ramps and look for cracks in any underbody sealant which could allow water to creep between the loosened sealing compound and the body metal, from where it can start hidden corrosion. Peel off loose sealant (1) and check the metal underneath. Surface rust can be treated with a rust preventive, painted, and the area then re-coated with fresh sealant, stippled on with an old paint brush. If the metal has been weakened by corrosion, have the damage put right by a body repairer – many underbody areas are load-bearing, and repairing them should not be regarded as a do-it-yourself task.

Check the brake pipes for rusting. Surface rust that can be removed with a wire brush is not important, but if the rust has pitted the surface (which will snag a finger-nail scratched along the pipe) have the pipe renewed by a brake specialist.

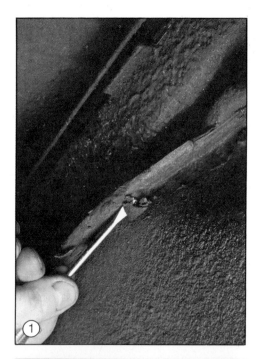

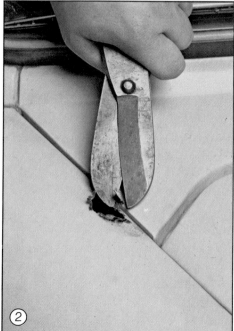

Cut away weak metal from around the hole with snips until the edges are sound

Patching a rust hole

Sooner or later all steel car bodies begin to go rusty. The first sign is usually blistering of the paintwork, and quite often when the paint is removed, the metal underneath falls away to reveal a rusty hole.

Provided it is not in a load-bearing section, a rust hole can be satisfactorily repaired by using a glass fibre repair kit and plastic body filler. Resin-bonded glass fibre is used to patch the hole, and filler is then applied to smooth the surface so that it blends with the surrounding metal.

Scrape away any loose or cracked sealant and inspect the metal underneath

Push expanded aluminium or perforated zinc through the hole and tack with filler

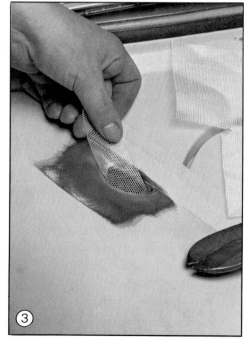

Use a paint brush to stipple on resin until the glass fibre becomes translucent

Start by grinding off blistered paint with a sanding disc. Remove weakened metal from the edge of the hole with tin-snips until all edges are sound (2). Grind off paint down to the bare metal to a point about 1in (25mm) back from the metal edge, then tap the edge inwards about $\frac{1}{4}$in (6mm) with a light hammer. If the hole is bigger than a 10p piece, a bridge will be needed to support the glass fibre. With old scissors, cut a piece of expanded aluminium or perforated zinc so that it is larger than the hole. If possible, pass it through the aperture (3) and support it against the inside edges while it is tacked in position with dabs of a fast-setting mix of body filler.

When the filler has hardened, cut two patches of glass fibre about $\frac{1}{4}$in larger all round than the hole. Mix a quantity of resin and hardener following the instructions.

Place the patch on the expanded metal and stipple on resin using an old paint brush until the glass fibre becomes translucent (4). If any resin drips on the surrounding bodywork, wipe it off immediately with a cloth dipped in methylated spirit. Before the resin can cure, apply a second patch over the first. Both patches should be below the level of surrounding bodywork.

When the resin has hardened (after about 20 minutes at 15°C) apply filler over the top (5). Blend it to the body shape as detailed on page 197.

Paint the area (see pages 198-199).

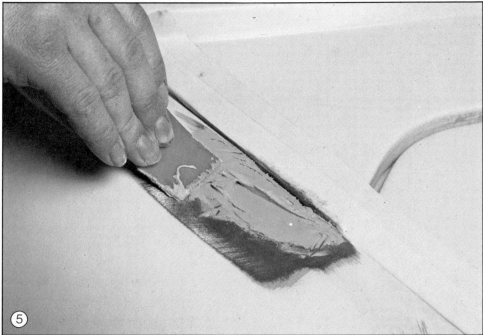

Once the resin has hardened, apply body filler and blend it into the body

ELIMINATING SMALL DENTS

The quickest way to smooth out a small dent or minor body damage that has stretched the metal is to fill the depression with a two-part plastic body filler. Filler kits are readily available from accessory shops.

To give maximum adhesion, filler should be applied to the bare metal and allowed to cure in a warm dry atmosphere at about 15°C. In winter, warm the area with an electric fire. Once it has hardened, the filler is blended to the body contour using wet-or-dry abrasive paper dipped in water to prevent clogging. Coarse grades, which have low identification numbers, are used for rough shaping, then the filler is rubbed down with finer grades until the final finish is achieved. This avoids scratching the finished surface.

A deep dent should be made as shallow as possible. If you can get behind it, partly tap it out with a hammer. Dents in double-skinned areas can be partially filled out by drilling a hole in the deepest part, inserting a self-tapping screw and pulling it outwards with a claw hammer (1). Rest the hammer head on a piece of wood to prevent further body damage. Remove the screw afterwards.

Use a wire brush or flap-wheel on a power drill to remove paint from the dented area (2). Feather the edge of the paintwork so that it meets the metal smoothly at the edge of the dent using 240-grit wet-or-dry paper dipped in water (3). Use a sharp implement, such as the tang of a file, to score the dented metal (4); this provides a key for the filler.

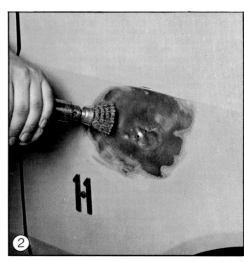

Pull out the dent with a hammer and screw, levering against a piece of wood.

Remove paint from the dented area with a wire brush, or use a power drill attachment.

Use wet-or-dry paper, dipped in water, to feather off the edges of the paintwork

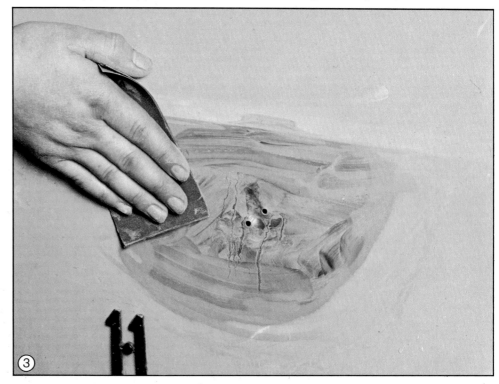

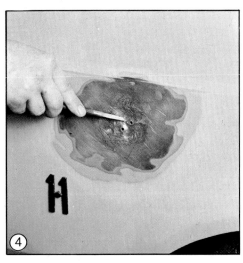

Mix the filler paste and hardener on a clean piece of hardboard according to the instructions. Smear it into the dent until the filler surface is proud of the surrounding bodywork (5).

When it has hardened, rough-shape it with a coarse file, then blend it to the body contour using coarse (120-grit) wet-or-dry paper, used wet. Change to about 240-grit paper as the shape improves, progressing to 320-grit and finishing with 400-grit as the final shape

is achieved (6). Make sure that the filler edge blends smoothly with the surrounding bodywork.

Wipe the filler with a clean cloth and allow it to dry. Fill any small blemishes or pin-holes in the surface (these are caused by air in the mixture) using a skim coat of freshly-mixed filler. Once this has hardened, rub it smooth with 400-grit paper, used wet.

Allow the repair to dry, then paint it (see pages 198-199).

Score the metal (left) to key in the filler, which should then be smeared quickly into the dent (below left)

When the filler is hard, rough shape it with a file, then smooth it into the bodywork with wet-or-dry paper

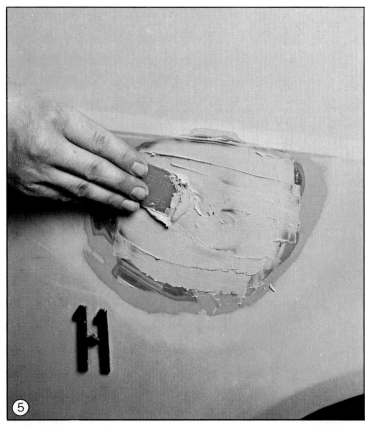

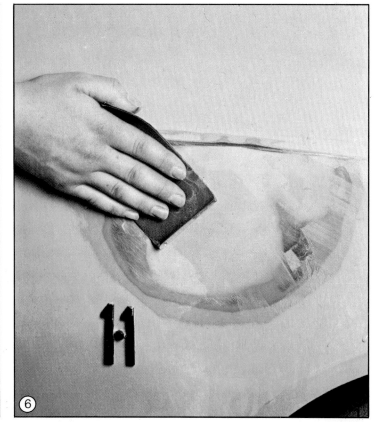

LOOKING AFTER WIPERS AND WASHERS

Windscreen wipers depend on a narrow unbroken strip of rubber on the wiper blade to squeegee water off the screen. If the strip is damaged or perished it will leave smears on the glass, which restrict vision.

In practice, wiper blades should be renewed every 12-18 months or when they do not wipe cleanly. Wiper arms need renewing when their weakened springs allow the blades to lift off the screen when travelling at high speeds. Usually they last longer than blades.

Changing wiper blades

There are three main types in use:

Push-on blades are released by hinging the arms away from the windscreen and pressing the blade mounting away from the small protrusion in the end of the arm and pulling it off (1).

Push-on blades slide on and off the arm

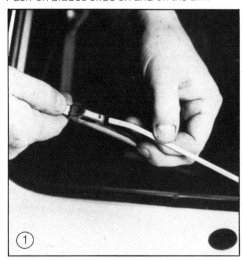

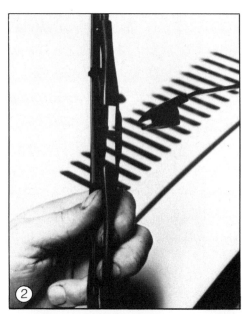

Hook-on blades can be disengaged from the hooked end of the wiper arm by first hinging the arms away from the screen and then rotating the blade towards the screen so it is at 90° to the arm. It will now slip off the hook (2).

Blades with pin mountings fit into a plastic mounting in the hooked arm. Hinge the arm away from the screen and move the blade and plastic mounting out of the hook. The plastic splits apart. (3) to release the pin.

On all types, fitting a new blade is a reversal of the dismantling procedure.

Twist the blade off the hook

Pull the plastic mounting out of the hook

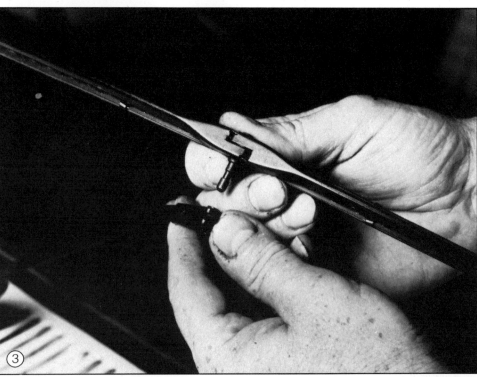

Changing wiper arms

Depending on your car, the wiper arm will be held by a single screw, a nut or a small spring clip.

Where the arm is held by a centre screw, undo the screw and draw the arm off its splined driving spindle. When fitting a new arm, make sure that the wipers are parked, fit the blade to the arm, align it so that it rests near the bottom of the windscreen, then fit the arm to the splined spindle. You may have to reset the arm on its spindle if the blades oversweep.

Some arms are held by a nut under a

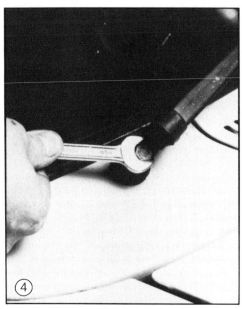

Lift the cover, undo the nut and remove the arm from its splines

This spring clip holds the arm to the spindle. Prise off the arm with a coin

hinged cover. With these, lift the cover and undo the nut (4) to remove the arm from its tapered driving splines. New arms may not have any splines at all. To fit this type, fit the arm on the spindle and do up the nut finger-tight. With the wipers parked, fit the blade and align it near the base of the windscreen. Tightening the nut will cause the spindle to cut new splines in the arm.

If the arm has no securing screw or lift-up cover, it will be held on the spindle by a hidden spring clip (5). Prise the arm forwards at the spindle, using a coin as a lever. It may be tight if the splines are corroded.

Fit the blade to the new arm and engage it with the splines on the spindle with the arm in the parked position. Press the arm firmly on to the spindle until the spring clip engages with the rear edge of the spindle.

Windscreen washers

Once an optional extra, windscreen washers are now obligatory and must always be in working order. In winter, windscreen washer anti-freeze should be added to water in the reservoir. In an emergency, two tablespoonsful of methylated spirit added to one pint of water will provide frost protection, but avoid using cooling system anti-freeze – it will cause streaking and can damage paintwork.

Water jets should aim a substantial quantity of fluid in the centre of the wiped area, about 4in down from the top. Most jets are aimed on a trial-and-error basis using a pin, although some can be directed by using a screwdriver in a slot while the washer is being worked by a helper.

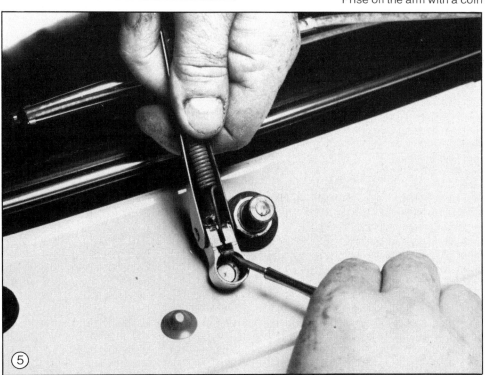

MINOR ADJUSTMENTS

Most of the body panels that move – the doors, bonnet and boot lid – have means of adjustment so that they can be aligned to shut correctly.

Door seals that have flattened with age will encourage wind noise and may let water in. The seal condition can be checked by closing the door on to a thin strip of paper. There should be a definite drag on the paper when it is withdrawn (1). If it slips out easily, the seal is not doing its job and is either worn out or the door needs adjusting. Try adjustment first. This is made by moving the striker plate, the pin or U-shaped piece of metal in the door-opening that engages with the latch. Loosen the fixing screws or hexagon section and slide it about ⅛in towards the centre-line of the car (2). Retighten the fixings and recheck the seal by shutting the door again on to the paper. If the seal grips the strip and the door closes easily, the job is done. If, however, the door will shut only with a powerful slam, fit a new seal and re-adjust the striker plate outwards until the door closes correctly on it without slamming. A similar adjustment is provided at the boot or tailgate lock.

A rear-hinged bonnet normally has a spring-loaded pin which holds it shut, and a hooked safety catch to retain it if the pin fails. The pin is adjustable by loosening the centre locknut (3) and rotating it clockwise to make the bonnet shut more tightly, or anti-clockwise to increase the clearance when it is closed. Tighten the locknut afterwards. Some cars have alternative positions for mounting the seats to provide extra adjustment for very tall drivers. To alter

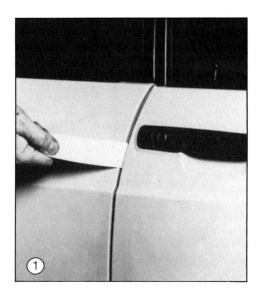

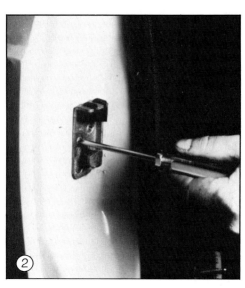

Try to pull out the trapped paper strip; there should be a definite drag on it

Loosen the fixing screws and move the striker in about ⅛in

Adjust the bonnet by slackening the locknut and screwing the pin in or out

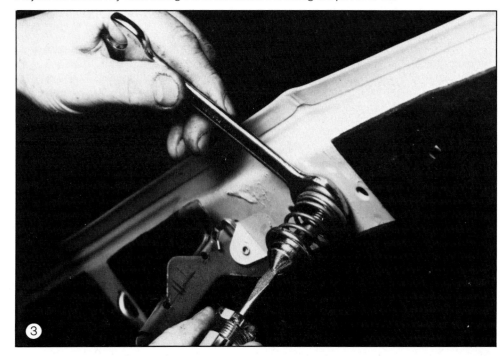

the position of the seat, remove the bolts and nuts, move the seat to the appropriate alternative mounting holes and refit the fixings.

Lubrication

Use an oil can to inject a little engine oil into the door hinges at regular service intervals. Some hinges have a small plastic cap above the hinge pin. These must be prised out with a screwdriver blade (4) and the oil injected into the hole. Replace the cap afterwards. Door check links (5) should also be oiled. The bonnet-release pin should be lubricated with grease, but the hinge of the safety catch (6) and the ends of the bonnet-release cable should be oiled (7) to ensure that they do not seize.

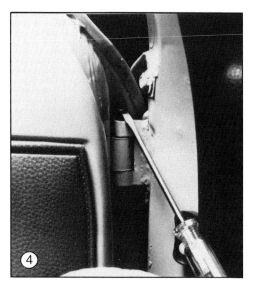

Prise out the hinge caps and squirt a few drops of oil into the hollow

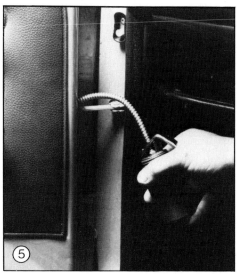

Oil the check links to prevent stiffness and noisy door operation

Grease the bonnet pin and apply a few spots of oil to both the safety catch pivot and the release cable

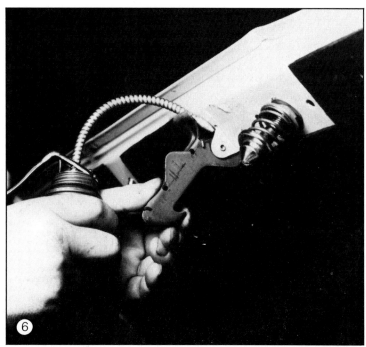

HEATING AND VENTILATION

What you can do: Pages

Check the airflow   216

Remove an air-lock   217-218

Check condition of all hoses   218

Check the operation of the tap   218

Deal with a blocked radiator   219

Free a seized air-control flap   219

Check the cowling   221

Check the thermostat   221

An efficient heating and ventilation system not only keeps the interior of the car warm and the passengers comfortable, but also plays an important part in making the car safe to drive in bad weather. Without it, the inside of the windows will mist up on cold and wet days and in winter ice can form on the outside – both drastically reducing vision and making driving difficult and potentially dangerous. Besides dispersing condensation and ice by blowing warm air on the glass, most modern heaters also provide face-level fresh air to discourage driver fatigue while warmth is supplied to the footwells. All car heaters provide warmth by passing air over a hot surface. The air may be blown by a fan or generated by the forward motion of the car. On cars with water-cooled engines the air passes through a small radiator linked into the cooling system, while on air-cooled engines the heat source usually employs part of the exhaust system. A few cars use petrol-burning heaters which are independent of the engine.

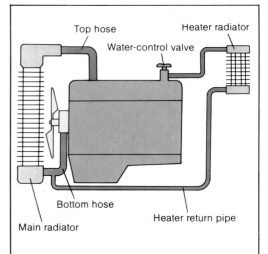

Water from the engine cooling system is diverted through the heater radiator which warms air passing through it into the car interior. Altering the flow of water through the heater/radiator provides a measure of temperature control

Where the heat comes from: Water-cooled engines

Cars with water-cooled engines use the hot water continuously circulating throughout the cooling system to provide warmth for the heater.

The water, driven by the engine water pump, is fed through a hose from the cylinder head to a heater radiator – virtually a main radiator in miniature – before being returned through another hose to the engine cooling system. Because the heater is connected directly to the engine water galleries, it is not dependent on the opening of the thermostat in the main cooling system. Consequently, it begins to receive heat very shortly after the engine has started from cold. Air which flows through the core of the heater radiator to the interior of the car cools the water inside by extracting heat. The temperature of air leaving the heating system can be adjusted by making some of it by-pass the radiator (the heater matrix) or by using a tap to regulate the flow of hot water passing through the matrix.

Recirculating heaters

Early heaters worked on a recirculating principle. The heater radiator was housed in a box mounted in the passenger compartment, with an electric fan to pass air through it. In this way, the same air in the passenger compartment was continually heated and recirculated. Airflow was controlled either by blocking off part of the matrix with small doors or by regulating the fan speed, using a rheostat switch. During summer months, a tap on the engine cylinder head was closed, preventing hot water from reaching the heater. The snag with recirculating heaters is that they are not particularly efficient and can make the interior of the car very stuffy after prolonged use. But they do not draw exhaust fumes into the car in heavy traffic, and for this reason some cars, mainly Japanese, with modern fresh-air heating systems have a separate control position which closes the fresh-air intake and enables the remainder of the system to work on the recirculating principle.

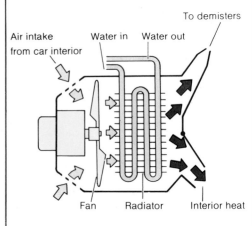

A recirculating heater is simply a radiator and an electric fan mounted in the car. It does not draw in fresh air from outside, but warms the air already existing in the passenger compartment

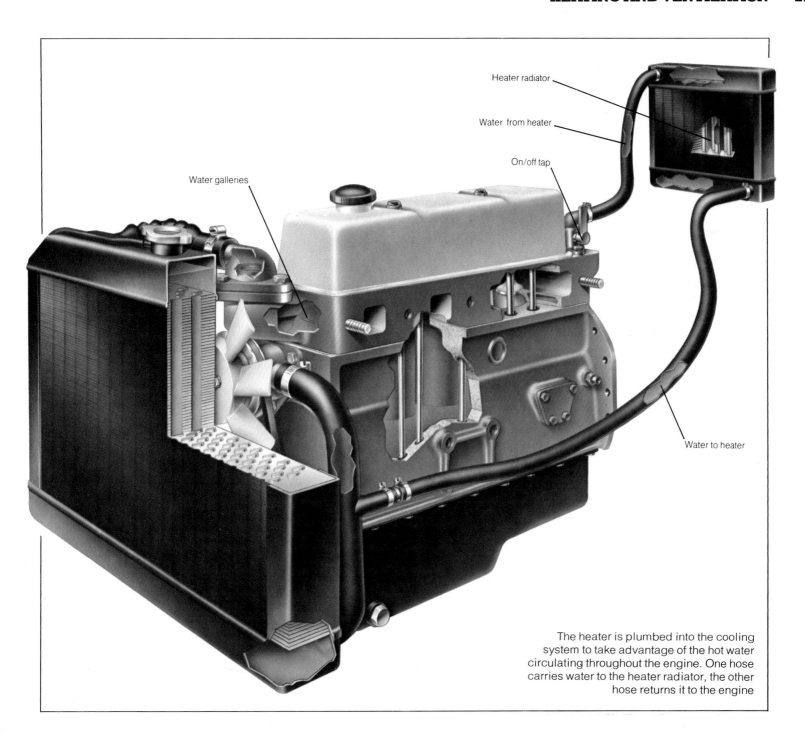

Heater radiator

Water from heater

On/off tap

Water galleries

Water to heater

The heater is plumbed into the cooling system to take advantage of the hot water circulating throughout the engine. One hose carries water to the heater radiator, the other hose returns it to the engine

Early fresh-air heaters

The first fresh-air heating systems obtained air from outside the car through a large diameter flexible trunking with its pick-up close to the front grille, or through a collector box, called a plenum chamber, positioned on the scuttle just ahead of the windscreen.

The plenum chamber is still the most frequently used pick-up on current cars because it is clear of the majority of exhaust fumes which tend to collect close to the ground.

Airflow through the heater is usually created by the forward movement of the vehicle. When the car is stationary, or to improve efficiency at low speed, a booster fan in the intake system can be switched on to speed up the airflow.

Air from the pick-up passes through the heater radiator and the temperature is adjusted by altering the flow of water through the radiator with a tap connected to one of the heater controls. Another control operates flaps which move to direct hot air on to the windscreen or to the interior. As there is no designed outlet for the heated air (except through badly-fitting door seals) these systems are not very efficient.

Full-flow ventilation

The full-flow system not only feeds fresh air to the heater radiator but also uses vents at the rear of the car to allow stale air to escape. To give the maximum throughput, the extractor vents are placed in the body where air rushing past the car creates a partial vacuum which helps suck out the stale air. To enable the temperature to be adjusted quickly, air is directed with

control flaps to pass both through and around the radiator. In this way the temperature can be instantly adjusted by altering the blend of hot and cold air. This type of heater requires a powerful booster fan.

On a full-flow ventilation system, the car maker usually also provides cool air

intakes which can be directed to provide refreshing face-level ventilation, while the heater system is supplying warm air to other areas. The increased airflow created by the extractor principle also allows the demisting function to be extended to the side windows.

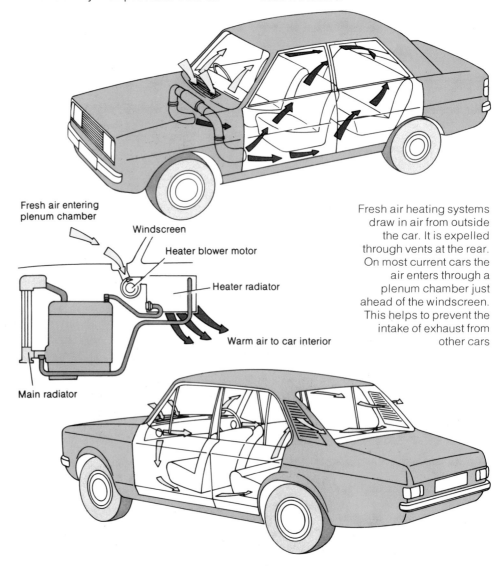

Fresh air entering plenum chamber

Windscreen

Heater blower motor

Heater radiator

Warm air to car interior

Main radiator

Fresh air heating systems draw in air from outside the car. It is expelled through vents at the rear. On most current cars the air enters through a plenum chamber just ahead of the windscreen. This helps to prevent the intake of exhaust from other cars

Heater controls

Heater controls vary from car to car, but are designed to enable the driver to alter the air temperature and direct the air where he requires it. First thing in the morning on a wet day when the windows mist up, he requires most of it to be blown on the inside of the windscreen. A few cars have vents below the front side windows—air from the heater is passed to these through tubes which join together and are sealed by a rubber ring when the doors are shut.

Some cars use one control to alter the air direction and another to adjust the air temperature. Others have two controls to direct the air—one to the windscreen and the other to the car interior, while a third control alters the air temperature. The operating levers or knobs are connected to the vent flaps and the variable water-control tap, if fitted, by rods and sometimes Bowden cables. Although forward movement of the car nearly always encourages a flow of air through the heater, at least one blower motor is provided. Most motors are built to operate at two speeds and sometimes three. This is achieved either by switching in separate circuits in the motor or by connecting it through electrical resistors of differing value. Most modern motors are fitted with propeller-type fans, but some older models have a 'squirrel-cage' fan. This has the appearance of a drum with a lot of vents in its outer surface. As it rotates, air in the vents is thrown outwards into a collector, which directs it into the car.

Air-blending heaters divert air either through the radiator or past it. This allows quick changes of temperature

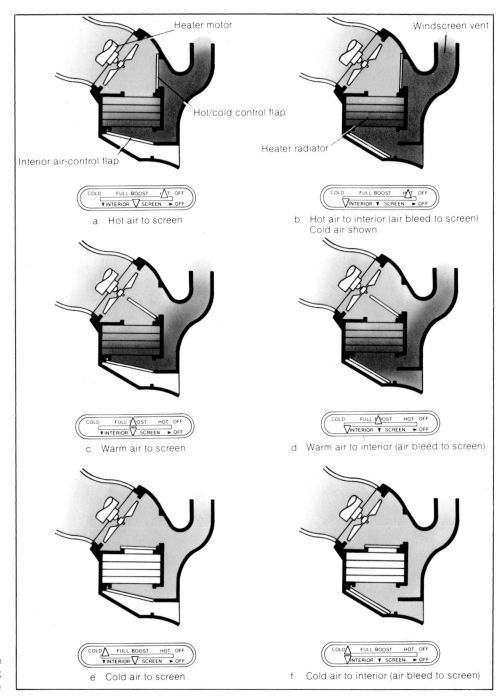

a   Hot air to screen

b   Hot air to interior (air bleed to screen) Cold air shown

c   Warm air to screen

d   Warm air to interior (air bleed to screen)

e   Cold air to screen

f   Cold air to interior (air bleed to screen)

Heater motor

Hot/cold control flap

Interior air-control flap

Windscreen vent

Heater radiator

Checking the airflow

Although the heater system does not normally need regular maintenance, the air intake on fresh-air heaters should be checked from time to time to make sure that it is not blocked by leaves or other debris, and that the drain tubes which allow water to escape from the plenum chamber are clear (1).

Each tube has a plenum valve, the end of which terminates in a slit which is intended to let water out without causing the chamber to leak air. Make sure that the flexible valve is not full of debris (2), and that the slit end reverts to the closed position after cleaning.

On heaters that pick up air through a flexible trunking, a sluggish airflow is sometimes caused by the inner lining of the trunking collapsing. As this is not apparent from outside, detach one end of the trunking so that the inside can be examined.

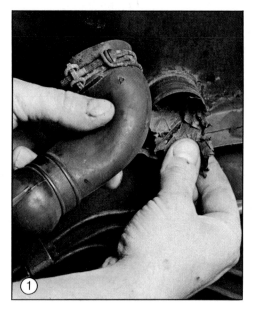

Make sure that the plenum chamber drain-tubes are not blocked

Check that there is no debris lodged inside the flexible valve

Sometimes a demister refuses to operate. If this happens after some work has been carried out under the facia, it is most likely that one of the flexible demister pipes has been displaced. If you are suspicious that one demister is inefficient but find it difficult to judge the airflow, tape some strips of tissue paper to each demister vent, then switch on the boost fan with 'demist' or 'defrost' selected on the heater controls. The tissue streamers will immediately indicate the relative strengths of the air flow through the vents.

The booster fan will generally last the life of the car, without maintenance.

If the heater blows cool . . .

When the heater warms up slowly or supplies cool air when it should be blowing hot, there is something wrong with the plumbing: either the pipework to the heater radiator is blocked, the radiator itself is blocked, the tap has stopped working, the system has an air lock or the thermostat is faulty.

Check the thermostat first. It is not necessary to remove any hoses, just start the engine from cold and with the bonnet open, rest your hand on the top hose of the main radiator (beware of the fan) while the engine warms up.

If all is well, the hose will remain cool for some time – maybe ten minutes on a cool day – and then will suddenly get hot, which indicates that the thermostat has opened. If the hose warms up very gradually, either the thermostat has been removed, which will mean the cooling system – and the heater – is operating at a lower temperature than it should, or the existing thermostat has jammed open. Fit a new thermostat.

Identify the return hose at either the main radiator, bottom hose or water pump

Run the engine at a fast idle until water flows from the return hose

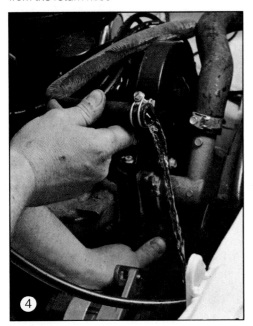

Quickly refit the return hose on to its stub and tighten the hose clip

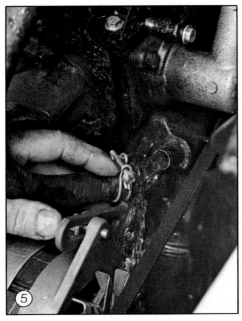

Removing an air-lock

If the engine passes the thermostat test the trouble may be an air-lock. The heater radiator is often higher than the top of the main radiator, and if the cooling system has been drained to add anti-freeze or to change a hose, filling the radiator again with water is not always sufficient. Any air trapped in the heater must be bled out.

Bleeding of the heater should be carried out when the engine is cold and the thermostat is shut, as this gives maximum flow through the heater. It is also inevitable that your hands will get wet – and it is better that the water is cold than scalding hot. The system can be bled as follows:

Use the heater controls in the car to select maximum heat.

Fill up the cooling system to the top of the filler neck and leave the filler cap off. Identify the heater hoses. One will start at the cylinder head and the other will be joined either to the base of the radiator, the bottom hose, or to the water pump. This is the return hose from the heater and the one you want (3).

Detach the front end of the return hose and raise it above the level of the bottom of the windscreen. With the other hand, block the stub it was joined to.

First check that your fingers are clear of the fan or fan belt, then have a helper start the engine and run it at a fast tick-over until water starts to come out of the return hose (4).

As quickly as possible, rejoin the return hose on to its stub with as little water loss as possible (5). Tighten the clip.

Top up the radiator and leave the filler cap off until the engine has warmed up. If necessary, top up again.

Curing heater air-locks on rear-engined cars

A few cars are fitted with a water-cooled engine at the rear, with the heater unit placed in the usual position ahead of the driver. On this layout, two long hoses carry the engine coolant to and from the heater radiator.

To simplify the removal of an air-lock in the pipework, most car manufacturers provide small bleed valves at the engine end of the heater system. This means that it is not necessary to disconnect the heater return hose to bleed out air.

Because of the length of the heater hoses, it is essential that bleeding is carried out with the engine cold, when the thermostat is closed. The heater controls should be set as recommended in the handbook – usually at the highest temperature.

A typical sequence is as follows:
Attach a length of transparent plastic tube to the bleed valve. The tube should be long enough for its end to reach the radiator cap (1). Top up the radiator. Start the engine and have a helper run it at a fast tick-over.

Open the bleed screw and allow water from the end of the bleed tube to run into the radiator (2). Close the valve when there are no air bubbles to be seen in the plastic tube.

Blockages and seizures

Sometimes when air is bled from a heater only a dribble of water emerges from the return hose. This indicates a blockage in the plumbing somewhere, and the most likely causes are collapsed hoses, a blocked water valve or a partially-blocked heater radiator.

Push transparent hose on to bleed valve

Open valve to allow flow into radiator

Hoses

It is normal for hoses carrying hot water to develop a few fine surface cracks where they bend or flex because of engine movement. But if these cracks seem more than skin deep, suspect that the hose has collapsed internally. Check by squeezing the hose firmly (3). If it is in good condition it will feel springy and will return to its original shape immediately it is released.

A hose that feels 'squashy' is breaking up internally and should be renewed before it blocks the flow of water.

Is the tap on?

The water valve or tap will be fixed to the cylinder head in an accessible place, or may be difficult to find in the heater assembly.

Where the valve can be seen, have a helper operate the temperature control in the car while you watch for movement at the valve or tap. If all is well with the linkage, the lever on the valve will move through its full travel as the facia control is moved from the hot to cold position. If nothing moves, disconnect the linkage at the valve and try operating the valve lever by hand (4). If it is jammed, the tap

Squeeze hoses to assess their condition

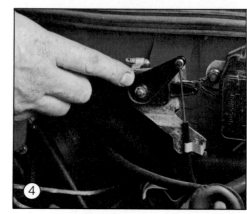
Try operating the heater valve by hand

or valve has seized – fit a new one. If the lever does move, the control linkage is either jammed or disconnected.

On heaters with cable controls, oiling the end of the cable at the tap or valve (5), and rerouting it to eliminate any sharp curves, often frees it. If the linkage is not easily reached for checking, leave the job to a professional. On some cars much of the heater must be dismantled to check the controls.

Dealing with a blocked radiator

If the heater valve is working, the hose leading from the valve to the heater radiator will gradually get hot. But if the radiator is partly blocked, it will be inefficient and not produce much hot air. It may be possible to clear a blocked radiator by using a proprietary radiator cleaning solution, following the maker's instructions. Usually these solutions are left in the cooling system for a few days for them to be fully effective.

Afterwards, the cooling system is drained by removing the bottom hose from the main radiator (not by unscrewing the drain tap) and the system is flushed out by hosing water at mains pressure into the filler (6).

To flush the heater, remove both hoses where they join the engine cooling system and with a mains hose set to deliver water at low pressure, run water through the heater radiator in both directions. Keep the water flowing until it runs clear (7).

If a sealing compound has been used to cure a water leak, the leak may re-open after the radiator has been treated with a cleaning solution. If this is the case, new sealant will be required.

Seized air-control flaps

If the heater controls move very stiffly – or remarkably easily – it is possible that one of the control flaps is not working. This is because it is either partially seized, or the linkage is disconnected or seized.

Check the airflow by switching the blower on, if necessary fixing tissue strips to the outlets (see page 216).

On most heaters the vent flaps and their linkages can be uncovered only after major dismantling. If you can reach the flap, oil the pivot and any control cables (see 'Is the tap on?').

⑥ Hose out the system at mains pressure

⑦ Run water through heater at low pressure

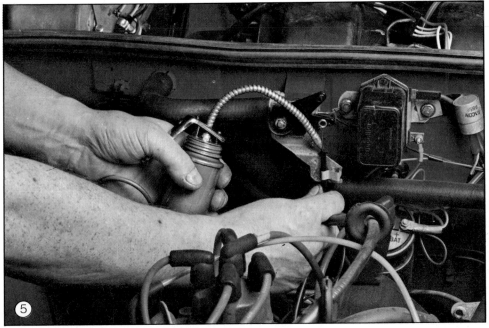
⑤ Where control cables are fitted, oil the end of the cable at the tap or valve

Petrol-burning heaters

Some cars with air-cooled engines have a separate petrol-burning heater that can heat the interior while the engine is stationary. It can also augment the normal heater when the engine is running.

This type of heater works in a similar way to warm-air central heating units used in factories and workshops.

A small quantity of petrol is injected by a metering pump into a large combustion chamber where it is ignited by a glow-plug. The chamber is shaped so that the burning petrol heats the maximum area of metal before leaving through the heater's own exhaust pipe.

An electric fan which blows fresh air into a casing fitting tightly round the outside of the combustion chamber.

The air picks up sufficient heat from the outside of the chamber to warm the interior and demist the windows.

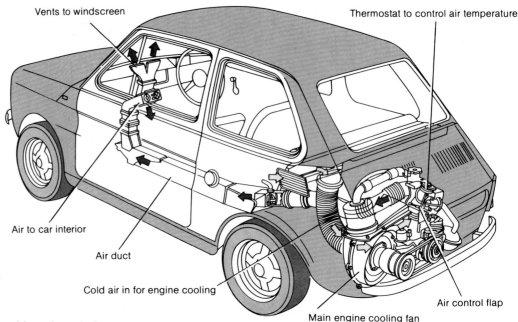

Vents to windscreen

Thermostat to control air temperature

Air to car interior

Air duct

Cold air in for engine cooling

Main engine cooling fan

Air control flap

Most air-cooled cars provide interior warmth by diverting some of the warm air from around the engine to the heater

Some air-cooled cars have a heater which can supply warm air when the engine is stationary. Heat comes from burning petrol and air in a combustion chamber. Air blown over the chamber by an electric fan provides 'central heating' in the car

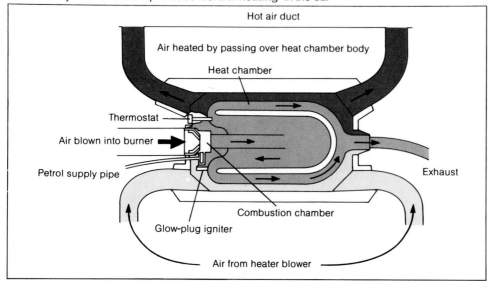

Hot air duct

Air heated by passing over heat chamber body

Heat chamber

Thermostat

Air blown into burner

Petrol supply pipe

Glow-plug igniter

Combustion chamber

Exhaust

Air from heater blower

Air-cooled engines

On these cars, engine cooling is provided by a large fan which blows air around the engine. To make maximum use of the airflow, the engine is shrouded in a tightly fitting cowling. In most cases, hot air is provided for the car interior by bleeding off some of the engine cooling air and diverting it inside through ducts. Extra heat is sometimes supplied by arranging for the exhaust pipes or silencers to pass through the ducts.

Heater servicing – air-cooled engines

The efficiency of the heater fitted to a car with an air-cooled engine is often dependent on the make of car. Some heaters are not very efficient due to their design rather than a fault.

When the heater is known to be efficient but does not function as well as it should, check the following points.

Checking the cowling

Often the loss of a screw or two holding a section of ducting or cowling in place will allow hot air to escape, or cool air to enter. Loose cowls are betrayed by rattling or buzzing sounds. Tighten their fixings firmly to cure the problem. Check any rubber plugs or sealing strips for leakage. Some engines have rubber plugs sealing the gap where the spark plug high-tension cables pass through the cowl. If one of these is damaged or missing (1), heater performance will suffer.

Is the thermostat working?

Check in the handbook to determine whether or not the engine has a thermostatically-controlled air-venting system. If it has, make sure that it operates. Normally the flap will be on the cowling and is usually closed when the engine is cold and opens progressively to spill air from the cowling and increase the flow past the engine as it warms up. If it is jammed open (2), because the thermostat is faulty, or the flap has seized, the heater – and the engine – will be slow to warm up. Fit a new thermostat or free off the flap as necessary.

Is the ducting blocked?

It has been known for waste rags, dusters and newspapers to get into badly fitted ducting and block the air-flow. If the ducting has gaps in it, check inside before closing them. Check also the air intake to the car heating system. Where the air flows through a large-diameter trunking, disconnect one end and look inside to ensure that it has not collapsed or is not blocked.

Replace any ill-fitting sealing plugs so that cooling air cannot escape

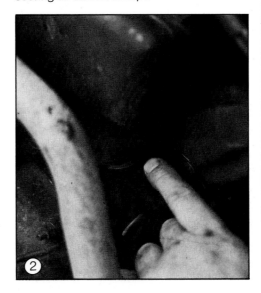

Check to ensure that the cowling flap is opening and closing correctly

Air conditioning

In this country, air conditioning is an extra fitted to comparatively few vehicles, although in hot countries it is considered essential. The air-conditioner cools and partially dries air entering the car and works on the same principle as the domestic refrigerator.

If a spirit such as petrol or alcohol is poured on the hand, it feels cold as it evaporates. This is because to evaporate, the spirit must change from a liquid to a gas and this requires heat. And some of the heat it needs comes from the hand.

The evaporation of Freon, the refrigerant used in a car air-conditioner, can be encouraged by altering the pressure acting upon it. Under high pressure it becomes a fluid, but if the pressure is lowered it evaporates.

In an air-conditioner, evaporation takes place in an evaporator – a device similar to a radiator – and takes warmth from the surrounding air in doing so. The cool air around the evaporator is then fed into the car interior. Once it has evaporated, the Freon gas is compressed by an engine-driven pump and passed through a condenser which changes it into a fluid again.

Apart from checking the tension of the compressor drive belt, and ensuring that any lubrication is carried out, there is little that a private owner can do to repair or service an air-conditioning unit. If a fault develops, seek expert help.

THE MOT TEST

What you can do: Pages   Pages
Pre-test checks   Suspension   229
Headlamps   227   Brakes   230-231
Stop lamps   227   Tyres   231
Direction indicators   227   Seat belts   232
Steering mechanism   228   Windscreen wipers and washers   232
Front wheels   228   Exhaust system   233
                                            Horn   233
                                            General vehicle condition   233

VEHICLE TESTING STATION

APPROVED BY THE MINISTRY OF TRANSPORT

The annual compulsory vehicle test, commonly known as the 'MOT Test', was introduced in 1960 on all cars more than ten years old. Since then the age limit has gradually been reduced and all cars now have to be tested once a year after they reach the third anniversary of their first registration.

The purpose of the test

The MOT test is a road safety measure which ensures that three year old vehicles are examined at least once a year and comply with certain important legal requirements. Many people erroneously assume that possession of a pass certificate means that their cars are perfectly serviceable and roadworthy for another 12 months. This is not so, and most testing stations display an approved poster which says, among other things: 'The MOT test for cars and light commercial vehicles does *not* mean that if the vehicle passes the test it is automatically safe and legal to drive on the roads. It means merely that certain specified items were up to a required standard. It does *not* follow that even these items will meet the required standards the following day'. The test standards are, in many respects, quite generous. The average new car has a brake efficiency of at least 80% but only 50% is needed to pass the test. Similarly, new tyres have a tread depth of up to 8mm, but only 1mm is necessary to pass the test.

A combination of both these factors, especially in poor road conditions, could result in a crash if a car in front had to brake suddenly.

To its credit, the test does keep dangerous old cars off the road and, as only one car in three passes the test first time, it ensures that much essential repair work is carried out.

Getting the car to a testing station

If your car does not have a valid test certificate after its third 'birthday', it is illegal to drive it on the road except to an authorised testing centre *where an appointment has been made in advance.*

Vehicle inspection form (VT 29)

For this journey the driver must be insured, but the vehicle does not have to be taxed. Imported cars can be driven to and from a test centre without number plates provided the import documents are carried.

If the car fails its test, it is easier if the test station rectifies any faults, retests the car and issues a pass certificate. Unfortunately not all garages that act as testing stations carry out rectification work and if one of these fails the car it could be illegal to drive it away—although it is normally acceptable to drive the car to a repairer.

If the car is considered dangerous to drive, the examiner will enter defects on the bottom of the test check list—form VT 29—and it would be unwise to drive away the car. Under these circumstances it is best to arrange for the repairer to collect it. Many of these problems can be avoided if you check that the testing station will do rectification work when making the appointment.

What the examiner looks for

At a testing station, the examiner makes a number of checks on the following main areas: lighting equipment; steering and suspension; the braking system; tyres and wheels; seat belts, and general items, including the chassis and structure.

These six headings are further divided into 32 individual checks that are itemised on a vehicle inspection list. A copy of this list is issued with each pass or failure certificate. In the event of a failure, the points on which the car has failed will be indicated.

The scaling of test fees encourages car owners to have any repairs done at the garage that carries out the test.

What it costs

At the time of writing, the current fee for the test is £6.70 and if a car fails the test and is left with the test station for repair and retest, no further fee is chargeable. If it fails and is removed from the test station but is taken to the same or another authorised test station for repair and retest within 14 days, one half of the fee (£3.35) is payable in addition to the original fee.

If you decide to take the car away and do the repairs yourself, or have them done by a garage that is not an authorised testing station, you must pay the full fee (£6.70) again when the car is retested. The full fee is also payable if the car is submitted for retest more than 14 days after the initial test.

About 12% of failures are due to minor defects which the vast majority of motorists could rectify themselves. To ensure that your car does not fail because the windscreen washer bottle is empty, or a sidelamp bulb has blown, it is worthwhile checking it yourself before taking it for test.

Unfortunately, even the most competent do-it-yourself owner cannot carry out a complete test beforehand as he does not have the special equipment that authorised test stations must have.

On the following pages the main points of the test are summarised. The guide can be used to make sure that your car does not have any obvious faults before it is submitted for test.

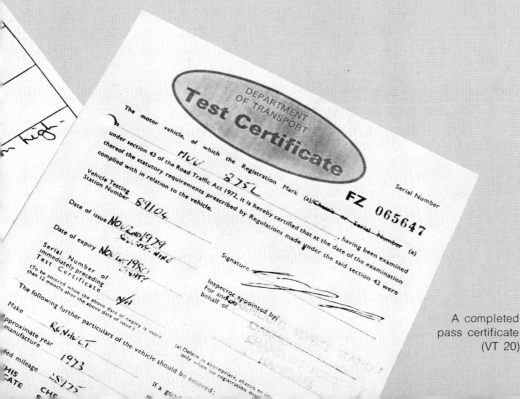

A completed pass certificate (VT 20)

Check your car yourself before the examiner does

The main items that the examiner checks are listed here. Many of them can be checked by the owner before taking the car to a testing station.

Lighting systems

All lights on the car must work, be unobscured and the lenses must be in position and undamaged (1).

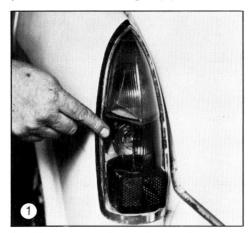

Replace any cracked or broken lenses

Obligatory front lamps (sidelamps)

Two white lights must be clearly visible from a reasonable distance. They may be incorporated in the headlamps, but must be independently switched. Make sure both of them work. If one is dimmer than the other, remove the lens and examine the bulb. If it is blackened, fit a new one.

Obligatory rear lamps

Two red lamps must be visible from a reasonable distance. Cars with lenses that have faded may be failed. If the lenses appear pale when compared with those on a similar car, fit new ones.

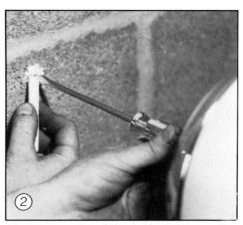

Mark the centre of the lamp on the wall

Mark two bold crosses on the wall

On dipped beam the 'hot-spots' should be below and to the left of the crosses

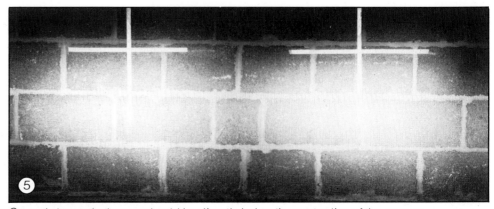

On main beam the beams should be directly below the centre-line of the crosses

Obligatory headlamps

One or two pairs of lamps, fixed with their centres between 24in and 42in from the ground, must clearly illuminate the road ahead yet must not dazzle oncoming drivers. They must give out a white or yellow light of equal intensity. Lamps with corroded reflectors should be renewed. The minimum height is important to owners of low-built sports cars where the headlamps are only just 24in above the road when the car is new. Any sagging of the suspension springs or the fitment of non-standard low-profile tyres can result in a failure—check with a tape measure.

Headlamp aim

Special equipment is best used to set the aim of headlamps accurately, but a rough check can be made as follows: drive the car on a flat surface as close as possible to a wall or garage. Mark the centre of each lamp on the wall (2), back the car up and then make two bold crosses (3). Reverse the car in a straight line 25ft from the wall. Switch on the headlamps. The brightest areas of light (hot-spots) should be below and to the left of the crosses on dipped beam (4), and directly below the crosses on main beam (5).

Headlamp aim can be altered by turning adjusting screws (6)—the owner's handbook or workshop manual will indicate where these are found. If the lamps dip to the right, check the fitting of the bulbs. On some foreign cars there is an adjustment on the bulb mounting to make the headlamps dip right or left. The handbook will indicate the correct adjustment for right-hand-drive cars.

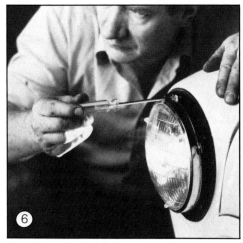

Turn the adjusters and watch the beam

Stop lamps

Two red lights at the rear must light when the footbrake is applied and go out when the pedal is released. Cars registered before 1971 need have only one stop lamp at the rear, but if two have been fitted, both must work. It is illegal to have rear fog lights connected to and operated by the stop lamps. Stop lamps work only when the ignition is on. Have a helper push the brake pedal while you check their action from behind the car.

Rear reflectors

Two rear red reflectors must be fitted. They are usually part of the rear light lenses (7). Reflective tape may be used in addition to but not as a substitute for reflectors. Make sure that the reflective surfaces are clean.

Direction indicators

Two front indicators may be either white or amber and two rear ones either red or amber and must operate at a speed of between 60 and 120 flashes per minute. A 'tell-tale' light clearly visible to the driver must operate in conjunction with the indicators. The rate of flashing can be checked with the second hand of a wrist watch—the indicators should flash between five and ten times every five seconds.

Older semaphore-type indicators must work smoothly, be amber in colour and clearly visible when illuminated to the front and rear. If they can be clearly seen by the driver (through a wing mirror, for instance) a 'tell-tale' is not needed.

Make sure that the two rear reflectors are clean and undamaged

Steering wheel and column

The wheel must be free from damage (1) and securely fitted to the column. When the wheel is pushed up and down and from side to side there must not be any free play.

Replace the wheel if it is damaged

Move the wheel to assess free play

Steering mechanism

All steering systems have some free play when the steering wheel is turned from left to right (2). Cars with steering boxes must not have more than 3in free play at the wheel rim, and on cars with rack and pinion steering the maximum allowance is $\frac{1}{2}$in. Check by standing alongside the car and gently rotating the steering wheel from side to side. The above limits must not be exceeded before the front wheels move.

When the wheel is turned firmly there should not be any excessive play in the joints and mountings. The steering box, rack assembly or power steering system must not be leaking and there should not be any serious corrosion within 12in of the mountings.

Front wheels

When jacking the front wheels, the examiner will check the suspension bushes for excessive movement as the weight of the car comes off them. It is difficult for an owner to do this, but it is reasonably easy to check the wheel bearings. Raise the front of the car, then spin each wheel to ensure that it runs freely without any roughness—on front-wheel-drive cars you must allow for some drag from the transmission.

Grip the tyre top and bottom and try to rock the wheel about its axle (3). A small amount of free play—about $\frac{1}{8}$in at the wheel rim—is allowable. More than this suggests that the wheel bearings are loose or worn out. Have them replaced by a garage.

Rock the wheel top and bottom. Only a trace of free play is permissible

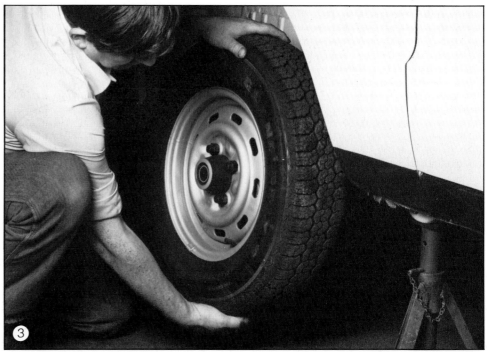

Lever the wheel to check for slackness

Check dampers here for oil seepage

Lower the wheels on to a smooth surface

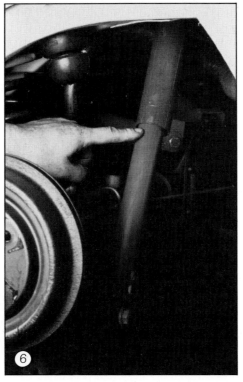

Suspension

The full examination of the suspension linkage varies according to the car, but on all vehicles the aim is the same—to look for looseness or wear in the joints and pivots.

Raise a front wheel and have a helper put a lever under the tyre and lever it up and down to move the suspension joints (4). Look for free movement at the pivots and mountings.

Sometimes wear that is not apparent with this check can be discovered when the helper vigorously rocks the wheel about the axle while gripping the tyre at the top and bottom. To do this effectively, the footbrake must be applied to eliminate wheel bearing free play. Examine all axle and suspension parts for damage and check for corrosion or damage to the areas within 12in of any mountings. Do not get under the car during any of the above suspension checks until the chassis is firmly supported on stands.

Lower the wheels so that they rest on smooth surfaces—two glossy magazines are ideal—and have a helper turn the steering wheel from lock to lock (5). Look underneath to ensure that the wheels do not foul anything, particularly the brake hoses. Examine all rubber gaiters for damage (including drive-shaft joint covers on front-wheel-drive cars) and check that there are no leaks (6) from the dampers (shock absorbers). Test damper action by pressing down firmly on each corner of the car in turn. When released, the suspension should not 'bounce' the car more than $1\frac{1}{2}$ times. If it does, the dampers are worn and should be renewed.

Parking brake

Apply the handbrake and ensure that it moves freely and cannot be accidentally knocked into the off position. There should be ample reserve travel when the brake lever is fully applied. If possible, look under the car and check that all cables, pivots and joints are undamaged, and make sure they move freely when the handbrake is moved on and off (1).

Footbrake

Operate the pedal until pressure is felt and ensure that it does not creep down from this point under sustained pressure. Test cars with servo brakes with the engine running. Check that the free play at the pedal does not exceed one inch (2). If it does, adjust the brakes or renew worn linings.

A car veering to one side or the other when braking will fail the test. If it pulls strongly to the nearside, for instance, there is probably a fault in the offside front brake—a leaking wheel cylinder, allowing fluid to reach the linings, is a likely cause.

Check all visible parts of the hydraulic system for corrosion and leaks, and make sure that the hydraulic reservoir is full. If it has needed frequent topping-up, there is a leak in the system—have a garage check it. Examine the flexible hoses near the wheels. Have new ones fitted if they are chafed or have any surface splits. The most likely area for damage is where the hose meets the metal union at each end. Bend it sharply away from the union and check for cracks (3). A brake hose covered in oil from a leaking back axle or damper will be failed.

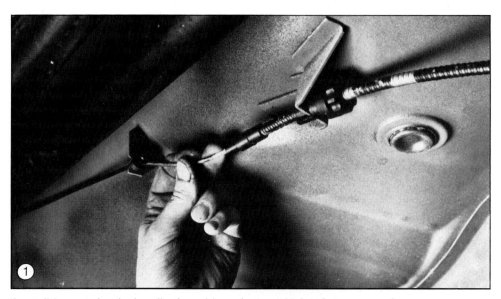

If possible, examine the handbrake cables, pivots and joints for wear or seizure

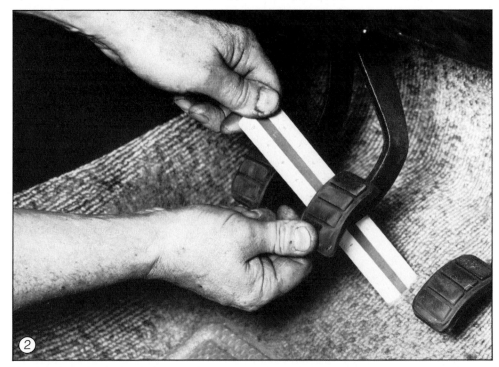

Measure free play at the brake pedal. It should not be more than one inch

Bend the hose sharply and look carefully for age cracks and surface splits

Examine the tyres for damage and use a depth gauge to assess tread wear

Brake testing

Test stations check brake efficiency and balance on a roller tester. The private owner can buy a small decelerometer, known as a Tapley meter, to check the efficiency of his own brakes on the road. The legal requirement is 50% for the footbrake and 25% for the handbrake (only 16% handbrake efficiency is called for on cars with split hydraulic circuits). A rough check can also be made on a quiet stretch of level road by applying the brakes at a given point and checking the stopping distance. From a speed of 20mph, a braking efficiency of 50% gives a stopping distance of 26.8ft. From the same speed, 25% brake efficiency will halt the car in 53.7ft and 16% in 84ft. The car should pull up in a straight line. If it does not, first check that the tyre pressures are equal on each 'axle', then try again. If the car continually pulls to one side, have a garage check the braking system.

Tyres

The size and type of tyre fitted to a pair of wheels on the front or rear of the car should be the same. If two radial- and two cross-ply tyres are fitted, the radials must be on the rear wheels. Examine each tyre for cuts, lumps or bulges and check that the minimum tread depth exceeds 1mm (4).
A wheel that is damaged where the tyre bead seals against it will be failed. Minor damage to the edges of the rims, such as may be caused by rubbing against a kerbstone, is not normally a reason for failure.
It is not only dangerous to use tyres on a car which have had their treads recut, it is also illegal.

Seat belts

All front seats on cars made after June 30 1964 must be equipped with seat belts which restrain the upper part of the body.

Examine the belts for signs of serious wear or cuts and make sure that the anchorages are secure (1). Webbing that has some surface fluff is probably sound, but if any strands are broken (2), have the belt replaced. Check that the belt buckle latches correctly and releases with the belt under tension. Retracting-type (inertia-reel) belts should be pulled out to check that they rewind freely. Where possible, check for excessive corrosion within 12in of the anchorages.

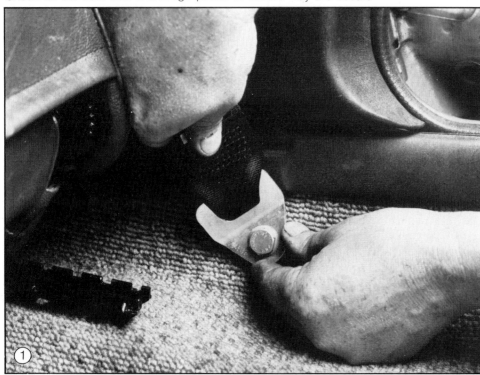

Replace a belt that has broken strands

Check all the seat belt anchorage points to ensure they are secure

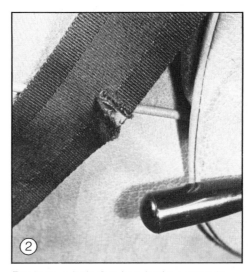

Windscreen wipers and washers

Make sure that the wipers work. The blades should not be split or perished (3) and must clear water from the screen effectively. Ensure that the washer bottle is full and that the pump puts an effective jet of water in the centre of each wiped arc about 4in down from the top. If necessary re-aim the jets (4).

Renew blades that are split or perished

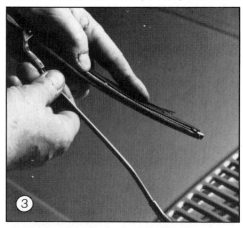

If necessary, re-aim the screenwasher jets

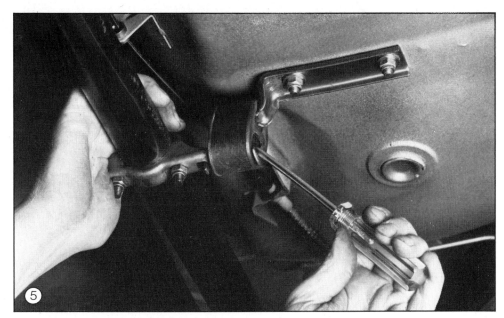

Apply a load to the exhaust mountings and look for breakages or damage

Make sure that there is no serious body corrosion, particularly at load-bearing areas

Exhaust system

If the exhaust leaks or parts are damaged or missing, the car will be failed. Ideally, the car should be driven over an inspection pit to inspect it. Pull the exhaust system downwards to put a load on the mountings (5). Renew any mounts that are broken or damaged. Start the engine and listen for the tell-tale hiss or chuffing sound caused by leaking exhaust gas. The leak can be pin-pointed by feeling for the escaping gas with the palm of the hand (do not touch the pipe—it may be hot). Small leaks that do not weaken the exhaust system can be repaired using a proprietory exhaust bandage kit. Leaks that weaken the system cannot be repaired—fit a new component.

Horn

Operate the horn and make sure it works properly. It is illegal to have a gong, bell, siren or a horn that does not sound a single tone.

General condition

This is best checked over an inspection pit. Ensure that there is no serious corrosion or damage to the main structure (6) or floor of the car—particularly where it could affect braking or steering.

In a summary as short as this, it is not possible to detail every check, although following this guide will enable you to prevent the car from failing the test because of an easily-rectified fault. Fuller details of the MOT test are to be found in 'The Testers' Manual' which is available from Government bookshops.

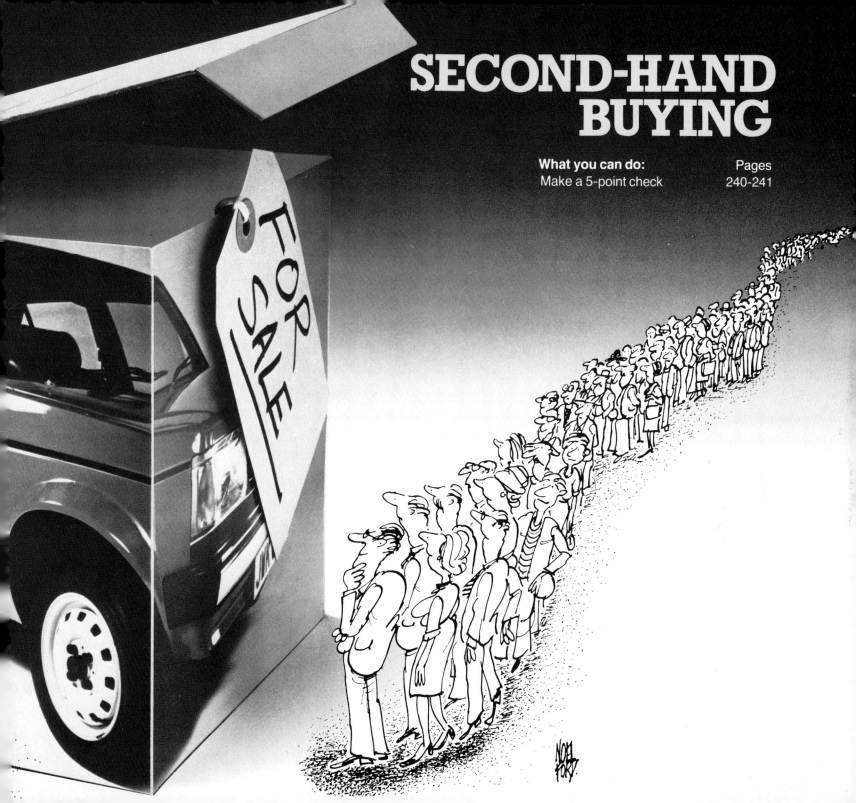

SECOND-HAND BUYING

What you can do: | Pages
Make a 5-point check | 240-241

Buying a used car is, to some, as fraught with risk as Russian roulette. The shady reputation of certain sections of the car trade and the feeling that some people have that they must be taking in another's dirty linen, makes a new car a much safer and more appealing proposition. Yet more and more motorists are finding themselves priced out of the new car scene, with even the Mini—Britain's symbol of basic motoring—costing the wrong side of £2,500. With one eye on his wallet and the other on his growing offspring, many a family man is having to resort to what he hopes is a good second-hand buy. But is there any way of being sure?

Deciding what to buy

Before you go anywhere, look at anything, or talk to anyone (particularly a salesman), take a long, hard look at your motoring needs and resources. Many people finish up with perfectly good cars that are, nevertheless, totally unsuited to them. To make sure that you get your priorities right, you must know the answers to the following questions:

How much do you want to spend?

In general, the more you pay in the first place, the cheaper it will be in the end. From an investment point of view, in times of new car price inflation, it does not pay to buy a car that is too old. Probably the best motoring investment these days is one of the popular hatchback 'superminis', about a year old, preferably first registered in the same calendar year and still covered by a maker's warranty. Such cars are available for perfectly genuine reasons, sometimes below their current list price, and make excellent buys.

How long do you intend to keep it?

The point behind this question is that older, higher mileage cars or those that enjoy a less-than-glowing reputation for longer-term reliability or rust-resistance could still give excellent service for a few years.

By the same token, the truth about their longer-term liabilities should be faced at the outset. It is no good buying an already 'mature' import that is as difficult to work on as its spares are costly, and delude yourself that it is a good long-term ownership prospect. AA road test reports, and some of those produced by motoring magazines, explore the question of constructional quality and reliability and are worth consulting. No second-hand buyer can afford to disregard this aspect of his purchase, especially the one who intends to keep the car a long time.

How big a car do you need?

Notice that the question is not what you fancy, but what you *need*.

Many people still assume that small cars are cheap but nasty, and bigger ones are invariably more comfortable but expensive. The used-car buyer in particular should recognise that this demarcation is no longer so clear cut, and with a limited budget it is foolish to buy a bigger, thirstier and more costly saloon than personal and domestic requirements demand.

Some of the better-equipped modern small cars have as much performance and refinement as their bigger stablemates, even if they are not as roomy. And they are not necessarily going to wear out any faster either.

What are your own special requirements?

For some people, choosing a car is a complex business. The car has to handle and accelerate well and project the correct 'image'. For others, car ownership is a necessary evil, and an easy-to-drive, undemanding-to-service tin box that always starts and keeps going is all they ask for.

Most of us probably fit somewhere between these extremes, but we all deserve a car that fits us, pleases us, and effectively performs the task we bought it to do. It is good sense, therefore, clearly to sort out your personal order of motoring priorities and draw up a short list of cars that will match them. Forget all your preconceived preferences and prejudices—sit down with pen and paper and try to list the qualities that matter to you in order of priority.

Do not be too influenced by what other people say

There are precious few people who are willing or able to tell you what they really think of their car—until they have sold it. And then some people exaggerate its faults to justify the change!

Do not be taken in by appearances—some sporty-looking jobs are not half as much fun to drive as other more domestic-looking family hold-alls of the current generation. Reading AA road test reports can be a help here, particularly if you have already made up your mind about the attributes you are looking for.

Do not be too brand-conscious—motor makers' ad-men spend a lot of time and energy encouraging 'marque-loyalty', but it really is not in the interest of a used-car buyer to narrow down his field of choice too much. In the final analysis it is the condition of the actual car you buy that will determine your satisfaction, and limiting your options too stringently is unwise. Marque loyalty is a new-car buyer's prerogative that the second-hand buyer cannot afford. It is better to get a good example of your second favourite model, in the wrong colour, than to buy your first choice in poor condition.

Where to buy

It is always the shady car dealer who gives the motor trade a bad name; yet the majority are honest traders anxious to give the public a fair deal.

A lot of the troubles used-car buyers suffer are as much a surprise to the sellers as they are to the unfortunate new owners! Not that that lessens the inconvenience, ill-will or expense to the owner of course.

Fortunately, those garages which are usually well established and hold a franchise with one of the larger manufacturers not only sell good quality used cars but go to quite a lot of trouble to get them that way. What is more, they back their efforts with a worthwhile guarantee that significantly lessens the buyer's risk. The plain fact remains, though, that such cars cost more than an identical example bought from a back street trader or direct from the previous owner. The more you stand to gain, the bigger the gamble.

Playing safe by paying more

Try to buy from a dealer with a reputation as impressive as his premises. What you need is a good car and caring after-sales service, not sumptuous surroundings and 'special offers'.

Look closely at the guarantee. Verbal blandishments like 'We'll see you're all right' or a closely worded document giving you, for example, a year's guarantee on half the cost of the parts but no labour costs, is virtually worthless. Prefer the clearly worded, written undertaking that covers everything without exception, for a much shorter period of time, say 3 months or 3,000 miles.

Try to buy from an agent who holds a franchise for the make of car you are buying. Excellent cars *can* be bought at keener prices from a good garage that does not normally deal with that make in his service or new car sales departments. However, do not be surprised if he cannot get the parts or carry out repairs as efficiently.

If you are playing safe, get your Ford from a Ford dealer or your Peugeot from a Peugeot agent—even if it is going to cost you more there.

Never consider the car until it is properly prepared for sale. Do not rush to sign the order form or accept the car until the agent has put everything right that he said he would attend to. If you have to compromise on anything, make sure that it is a mere detail such as a defective cigarette lighter rather than a bent bumper or a noisy gearbox.

What about a discount?

Find out what the car is worth—used-car advertisements in the local paper indicate how much popular models are fetching. Even the dealer with the highest reputation is open to offers—you do not have to pay the price on the windscreen without question. Indeed, if you have no car to part-exchange, he may well give you discount in consideration of the fact that once he has sold to you, he has less of his money tied up in stock. There is no need to be coy even if you need HP facilities—the dealer will actually enhance his profit on the deal with the commission he collects from the finance house, so a discount should be even more feasible. At this point, we should consider the reputable dealer's dilemma about trade-ins. If you have gone to a first-class concern to buy a good and fairly priced car, they are unlikely to welcome your tired and rusty cast-off with a high part-exchange value. On the other hand, a flattering trade-in value offered by a less scrupulous dealer may indicate that he has no scruples about reselling a low quality car on his own used-car lot rather than disposing of it for less money in the trade. But do you want to buy from someone like that? It could be more expensive in the end.

Calling in the professionals

Even if all the foregoing conditions are met, test the garage's reaction to the prospect of the car being given an independent professional inspection such as the AA provides. If they welcome the idea, the car is probably as good as it looks. If they do not, it could well be that the car is in poor condition. Be suspicious. Really efficient garages are confident of the satisfactory condition of their stock, and are not afraid of an independent engineer's inspection. Some actually submit their cars to an inspection scheme before they are offered for sale to the public. If the vendor is happy to have his wares inspected, he may ask you to put a deposit on the car, which would be returnable only if the inspection report was generally unfavourable. (He does this to protect himself from the opportunities he might lose to sell the car to someone else while he is waiting for the engineer to come).

In other words, the buyer enters into a contract to purchase, subject to a satisfactory report, and must be prepared to forfeit his deposit if he opts to withdraw for other reasons.

Before you call in an engineer

Before calling in an expert to check a used car it pays to make sure that you are not wasting his time—and your money. Make this five point check. If the car fails any of them, look for another car.

1. Does it sit straight?

Cars that have been repaired after a serious accident sometimes refuse to sit squarely on their four wheels. With the car on level ground, stand about 20ft away and look at it critically from the front, rear and both sides. If it seems lop-sided, ask why. British Leyland cars with Hydrolastic or Hydragas 'float on fluid' suspension will lean to one side if suspension fluid has leaked out (1). A garage can correct this, but it often means replacing some fairly costly suspension components.

2. Is the paint original?

While you are standing back, check that all the body panels are the same colour. Spray painters finish repair work at body joins to disguise any slight mis-match. If a mis-match is obvious, ask about the repair work. If the complete car has been resprayed, all the panels will be the same colour, but there is almost certain to be a trace of the new paint on a window sealing rubber where it has crept under the masking tape (2). Ask why it was resprayed.

3. Is it rusty?

The most likely rust spots are the bottoms of doors, the front and rear top edges of the front wings, and at the edges of the wheel-arches. Any bumps or bulges in the paintwork (3) suggest that there is rust or a rust repair.

Beware of a leaning Leyland—its Hydragas suspension is probably leaking

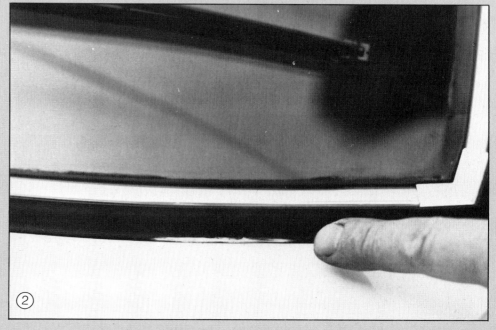

Carefully examine window sealing rubbers for signs of paint overspray

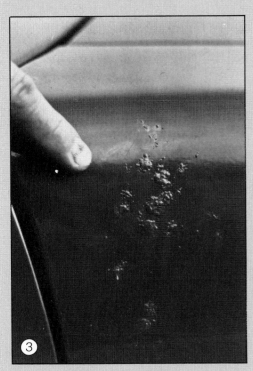

Watch out for bubbling caused by rust

Engineers check for the presence of plastic body filler under the paintwork by using a small magnet. This is attracted to sound metal, but does not react when placed on paint covering plastic body filler—it is a simple trick you can use yourself.

4. How is the interior?

It is best to avoid a car with a tatty interior, for although in theory it is possible to spruce up the inside by replacing damaged trim panels, few dealers carry such items in their spares stock and they can take months to order. Renewing a torn headlining is very costly and often involves taking out the windscreen and rear window. This means it is not a do-it-yourself job.

5. Listen to the engine

With the bonnet up, ask the owner to start the engine. It should start without too much bother (be suspicious if the engine has been warmed up in advance) and should run without excessive mechanical clatter. Air-cooled engines are noisier than water-cooled ones, but should run smoothly. An engine that is covered with oil is leaking and has probably been neglected. Ask who services the car.

Buying privately

It will be obvious by now that buying a used car from a reputable concern does a lot to lessen the risk. However, those with an eye to a bargain or whose financial position is pressing, may decide to buy privately.
There are some excellent second-hand buys sold at car auctions or in the classified ads—if only you can separate the good from the bad. Two similar cars of similar age may have been subjected to widely different treatment—and it is the second owner who will reap the results, for good or ill. There are, of course, some conclusions to be drawn—some obvious, some not so obvious—from this situation.

Buy a car you know

'Never sell a car to a friend,' may well be sound advice, yet by the same token buying from someone known to you could be a real advantage. In private deals the onus is on the buyer to ensure that the car is fit for his purpose. So long as the car is roadworthy, and the vendor has not made any false claims for it to help him sell it, the cost of repairing anything the buyer subsequently finds faulty, is clearly his responsibility—not the seller's.

It is a great advantage, therefore, to buy from someone whose word can be trusted and whose period of ownership has been observed, if only from a distance. 'Only used by two ladies to go to church,' and, 'Never been involved in an accident,' are reassuring statements only when you know they are true.

Get a reliable second opinion

Most private sellers will be relieved if you tell them that you know little about mechanics and do not intend to blame them if anything goes wrong later, and would prefer to let a mechanic or an AA engineer look it over—at your expense, of course.

Another worthwhile feature of a more elderly car is a recent MOT pass certificate. This by no means covers everything but should, in theory, ensure that essential repair work has been carried out; see pages 222-233.

Offer to pay by banker's draft

In private transactions, especially if the parties do not know each other, payment and exchange of the vehicle can be an embarrassment. The vendor may well seek time to clear a cheque, and on the

other hand the buyer may feel uneasy about handing his good cheque over without receiving the goods—the vendor could disappear with the car after cashing it. A banker's draft or even a building society cheque, made out in favour of the seller and handed over in exchange for the car, is usually a mutually satisfactory solution.

Do not spend all your money on the purchase

Try to buy the car of your choice for rather less than your total buying budget. In private purchases, particularly, an otherwise sound buy will often need minor attention, plus a thorough service to get it in good running trim. It even pays sometimes to have the car well cleaned and polished (inside, outside and underneath!) by professionals. This will not only make you a proud owner but will bring to light any minor blemishes which will only get worse if neglected.

Do not be side-tracked by gimmicks

Remember that you need a reliable car more than a stereo sound system or fancy number plates. Even the fact that a car has been 'rustproofed' is in itself no guarantee that it is not going rusty. Constant care and attention are more reassuring than a recent £100 repair bill, and even quite low mileage cars quickly become the unreliable victims of neglect and misuse. Conversely, do not dismiss the higher mileage car just because of its speedo reading; short journeys with a bad driver and infrequent oil changes can play far more havoc with a car's mechanical components than careful driving over long distances.

In a nutshell, buying a second-hand car does have its risks, but they can be reduced by careful forethought and wise negotiation. There will always be those who prefer 'new' to 'used', but for those whose assets fall short of what they know would make them happy, a well chosen, used example can be the best of all compromises.

Is the car his or hers to sell?

There was a time when you could buy a car from someone only to find it belonging to an HP company who promptly reclaimed it, leaving you with no car and no money. Nowadays, if you seek and obtain written reassurance from the vendor that the car is his own property, this confirms a good title to the vehicle on purchase and an HP company cannot 'snatch it back' even if the seller was lying.

ACCESSORIES

What you can do: Pages
Fit rear fog lights   254-255
Fit trailer-lighting sockets   256-257
Reverse the car's polarity   257
Fit an ammeter   258-259

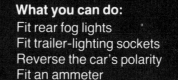

Although cars of the same make and model may look very much alike, they are bought by people who are completely unalike in their habits, tastes and personal preferences.

Fortunately, cars can be altered to suit the personality of the owner by adding accessories. A keen driver may fit high-power driving lights, rally-type seats and, perhaps, change to firmer dampers to improve the roadholding. A caravanning enthusiast will add all the necessary towing equipment, while a family motorist may add a child safety seat. Most owners will fit a radio or tape player.

Except for the more complicated extras such as sun-roofs and some high-security anti-theft systems, most accessories are designed so that they can be fitted by the average owner using a simple toolkit.

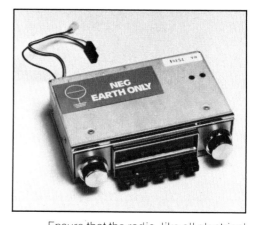

Ensure that the radio, like all electrical accessories, will suit the car's polarity

Choosing the right accessory

Before spending any money, make sure that you know exactly what you need. There is little point in buying a car radio with an FM band if you live in an area with poor FM reception, or buying an electrical extra that is designed for use on a car having the opposite battery polarity to your own.

Many of these problems can be avoided before you leave the accessory shop. Car radios and tape players, for instance, are clearly marked to indicate their suitability for positive- or negative-earth electrical systems, and the staff of a reputable accessory shop will always advise on the most suitable accessory for a particular purpose. Having decided that a certain accessory is suitable and can be fitted to the car, it is important to decide whether or not you can actually fit it yourself. Will special tools such as a soldering iron be needed, for example, and if so, will a suitable power supply be available?

It might be a better idea with complicated accessories, such as electronic ignition and anti-theft devices, to employ a garage to fit them.

Instructions

Although most accessories come with fitting instructions, simpler components, such as wing mirrors, are sometimes supplied without any. With these it pays to check where they are fitted on similar models before drilling any holes in the bodywork. The bonnet-opening arrangement on some cars, for example, means that a radio aerial cannot be fitted at the front – it must be fitted at the rear and an extension cable used to reach the receiver. Similarly, it is all too easy to position a wing mirror wrongly, where it is partly masked from the driver's view by a vertical window channel or a parked wiper blade. When the job is finished, keep any notes or fitting instructions in a safe place – they may be useful at a later date.

An aerial can be mounted at the front or rear, depending on the make and model of car

How accessories are fixed

Most add-on components are fixed to the bodywork and this involves drilling holes in the metal. But before you even plug in a power drill, find out if there are any regulations that specify where the accessory must be fitted. For example, rear fog lights must not be positioned closer than 100mm to a stop light. This sort of information should be given in the instructions.

Complying with regulations can involve you in extra expense. All road wheels, for instance, must be covered by 'mudguards', so if extra wide wheels are fitted, wing extensions must be added to make them legal.

Once you have decided on the correct position for an accessory, make sure that it will, in fact, fit. Remember to check behind any panel to be drilled for such items as brake pipes, electrical cables, the fuel tank, the fuel line or window glass, and make sure that any mounting bolt that protrudes through the panel cannot foul any of the moving components such as a window-winder mechanism.

Some body panels are double-skinned; this means that they consist of two panels that are separated by a small air gap. Conventional nuts and bolts cannot be used to fix an accessory to these areas because the nuts cannot be tightened, so self-tapping screws of the correct length must be used.

Double-skinned areas can be identified by pressing the outer panel inwards with one hand while feeling for movement on the inside with the other.

Heavy accessories should not be fitted to thin metal without extra bracing or reinforcement, otherwise the metal will flex each time the car goes over a bump, and eventually crack.

End view of fixing

If extra wide wheels are fitted, wing extensions
are needed to make them legal

MAKING HOLES

To some people, drilling a hole in a new car feels like a deliberate act of vandalism. And it can be if the hole is drilled in the wrong place or the job is botched. However, by following a few simple rules, all will be well.

First, work out where the hole is to be drilled and then, particularly where external bodywork is concerned, take steps to ensure that the drill cannot slip and score the surrounding paintwork.

Do not use a centre punch because it makes a dent in thin body metal. Instead, drill through a piece of masking tape stuck on the bodywork – this discourages the drill from slipping and provides a surface on which the hole position can be clearly marked (1).

Use a small drill first to provide a pilot hole (2) and gradually enlarge the hole by using progressively larger drill-bits. Large drills will often cut an untidy triangular-shaped hole in thin sheet metal and for this reason it is better when cutting large holes, such as are required for mirrors and aerials, to use a special hole-cutting tool, or to enlarge a small hole to its final size by using a round file (3).

Because it is very easy to withdraw the file from the hole accidentally and score the paintwork, wrap tape around it about $\frac{3}{4}$in from the end. This will prevent it from jumping out (4).

Where self-tapping screws are to be used, the fitting instructions will normally indicate the correct drill-bit diameter. It must make a hole slightly smaller than the diameter of the screw thread, but fractionally larger than the solid metal part of the screw in the centre.

Once the hole is made, protect the bare metal with a rust preventive and seal it with paint (5). If this is not done the paint around mirror and aerial mountings is likely to bubble and lift as rust creeps under the unprotected edges. If self-tapping screws are fitted while the paint is still wet, a better seal is provided.

A keyhole saw is used to make the large diameter hole for a radio speaker in a trim panel. After checking that there is sufficient room for the speaker to be mounted behind the panel without fouling anything, mark the size of the hole required, then drill a $\frac{3}{8}$in pilot hole just inside the line of the hole.

Use the keyhole saw to cut round the line (6), starting from the pilot hole.

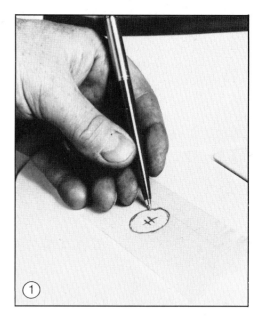

Place masking tape in position for drilling and mark the target on it

Use a small drill first, then enlarge the hole with progressively larger ones

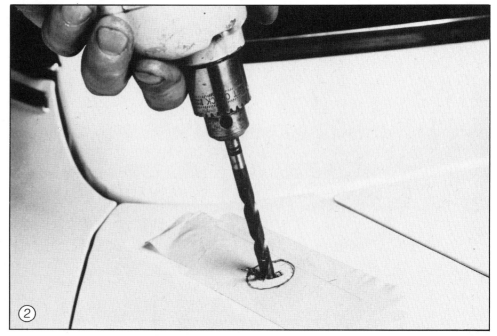

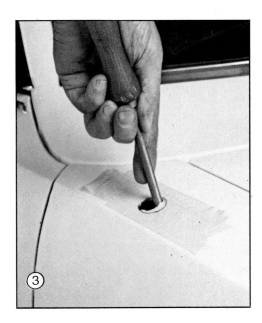

Do not try to make a hole with a large drill—it may cut a triangular-shaped hole. Use either a proper hole-cutting tool or drill a small hole and enlarge it with a round file

Having made the hole, protect the bare metal with a rust preventive and seal it well with paint. Failure to do so will mean that rust will creep under the unprotected edges

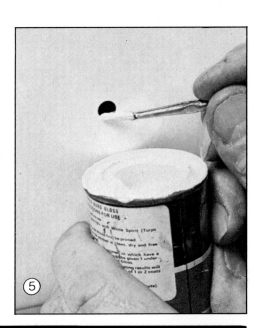

A keyhole saw is used for a large diameter hole needed for a radio speaker. Start from the pilot hole, and with the panel supported, use the saw from above to cut round the marked line

A length of insulating tape wrapped around the file near its end (about ¾in will do) will prevent it from jumping out and marking the paintwork

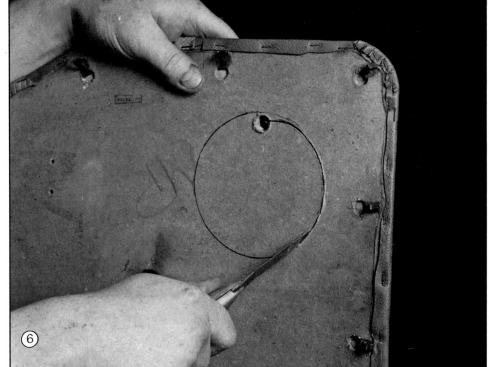

ELECTRICAL ACCESSORIES
Calculating the current

Before fitting an electrical accessory it is important to work out how much current it will need. If it is rated in watts, divide these by 12 (for cars with 12-volt systems) to find the current consumption. For instance, a 60-watt driving lamp will consume $\frac{60}{12}=5$amps. Knowing the current consumption enables you to decide whether or not the car can be fitted with certain types of accessory. The current consumption of the car's standard electrical equipment will have been calculated by its manufacturer, who then provides a suitable generator.

A typical electrical circuit has two headlights (approximately 60 watts each), a number of side, rear and panel lights (30 watts), heater and wiper motors (50 watts each), an ignition system (20 watts) and other items such as a clock and radio (about 20 watts). When everything is switched on, the total consumption of this layout is 290 watts or about 24amps.

If this car has a generator with a continuous maximum output of 30amps, there would be about 6amps left to operate any electrical accessories. So if an owner added a rear window heater (about 80 watts), two rear fog lights (21 watts each), and two driving lamps (40 to 60 watts each), a total of about 220 watts or an extra 18amps would be needed to cope with them. As this is not available, it will be necessary to fit a generator which has a higher continuously-rated output or at least an ammeter which will give the driver warning if current consumption exceeds generator output.

An ammeter will give warning if current consumption exceeds generator output

Making the right connections

Some electrical accessories, such as a rear window heater or an electric cooling fan having their own on/off switches, are best connected in such a way that they are automatically switched off with the ignition key. This prevents them from being left on and draining the battery.

However, before doing this, the current consumption of the accessory and whether or not it is inductive (contains coils of wire like an electric motor) must be considered. When inductive devices are switched off, arcs are produced by their windings which burn the switch contacts; this can lead to early failure of the ignition switch. As a rule, any accessory which is inductive (except a relay) and any accessories which together use more than a total of 3 to 4amps, should be supplied through an appropriate relay controlled by the ignition switch.

Accessories that are required to operate at all times, like a clock, or at any time, like an emergency four-way flasher system or an interior light, should be connected to a permanently live circuit so that they operate irrespective of the ignition switch position.

The easiest way to separate the ignition-switched and permanently live circuits is to study the car's wiring diagram and identify the different wires on the car by their colour. Where this is not possible, the fuse box lid or holder is normally marked to show the equipment supplied through each fuse. Connections can be made to the fuse box, which usually has spare connecting points.

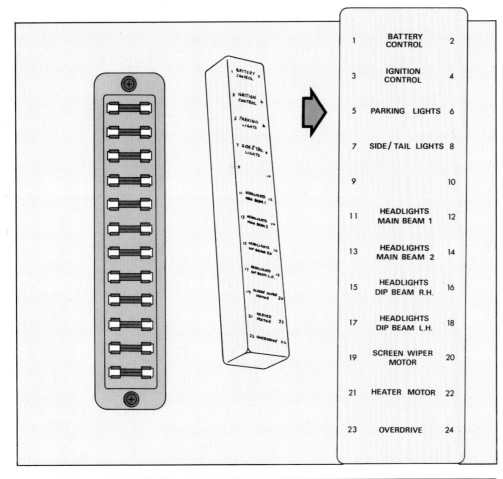

1	BATTERY CONTROL	2
3	IGNITION CONTROL	4
5	PARKING LIGHTS	6
7	SIDE / TAIL LIGHTS	8
9		10
11	HEADLIGHTS MAIN BEAM 1	12
13	HEADLIGHTS MAIN BEAM 2	14
15	HEADLIGHTS DIP BEAM R.H.	16
17	HEADLIGHTS DIP BEAM L.H.	18
19	SCREEN WIPER MOTOR	20
21	HEATER MOTOR	22
23	OVERDRIVE	24

The detachable fuse box lid or holder is normally marked to show the equipment supplied through each of the fuses

Wiring

The sort of wiring used in a car's electrical system has many thin strands of copper twisted together and covered with coloured PVC, which insulates it and aids identification. The thin strands resist work-hardening caused by vibration and movement which would break the sort of three-strand wire used for household appliances. A wire's current-carrying capacity can be determined by counting its strands. Low-capacity wire used by such circuits as sidelights, flashing indicators and rear fog lights, has 14 strands and is continuously rated at about 6amps. Medium-duty wire, as used for components such as the headlights, spot lights and wiper motors, has 28 strands and is continuously rated at approximately 17amps. Heavy-duty wire, which is used in the car's charging system, has 44 strands and is continuously rated at about 28amps. When wire is sold, the number of strands it contains is quoted. For instance, 28/0.30 wire has 28 strands, each of them with a diameter of 0.3mm.

The main wires used for connecting the battery are made from much heavier wire. The earth wire, which joins one battery terminal to the car body, is often braided and usually has no insulation. The main supply lead connecting the other battery terminal to the solenoid is about 10mm thick and insulated.

The current-carrying capacity of a wire is determined by the quantity and the diameter of the strands it contains

WIRE GRADES

Imperial	Amperage	Metric	Conductor Section
14/010″	6	14/0.25	0.7 m/m²
14/012″	8.75	14/0.30	1.0 m/m²
28/012″	17.5	28/0.30	2.0 m/m²
35/012″	21.75	35/0.30	2.5 m/m²
44/012″	27.5	44/0.30	3.0 m/m²
65/012″	35.0	65/0.30	4.5 m/m²

Connectors

Most car manufacturers use either 'bullet' or spade-type connectors to join wires together. Where equipment is joined with multi-wire connecting plugs it will be found that these have a number of bullet or spade connectors, some being reversed (male and female) to ensure correct plug and socket location. The various types are available from accessory shops.

Tapping into the wiring

The tidiest way to connect an accessory into the car's electrical system is at an existing connector. A straightforward single bullet connector sleeve can be replaced by a double sleeve which leaves two spare connecting points, both ready to accept additional accessory wires. Spade connectors can be made to take an extra wire by fitting a 'piggy-back' connector.

When an existing connector is unavailable, a blade-type connector can be used. The wires to be joined are held in the connector and a steel blade which cuts through their insulation is pressed into place with pliers. The blade makes contact with the copper core of each wire, connecting them together.

The principal advantage of blade connectors is that no soldering or special tools are needed to make a sound connection. Blade connectors for car electrics are usually pale blue in colour and have a current-carrying capacity of approximately 5amps.

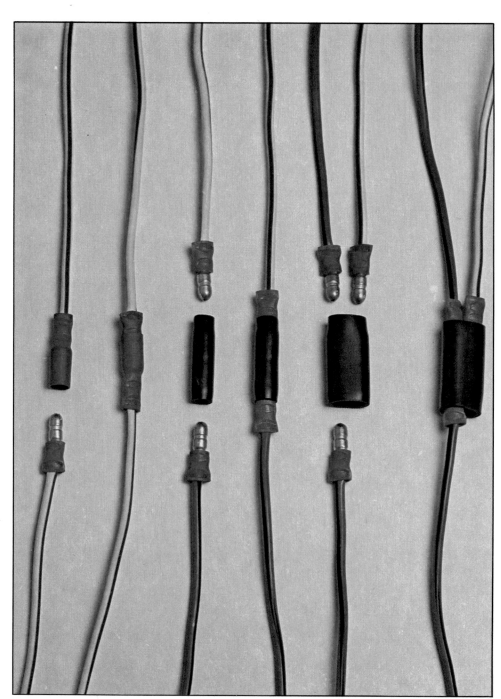

A single bullet connector sleeve may be replaced by a double sleeve, leaving two spare points for accessory wires

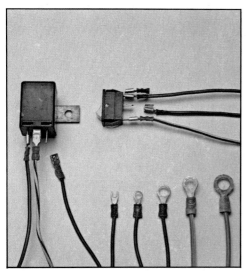

Push-on Lucar connectors are used for most vehicle electrical components

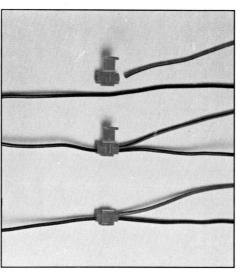

A blade-type connector joins two wires. The steel blade cuts into both

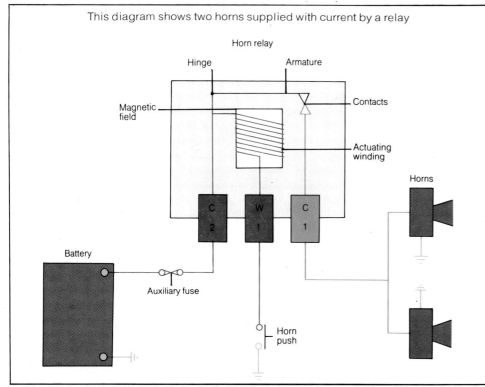

This diagram shows two horns supplied with current by a relay

Horn relay

Hinge — Armature

Magnetic field

Contacts

Actuating winding

Horns

C 2 — W 1 — C 1

Battery

Auxiliary fuse

Horn push

Relays

A relay is simply a remote controlled electrical switch. When a small current is passed through the relay-actuating winding it produces a magnetic field which attracts a flap of metal, known as an armature, closing two or more contacts together. These contacts can pass sufficient current to drive high current-consumption devices such as a pair of horns, without damaging the horn button which has only to provide the small relay-coil current.

While there are many different relays with many combinations of connecting terminals and markings, there are only two basic types, known as either continuously- or intermittently-rated relays. A continuously-rated relay is designed to be left for long periods of time with current passing through its actuating winding. It is used for fog and spot lamps or engine cooling fans. The actuating winding in an intermittently-rated relay will overheat and be damaged if current is passed through it for too long a period. This type of relay is designed to operate very fast, closing its contacts together very quickly to prevent, so far as possible, any arc occurring. It is used in high current applications, such as horn and main beam flasher circuits which are used for only short periods.

It is important, therefore, when buying a relay, and particularly when using one found in a junk box, to make sure that it is suitable for the intended application—continuous or intermittent. The relay-type can usually be checked by quoting its part number to one of its manufacturer's agents who will normally have reference information.

FITTING REAR FOG LIGHTS

All new cars manufactured since October 1979 or first used on or after 1 April 1980 must be fitted with at least one, but not more than two, rear fog lights. The regulations also make it an offence to connect rear fog lights in such a way that they operate as brake lights. This used to be a common practice.

The rear fog light is specially made with a large-area red lens and a 21-watt bulb (more than 25 watts are not allowed). It has to be 'E' marked and must be fitted to the car in such a way that no part of its lens is closer than 100mm from any part of a stop light lens. It should also be fitted between 1m and 250mm above the ground. If only one rear fog light is fitted it has to be mounted on the offside; two rear fog lights should be mounted symmetrically, one on each side (1).

Wiring connections

Regulations state that rear fog lights should be controlled by a switch which must also operate a warning light, and that they can be illuminated only when any front obligatory lamps, such as front side lights, are on.

First fit the lamps in a position where they comply with the regulations, and where they have some impact protection by being closer to the car than the outer face of the rear bumper. It is usually possible to mount them upright with the fixing bolts underneath (see 'Making holes' page 248) or upside down with the fixing bolt on top (2).

When inverting lamps it may be necessary to turn the front lens the other way up if it has a water drain hole in its mounting face.

Before making electrical connections, check with an agent for the car, because

If the red lens has a water drain hole in its mounting face the hole should be located at the bottom

Where to fit rear fog lights

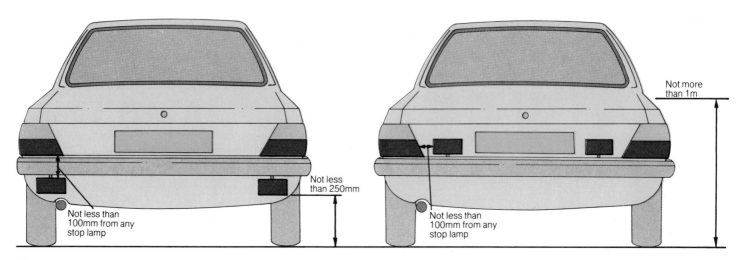

Not more than 1m

Not less than 250mm

Not less than 100mm from any stop lamp

Not less than 100mm from any stop lamp

When two rear fog lights are fitted ensure that they are symmetrical a spare wire for the rear fog lights may have been included in the wiring loom during manufacture.

Where an extra wire has to be fitted, always route it inside the car. A length of good quality, three-core PVC-covered mains cable, of the sort used for an electric lawn mower or a vacuum cleaner, is ideal as it will provide two spare feeds for any future electrical accessories.

Starting from behind the instrument panel, pass the wire under the carpets—preferably where they fold up the side of the inner door sill—under or around the rear seat and from there, into the boot.

Make sure that the wire cannot be trapped by the rear seat edge or seat belt mountings, and that it does not pass directly under a carpet where the occupants' feet are likely to tread.

Where the wire passes through a metal panel, make the hole larger than the wire and fit a rubber or plastic grommet to prevent chafing (3). Connect the wire to the fog lights.

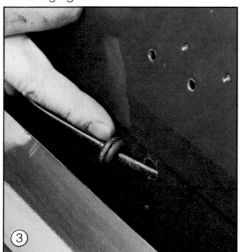

Connect the right fog light switch into the side lights circuit using a blade-type connector and a line fuse

The switch

Many cars are supplied with blanked-off switch positions on or near the instrument panel. For these, the car's franchised dealer may be able to provide a switch containing a warning light. If not, buy a sub-panel and an illuminated switch from an accessory shop and fit them in clear view at a convenient point under the facia.

Tapping the power

The rear fog light switch should be connected into the car side lights circuit (check the cable colour from the wiring diagram in the handbook) through a line fuse (4).

The fuse must have a value sufficient to supply the rear fog lights but not as high as the fuse protecting the side lights circuit. The actual connection to a side light wire can be made with a blade-type connector.

Connect the power supply to one switch terminal. The other terminal is connected to the wire feeding the fog lamps. A third terminal may be provided to give an earth return for the warning lamp (5). Test the lamps by turning on the side lights and operating the switch.

The warning light bulb is an integral part of a modern accessory switch. It is provided with its own earth terminal

To pass a wire through a metal panel, make the hole larger than the wire and fit a rubber or plastic grommet

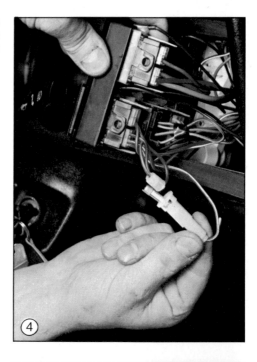

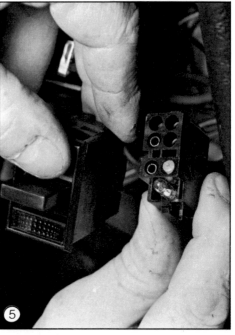

TRAILER OR CARAVAN ELECTRICS

Before the October 1979 rear fog light regulations, one seven-pin socket at the rear of the car supplied all the trailer's electrical needs, including current for accessories such as interior lights. Since the regulations, if the trailer requires an accessory supply, two sockets are needed. The seven-pin trailer-lighting socket is made to ISO (International Standards Organisation) Standard 1724 and is known as a 12N socket (1). The connection to pin 2 (blue wire) which once provided the trailer accessory supply, now feeds current to the trailer's rear fog lights. Some 12N sockets have an automatic cut-out which prevents the rear fog lights fitted to the car from lighting while a trailer is on tow (2).

Accessory socket

To supply current for trailer accessories or reversing lights, another seven-pin socket made to ISO 3732 – a 12S socket – is used. Both the 12N and 12S sockets look similar but have different pin arrangements which prevent them from accepting each other's plug.
To make the electrical connections to the car, pass the seven-core cable from the 12N socket and the cable from the 12S socket (if fitted) into the boot through holes with their edges protected by rubber grommets. Identify the different wires which supply the car's rear lights and direction indicators, and connect them to the socket, following the fitting instructions, and using bullet connectors.
Accessory supply current can be provided to the 12S socket (if required) by a wire passed through the car and

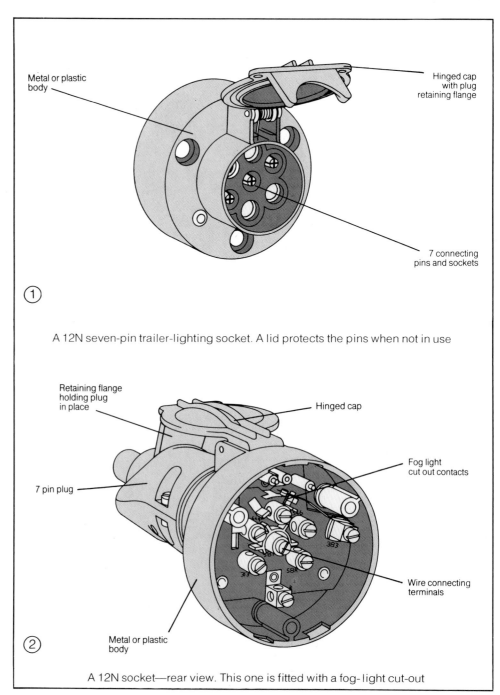

Metal or plastic body

Hinged cap with plug retaining flange

7 connecting pins and sockets

① A 12N seven-pin trailer-lighting socket. A lid protects the pins when not in use

Retaining flange holding plug in place

Hinged cap

7 pin plug

Fog light cut out contacts

Wire connecting terminals

Metal or plastic body

② A 12N socket—rear view. This one is fitted with a fog-light cut-out

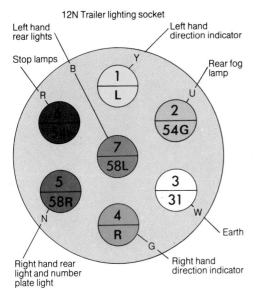

12N Trailer lighting socket

- Left hand rear lights
- Stop lamps
- Left hand direction indicator
- Rear fog lamp
- Right hand rear light and number plate light
- Right hand direction indicator
- Earth

Wire colour
Y = Yellow
U = Blue
W = White
G = Green
N = Brown
R = Red
B = Black

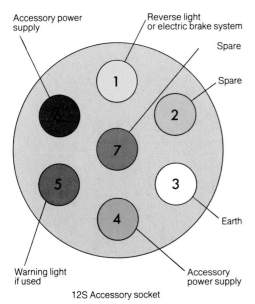

- Accessory power supply
- Reverse light or electric brake system
- Spare
- Spare
- Earth
- Accessory power supply
- Warning light if used

12S Accessory socket

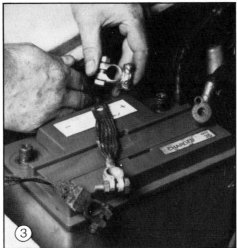

(3) Connect the battery the 'wrong' way round

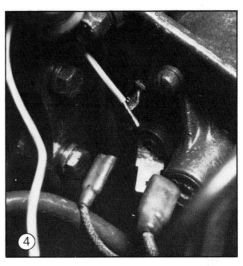

(4) Briefly touch the small dynamo terminal

connected to the battery through a line fuse, in much the same way as it is for the rear fog lights (see pages 254-255).

REVERSING POLARITY

Most cars have a 'negative earth' electrical system in which the negative terminal of the battery and negative output terminal of the generator are connected to the vehicle body which acts as a current-return system for all the electrical components.

Older cars fitted with dynamos may be positively earthed. This can be inconvenient because nowadays positive-earth radios, tape players and other electrical accessories are becoming increasingly rare.

It is surprisingly simple to convert a car from positive to negative earth operation. First connect the battery the 'wrong' way around, so that its negative terminal is earthed, if necessary using new wires and terminals (3).

The next step *before starting the engine*

is to repolarise the dynamo. To do this, remove the wire which is connected to the smaller of the two spade connectors on the end of the dynamo, then with a piece of wire, briefly touch the exposed dynamo terminal (4) to the positive battery terminal.

A small spark as the wire is removed indicates that a satisfactory connection has been made. The brief connection changes the polarity of residual magnetism in the dynamo field windings so that when the engine is started it will produce positive current from its output terminal. The two low-tension wires on the ignition coil should be swapped over.

Do not change the polarity if the car is already fitted with a radio or transistorised equipment as these will be damaged unless they, too, are changed to negative earth. All but a few alternators are designed for use with negative-earth systems and cannot have their polarity reversed.

FITTING AN AMMETER

An ammeter indicates whether or not the battery is receiving or supplying current. For example, if the headlights and heated rear window are in use and the fan belt is slipping, the generator may not be providing as much current as is being used. This will be shown on the ammeter as a discharge because the battery is supplying current to supplement the generator output.

The result is that eventually the battery would become flat.

When fitting an ammeter, remember that all the current passing to and from the battery, with the exception of that used by the starter motor, will pass through it. There are no fuses, and a short circuit with its connecting wires will most certainly cause a fire, so care and adequate insulation and protection are essential. The wire used for the ammeter must be capable of carrying maximum generator output. Cars with a generator output of 35amps, for instance, will need 65/0.30 cable (see table on page 251). Generator output will be given in the car handbook or workshop manual.

First examine the battery live terminal and ensure that it has only one very thick wire connected to it, which goes to the starter motor solenoid. At the solenoid, mark with sticky tape all the wires connected to the same terminal as the battery lead (1). Wires connected to other solenoid terminals should not be disturbed.

Disconnect the battery and remove all the marked wires (but not the main battery lead) from the solenoid. Bare the ends, twist them together, then solder them to a wire leading to the ammeter (2). Make sure that the joint is well insulated. At the other end of the wire, solder on a terminal tag and connect it to one ammeter terminal. From the other ammeter terminal connect a second wire of the same length, using a suitable tag. The second wire should then be connected to the solenoid terminal using a suitable terminal tag, together with the main battery lead (3). This connects the ammeter in series between the removed wires and the battery. Any extra wires found connected to the battery terminal in the first inspection should be joined to the wires removed from the solenoid terminal, which are soldered to the ammeter wire.

Test the ammeter by reconnecting the battery and switching on the headlights; if it shows a charge instead of a discharge it is connected the wrong way round. Disconnect the battery and interchange the ammeter connections to make it indicate correctly (4). Reconnect the battery.

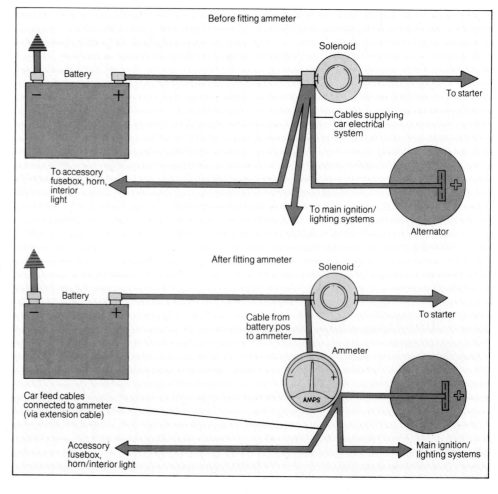

Before fitting ammeter

Battery
Solenoid
To starter
Cables supplying car electrical system
To accessory fusebox, horn, interior light
To main ignition/ lighting systems
Alternator

After fitting ammeter

Battery
Solenoid
To starter
Cable from battery pos to ammeter
Ammeter
Car feed cables connected to ammeter (via extension cable)
Accessory fusebox, horn/interior light
Main ignition/ lighting systems

Identify all the wires at the solenoid

Solder the wires to the ammeter wire

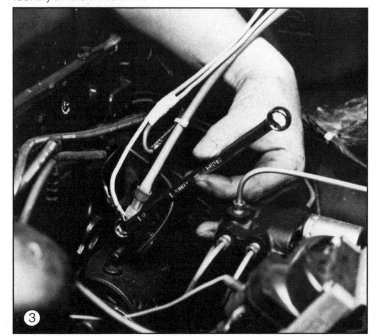

Connect ammeter wire to the solenoid

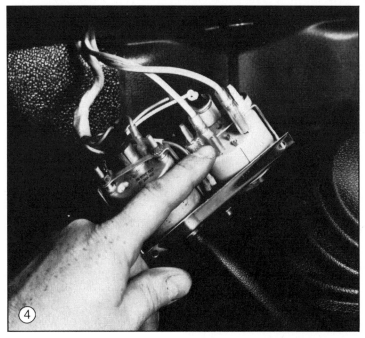

If necessary, reverse the connections

MUSIC ON THE MOVE

What you can do: Pages

Fit radio or tape-player   262-263
Fit the aerial   264-265
Fit the speakers   266-267
Cure interference   267-269

The most commonly fitted car accessory is some sort of audio system—either a radio, a cassette tape-player, or both. But, unless the system is properly planned and fitted, reception can be disappointing. Fitting an audio system falls into four distinct areas: wiring up the receiver or cassette player; fitting an aerial; fitting speakers; eliminating interference.

All these are dealt with on the following pages.

FITTING A RADIO OR TAPE-PLAYER

Before choosing a car radio you should decide if you need one with an FM stereo channel as well as the usual long and medium AM channels. FM sets are more expensive than AM-only receivers and can be unsatisfactory if you live in an area where FM reception is poor. Take advice from a radio specialist. FM sets also pick up interference more easily than AM receivers.

Car radios fitted with a tape-player are large and fairly heavy. Before buying one, decide where it is to be fitted and take measurements. This is particularly important if you intend using the radio aperture normally provided in the facia panel. Remove the blanking plate and measure the area behind it (1).

Make sure there is enough room behind the facia to accept the receiver

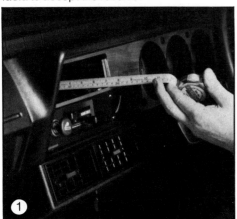

Fitting kits

On most modern cars provision is made for fitting a radio. But few sets are sold with a loud-speaker, mounting brackets or fitting instructions. These are provided separately as part of a fitting kit and will be tailored to fit a particular car.

If the radio is being moved from one car to another of a different make or model it is worth buying a new fitting kit (2) so that it can be properly fitted with the minimum amount of trouble. A radio

If the fixing screws are too long they could easily damage the set

A new fitting kit makes it neater and easier to relocate the set in a different car

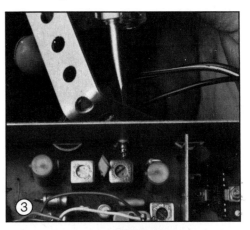

simply bolted up under the facia or parcel shelf is easy to steal and could cause leg injury in an accident.

All but very lightweight radios will need to be fixed by rear and possibly side mountings, as well as those at the front. Make sure that bolts screwed into the side or rear of the set are not too long. If they protrude into the set by more than about 1/16in (3) they may touch something vital.

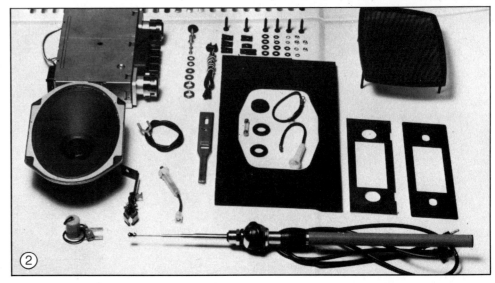

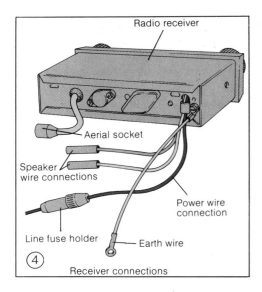

Radio receiver

Aerial socket

Speaker wire connections

Power wire connection

Line fuse holder

Earth wire

④ Receiver connections

Connecting up

The type of electrical connections used on radios and tape-players are usually quite straightforward (4).

The speaker hook-up is normally made with a plug and socket, and where two speakers are used the wire colours or the shape of connector plugs prevents a wrong connection from being made. Make sure that when positioning speaker-connecting wires under carpets and across door jambs they are protected and cannot get trapped or damaged.

Plug and socket connectors make it easier to wire up the receiver

The earth connection between the radio case and bodywork should be well made using a short, braided earth-strap. Do not rely on the aerial lead's screening braid for an earth—this makes interference suppression much more difficult.

Power for the radio normally comes from a circuit connected to the accessory position of the ignition switch. This ensures that the radio is turned off when the ignition key is removed but enables the driver to listen to it when the car is parked, by turning the key to the accessory position.

Most cars have a combined ignition switch and steering lock which has its connecting wires soldered on. A radio connection is made at the multi-pin plug and socket assembly containing the switch wires, which is normally found just under the facia near the steering column.

The colour of the accessory wire can be found in the car wiring diagram or it can be identified with a test lamp. The wire will become 'live' and light up a test lamp when the key is turned to the accessory position (5). Connections can be made directly to the plug and socket with a bullet or spade connector or to the wire with a blade-type connector (see page 252).

The radio supply lead will almost certainly contain a line fuse having a value of 1 or 2amps, and there may also be a radio suppression choke in another fuse holder, provided as part of the fitting kit. The supply lead should be cut to the required length. If extra lead is coiled up and tucked behind the facia panel it can make interference suppression difficult.

If you do not know the colour of the accessory wire, it can be identified with a test lamp

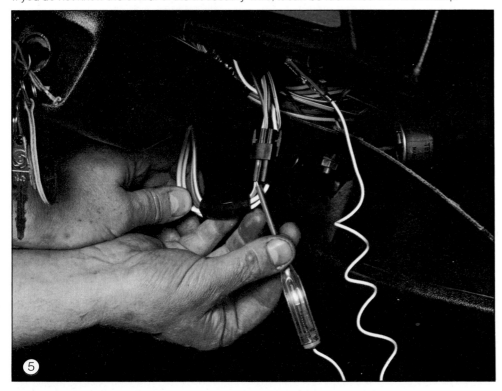

⑤

PICKING UP THE SIGNAL

Most cars are virtually a metal box which prevents the entry of radio signals and, to a large extent, keeps in any interference generated by its electrical equipment. The only way that a radio can perform satisfactorily in this environment is to pass any outside radio signals to it through a metal 'tunnel', which prevents the entry of interference or the escape of the signal.

The car aerial does this, with its co-axial connecting lead (covered by an outer braided screen) acting as the tunnel. The best quality aerials combine good signal collecting properties with a co-axial cable that does not allow signal losses.

Aerial position

To help the aerial collect signals efficiently and to prevent the entry of radiated interference, the position of the aerial on the car bodywork is an important factor.

Most car manufacturers provide good quality aerials, with fitting instructions for correct aerial positioning on their different models. Where this information is not available, see where the aerial is fitted on the majority of cars of the same make and type as your own. Where the aerial is to be fitted on steeply sloping bodywork, make sure that it has the correct mounting.

Before drilling any holes, check that there is room below the panel to accept the aerial (1). Remember also that the lead must reach the radio set—sometimes a good quality extension lead may be required.

When planning the route of the lead, try to keep it out of the engine compartment as much as possible and do not pass it through holes with other wires, as these may introduce interference. Fit a rubber grommet into any hole before threading through the lead.

Ideally, the mounting hole in the bodywork should be made with a hole-cutting tool after a pilot hole has been made with a drill (2). To prevent the drill from slipping, stick a piece of masking tape to the bodywork (see page 248).

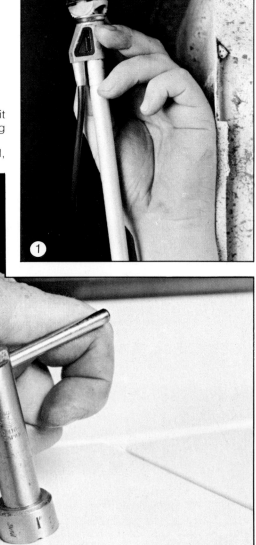

Check that the aerial will fit up under the wing

To make a clean, accurate hole for the aerial, use a hole-cutting tool

Earthing the aerial

It is important that the aerial outer cover makes a good electrical connection with the bodywork. Remove thick underbody sealant, but rather than cleaning it all away as is often advised, make sure that the points on the earthing plate are sufficiently proud, bending them and filing them sharp if necessary (3). As the aerial-mounting nut is tightened (4) they will press through the body sealant and paint to make contact with the metal body. Remember to fit the bottom stay provided with the aerial (5). This prevents it moving and disturbing the earth connection with the bodywork.

The last job is to trim the aerial using the trimming screw on the radio set (6). The radio maker will usually suggest that a weak signal near the lower frequency end of the medium waveband is used.

Check the earthing plate points

Tighten the aerial-mounting nut

Fit and adjust the bottom stay

Use a weak station to trim the set

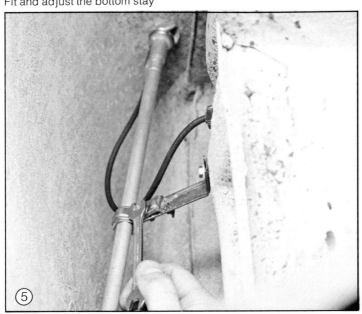

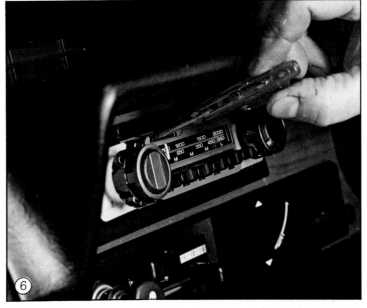

WHAT YOU SHOULD KNOW ABOUT SPEAKERS

Even the best possible radio, fitted in an interference-free car with an efficient aerial, will produce only mediocre sound quality if the speaker is not positioned properly, if it does not match the system, or it is in any way damaged. Speakers have a delicate diaphragm made from a type of thin card that is easily damaged. If they are fitted in doors without proper protection from the water which inevitably runs down the door window glass, they can be ruined in a very short time.

Even sudden changes in air pressure can wreck the diaphragm. A speaker fitted in the rear parcel shelf between the interior of the car and the boot should have large gaps or holes around it under the grille, otherwise the diaphragm can be damaged by air pressure trying to turn it inside out when the boot lid or a car door is slammed.

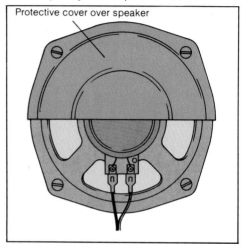

Fit covers over door-mounted speakers to stop them being ruined by rain water running down the windows

Check that the speaker impedance is suitable. One of the terminals is marked for stereo use

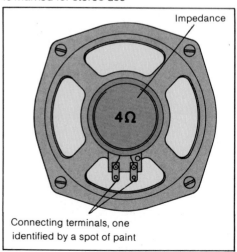

Connecting terminals, one identified by a spot of paint

Impedance

Speakers provided in a radio-fitting kit will be of the correct shape to fit any speaker location built into the car. They will also be of the correct impedance to match the type of radio used. Where a fitting kit is not being used, it is important that the speaker impedance (stated in ohms) is suitable for the radio in question. Speaker impedances are usually 3, 4, 8 or 15 ohms. It is usually possible to fit a speaker of higher impedance than recommended (though performance may be affected), but a lower impedance speaker should not be used as it can damage the radio output circuit. The output circuit may also be damaged if the radio is turned on with the speaker disconnected or its connecting leads are short-circuited.

Holes under the grille prevent air pressure from damaging the speaker

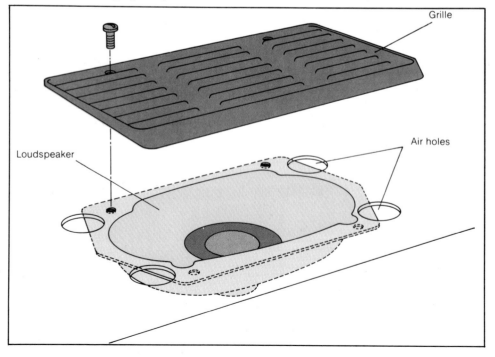

STEREO SYSTEMS

When two speakers are used for a stereo system, it is important to connect them so that they operate in phase with each other. This means that their diaphragms move to and fro together rather than one forward as the other goes back—in effect, trying to cancel each other out. Most speakers are connected with a twin wire which has black insulation. The wires can be identified individually because one usually has a white stripe down it, or one wire will be of plain copper and the other of tinned copper. It is normal for one of the two terminals on the speaker to have a red spot of paint or some other mark on it. Both speakers should be connected so that the speaker wires with the same identification are connected to the marked speaker terminals.

Where two speakers are used with a mono system, one is usually fitted at the front of the car and the other at the rear. A balance control can be added which enables speaker outputs to be varied in relation to each other, although the overall volume is adjusted at the set.

Interference—and how to cure it

A radio transmitter sends a signal by feeding a rapidly changing high-frequency electrical current to a suitable aerial. Similarly, any rapidly changing electrical current produced in the supply wires of equipment, such as a car's ignition and charging systems,

For stereo use, join the same terminal on each speaker to the radio

instrument stabilizer and wiper motor, will also transmit radio signals. The differences between these signals and those transmitted by a radio station are their strength and the fact that when they are processed by a radio receiver they produce a disorientated noise.

Unwanted radio signals usually enter the receiver in two ways: as radiated interference through the aerial or as power supply interference through the radio connecting leads. There are three ways of reducing it:

Screen the source of interference and prevent it escaping.

Make any 'aerial' it is using (its supply wires) as inefficient as possible to reduce the transmitted signal.

Slow down the rate of current change, thus preventing transmission.

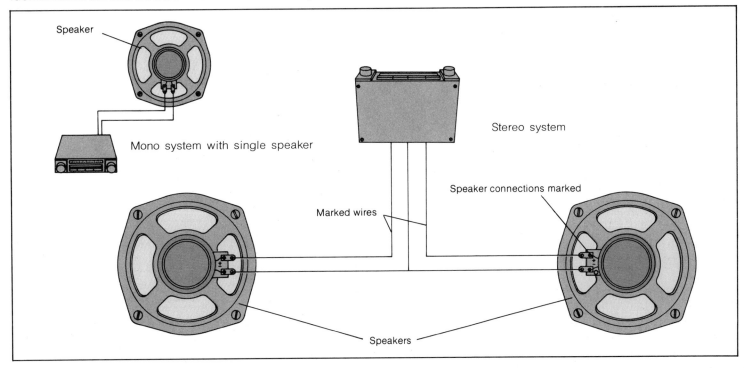

Speaker

Mono system with single speaker

Stereo system

Speaker connections marked

Marked wires

Speakers

Ignition interference

The ignition system is the biggest cause of interference and all three methods of suppression are normally required. The engine compartment is itself a metal box and will contain most of the radiated interference while the bonnet is closed. In this respect, replacement glass-fibre bonnets and wings can produce a radio interference problem because they are 'transparent' to radio signals.

High tension leads from the ignition coil, spark plugs and distributor are made of resistive cable. This is because a resistor makes an inefficient aerial. If the cables are old and their internal conductors are broken, the plug caps are ill-fitting or the leads have been replaced with copper-core cable in a misinformed attempt to cure an ignition problem, interference will be excessive. Check the leads and plug caps carefully. Change them if in doubt.

The ignition coil is connected to the ignition switch from which the radio supply is also normally provided. Pulses produced by the coil have to be reduced and this is done by a capacitor which absorbs the sharp pulses to reduce interference.

On a coil, a radio suppression capacitor is connected between a good earth (usually the coil-bracket bolt) and the ignition switch supply terminal on the coil. In the same way, a capacitor will often be required between the output lead of the generator and a good nearby earthing point.

Alternators may need a capacitor with a higher electrical value than the type used for the ignition coil. These can be bought from a car radio or vehicle electrical specialist.

INTERFERENCE CHECK-CHART

CONDITION	CAUSE	CURE
Clicking, crackling noise keeping pace with engine	Ignition system	1. Ensure resistive plug leads are fitted 2. Check for badly fitting plug caps 3. Fit suppression capacitor to coil supply terminal 4. Make sure the metal body of the coil makes a good earth 5. Check that there is a good earth connection between bonnet lid and car body. If necessary make one using an earthing strap 6. Ensure that the aerial lead is not passing through holes with other wires 7. Fit a choke in radio supply lead 8. Check that the aerial is fitted in the right position
Whining noise (above engine tickover speed)	Generator	Fit suppression capacitor between main output lead and earth
Regular clicking/grating noise every 1 to 3 seconds (ignition switched on)	Instrument voltage stabilizer	Fit suppression capacitor and choke in stabilizer supply lead
Crackling when wipers are in use	Wiper motor	Ensure that the motor body is earthed; fit supply lead choke-cluster kit
Whine or crackling when heater in use	Heater motor	Fit a choke and capacitor to supply lead
Regular clicking noise (ignition switched off)	Clock	Fit a suppression capacitor and choke in supply lead

Chokes

To eliminate interference from some components, a choke is needed as well as a capacitor. The choke is a small coil of wire which produces a magnetic field when fitted in the supply lead of a component. The strength of the field changes as the interference pulses occur, effectively cancelling out the pulse. Chokes can be bought with suitable connectors which enable them to be fitted easily to wiper motors, tachometers, clocks, heater motors and fuel pumps.

General

Tidiness can be a fault. It is important not to coil together extra aerial, speaker and radio supply leads and tuck them behind the instrument panel.
Interference will be passed between them, because coiling the wire creates a crude transformer.
If possible, ensure that speaker and aerial wires do not pass through the same holes in the bodywork as other wires in the car's electrical system.

NINE WAYS OF CURING INTERFERENCE

Radio interference can be subdued by fitting suitable capacitors or chokes—sometimes both—to the component causing the trouble. The chart on the previous page will enable you to identify the source of the interference: the drawings on the right show where the capacitors should be fitted.
Interference from resistive ignition leads can usually be cured by fitting a new set of leads.

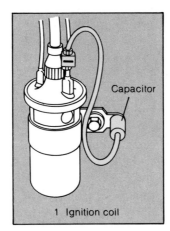

1 Ignition coil

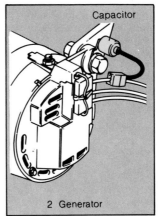

2 Generator

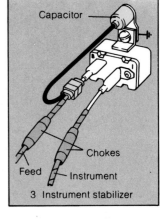

3 Instrument stabilizer

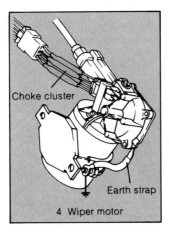

4 Wiper motor

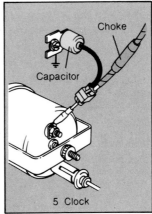

5 Clock

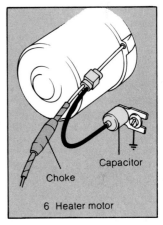

6 Heater motor

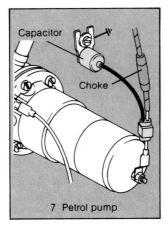

7 Petrol pump

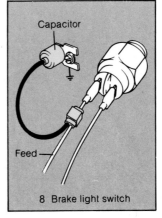

8 Brake light switch

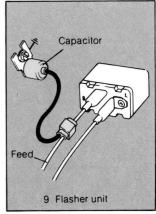

9 Flasher unit

CURING FAULTS

Fault-finding charts   272-277
Diagnosis in detail   278-285

No amount of understanding of the mechanical and electrical systems of a motor car can compensate for the ability to recognise a fault, trace its origins, and find out how to put it right.

That is why this book, which as its title suggests, is designed to inform on a broad spectrum of motor engineering, would be incomplete without a detailed diagnosis of the most common engine faults that can occur during the lifetime of the vehicle.

Many owners possessing only limited mechanical knowledge are tempted, when something goes wrong, to make quick assumptions which can lead to false conclusions. Faults rarely present themselves in an orderly way, and it is therefore only too easy to miss vital clues to the source of the problem.

The quick-reference charts in this section will give an at-a-glance opportunity to make a quick diagnosis of the trouble and help you to find out how to rectify it.

The charts cover virtually all the engine faults you can meet—from the mild irritation of an erratic idler to the ultimate frustration of a non-starter. Each chart is drawn up in the form of a series of questions which need either a YES or NO answer.

If the answer is YES, follow the green arrows; if it is NO, follow the red arrows. Every 'car' in the charts has a number which relates to a numbered step in the text that follows, in which the most likely causes are detailed.

It is important to remember that the charts are designed to be read from the

START point and should be followed through to the point where the fault applies. For example:

If the engine will not start, refer to the start point (extreme left) in Chart 3, *Does starter turn the engine?* asks Car 43. Turn to the note in Step 43. If the answer is YES, follow the green arrows to Car 19, *Slowly press throttle to floor, return choke and try again. Does engine start?* Turn to Step 19 for further symptoms. Armed with this additional information, it should be possible to give a second YES or NO answer, and so follow the arrows to the next question.

Continue the procedure until the trouble has been satisfactorily diagnosed by means of either the chart or the text, or by deduction made by piecing together the clues gleaned from both sources.

Chart 1 Engine will not turn

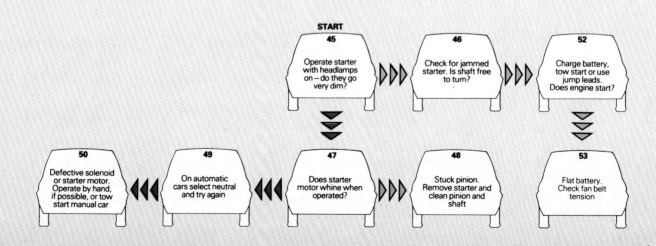

Chart 2 Engine will not start (electrical faults)

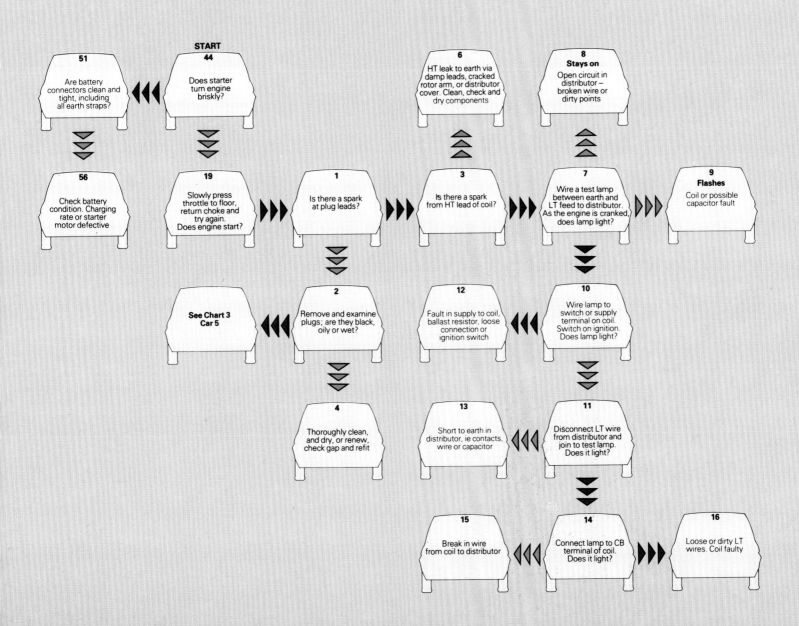

51 Are battery connectors clean and tight, including all earth straps?

START 44 Does starter turn engine briskly?

6 HT leak to earth via damp leads, cracked rotor arm, or distributor cover. Clean, check and dry components

8 Stays on Open circuit in distributor – broken wire or dirty points

56 Check battery condition. Charging rate or starter motor defective

19 Slowly press throttle to floor, return choke and try again. Does engine start?

1 Is there a spark at plug leads?

3 Is there a spark from HT lead of coil?

7 Wire a test lamp between earth and LT feed to distributor. As the engine is cranked, does lamp light?

9 Flashes Coil or possible capacitor fault

See Chart 3 Car 5

2 Remove and examine plugs; are they black, oily or wet?

12 Fault in supply to coil, ballast resistor, loose connection or ignition switch

10 Wire lamp to switch or supply terminal on coil. Switch on ignition. Does lamp light?

4 Thoroughly clean, and dry, or renew, check gap and refit

13 Short to earth in distributor, ie contacts, wire or capacitor

11 Disconnect LT wire from distributor and join to test lamp. Does it light?

15 Break in wire from coil to distributor

14 Connect lamp to CB terminal of coil. Does it light?

16 Loose or dirty LT wires. Coil faulty

Chart 3 Engine will not start (fuel faults)

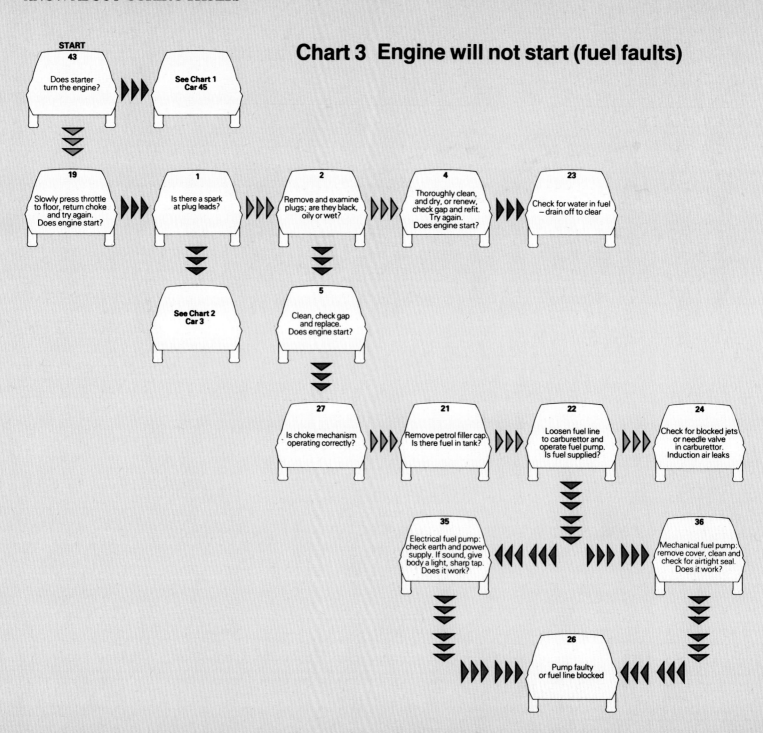

START
43 Does starter turn the engine?

See Chart 1 Car 45

19 Slowly press throttle to floor, return choke and try again. Does engine start?

1 Is there a spark at plug leads?

2 Remove and examine plugs; are they black, oily or wet?

4 Thoroughly clean, and dry, or renew, check gap and refit. Try again. Does engine start?

23 Check for water in fuel – drain off to clear

See Chart 2 Car 3

5 Clean, check gap and replace. Does engine start?

27 Is choke mechanism operating correctly?

21 Remove petrol filler cap. Is there fuel in tank?

22 Loosen fuel line to carburettor and operate fuel pump. Is fuel supplied?

24 Check for blocked jets or needle valve in carburettor. Induction air leaks

35 Electrical fuel pump: check earth and power supply. If sound, give body a light, sharp tap. Does it work?

36 Mechanical fuel pump: remove cover, clean and check for airtight seal. Does it work?

26 Pump faulty or fuel line blocked

Chart 4 Engine will not tick-over smoothly

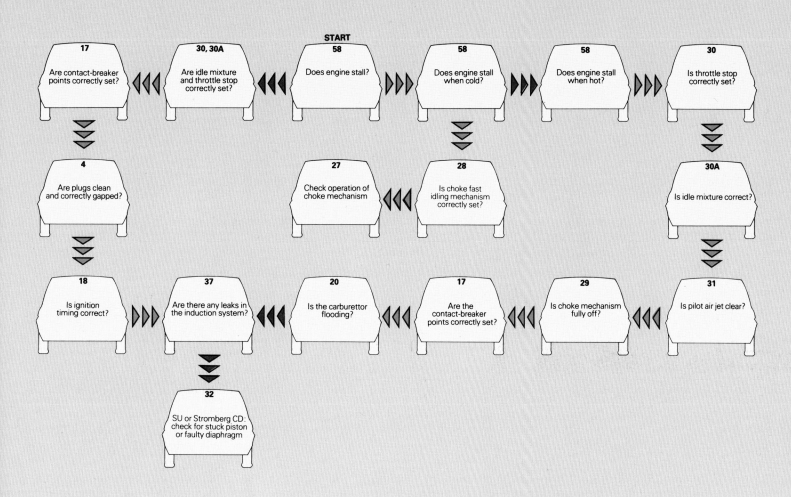

17 — Are contact-breaker points correctly set?

30, 30A — Are idle mixture and throttle stop correctly set?

START **58** — Does engine stall?

58 — Does engine stall when cold?

58 — Does engine stall when hot?

30 — Is throttle stop correctly set?

4 — Are plugs clean and correctly gapped?

27 — Check operation of choke mechanism

28 — Is choke fast idling mechanism correctly set?

30A — Is idle mixture correct?

18 — Is ignition timing correct?

37 — Are there any leaks in the induction system?

20 — Is the carburettor flooding?

17 — Are the contact-breaker points correctly set?

29 — Is choke mechanism fully off?

31 — Is pilot air jet clear?

32 — SU or Stromberg CD: check for stuck piston or faulty diaphragm

Chart 5 Engine is noisy and sluggish

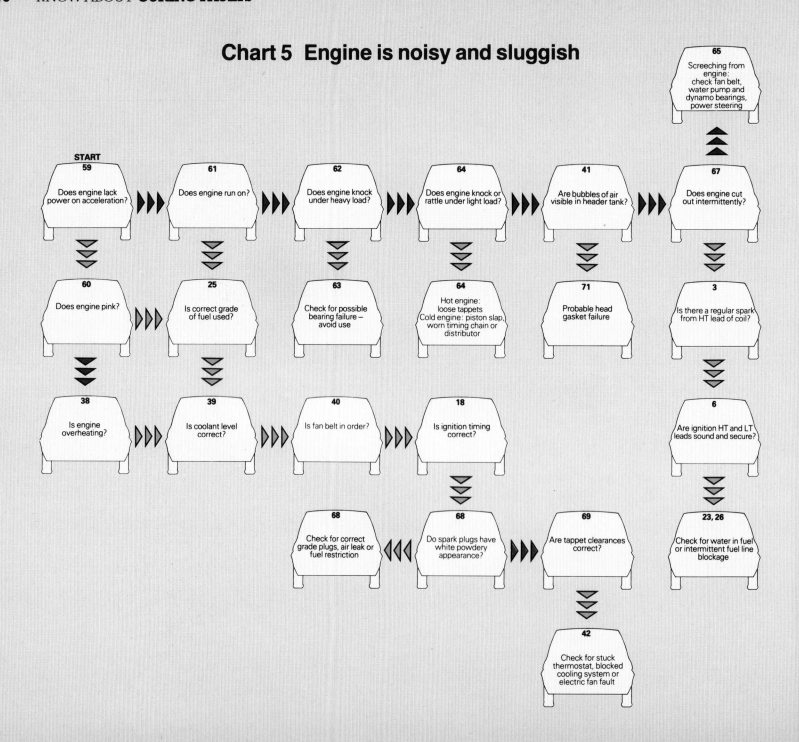

65 — Screeching from engine: check fan belt, water pump and dynamo bearings, power steering

START

59 — Does engine lack power on acceleration?

61 — Does engine run on?

62 — Does engine knock under heavy load?

64 — Does engine knock or rattle under light load?

41 — Are bubbles of air visible in header tank?

67 — Does engine cut out intermittently?

60 — Does engine pink?

25 — Is correct grade of fuel used?

63 — Check for possible bearing failure – avoid use

64 — Hot engine: loose tappets Cold engine: piston slap, worn timing chain or distributor

71 — Probable head gasket failure

3 — Is there a regular spark from HT lead of coil?

38 — Is engine overheating?

39 — Is coolant level correct?

40 — Is fan belt in order?

18 — Is ignition timing correct?

6 — Are ignition HT and LT leads sound and secure?

68 — Check for correct grade plugs, air leak or fuel restriction

68 — Do spark plugs have white powdery appearance?

69 — Are tappet clearances correct?

23, 26 — Check for water in fuel or intermittent fuel line blockage

42 — Check for stuck thermostat, blocked cooling system or electric fan fault

Chart 6
Engine lacks power

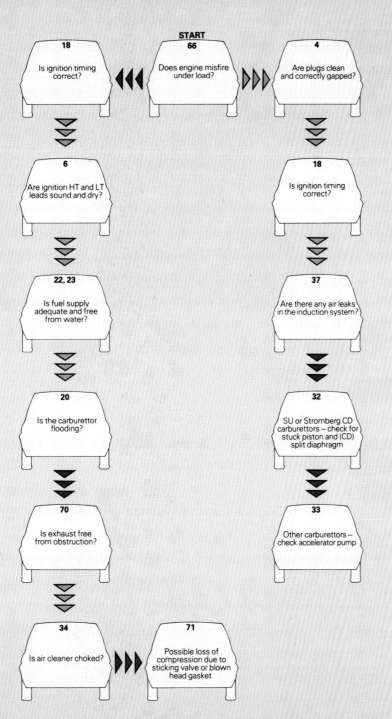

18 Is ignition timing correct?

◄◄◄ **START 66** Does engine misfire under load? ►►►

4 Are plugs clean and correctly gapped?

6 Are ignition HT and LT leads sound and dry?

18 Is ignition timing correct?

22, 23 Is fuel supply adequate and free from water?

37 Are there any air leaks in the induction system?

20 Is the carburettor flooding?

32 SU or Stromberg CD carburettors – check for stuck piston and (CD) split diaphragm

70 Is exhaust free from obstruction?

33 Other carburettors – check accelerator pump

34 Is air cleaner choked? ►►►

71 Possible loss of compression due to sticking valve or blown head gasket

STEP 1 Test for a spark by asking a helper to work the ignition switch while you check the spark plug leads. Take off a lead from one of the plugs and hold it about ⅛in away from a good earth point—the exhaust manifold, for example. Do not hold it close to the carburettor or a breather vent. With the starter turning the engine, you should see and hear a crisp spark jumping from the lead to earth.

If the plug lead connector is deeply recessed in a rubber shroud, push a piece of wire or a nail into the connector to form an improvised conductor.

 2 Before detaching the plug leads, label them so that they can be refitted in the correct order. Remove the spark plugs, keeping these in order, too.

Examine the plug electrodes to see if they are choked with carbon deposits or are black or oily. A plug in good condition should be light brown or grey in colour; soot or oil on an electrode may prevent a spark from passing.

Sooty plugs indicate that the carburettor mixture is too rich. Wet plugs suggest excessive use of the choke, causing petrol flooding. Oily plugs mean worn valve guides or piston rings.

 3 Remove the HT (king) lead from the centre of the distributor cap and pull back its insulating sleeve to expose the metal connector. With the ignition switched on, carry out the spark test as described in Step 1. If you can see and hear a spark the ignition coil is operating correctly.

4 Wet plugs smelling of petrol mean that fuel is reaching the cylinders. A wet plug but no smell of petrol can mean that there is a water leak past the cylinder head gasket, or there is water in the fuel system. Spark plugs that are sooted up or choked with carbon deposits can be thoroughly cleaned by a sand-blasting machine used by garages. But make sure that the plugs are well washed in petrol afterwards, to remove all traces of loose grit.

Examine the plug outer electrodes. If the tips and/or the centre electrodes are burnt away, the plugs should be renewed. It is always best to renew the plugs in sets.

Before fitting new or cleaned plugs, check and, if necessary, adjust the gap by bending the side electrode to the correct figure (usually 0.025in) as shown in the car handbook or workshop manual. Also ensure that the sealing gaskets are in good condition, then refit the plugs. Connect the HT leads in the correct order.

 5 Check the condition of the plug electrodes: if necessary, clean them. If the tips of the centre electrodes are dome-shaped, use a small contact file to square them off. Check the gaps and refit the plugs as detailed in Step 4.

 6 If Step 3 showed the coil to be working correctly but there is no spark at the plug leads (Step 1), high-tension current is leaking to earth somewhere between the coil and the plugs.

Ask a helper to operate the starter while

you listen along the leads for a sharp clicking sound, especially near places where they may be attached by clips. At night or in a dark garage, a spark or blue flash may be visible, indicating where the short is occurring. If you cannot see or hear the wayward spark, remove the distributor cap and dry it thoroughly inside and out. Also dry the top of the coil and all the HT leads and plug covers.

With the distributor cap removed, check inside it for fine random lines or cracks along which HT current could run to earth.

Examine the rotor arm for similar faults, too. If either the cap or the rotor arm appears faulty it should be renewed.

7 Connect a test light (available from any good accessory shop) between a sound earth point and the low-tension wire from the coil to the distributor. Watch the test light while operating the ignition/starter. It will either light up and stay on, flash on and off, or not light up at all.

8 If the light stays on, the contact-breaker points are dirty or not closing, or there is a break in the LT circuit in the distributor. First check that the contact-breaker points' gap is not too wide. It is usually about 0.018in, but check the figure in the car handbook. Then ensure that the spring strip on the contact is not broken, or that the moving contact has not seized on its pivot.

Check that all low-tension wire connections are sound and that no wires are broken.

If the light flashes as the engine turns, there is nothing wrong with the ignition LT circuit. The absence of any HT spark from the coil lead could mean that the capacitor in the distributor is defective or there is a fault in the coil.

 If the light does not come on, check the bulb and wiring by connecting it between the battery and a good earth.
If the light comes on, connect it between the coil's LT terminal (marked SW or +ve) and earth. Then turn the ignition switch.

 If the light comes on when test 10 is made, disconnect the LT wire from the distributor and connect the light between the end of the wire and a sound earth.

 If the light does not come on when Step 10 is made, no LT current is reaching the coil from the ignition switch—even though the ignition is on. This could be due to a faulty ignition switch, a loose connection or a defective ballast resistor.
Do not try to make a connection between the coil and battery—it is advisable to call in professional help.

 If the test light comes on when Step 11 is conducted, there is a short circuit to earth in the distributor. Remove the cap and make sure that all the LT wire connections are sound. Check also that the insulating washers under the contact assembly are in position.

 If the light fails to come on when Step 11 is made, connect it between the distributor contact terminal on the coil and earth.

 If the light now comes on, the LT wire from the coil to the distributor is broken. A length of insulated wire connected between the two terminals will serve as a temporary repair.

 If the light does not come on when Step 14 is made and the coil's LT terminals are clean, the coil should be renewed.

 With the ignition switched off, remove the distributor cap and rotor arm. Turn the engine until the points are fully open (ie with the heel of the distributor moving-contact on top of one of the cam lobes). You can turn the engine either by moving the car to and fro in top gear or by using a spanner on the crankshaft pulley fixing.
Place an appropriate feeler gauge between the contact points. The gap on most cars is about 0.018in, but check the correct figure in the car handbook. Hold the points apart and examine their condition. There should be no pips and craters on the surfaces. If they are in a bad state they can be filed flat as an emergency measure, but it is always best to fit a new set. Make a careful note of the position of the points and wiring before removing them so that they can be reassembled in the correct order.
It is worth checking the contact-breaker points between servicing intervals. This is a simple job that will reveal any excessive wear before they fail.

 To check static ignition timing with a test light, connect one of the wires on the light to the distributor LT lead connection at the coil and the other to earth.
Remove the distributor cap and mark the position of no.1 spark plug on the cap in relation to the distributor body. Switch on the ignition and turn the engine in its direction of rotation by pulling the car forwards in top gear or by using a spanner on the crankshaft pulley fixing. Keep turning the engine until the timing marks on the crankshaft pulley are correctly aligned. (Their exact location should be given in the car handbook or workshop manual). The test light should now come on. Turn the engine back in the opposite direction until the light goes out—when it does, the points have closed. Now turn the engine forwards again, stopping the instant that the test light comes on. The relationship of the timing marks will show whether or not the setting is correct. Check in the car handbook for the right setting, eg 6° BTDC (before top dead centre).
This means that the contact-breaker points should just be opening and lighting the test light when the crankshaft has 6° to rotate before the top dead centre (TDC) position is reached. If the marks line up correctly, all is well. If the light comes on before the timing marks align, the ignition is too far advanced and should be retarded. The way this is done depends on the type of distributor fitted.
Some distributors have a very fine adjuster screw on the side of the distributor which will advance or retard the ignition by very small amounts. If

there is no such adjuster, the distributor clamp must be slackened slightly so that the distributor body can be turned a little until a test light check shows that the timing marks are correctly aligned. To retard the ignition in this way, turn the distributor in the direction of the rotor arm's rotation. To advance the ignition, turn it in the opposite direction.
After the timing has been adjusted, check it again with the test light.

 If the accelerator has been pressed a few times during starting with the choke in operation, the engine is likely to flood with an overdose of petrol from the carburettor (particularly fixed-jet types). This excess fuel can usually be cleared by slowly pressing the accelerator to the floor and holding it there while operating the starter with the choke in. The engine should fire within seconds. On a car with an automatic choke, remove the air cleaner assembly and ask a helper to hold the choke flap fully open until the engine fires. If the flap is then released, the engine should idle normally.
Persistent flooding is usually caused by a float-needle valve sticking or jamming open, or by a punctured float.

 If petrol flooding occurs while the engine is running, the symptoms will be blackish exhaust fumes and a rhythmical misfire. The engine will probably run slower and slower until finally it stalls. To confirm your suspicions, take a look at the carburettor body; it will be wet with fuel, or stains caused by leaking petrol will be seen around the float chamber.

The needle valve inside the float chamber is operated by the float and controls the fuel flow into the carburettor. A worn or sticking valve or a punctured float will prevent the needle from shutting off the supply from the fuel pump and flooding will occur.
Remove the float chamber or the cover from the carburettor and check the float and needle valve assembly. Detach the float by removing the float pivot pin, and shake it to determine whether or not there is any fuel inside. If there is, a new float is needed. Unscrew the needle valve and try to blow through it while holding it in the closed position with one finger. A hiss of air past the valve means that there is a leak—a distinct wear ridge near the point may be visible.

 Before dismantling the carburettor or fuel pump, always make sure that there is petrol in the tank—the fuel gauge could be faulty. Check by removing the filler cap, rocking the car from side to side and listening for the splash of fuel inside the tank. *Never use a naked light when looking into the tank.*

 Test for fuel reaching the carburettor from the pump by detaching the feed pipe at the carburettor. Put the end of the pipe into a container to prevent petrol spraying over the engine. If an electric pump is fitted, this should work immediately the ignition is switched on. With a mechanical pump, you will need someone to operate the starter to turn the engine. Whichever type of pump is fitted, fuel should spurt out of the feed pipe if the pump works.

 If traces of water can be seen on the spark plugs (see Step 4) the cause is probably water in the fuel tank or it may be due to a blown cylinder head gasket.
To check for water in the fuel, remove the carburettor float chamber or the cover. Water is heavier than petrol so it collects at the bottom of the float chamber. If water is present, tip the contents of the float chamber away or soak it up with a piece of non-fluffy rag. Clean any jets that can be removed by blowing through them.
If no water can be seen in the float chamber, check the coolant level in the radiator. Top it up if it is low, then run the engine. If it starts to misfire and overheat and bubbles are visible near the filler cap hole, the head gasket has blown.

 If fuel reaches the carburettor but does not actually get to the engine, take off the carburettor cover or remove the float chamber and check the operation of the needle valve assembly (see Step 20).
With SU or Stromberg-Zenith carburettors, ensure that the suction piston is not stuck open. There is often a pin which, when lifted, raises the piston a little. When it is released, the piston should fall with a distinct 'clonk'. If there is no pin, remove the air cleaner assembly and lift the piston carefully with a screwdriver. If the piston does not drop sharply when the screwdriver is withdrawn, remove the suction chamber from the top of the carburettor and try to free the piston by sliding it up and down. If necessary, remove and clean it, but always take great care not to bend the jet needle.

Using petrol with an octane rating lower than that recommended by the manufacturer is very likely to cause constant engine 'pinking' (a sort of tinkling noise) on hard acceleration. It may also cause running-on after the ignition has been switched off. Always use the correct grade of fuel for your car (see the handbook or workshop manual, or check with a dealer). Where this is not possible, retard the ignition by 4°-5° (see Step 18) and run the car at lower speeds.

 If the car has a reserve fuel supply, check that its control is not in the reserve position and the tank has emptied. Make sure that the fuel tank vent is clear, and that the filler cap is of the correct type.
Any fuel-line filters that are fitted should be examined for blockages or leaks. Look also for dents or kinks in the pipes. If no obvious fault is found, disconnect the inlet pipe from the fuel pump and blow down it—a length of rubber or plastic hose will help. Listen for air bubbling into the fuel tank. Blow as hard as you can, but if no bubbling can be heard there is a blockage in the pipe. The blockage will be in the feed pipe between the fuel pump and carburettor if the pump works but petrol does not reach the carburettor. Check the pipe by disconnecting it at both ends and blowing through it. Blow through the inlet side of the fuel pump too, if necessary. Grit may have jammed under one of the fuel pump valves if the car has previously run out of petrol. After the pipe has been refilled, blowing into the tank will help to prime the system.

 If you are satisfied that there is nothing wrong with the ignition system but the engine still will not start and the spark plugs are dry, it is likely that insufficient mixture is being drawn into the cylinders. Check that the choke mechanism at the carburettor is working correctly. On a car with an automatic choke, remove the air cleaner cover and check that the choke plate closes properly. If the plate is in the vertical (hot) position, it may be possible to close it by lightly touching it. Do not force it closed.

 Make sure that the linkage opens the throttle slightly to a fast-idle position. There is often a cam on the side of the carburettor which operates this linkage as the choke control is pulled out. The fast idle setting can sometimes be adjusted in an emergency, either by bending the choke interconnecting rod or by turning the small screw which bears on the cam. Usually, there should be a clearance of about 0.015in between the end of the screw and the cam when the choke is pushed in.

 If the engine stalls when it is hot, remove the top of the air cleaner and make sure that the choke plate is vertical when the choke control is pushed fully in.
On a carburettor with an automatic choke, remove the top of the air cleaner and simply check that the choke plate is vertical. If it is not it may be stuck. Touch it lightly: if this does not make it open fully the mechanism is faulty and should be repaired by a garage. Do not try to tie or wedge the choke plate open.

 If DIY settings can be made to the carburettor, both the throttle stop and the idling volume control screws should be adjusted when the engine is at its normal operating temperature. But first ensure that other vital adjustments, such as valve clearances and ignition timing are correctly set. Adjust the idling speed by turning the throttle stop screw in or out until a reasonable idling speed is achieved. This is usually between 600-800 revs per minute.
Fixed-jet carburettors which have a volume screw can be adjusted to meter the fuel and air at idling speed. The volume control is a small sprung screw in the side of the carburettor body. To set the idling mixture, turn the screw in until the engine revs drop, then turn it out again until the engine runs smoothly at the highest engine speed. It may now be necessary to readjust the throttle-stop screw in order to achieve the correct idle speed.

 On the underside of certain types of variable-jet carburettor there is a jet-adjusting nut. Screwing this nut upwards weakens the idling mixture; screwing it downwards richens it. The idling mixture is set by screwing the adjusting nut upwards by small amounts at a time until the engine revs begin to drop. Then screw it downwards until the engine idles smoothly at the highest speed. Raise the piston-lifting pin about 1/16in to check the mixture strength. The engine should speed up slightly and then idle normally. If the engine speed rises and continues to do so, the mixture is too rich.

If the engine speed drops, the mixture is too weak. On most cars, engine idling can be affected by the condition of the crankcase ventilation valve. Pinching the valve's rubber tube should slow the engine noticeably. If the tube is released and the oil filler cap is removed the engine should run noticeably faster.

 Certain of the Solex by-pass carburettors also have an additional adjusting screw. This allows air to mix with the fuel and makes it easier to control the idling mixture. Normally located halfway down the side of the carburettor body, the screw is turned in or out by small amounts to give the correct idling speed and mixture. With this type of carburettor, the normal volume control screw is factory-set and should not be tampered with.

 On SU and Stromberg-Zenith carburettors the piston inside the upper part of the carburettor body controls the air/fuel mixture. Check that the piston is free to slide up and down, and falls with an audible 'clonk'. To do this, remove the air cleaner and lift the piston with a screwdriver or a finger inserted into the air intake, or take the top off the carburettor. Sometimes the piston sticks because the jet assembly is off centre. If so, the complete assembly should be unscrewed and centralised by a carburettor expert.
Stromberg-Zenith carburettors have a diaphragm attached to the air-valve body. Check that this diaphragm is not perforated or damaged in any way.

 In order to inject extra fuel into the airstream when the throttle is opened quickly, fixed-jet carburettors have a small piston or diaphragm accelerator pump in the side of the carburettor body. If the piston or diaphragm is worn or damaged, a 'flat spot' will result.

 Take off the top of the air cleaner and check the condition of the air filter. If it is choked with dust and dirt the air supply will be restricted, so making the mixture richer and upsetting the carburation. The engine can be run with the filter removed, but this should be done only in an emergency. Fit a new filter.

 A faulty electric fuel pump can sometimes be made to work by giving the pump body a tap with a spanner. An audible, fast ticking sound means that there is an air leak in the supply pipe, or that the fuel tank is empty. If the pump does not work, check the feed and earth connections, using a test light with the ignition switched on.

 The first thing to check on a mechanical fuel pump that fails to deliver petrol to the carburettor when the engine is turned, is that the filter cover sealing-ring fits properly.
To test that the pump is operating correctly, remove the feed (inlet) pipe, blocking it to prevent loss of fuel. Place a finger over the pump's inlet stub and ask a helper to turn the engine again. If you cannot feel moderate suction on your finger, the pump is probably faulty and should be replaced.

 If there is an air leak into the inlet manifold between the carburettor and the cylinder head, it will weaken the mixture and upset the carburation. This can increase combustion chamber temperatures which may damage the engine. Carefully check for leaks around the carburettor flange and inlet manifold gaskets, brake servo pipe or connections, vacuum pipe connections or the crankcase emission-valve connection. Leakages may be pin-pointed by smearing a drop of washing-up liquid over a pipe or joint. If it bubbles there is a leak. Any faulty parts should be renewed.

 One of the main causes of breakdown and engine damage is due to overheating. To prevent it, make sure that any fault which develops in the engine or cooling system is corrected immediately. A water temperature gauge is invaluable. But if the driver does not notice an increase in temperature and coolant leaks away, there may be no water around the gauge sender unit in the cylinder head. If this happens the engine may continue to overheat without the correct temperature showing on the gauge. One sign that there has been a loss of coolant is that the car heater may run cold when set to the hot position.

 The water level in the radiator is the first thing to check if engine overheating is suspected. But allow the engine 10-15 minutes to cool before doing so to avoid the chance of being scalded. Release the pressure cap slowly to allow any pressure remaining in the system to escape, then check the level. If it is low or no water is visible do not immediately fill up with cold water—this could damage the radiator or the cylinder block. Pour water in after 10 minutes.

 In most cases the fan belt drives the water pump. If the belt breaks, the ignition warning light will come on and the engine is likely to overheat almost immediately.

It is good sense always to carry a spare belt, but if one is not available a temporary one can sometimes be made from thick doubled-up string or nylon. Run this temporary belt only between the crankshaft and water pump pulleys. Drive slowly and keep an eye on the water temperature gauge. If you are lucky, you will get to a garage for a replacement belt.

 If, with the radiator cap removed, a lot of small bubbles can be seen floating on top of the coolant but the coolant is not boiling, the cylinder head gasket is probably leaking. When this happens, combustion gases enter the engine water jacket and hence to the radiator. Water may also run into the sump.

 There are other faults which can affect the efficiency of the cooling system besides a broken fan belt, faulty hoses and a loss of coolant. Today, a lot of cars have electrically-operated cooling fans. These are controlled by a temperature-sensitive switch in the radiator and operate via a relay. Using

insulated wire, connect the switch terminal to earth (or between the switch terminals if there are two). The fan should operate. If it does not, even though the radiator is still very hot, the switch is probably at fault. If the fan does not work when the test is made, suspect the relay or look for a break in the fan supply circuit, checking the connections in each case.

Make sure that the radiator core is free from leaves, dirt or other obstructions so that airflow is not impaired. If the thermostat sticks in the closed position, take it out and check its operation. Radiator sediment that has built up over the years can block or slow down the circulation of coolant in the radiator. Flush out the radiator at regular intervals, preferably with it removed from the car.

 Ensure that the gear lever is in neutral, then switch on the ignition and attempt to turn the engine with the starter motor.

 Listen to the speed with which the starter operates. If it sounds sluggish the fault is likely to lie in the condition of the battery or its connections.

 Turn on the headlamps and operate the starter motor. Dimming of the lights indicates that current is being passed to the starter motor.

 If the lights go very dim, the starter does not operate or there is a rapid clicking sound from the solenoid, the battery may be

flat and need charging or replacing. A single loud click from the starter solenoid when the motor does not turn indicates that the starter motor is jammed or defective. Rock the car backwards and forwards in top gear or turn the squared end of the armature shaft with a spanner. (See also Steps 54 and 55).

 If operation of the starter is accompanied by a droning noise, the starter motor is working but the pinion gear is not engaging with the flywheel ring gear.

 If the starter motor pinion will not engage, try freeing it by using a heavy object to tap the motor body while a helper operates the starter. Failing this, the starter will have to be removed from the engine.

Use paraffin to clean the Bendix pinion gear on the end of the shaft and dry it thoroughly. This removes any oil or metal particles. Ensure that the Bendix assembly is free to rotate on the shaft and that it returns to its stop position under the return-spring pressure. The pinion threads must not be oiled as this could lead to a further sticking problem.

 Automatic cars have a gear-selector inhibitor switch which prevents the engine from starting unless it is in the Neutral or Park positions. Moving the gear selector lever through all gear positions may free this switch if it is faulty or needs adjusting.

 Test the starter solenoid if the starter motor does not operate. A button on the solenoid operates the starter manually in some older cars. *Make sure that the gear lever is in neutral,* and the handbrake applied, switch on the ignition and press the solenoid button. If the starter now operates, there could be a defect in the wiring to the solenoid from the ignition switch, or the ignition switch or solenoid could be faulty.

Since modern cars have no solenoid button, it is necessary to bridge the two large solenoid terminals with heavy gauge wire. With the gear lever in neutral and the ignition switched on, touch the wire between the two terminals. It may get very hot. The fault is in the starter motor itself if the starter still fails to turn.

 A loose or badly corroded battery connection can sometimes fail to pass the large current required by the starter motor. A terminal in this condition will usually feel hot to the touch after attempting to operate the starter. Check all the battery leads and after cleaning off any corrosion down to bare metal, remake the connections firmly. Engine and battery earth connections to the car body also affect starting, so make sure that they are tight and clean.

 If you do not own a battery charger, a garage can give a flat battery a boost charge. The engine will start after about 30 minutes of charge. If you do own a charger, an overnight charge of 3-4amps should produce enough power in the battery to start the engine. If this fails, a car with manual gearbox can be started by pushing or towing. On an automatic car with a flat battery use jump leads.

 Batteries benefit from use, unlike many other motor car components. An occasional complete discharge will not damage it, provided the discharge or charge is not too rapid. The unit must never be left in a discharged condition.

 An excessive load is imposed on the starter motor if an attempt is made to start a very stiff engine. If the cause of the stiffness is not apparent and the defect is not cured, the engine must not be started—this could damage the starter motor. Call your motoring organisation for roadside help, or contact a garage.

 If the engine seems particularly stiff, instantly switch off the ignition. Try to turn the engine by placing a spanner on the crankshaft pulley fixing. If a lot of leverage on the spanner is needed to turn the engine, it is partially seized. Check for water in the combustion chambers by removing the spark plugs. If water spurts out as the engine is turned, the fault may be a leaking head gasket.

 A battery which goes flat after a recent full charge could be too old to hold its charge. Another possibility is that the generator may not be charging at the correct rate. A faulty voltage regulator, a slipping fan belt, worn brushes or a fault within the generator are frequently to blame. If both battery and generator appear to be in good condition, check the engine earth connections and the starter motor brushes.

 If the power fault is cured but the engine will still not run smoothly, see Chart 4, Cars 58.

 Make sure that the engine idles smoothly at the correct speed. Allowance must be made for very cold weather. If it is not possible to detect a fault that is apparent when the engine is idling but not under load, see Steps 30 and 30A and then carefully follow the checking procedures.

 When the fault persists above idling speed, or becomes obvious only on acceleration, rev up the engine with the car stationary but do not race it. Note the result. Problems such as rattling and misfiring often become apparent at higher engine speeds.

A carburettor hesitation (flat spot) which occurs when the throttle is opened rapidly may be due to blocked jets or venturi progression holes, a weak mixture, or a worn accelerator-pump piston, jet or diaphragm. A sticking piston may be the cause on variable-jet SU and Stromberg-Zenith carburettors. Other possibilities include retarded ignition or an air leak in the inlet manifold or in the carburettor.

 'Pinking' describes a metallic, tinkling noise heard from the engine when climbing a steep hill or during hard acceleration. If this defect persists over a long period, it may damage the pistons and valves. Causes include the use of lower octane fuel than that specified for the car and over-advanced ignition timing. An overheated engine may exhibit this fault. Certain cars are more prone to pinking than others.

 The term 'running on' is used when the engine continues to run lumpily or irregularly after the ignition is switched off. Common causes of this include a weak carburettor mixture, incorrect fuel grade, and excessively high combustion chamber temperatures resulting from incorrect ignition timing.
Now that fuels and oils contain special additives, a less common cause of running-on is the build-up of carbon deposits in the combustion chamber. These deposits glow incandescently and continue to ignite the fuel until they cool down. Removal of these deposits used to be referred to as a 'decoke'.

 Knocking noises from the engine can cause concern; they may be due only to the engine oil level being low. For other causes and sources of engine noises see page 35.

 Initial damage to the engine may not be serious, but it may rapidly worsen and could cause a broken connecting rod and damage to the block. The car must not be used until the cause of the noise is detected.

 Light tapping or rattling noises from the engine are normally less critical, but the cause must be promptly investigated before the car is used.

If the noise is apparent when the engine is at normal running temperature, check that the tappet clearances are correct. On a cold engine, the noise may be due to piston slap, a faulty timing chain and/or its adjuster, or a worn distributor.

 A worn or slipping fan belt is the usual cause of a high-pitched screaming noise coming from the front of the engine. Slipping overheats the belt, causing it to disintegrate.
On hearing this noise, check the tension of the belt and replace it if it is worn. If the belt is all right, the noise may come from a squeaking or frozen water pump. A water-soluble lubricant introduced into the coolant will usually cure a squeaking pump. Power-steering drive belts or pumps sometimes squeak, but if the reservoir oil level and belt tension are correct, the pump should be checked by a garage.

 A breakdown of the spark plugs or coil can cause engine misfiring on hard acceleration. Higher combustion pressures exert a greater strain on the ignition system. Spark plugs need changing after 10,000-12,000 miles.

 It is difficult to check an engine which cuts out intermittently without warning since it may be satisfactory when you investigate it. The fuel or ignition systems are worth checking. Possible causes include a blockage in the fuel tank venting system or, on a hot day, the fault could be due to a vapour lock in the fuel line.

 Extremely high operating temperatures make the spark plug tips white and powdery (see Step 2). The car handbook will indicate if they are the correct grade for the engine. An air leak at the manifold or a very weak carburettor mixture will also cause the plugs to overheat. Both the piston and the valves can be damaged by an overheated, incandescent plug.

 A valve with insufficient rocker or camshaft clearance will overheat. Consult the handbook and ensure that the valve clearances are correctly adjusted, as specified. The engine must not be noticeably warm if the valve clearances should be set cold. The engine should be at normal operating temperature if a hot setting is specified.

 If you reverse the end of the tailpipe into a roadside verge, the exhaust may become partially blocked. This will reduce engine efficiency.

 The following symptoms will usually be shown by a blown or defective cylinder-head gasket: rough running, chuffing or similar noises when idling, and loss of power. A sticking valve will also cause the engine to misfire. If not quickly discovered, the valve will get damaged, with consequent loss of power.
Check the compression of each cylinder by placing a spanner on the crankshaft pulley fixing and turning the engine. With a four- or six-cylinder engine you should detect the compression on all cylinders. Now check Step 57.

WEEKEND WORKSHOP

JOB NO.	FRIDAY	PAGES
1	Fit new steady-bar rubbers	288
3	Remove the trim	290
11	Free an inertia starter pinion	296
13	Free a jammed inertia pinion	298
13	Dismantle an inertia pinion	298
15	Change a headlamp bulb	300
16	Change a sealed beam headlamp	301

18	Renew a steering rack gaiter	302
20	Paint with a spray gun	304
22	Trace and cure a water leak	306-307
24	Renew a bolt-on front wing	308-309
26	Fit a child safety seat	310
28	Renew a mechanical fuel pump	312
29	Fit a new steering ball-joint	313
31	Fit mudflaps	315

JOB NO.	SATURDAY	PAGES
2	Clean a crankcase ventilating system	289
4	Service an air filter	291
6	Replace an exhaust manifold gasket	292
9	Renew drum-type starter motor brushes	294-295
12	Repair a front seat	296-297
14	Replace a screenwash electric motor	299
17	Change a capacitor	301

JOB NO.	SUNDAY	PAGES
5	Adjust OHC and finger clearances	291
7	Renew an electric fuel pump	293
8	Check a solenoid	293
10	Clean a mechanical fuel pump	295
19	Fit electronic ignition	303
21	Brighten up shabby road wheels	305
23	Renew engine mountings	307
25	Clean a bowl-type oil filter	309
27	Add a rear window wiper and washer	311
30	Add a rear window heater	314-315

Although all the jobs described in this book can be tackled in any part of the week and all through the year, the 31 presented in this section will be of particular interest to the weekend DIY man. Each has been selected with an eye to the most convenient period of the weekend when any competent motorist can expect to complete the work efficiently and safely. Some tasks, for instance, are considered more suitable for evenings than others, as they depend less on daylight than those which take longer and may need a full morning or an afternoon to finish.

The accompanying photographs are numbered to correspond with the numbers in the text. In cases where different methods apply, the action to take is preceded by an exclamation mark.

At the start of each job an assessment of how long the job will take is given, together with the tools and materials required. The times quoted for these jobs are only a guide and do not take into account unexpected snags or complications caused by the type of car under repair and its condition. Although most types of components are covered, some are bound to be different from those illustrated. In such cases it is advisable to consult the car workshop manual.

	FRIDAY EVENING
	SATURDAY
	SUNDAY

1 FIT: NEW STEADY-BAR RUBBERS

FRIDAY EVENING
Allow about: 30min
You need: Spanners to fit fixing bolts; new rubber bushes; washing-up liquid

Excessive engine rock can cause clutch judder and strain the exhaust system. The problem can be caused by worn steady-bar rubbers. The illustrations show the job being carried out on a Mini.
a Remove the fixing bolt and loosen the cover-bracket bolt on the cylinder head (1).
b Pull the bar out and remove the old bushes (2).
c Fit the new rubbers and sleeve. If necessary, use washing-up liquid as a lubricant (3).
d Fit the centre sleeve, replace the bracket and fixing bolt and tighten both the bolts (4).

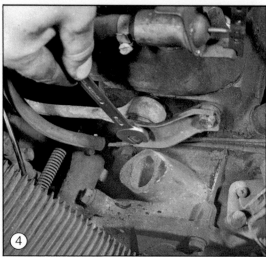

2 CLEAN: A CRANKCASE VENTILATING SYSTEM

SATURDAY MORNING
Allow about: 30min
You need: Screwdriver; old paint brush; stiff wire; paraffin; rag

Crankcase ventilation systems generally incorporate an oil separator and a valve or flame trap. Their purpose is to relieve crankcase pressure and avoid a fire, by preventing oil from being blown on to the exhaust manifold. Breathers should be cleaned every 10,000-12,000 miles. If this is not done, oil leaks can develop as a result of pressure.

a If your oil filler cap is the type with vent holes and a gauze filter, wash it thoroughly in paraffin and shake off as much of the surplus as possible before refitting it (1).

! If there are no vent holes, check the condition of the sealing ring. If it is damaged, fit a new seal or renew the cap.

b Locate the breather assembly—it will probably be at one end of the ventilation hose joining the crankcase to the inlet manifold or carburettor air cleaner (2).

c Remove the assembly and brush it clean with paraffin (3).

d Try pressing the valve into the housing. If it has a sticky action, fit a new valve. If the valve can be dismantled for cleaning (see the workshop manual) this expense can be saved.

!! Some ventilation valves are mounted on the inlet manifold. These are disc-shaped and contain a spring-loaded diaphragm. They should be dismantled and cleaned at the recommended intervals. Remove the spring clip to release the top cover then lift out the diaphragm and the spring below it. Wash all parts thoroughly in paraffin, wipe dry and re-assemble the valve in the reverse order of assembly.

e Ventilation valve hoses can be cleaned by hooking a length of wire round a small piece of non-fluffy rag and using it as a pull-through (4). Renew any damaged hoses and check that they are firm and airtight—air leaks cause poor idling.

3 REMOVE: THE TRIM

FRIDAY EVENING
Allow about: 1hr
You need: Screwdrivers; hooked wire or skewer to remove door handle

Replacing a window-winder mechanism or installing door-mounted speakers are both reasonable jobs for a DIY owner to tackle. But to do so it is necessary to remove the door trim. This calls for a certain amount of care because brute force can easily damage the plastic and fibreboard materials. If the trim does not respond to the treatment illustrated, seek expert help.

a Remove the door fittings. Armrests are usually held on by screws (1). Some screws may be hidden under a plastic finisher but if there are no screws, try to remove the armrest with the panel attached.

b Window-winder handles are screwed, pinned or clipped to the winder shaft. The fixings can usually be reached by prising off the plastic cover (2).

c Where door handles are held by a spring clip or a cross pin, press the trim inwards to gain access. Push out a cross pin with a skewer or try a small screwdriver.
A spring clip can often be hooked out with a piece of bent wire or pushed out with a piece of shaped metal (3).
With the fixing removed, the handle can be pulled off the shaft.

d Remove the trim around the door handle (4). Plastic surrounds can be gently prised off or they may be held by clips or pegs, released by slightly distorting the moulding.

e Where the trim hooks over the top of the door it may be necessary to remove the lock button. This is simply unscrewed by hand.

f Prise off the trim using a large screwdriver, taking care not to damage surrounding paintwork (5). Place your hand behind the blade to act as a fulcrum. Remove the trim (6).

! On some cars one edge of the panel will be slotted into a metal channel. Work round the other sides before finally sliding the panel clear of the groove.

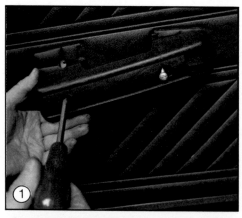

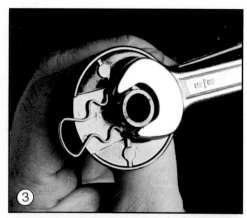

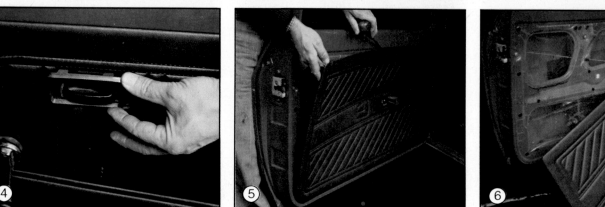

4 SERVICE: AN AIR FILTER

SATURDAY EVENING
Allow about: 15min
You need: Tools to remove air cleaner lid; paint brush; new air filter

Most modern cars have a paper element inside the air cleaner to prevent dirt from being sucked into the engine. The element should be checked and changed according to the car's service schedule.
a Remove the cover of the air cleaner (1).
b Extract the paper element. If it is less than 12,000-miles old,

clean off the dust by tapping it against a wall.
c If the element is oil-fouled, discard it but locate the source of the leak. The crankcase breather may need cleaning.
d Clean the inside of the air cleaner and reassemble.
! With cars equipped with wire-mesh filters, the mesh should be extracted and washed in petrol. Dip it in engine oil and allow it to drain thoroughly before refitting.
!! Oil-bath air cleaners have to be removed from the carburettor. After removing the lid and pouring out the old oil, the cleaner should be cleaned with a petrol-soaked paint brush. Dry it carefully, then refit and replenish the oil before refitting the lid.

5 ADJUST: OVERHEAD CAMSHAFT AND 'FINGER' CLEARANCES

SUNDAY MORNING
Allow about: 1½hr
You need: Set of spanners; screwdriver; feeler gauges

See pages 15-17 for overhead camshaft details and how to

renew a rocker cover gasket. When a follower or 'finger' is interposed between the valve and camshaft lobe, the clearance is checked between the 'finger' and the cam heel.
a Identify the inlet and exhaust valves, then check the gap with a feeler gauge (1).
b To adjust the clearance, loosen the locknut. Turn the stud clockwise to widen the gap, anti-clockwise to reduce it (2).
! On certain Ford single overhead camshaft engines the carburettor may obstruct access to the locknut. The carburettor may need to be removed.

6 REPLACE: AN EXHAUST MANIFOLD GASKET

SATURDAY AFTERNOON
Allow about: 1½hr depending on engine type
You need: Spanner; socket and bar or box spanner to fit manifold nuts; old knife and, if applicable, spanners and screwdriver to remove air cleaner and carburettor controls; new gasket; penetrating oil

A leaking manifold can mean a car full of carbon monoxide. Small doses will cause headaches and drowsiness, so this is a priority job. Fortunately, a leak can be heard. The cure is a new gasket. Where exhaust and inlet manifolds are combined, the carburettor and air cleaner may have to be removed, if necessary disconnecting throttle and choke controls.

a If the manifold nuts cannot be moved, soak the threads overnight in penetrating oil.

b Remove the nuts or bolts holding the manifold (1).

c Pull the manifold away from the cylinder head and extract the old gasket. On some cars it may be necessary to loosen the manifold-to-downpipe clamp.

d Clean off the head and manifold faces with the knife (2) and fit the new gasket (3). Refit the manifold and fixings, working outwards from the centre.

e Re-tighten downpipe fixings, and connect the throttle and choke controls.

7 RENEW: AN ELECTRIC FUEL PUMP

SUNDAY, AFTERNOON
Allow about: 30min-1hr depending on the location of the pump
You need: Ramps; jack and axle stands; spanners; screwdrivers; pump wiring; fuel pipes and bracket; new or reconditioned pump; two sharp pencils

Electric pumps are often in the boot near the fuel tank or they may be under the bonnet. They can be overhauled provided the bodies are not one-piece but new units are not expensive. Pumps are often sold by dealers on an exchange basis. When ordering a new pump, the dealer will need to know engine and chassis numbers.

a Disconnect the battery.
b If necessary, raise the car to gain access to the pump.
c Release the pump and, if fitted, detach the plastic pipe from the end cover (1).

d Disconnect the live cable and the earth wire from the pump body (2).
e Disconnect the fuel line which comes from the tank, stemming the petrol flow with a pencil. Repeat the procedure with the other pipe.
f Clamp on the new pump, ensuring that it is the right way round.
g Reconnect the wiring and fuel pipes. Ensure they are correct. One pipe stub on the pump will be marked 'inlet'.
h Reconnect the breather and finally the battery.
i Turn on the ignition to test the pump—it will click as it pumps fuel to the carburettor.

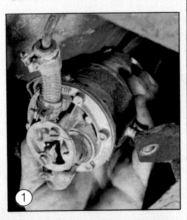

8 CHECK: A SOLENOID

SUNDAY AFTERNOON
Allow about: 5min
You need: Stout screwdriver with an insulated handle

Starter motors are of the inertia or pre-engaged type and both are activated by a solenoid. For a pre-engaged starter motor the solenoid is on the motor body.

For an inertia starter it is mounted on the car bodywork. Before checking the solenoid when a starter motor fails to operate, make sure that the battery leads are tight, and there is a good earth.

a Test the solenoid with a screwdriver by short-circuiting the two main terminals (1). If the motor turns, the solenoid is defective.

! With automatic cars, the solenoid is supplied via a switch on the gearbox. This prevents the engine from being started while a gear is selected. Check that the selector is in neutral, and also check with a test light that current is reaching the solenoid winding when the starter switch is operated. If it is, the solenoid is faulty.

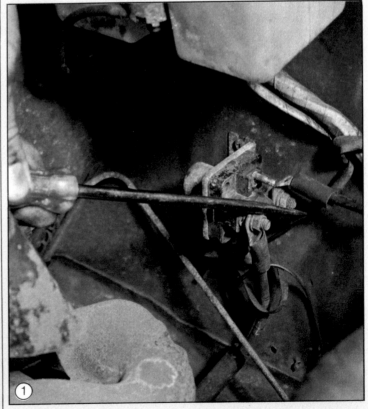

9 RENEW: DRUM-TYPE STARTER MOTOR BRUSHES

SATURDAY AFTERNOON

Allow about: 2½hr

You need: Screwdriver or spanner to disconnect battery; spanners to disconnect starter; screwdriver to loosen through-bolts; vice (if necessary); wire cutters or pliers; soldering iron and resin-covered solder; fine file; starter brush set; methylated spirit; cloth; fine glasspaper

Most modern starter motors are of the face-type and new brushes are simply pressed into the holder.

Never clean the commutator on a face-type motor with abrasive paper as the segments are thin and you may damage the unit. With the older drum-type motors, shown here, the brushes, similar to those used in a dynamo, should be renewed if they are worn down to less than ⅜in when measured from the top of the brush. Worn brushes will create arcing and subsequent damage to the commutator.

Because they draw a heavy current, most starter motors have four brushes, mounted on the inside of the commutator end plate. Two are connected to terminals on the end plate and two to the motor field-windings on the casing.

a Remove the starter motor (see Job 11, page 296).

b Prevent the terminal stud from rotating, then remove the fixing nut and washers and the cover band (1).

c Undo the pair of through-bolts at the end plate. If they are very tight, grip the bolt heads in a vice and turn the motor body. Remove the bolts (2).

d Remove the end plate (3). The assembly is tethered by two field-brush wires. Pull the armature assembly out of the casing.

e Lift the springs and remove the brushes from their holders to release the plate.

f Clean the segments of the commutator with fine glass-paper (4), and wash in methylated spirit. If the commutator is badly worn, the motor will need to be replaced.

g There will be four new brushes, two of them with uninsulated, plaited leads and two with insulated ones.

One of the insulated leads will be longer than the other (5). The brushes with insulated leads have to be connected to the armature windings, but the leads

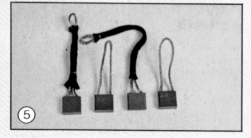

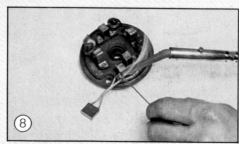

are copper and the windings are aluminium.

h These will not solder together so leave at least ½in of old lead when cutting through the existing brush leads (6).

i Hook the cut leads through the loops at the end of the brushes with insulated leads. Connect the ends of the wires with resin-core solder (7).

j Cut through the two old leads on the end-plate brushes and solder the new brushes with uninsulated leads to them (8).

k Fit the new brushes in their holders, filing if necessary so that they slide easily. Raise each brush until its working end is flush with the bottom of the holder and hold it in place by resting the spring on the side of the brush (9).

l Refit the casing and the end plate, engaging their locating notches correctly. Do not forget to fit the nylon sleeve to the terminal connected to the main feed wire. If the terminal touched the end plate it would cause a short circuit.

m Position the bush springs using a small screwdriver (10) and refit the cover band.

n Refit the starter motor to the engine. Testing the motor before it is fitted to the engine is not advisable. It is very powerful and requires a lot of operating current.

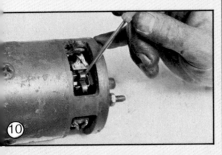

10 CLEAN: A MECHANICAL FUEL PUMP

SUNDAY EVENING
Allow about: 25min
You need: Spanners and screwdrivers to remove pump cover; cloth; clean paint brush

All a mechanical pump needs is to be kept clean and free from sediment trapped by the filter. Normally, the pump should need attention only at major services or if it is dismantled due to a breakdown.

a Disconnect the battery.

b Unscrew the retaining bolt on top of the pump and remove the domed cover and gasket (1). The cover may be made of either glass or metal.

c Remove the wire mesh filter and wash it in petrol (2).

d Clean the sediment chamber with a paint brush dipped in petrol and wipe clean (3).

e Refit the pump cover with a new gasket, if necessary.

f Be careful not to overtighten the cover but ensure that the seal is airtight (4).

g Reconnect the battery and run the engine, looking for possible fuel leaks.

11 FREE: A STICKING INERTIA PINION STARTER

FRIDAY EVENING
Allow about: 1hr
depending on accessibility
You need: Screwdriver or
spanner to disconnect
battery; spanners; methylated
spirit or petrol; clean cloth

If the starter motor pinion rotates
at high speed without turning the
engine, the cause of the trouble
may be that the starter motor
shaft is caked with dirt. The
pinion must be able to slide
freely along the helical screw or
quick-thread to connect with the
ring-gear teeth on the flywheel.
a Disconnect the battery.
Remove the feed cable from the
motor and undo the mounting
bolts. Take the starter motor to
the work bench.
b Check that the pinion can
move freely and return to its
starting position under pressure
from the restraining spring (1).
c Clean the pinion shaft with
methylated spirit or petrol, being
careful to keep the cleaning fluid
out of the motor (2). Remove
excess fluid and, when dry,
re-check the pinion movement.
Never oil the pinion as oil
collects dust and will cause the
pinion to stick again.
d If cleaning does not improve
matters, the pinion must be
taken off the shaft for further
investigation or replacement.

12 REPAIR: A FRONT SEAT

SATURDAY EVENING
Allow about: 3hr
depending on the type of
seat
You need: Large-bladed
screwdriver; pliers;
hooked wire

If the metal frame inside a seat
breaks, a garage will generally
regard it as being beyond repair.
What they mean is that because
of high labour costs it is as well
to buy a new seat.
Do not be put off, however.
Removing the seat upholstery is
a fiddly but feasible job for the
amateur.
Once the frame has been bared,
a blacksmith or an engineering
workshop will be able to weld or
braze the break together for a
small charge.
Remove the seat from the car
and tackle the job indoors.
a Separate a reclining backrest
from the cushion (1). This one
has spring clips on each pivot
which can be prised out with a
screwdriver.
b Disengage the backrest (2), if
necessary using a large
screwdriver to lever the hinge
plates off the locating pins.
c This backrest cover is held by
staples at its base. Lever them
up with a screwdriver (3).

d It should now be possible to slide off the cover. On this seat the trim surrounding the backrest-locking lever first had to be tucked under the fabric (4).

e The padding underneath, consisting of a layer of felt on a semi-rigid fibre base, is easy to remove (5).

f The seat cushion presents more of a challenge. In this case, a wire stiffener runs round the bottom of the upholstery and the ends are wrapped round the frame. Unhook it with the aid of long-nosed pliers (6).

g Prise out staples or clips securing the rest of the fabric (7). Proceed carefully—spares may be difficult to obtain.

h A shaped cushion may well have wire inserts pulling it on to the spring base. The inserts will probably be held in place by split-rings. Before opening these (8), sketch their positions.

i Remove the cover (9).

j Strip off the felt, foam and fibre padding (10). If the foam sticks to the base, peel it off carefully using a knife. It can be stuck back with double-sided tape.

k Reverse the process to re-assemble. A small hooked tool (11) can be made from an old wire coathanger and used as a puller to locate the trim rods. Once in position, the ring can be closed with pliers.

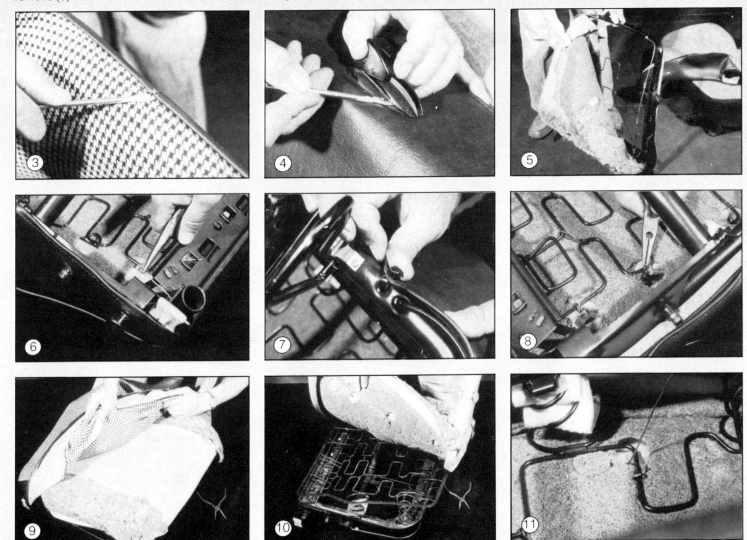

13 FREE: A JAMMED INERTIA PINION. DISMANTLE: AN INERTIA PINION

FRIDAY EVENING
Allow about: 10min if only jammed, 2hr to dismantle
You need: Bladed screwdriver to prise off cover; small open-ended spanner to fit the end of the armature.
Screwdriver or spanner to disconnect battery; spanners for terminal nuts and mounting bolts; compressor for buffer spring; pliers; carborundum stone; replacement pinion parts

a If the starter motor fails to turn the engine, it could be that its pinion is jammed. Remove the end cover on the starter motor (if fitted) to expose the motor shaft.
b Fit a spanner to the squared end of the shaft and turn it clockwise to wind the pinion out of mesh (1).
c Check the motor mountings for tightness.
If the pinion continually jams or cannot be freed easily it will have to be dismantled—the cause may be a broken return spring. Pinion teeth can be damaged by constant contact with the ring gear of the flywheel, in which case the only solution is to fit a new pinion.
a Disconnect the battery and remove the starter motor from the engine using a socket-wrench if necessary.

When unscrewing the nut that holds the power lead, make sure that the connecting bolt does not turn, because if this happens, damage to the field-winding connections could result.
b Remove the circlip from the end of the shaft. This can be prised off (2) when the buffer spring is compressed.
! Older pinions can be secured by a nut, often with a left-hand thread. Use pliers to remove the split pin and undo the nut.
c Remove the buffer spring with the compressor in situ, then take off the quick-thread sleeve and pinion (3), and (where separate) the restraining spring.
d If the pinion is worn, fit a new one (4). It is cheap compared with a new starter motor.

e If the buffer spring is cracked or broken it should be replaced at the same time.
Before reassembling the unit remove any burrs from the starter shaft splines using a small carborundum stone.
f Fit the pinion, compress the spring and replace the circlip. Check that the pinion slides freely along the thread.

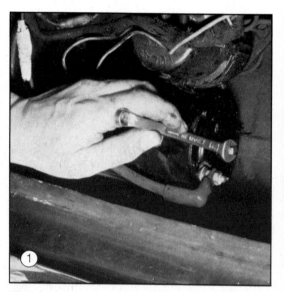

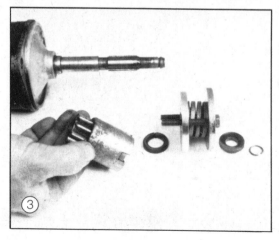

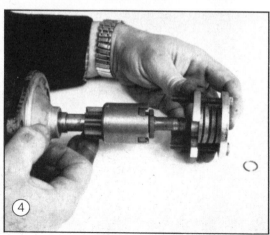

14 REPLACE: A SCREENWASH ELECTRIC MOTOR

SATURDAY MORNING
Allow about: 1hr
You need: Drill and bits; screwdriver or spanner to disconnect battery; pliers; replacement pump kit

If your electric screenwasher fails to operate, make sure that the motor is faulty before buying a new one.

a Check the power supply with a test lamp and ensure that the earth lead is secure. Try operating the washers with the outlet pipe disconnected. If water spurts out, there is a blockage in the feed pipe or the jets (1). These should be cleaned out.

b If no water comes out, the pump is faulty. Service kits are available from accessory shops. Fix the new pump in place of the old one, disconnect the battery and transfer the wires and pipes to the new pump.

! Many cars have a gravity-fed pump at the base of the reservoir (2), and the part should be obtained from a dealer. If a replacement cannot be obtained, a service kit will be needed.

Pull off the outlet pipe from the old pump and block the stub by inserting a tight-fitting woodscrew.

!! Fit the new pump as close to the reservoir as possible (3).
!!! Disconnect the battery.

Connect the wires from the old pump to the new one (4). If necessary, lengthen them and fit new connectors. Join the original pump outlet to the replacement pump.

!!!! Pull off the suction pipe from the old pump and join it to the inlet stub of the replacement one. If this cannot be done, fit a new suction pipe down to the bottom of the reservoir through a hole drilled in the cap.

c Reconnect the battery, top up the reservoir and test that the system is working properly.

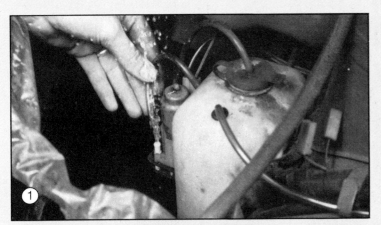

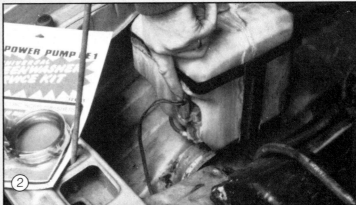

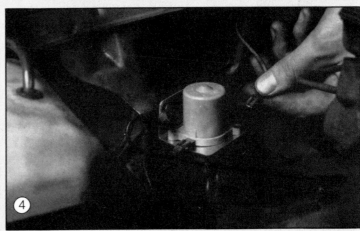

15 CHANGE: A HEADLAMP BULB

FRIDAY EVENING
Allow about: 15min
You need: Screwdriver

Two types of bulb are used in modern headlamp units. These are quartz-halogen and tungsten-filament. The quartz-halogen bulb has a filament in a quartz envelope filled with a halogen gas. The tungsten-filament bulb has a much larger glass envelope and is filled with an inert gas.

Filaments in both bulbs are accurately located so that they are always in focus. The design ensures that it can only be fitted in the correct position. Quartz-halogen bulbs can be fitted in place of the tungsten type and provide much brighter light.

a Remove the headlamp trim and release the lamp-fixing screws if the bulb cannot be reached from behind (1).

b Unplug the bulb-holder wires (2) and remove the spring clips holding the assembly to the reflector (3). Discard the old bulb.

c Fit the new assembly, checking that the wires are in good condition.

Do not touch the glass on a quartz-halogen bulb directly with your hands (4) as this will damage the quartz. If touched accidentally it should be wiped clean with methylated spirit.

d Refit the lamp unit and renew the rubber sealing ring if it is worn. Check that the lamp alignment is correct.

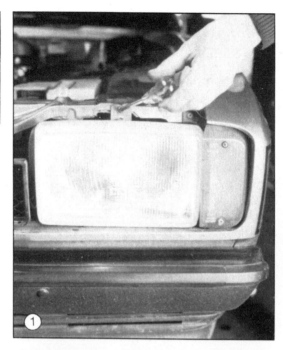

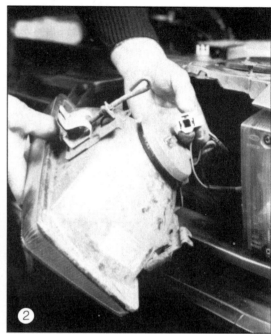

16 CHANGE: A SEALED-BEAM HEADLAMP

FRIDAY EVENING
Allow about: 30min
You need: Screwdriver; new sealed-beam unit

In effect, this unit is a large bulb, sealed for life against ingress of dirt or moisture. The back is a reflector and the glass is moulded in the shape of a lens.
a Remove the light trim or, if necessary, the radiator grille (1). Some trims are held by a screw, whereas grilles have numerous fixings. When in doubt consult your vehicle handbook.
b Undo the screws round the lamp unit (2). Do not loosen the beam-adjusting screws.

c Pull out the lamp unit (3) and disconnect the bayonet fitting from the back.
d When fitting the new unit, line it up with the locating tabs. Refit the screws and trim in reverse order, then check the headlamp alignment.

17 CHANGE: A CAPACITOR

SATURDAY EVENING
Allow about: 20min
You need: Spanner to fit terminal post nut; screwdriver; new capacitor

The job of the distributor is to send high-voltage current to each spark plug in turn. A capacitor (often referred to as a condenser) 'stores' electricity until it is required, when it then helps speed the current flow to the spark plugs. The capacitor, a tube-shaped component, is screwed to the distributor body and is connected to the spring of the contact-breaker points by a short wire.
A failed capacitor produces burning at the points which will become blackened by carbon deposits in a few hundred miles. The first indication of this can be poor starting.
The photographs show how the job is done in a Lucas distributor but there are many other makes which can be tackled in a similar way. When in doubt, sketch the parts as they are removed to ensure correct reassembly.
a Remove the distributor cap and rotor arm. Undo the terminal-post nut, lift out the insulator and disconnect the capacitor wire from the top of the spring (1).
b Remove the capacitor-retaining screw (2).
c Reassemble in reverse order. When attaching the capacitor wire to the terminal post, ensure that the terminal (and the low-tension wire terminal) makes contact with the spring.
Fit the insulator and tighten the fixing nut before checking the tightness of the capacitor-retaining screw.

18 RENEW: A STEERING RACK GAITER

SATURDAY MORNING
Allow about: 2hr
You need: Wheelbrace; jack; axle stands; chocks; pliers; wire brush; spanners to fit ball-joint nuts; taper-breaking tool; hammer; self-grip wrench; lever; wire cutters; screwdriver; oil can; new gaiter and clips; grease; paraffin; EP90 oil

g Refit the gaiter clip (4) or wire and position the other end in the appropriate recess.
h Raise the inside end of the gaiter and feed in $\frac{1}{3}$ pint of EP90 oil (5), then fit the sealing wire or clip.
i Screw on the locknut using the correct number of turns, then refit the ball-joint to the steering rod and arm (see page 313).
j Lower the car to the ground. As the operation could have affected the car's wheel alignment, resulting in steering wheel shake and increased tyre wear, have the steering checked professionally on specialist equipment at a garage.

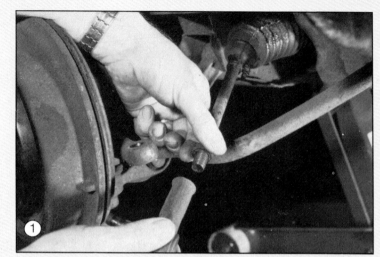

The inner ball-joint in the steering rack housing is protected by a rubber gaiter. A split will allow water, dirt and grit to get in and let lubricant get out, resulting in premature wear. Nearside and offside gaiters may differ, so specify the correct one when you buy.
a Chock the rear wheels and jack up the front of the car on the appropriate side. Fit an axle stand and remove the wheel.
b Clean the parts around the rubber gaiter with a paraffin-soaked rag.
c Remove the outer ball-joint (1) and take off the locknut from the end of the steering rod. Count the number of turns needed to remove the locknut.
d Remove the clip or wire grip from the end of the rubber gaiter.
e Loosen the inner clip, peel the gaiter out of its recess and slide it off the rod (2).
f Smear a little grease around the sealing surfaces of the new gaiter (3) and slide it over the steering rod.

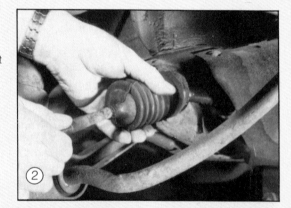

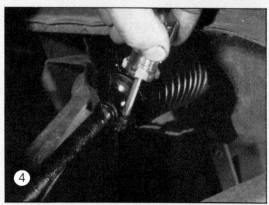

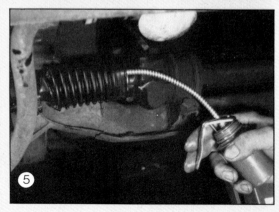

19 FIT: ELECTRONIC IGNITION

SUNDAY MORNING
Allow about: 2½hr depending on the type of system
You need: Cross-head and bladed screwdrivers; drill and 9/64in bit; small electrical spanner; electronic ignition system to suit your car; insulating tape

Exaggerated claims have been made by makers of electronic ignition systems about their products, not least in the area of fuel economy. In fact, an electronic system will produce no fuel saving over a well adjusted conventional system, and a buyer is unlikely to save enough money on running costs to recover the cost of the equipment.

However, by doing away with the contact-breaker points, electronic ignition systems will make your car more reliable and reduce the amount of maintenance work required. Not all electronic systems do away with the contact-breaker points, so their usefulness is somewhat limited.

The kit shown here is one of the better sort, readily available from accessory shops. Once fitted it can be forgotten.

A slotted disc rotated by the distributor cam chops through a tiny light beam to switch a light-sensitive transistor on and off. It does exactly the same job as a set of contact-breaker points but no wear takes place.

a Disconnect the negative battery terminal. Pick a suitable mounting point for the control box, ensuring that the wires will reach the distributor and coil. Ideally, the box should be placed away from the battery and the exhaust system.

b Drill the holes required and attach the control box using self-tapping screws (1). Remember to earth the control box by attaching the short black wire to one of the screws.

c Remove the distributor wire at the coil and replace it with the wire from the unit (see the instructions supplied). If the car has a tachometer (rev counter), connect the wire to the wire from the distributor.

d Connect the supply wire to the ignition switch. This lead must have a 12-volt feed and must not have its voltage cut down by a ballast resistor.

e Remove the distributor cap, rotor arm and contact-breaker points (2). Fit the optical unit and light-chopping disc. Ensure that nothing will impede the disc as it spins and that the vacuum-advance mechanism will still work (3).

f Connect the three-pin plug from the control unit to the three-pin socket from the optical unit.

g Tidy up any excess wire, fixing it with insulating tape so that it cannot contact anything hot or moving.

h Reconnect the battery.

i If necessary, adjust the car's timing (see pages 98-100).

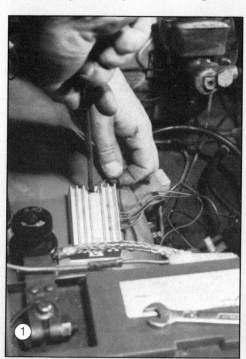

20 PAINT: WITH A SPRAY GUN

SATURDAY MORNING
Allow about: 1½hr per wing
You need: Spray gun; viscosity cup; primer; top coat and suitable thinners; 400-grit wet-or-dry paper; lint-free cloth; 'tacky rag'

Large-sized aerosol cans are available for tackling a complete body panel, but it may be more economical to hire a spray gun and buy a can of paint. In any case, a spray gun can give more professional results by applying the paint quicker and more evenly than an aerosol.

If you have the space to work, this is a job that should certainly be done in the garage as airborne dust and insects could ruin your efforts.

If your car has a metallic paint, think twice about spraying it. Even professionals have a hard task to achieve a good match. Some paints need to be baked on in a large oven, so check before purchase.

For indoor spraying, a protective face mask and goggles are essential. A fine paint mist is harmful if breathed in.

Do not practise painting on your car. If you are unskilled it can come as a shock to find that a spray gun is either on or off with nothing in between. A gentle squeeze on the trigger is all it takes.

Before the spray gun settles down, paint can spatter out in blobs, so start the work by spraying on to a piece of old board.

Professionals do not wait for each coat of paint to dry but do not be tempted to do the same in the interests of speed. If you have no experience, the layers of paint will go on too thickly and run down the panel, forming ugly tear-drops. Spray the edges of the panel first and then fill in the rest with even, sweeping strokes, overlapping all the edges by about two inches. Stop the spray gun at the end of each sweep.

To paint a horizontal panel (a bonnet or boot, for example), the spray gun should not be angled at more than 45°. And do not let the spray gun run dry. If air is blown through with the paint, the gun will spatter large blobs of paint on to the work.

a Ensure that the garage is ventilated—some paints give off unpleasant petroleum vapours—and lay the dust by spraying water on the floor. The surface to be painted must be spotless and here you can copy the professionals. A special 'tacky rag' sold by accessory shops and paint suppliers prevents a build-up of dust-attracting static electricity on the panel to be painted, and its sticky surface picks up any dust.

b Mask off surrounding bodywork. Painting up to a waistline or body join will disguise a slight mismatch (1).

c Stir the primer thoroughly and dilute it with thinners (2). A viscosity cup will show if this has been done correctly—paint manufacturers quote a time in seconds for a specific amount of paint to run through a hole in the cup (3).

d Strain the mixture into the gun through a nylon stocking and then make a test spraying. If the paint blobs, thin it a little more and test again.

e Hold the spray gun about 18 inches away from the work (4), spraying as explained in the introduction.

f Allow the primer to dry, then rub it down carefully with the wet-or-dry paper to smooth it. While the primer is drying, clean the gun with fresh thinners (5).

g Some primers need to 'cure' as well as dry, and it may be necessary to wait 24 hours before applying the pigment.

h Mix the colour with thinners according to the instructions (usually 40% paint to 60% thinners) and strain it.

i Spray as before, building up the finish slowly and with great care to match the surrounding paintwork (6).

j Clean the gun and leave the paint for a week before polishing it with cutting compound if it lacks gloss.

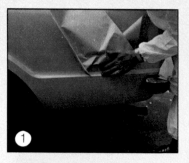

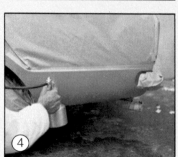

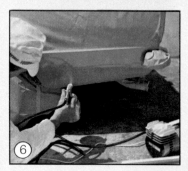

21 BRIGHTEN UP: SHABBY ROAD WHEELS

SUNDAY EVENING
Allow about: 30min per wheel
You need: Wheelbrace and jack; power drill and rotary wire brush; aerosol paint spray; masking tape; newspaper

Painted road wheels collect stone chips and scuffs, and suffer more than most other painted parts of the car. Repainting the wheels every year takes only a short time and can keep the car looking smart—and make it easier to sell when the time comes.
Special aerosols containing enough paint to tackle five wheels are sold specifically for this job. Failing this, you will need one small aerosol per wheel, which will prove much more expensive.
Time should be spent removing rust, dirt and paint flakes before painting, as this will make the job more permanent.
a Inspect the wheels for damage. Cracked steel wheels must be replaced.
b Remove each wheel in turn and using the wire brush, clean off the rust and loose paint (1) to achieve a smooth surface.
c Leaving the rim exposed, tape sheets of newspaper around the wheel (2).
d Lean the wheel against a wall and give it three light coats of paint (3).
e Allow the paint to dry thoroughly before refitting the wheel to the car (4).

22 TRACE AND CURE: A WATER LEAK

SATURDAY
Allow about: A full day
You need: Hose jet and sprinkler; impact adhesive; mastic-type sealant; stiff wire; talcum powder; if necessary, hair dryer

Water will not cause a car to rust unless it can collect in one spot. If, for example, it can find its way into the passenger compartment it can soak into the carpet, causing mildew and a rusted floor pan. But finding where the water comes in, and there are numerous places where it can, is often more difficult than stopping the rot.

Start by poking out the drain holes in the doors and the heater-intake area, and examine door seals for damage.

The next move is to remove the wet carpets—it may be necessary to remove the seats first—and then give the car a good drenching.

One way to achieve this is to replace the seats and head for the nearest car-wash with a helper. As the water pours over the car take note of where it comes in.

You can, of course, always check for interior leaks when the car is cleaned.

a Pour water on to the outside of the closed window. It should come out through the drain holes straightaway (1).

b Water is normally kept off the inside of the door trim by a sheet of plastic (2). Water will seep through this if it is ruptured.

c The plastic sheet can be repaired by sticking on a patch

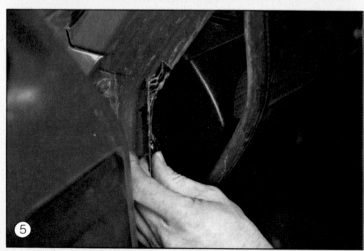

cut from a polythene bag (3).
d If a fibreboard trim panel is distorted by water it can probably be straightened. Wipe the back of the board with a wet cloth and, using weights to press it flat, leave it to dry thoroughly.
e Refit loose door and window seals, first cleaning and drying the seating slot (4). (Wet surfaces can be best dried using a hair dryer.)

f Use mastic sealant or impact adhesive to secure the seal (5).
g If the seals still leak, the source can often be traced by using talcum powder (6). It may be that the only course of action is to renew the complete seal.
h If you suspect that there is a leak in the floor, ask a helper to watch inside while you hose water all over the underside of the car and into the wheel arches.

23 RENEW: ENGINE MOUNTINGS

SUNDAY MORNING
Allow about: 1hr
You need: Trolley or bottle jack; spanners to undo mounting bolts; screwdriver, pliers or spanners to undo hose clips and remove radiator or fan fixings; new engine mounting; packing wood

Rubber engine mountings prevent vibrations from reaching the body. If these are damaged either by leaking oil or old age the engine will be able to rock excessively, causing severe juddering when the clutch is engaged.

a Place the jack under the engine sump, spreading the load by using a piece of wood at least 1in thick and measuring about 9in×6in.
b Operate the jack until it is supporting the engine (1).
c Remove the fixing bolts from the damaged mounting (2).
d Jack up the engine very gently.
! On some cars it may be safer to drain the cooling system and remove the hoses to avoid overstretching them.
!! In rare cases it may also be necessary to remove the radiator or fan to prevent damage.
e Replace the defective mounting, screwing the nuts and bolts up finger-tight.
f Lower the engine very slowly. When the strain is being fully taken by the mounting, tighten all the fixings.

24 RENEW: A BOLT-ON FRONT WING

SATURDAY MORNING
Allow about: 4hr
You need: Penetrating oil, spanners and screwdrivers to remove bumper, wing and light fixtures; blunt knife; wire brush; rat-tail file (if necessary); nut splitter; new wing and set of bolts; rust preventive; mastic sealant; paint; cloth

Increasing numbers of modern cars are being built with bolt-on front wings for ease of repair. If a wing is badly damaged in an accident or has rusted beyond the filler and aerosol stage, it can be unbolted and replaced quite easily.

However, if the car's wings are welded on, replacement is a job for a body-shop.

The bolt heads are usually visible once the bonnet is lifted but concealed bolts also attach the wing to the door pillar and to the body under the headlamp. Some bolts are mounted horizontally and can be seen from inside the wheel arch.

a Wire brush the bolts clean and keep them well soaked with penetrating oil for at least three days before starting work. Bumper fixings, too, can rust so give them a similar dose of oil. The new wing will come ready primed but do not be fooled by the manufacturer's quick blow-over. Immediately the wing is fitted it should be re-primed and painted.

b Disconnect the battery and the wiring to the light fittings. Wiring connectors should be located under the wing or inside the engine bay.

c Remove any trim strips and take off the bumper (1).

d Remove the light units—side, head and indicators (2).

e Loosen the wing screws and bolts (3). This can be a two-man job. Seized nuts are best tackled with a nut splitter but you may have to drill them out.

f Gently separate the wing from the body, first making sure that all the fixings have been properly removed (4).

g Clean up all the flanges to which the wing is bolted, using a blunt knife and a wire brush. Paint on a generous coat of rust preventive (5).

h Prime and paint the flanges. When the paint is dry, offer up the new wing and bolt it in place. It may be necessary to elongate some of the holes with the rat-tail file (6).

i Remove the wing again and coat the body flanges with mastic sealant (7).

j Refit the wing and tighten all the bolts evenly, then wipe away left-over sealant (8).

k Prime and paint the new wing (see page 198).

l Refit the bumper and light fittings.

m Re-align the headlamp (see page 227).

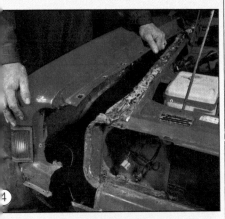

---

25 CLEAN: A BOWL-TYPE OIL FILTER

SUNDAY AFTERNOON
Allow about: 20min
You need: Spanner; sharp skewer or similar pointed instrument; mirror, if necessary; waste oil container; paraffin; cleaning rag; new filter element

This can be a messy job on some cars, so be warned.

a Place a tray under the filter to catch spilt oil and loosen the securing bolt. This will be at the base of the bowl (1) or on top of the filter housing.

b Remove the bowl (2), noting the arrangement of any springs or washers on the centre bolt.

c Locate the sealing ring in the filter housing and ease it out with a skewer or a thin spike (3).

d Clean out the groove and insert the new rubber ring, taking care not to twist it. A mirror and a torch may help you to check on this if access is awkward.

e Clean the filter bowl thoroughly in paraffin; dry it and insert the new element (4).

f Hold the bowl against the sealing ring and tighten the fixing bolt, first by hand and then by spanner. Do not overtighten.

g Fill the sump to the correct level, run the engine and check for leaks. These are most likely to be due to a loose fixing bolt or a poorly fitted sealing ring.

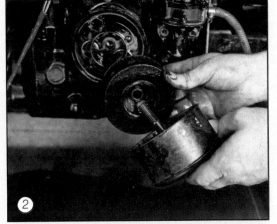

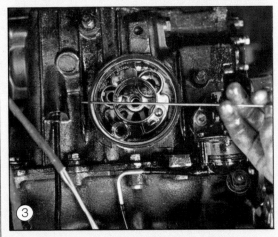

26 FIT: A CHILD SAFETY SEAT

SATURDAY AFTERNOON
Allow about: 3hr
You need: Screwdriver to undo rear seat mounting screws; drill and suitable bits; centre punch; spanners or sockets to fit mounting nuts and bolts; safety seat with fixing kit

A child safety seat must be mounted to suitably strong sections of a steel-bodied car or to the steel framework of a glass-fibre-bodied car. In an accident, the tremendous deceleration forces can increase a child's weight many times over and a badly mounted seat—simply hooked over the seat back, for example—would be useless.

If the rear shelf is made of fibreboard or plastic, as on modern hatchbacks, the seat-retaining straps must clear it so that they can be fastened to the boot floor. The straps should also be secured as far behind the back of the seat as possible. Check first with your car handbook as many modern cars have threaded attachment holes for rear seat belts and these are ideal for your purpose.

For cars with a fixed back seat proceed as follows:

a Undo the screws securing the seat cushion and lift it out (1).

b Undo the screws holding the bottom of the seat backrest, unhook it from the parcel shelf and take it out (2).

c Locate the rear seat belt mounting holes that you intend to use and remove the plastic plugs or blanking plates (3).

d Bolt the two lower fixing straps to the belt-mounting holes (4).

! If there are no holes they will need to be drilled.

Before drilling, look behind the panel to be sure that you will not hit anything vital, such as the fuel tank and brake pipes.

!! Drill a pilot hole with a small bit and then follow through with the recommended larger one. Screw on the anchorages using the recommended spacers and washers while a helper holds the head of the bolt.

e If the slope of the rear window makes it impossible to drill down through the parcel shelf—and you do not have a flexible drill-drive—drill up from the boot (5). Again, drill a small guide hole first.

f From inside the car, fit the anchor bolts with the necessary washers and spacers (6).

g Thread a large washer and nut (7) on to the bolt protruding into the boot and tighten the nut fully, with a helper holding the bolt.

h Refit the seat, ensuring that the lower mounting straps are not trapped.

i Connect the straps to the seat and adjust them as tightly as possible (8).

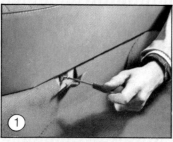

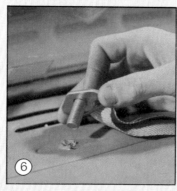

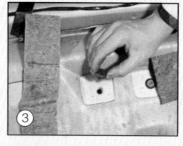

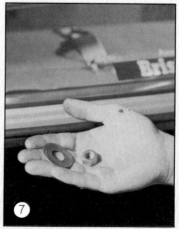

27 ADD: A REAR WINDOW WIPER AND WASHER

SUNDAY AFTERNOON
Allow about: 4hr
You need: Screwdrivers to fit pump-fixing screws and battery connections; drill and bits; rat-tail file; pliers; test lamp; 3ft of stiff wire; rear wash/wipe kit; insulating tape

Most modern hatchbacks and estate cars have rear wash/wipe equipment as standard. This is a necessity rather than a luxury on some cars as their body design creates a vortex at the back which sucks road spray on to the window.

Ensure that the kit you buy is suitable for your car. A front-mounted pump must be powerful enough to push water through a very long pipe. Some kits will provide a separate rear-mounted reservoir.

a Remove the trim panel from the tailgate.

b Rear wiper kits contain a template to ensure correct drilling of the motor spindle hole. Drill a pilot hole and enlarge it, if necessary, using the rat-tail file (1).

c Remove the template and thread the motor shaft through the hole (2), securing the assembly with the appropriate washers, nuts and seals.

d Find an ignition-controlled supply using a test lamp and then disconnect the battery.

e Connect the two-position switch (3). The picture shows a short cable making a suitable connection with a nearby switch.

f Wire the wiper and washer motors to the remaining switch terminals and fit the switch into the facia (4).

g Fix the washer motor close to the reservoir (5).

h Drill the top of the reservoir and insert the feed pipe (6). Secure it with a rubber grommet and connect the other end to the motor inlet stub.

i Connect the wires to the pump (the switch wire goes to the positive motor terminal and the other one goes to earth).

j Route the wiper motor wire and the long plastic pipe through to the back of the car, under the carpet. If possible, tape them to the wiring loom.
Check that the pipe is not going to be damaged or kinked.

k Both pipe and wire can be threaded up inside the rear pillar to the hinge (7). Drill an exit hole and pull them through using a piece of bent wire. Tape the exposed pipe and wire with plastic insulating tape and thread on a rubber grommet.

l Repeat the procedure with the tailgate, making sure that it can be opened and closed without fouling the wire and pipe.

m Connect the wire to the live terminal of the motor. If necessary, earth the motor to a self-tapping screw on the tailgate shell (8).

n Drill a hole and fit the jet, then join a short tube to it with a non-return valve at the end. The valve operation can be checked by sucking on the end (9).

o Connect the tube from the pump to the valve (10).

p Reconnect the battery, switch on the ignition and operate the wiper to test. If the motor is not self-parking, fit the arm and blade when the spindle is at the end of one arc.

q Top up the reservoir with water and direct the jet at the centre of the wiped area.

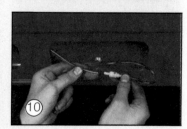

28 RENEW: A MECHANICAL FUEL PUMP

SATURDAY MORNING
Allow about: 1hr
You need: Spanners and screwdriver; new pump and gaskets; scraper and sharpened pencil

If fuel is not reaching the carburettor the fuel pump may have failed. Disconnect the fuel inlet pipe at the carburettor and operate the starter. If no fuel comes out there may be a blockage that can be cleared by blowing air through the system. If the pump is faulty, change it as follows:

a Disconnect the battery.
b Remove the fuel pipes from the pump, plugging the inlet pipe with the point of a pencil (1).

c Unbolt the pump (2). If it is rod-operated, pull out the rod.
d Withdraw the pump (3) and scrape any remains of old gasket from the pump mounting, taking care not to damage any of the spacer surface. Fit new gaskets.
e Fit the new pump, ensuring that the operating lever fits over the camshaft.
f Screw up the fixings finger-tight and, while the pump is loose, push it towards the block. The spring inside should push it back. If this happens, tighten the nuts. No resistance indicates that the pump lever is underneath the camshaft, in which case remove the pump and refit.
! If the pump is push-rod operated, fit the rod and pump using new gaskets, ignoring **f**.
g Refit the fuel pipes, reconnect the battery, run the engine and check for leaks.

29 FIT: A NEW STEERING BALL-JOINT

SUNDAY MORNING
Allow about: 1hr
You need: Wheelbrace; jack; axle stands; chocks; wire brush; pliers; spanners to fit ball-joint nuts; taper-breaking tool; hammer; self-grip wrench; lever; new ball-joint assembly; penetrating oil

If the steering suffers from excessive play, it may be that a ball-joint is worn out. Garage equipment is needed to measure the exact amount of play, but renewing ball-joints is a straightforward DIY job.
Do not economise on steering parts—buy only those approved by the manufacturer.
Ball-joints are protected by a rubber seal and trouble starts if this becomes damaged. Water and dirt get in, causing rusting and wear.
You can test a ball-joint for wear by placing a hand on the joint

while a helper turns the steering wheel back and forth. A damaged ball-joint can be felt by gripping it in the hand and with the aid of a torch, may possibly be seen, too.
The new joint will probably come with a new self-locking nut on the end of the tapered pin. If this nut is not included you should buy one.
a Chock the rear wheels and raise the front of the car on a jack. Remove the road wheel and fit an axle stand.
b Wire-brush the threads above the ball-pin nut and find a spanner of the correct size.

c Remove the nut (1), saving any washer underneath for use with the new joint.
d Fit the taper-breaking tool between the top of the ball-pin and the underside of the steering arm and tighten the bolt (2) until the pin drops.
e If the pin is really stubborn, tap the head of the taper-breaker bolt with a hammer once or twice. Do not attempt to hit the ball joint's connecting bolt thread with a hammer.
f Disconnect the joint (3) from the track-rod after loosening the locknut. Remember that the left-hand ball-joint will

have a left-hand thread.
g Prevent the track-rod from rotating by use of a self-grip wrench. Unscrew the joint (4), counting the number of turns to remove it.
h Fit the new ball-joint to the rod using the same number of turns, then tighten the locknut.
i Fit the tapered pin into the housing and replace the ball-joint washer and nut while holding the pin firmly in position with a lever (5).
Modern ball-joints are sealed for life so do not try to add grease.
j Lower the car and have the wheel alignment checked.

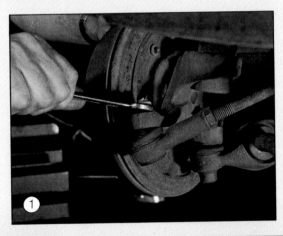

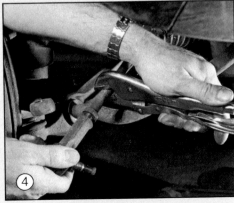

30 ADD: A REAR WINDOW HEATER

SUNDAY AFTERNOON
Allow about: 2hr
You need: Drill and small bits; screwdriver; pliers; spanners; heated rear window kit; clean cloth and, if necessary, a relay; a hair dryer

A heated rear window is regarded by most drivers as a necessity rather than a luxury. It is hard to find even a new basic model without one, but there are many older cars that can be made safer to drive by having DIY heating elements fitted.

Remember that the device consumes a lot of current, so if it is to be wired through an ignition-controlled circuit, it may be necessary to include a relay in the circuit to prevent the ignition switch from being overloaded.

a Check the best position for the heater by taping it to the outside of the window and looking in the rear view mirror. Mark the position with tape (1).

b Clean the inside of the back window with a dry cloth. If necessary, use a hair dryer to remove every trace of moisture from the glass (2).

c Place the heater on a flat surface and remove the backing paper (3). Cut the paper in half, then replace it leaving a 2in gap down the middle.

d Place the heater on the back window and peel off the protective paper (4), while pressing the element against the glass with your palms.

e Fit the illuminated switch to a convenient place on the car facia, and then identify an ignition-controlled feed by using a test lamp.

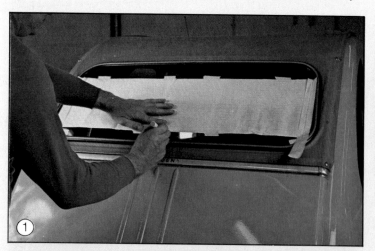

f Disconnect the battery and with a splice connector, join an additional wire to the chosen ignition-controlled cable. Next connect the other end of the extra wire to the switch.

g Earth the switch to the car body and route a wire from the switch output to the rear parcel shelf.

h Remove the adhesive strips from the lead-out wires on the element and press them firmly on to the screen. Connect one to the cable from the switch or relay, and earth the other using a short piece of cable and a self-tapping screw.

i Re-connect the battery and switch on the heater, carefully smoothing out the element as it warms up. Peel off the backing after 10 minutes (5) and switch off.

j As it is cooling, press the element on to the glass with your thumbs.

Leave the adhesive to set for at least two or three days before cleaning the glass.

31 FIT: MUDFLAPS

SATURDAY EVENING
Allow about: 1hr per pair
You need: Sharp knife; stiff brush; spanners or screwdriver to tighten clamps; drill and bit (if using self-tapping screws); mudflap kit

Mudflaps protect the lower bodywork from flying stones, but metal to metal contact at the fixing points can lead to corrosion. Flaps with plastic inserts are now available to prevent this.

Considerable time can be saved by buying flaps from a dealer specialising in your make of car, but these will probably be more expensive than the universal type generally available from accessory shops.

This job covers fitting the universal type (see right).

a Clean up the wheel arch flanges with a stiff brush.

b Align the mudflaps, enlisting a helper to stand behind the car. When the first flap is in position, mark the outline of the edge of the wheel-arch flange on to the rubber.

c Carefully cut away the surplus rubber, then use the cut flap as a template to cut the other flap (1). Remember that the flaps are handed—one left, one right.

d Clamp the mudflap securely to the wheel arch flange (2).

! If the clamps are not suitable for use on your particular car, the flaps will have to be held in place by two or three self-tapping screws. Ensure that the flap is correctly aligned before drilling the mounting holes.

!! If the shape of the wheel arch skews the mudflap, use the small wedges in the kit to straighten it. These should be packed between the wheel arch and the flap. If there are no wedges in the kit, use offcuts from the rubber that you have cut away from the flaps.

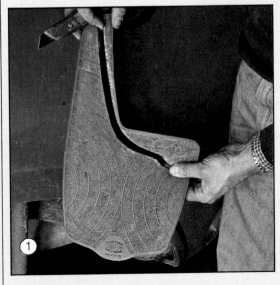

INDEX

A

AA vehicle inspection	239
Accelerator pump	22-23 275 282 284
Accessories	110-115 206-207 232 244-259 299 311
Accident safety	3 144-145 194-195
Ackermann steering	154
Additives, oil	30-31 285
Adjuster, brake	168
Aerial	246 264-265 267-268
Aerosol spray painting	198-199 305
Air cleaner/filter	26-28 34 277 280 282 291
Air conditioning	221
Air-cooled engine	9 14 68 82-83 220
Air flow	212-216 221
Air/fuel mixture	8-10 18-19 22-27 94-95 278 281-282 284-285
Air intake valves	28
Air lock	75 84 216-218
Air-regulating screw	26-27
Alignment of propeller shaft	56
Alignment of wheels	154-157
Alternator	101-106 257
Ammeter	110 250 258-259
Amps	107 110
Annulus	51-53
Anti-corrosion treatment	196-197 201-202
Anti-dieselling valves	23
Anti-freeze	69 72-73 82-83 207
Anti-roll bar	120 124 137-138
Aquaplaning	182
Armature	101-102 106-108 253 283 294
Aspect ratio	181
Audio	262-269
Automatic advance systems	94-95
Automatic choke	23-25 280-281
Automatic ignition timing	94-95
Automatic transmission	50-54 59 65 272 283-284
Axle wind-up	126-127 138

B

Backplate	160-161 168
Backrest	296
Balancing wheels	156 186
Ballast resistor	94-95 273 279
Ball-joint, steering	142-143 145 148 157 302 313
Ball-joint, suspension	123
Battery	3 88-91 258-259 272-273 283-284
Battery charging	91 272-273 283-284
Battery condition indicator	110
Baulking mechanism	39 64
Bearings	30-31 62-63 65 76 276 285
Bell-housing	42 44-45 59 64
Bellows thermostat	77
Bendix pinion gear	283
Bias-belted tyres	179 183
Big end	31 35
Bi-metallic spring/strip	23 28 83 109-110
Birfield constant-velocity joint	56-59
Bleeding a hydraulic clutch mechanism	47
Bleed valves	84 165
Blockage in heating system	218-219 221
Blown cylinder-head gasket	34 276-277 280 285
BL suspension systems	130 132-133 137 240
Body roll	123-124 128-129 137-138
Bodywork	190-209
Bolt-on front wing	308-309
Bonnet	208-209
Boot lid	208
Bores	8-9 35
Bowl-type oil filter	30-32 309
Brakes	158-175 230-231
Brake adjuster	168
Brake failure	160 170-171
Brake fluid	160 164-165 168-170 172-173
Brake lights	115 227
Brake testing	231

Braking distance	231
Braking in wet weather	182
Brush, distributor cap	94-95
Brushes, generator	102 284
Brushes, starter motor	107 284 294-295
Bulbs	114-115 300
Burst coolant hose	72-73 83 85
Buying a used car	236-243
By-pass hose	71 80
By-pass oil system	30

C

Cables, electric	112-113 247 250-259 273-274 276-279 282
Cables, handbrake	174-175 230
Calipers	160 162-167 174
Cam-and-peg steering	146-149 157
Camber angle	123 128 155
Camshaft	15-18 31 285
Capacitor, ignition	92 273 279 301
Capacitor, suppression	268-269
Caravans	52 256
Carburettor	22-29 34 274-275 277 280-282 284
Car sales	236-243
Cartridge oil filter	30-32
Cassette player	262-263
Castor angle	155
Changing spark plugs	20-21 101
Changing a wheel	189
Child safety seat	310
Chipped paintwork	197
Choke, carburettor	22-27 34 274-275 280-281
Choke, electrical	269
Choosing a car	236-243
Circuit-testing lamp	96 98 273 278-280 282
Citroen power brakes	172
Citroen suspension system	131 134
Clearances, valve	16-17 285 291
Close-ratio gears	40
Clutch	42-49 52-54 64-65
Coil, ignition	18 92-95 257 268-269 278-279 285
Coil springs	120-121 123-125 128-129 134 137
Coil-spring clutch	43
Cold starting	24 28-29 68-69 81
Combustion chamber	12-13 15 18-19 34-35 285
Commutator	102 106-107 294
Components, electrical	108-115
Compound carburettor	26-27
Compression ratio	12
Compression rings	8-9 34-35
Compression stroke	10-11
Condenser	301
Connecting rods	14 30-31 285
Connections, electrical	250-259 262-265
Connectors, spark plug	278
Connectors, wiring	252-253
Constant fuel/air ratio	22-23
Constant-mesh gearbox	38-39

Constant-velocity joint	55-59 65
Contact-breaker points	18 92-99 273 275 278-279 303
Control box, generator	106
Cooling fan	68 78-80 82-85 283
Cooling system	9 34 66-85 276 280 282-283
Cornering	137-138 142 181 186
Corrosion	69 82 90-91 132-133 137 156 192 196-197 200-203 229-230 232-233 240-241 284
Couplings and joints	55-58 65 123 128-129 142-145 148-149 156-157
Cowling	221
Crankcase and crankshaft	8-11 14 16 30-31 38 279
Crankcase fumes/ventilation	31 282 289
'Crash' gearbox	39
Crash test	194
Cross-ply tyres	179 181-183 231
Crownwheel and pinion	60-61
Cubic capacity	9
Curing faults	278
Cut-out, dynamo	106
Cutting compound	197 199 304
CVT system, Daf/Volvo	54
Cylinder block	8-9 14 31
Cylinder head	8-9 14-15 31 34 276-277 280 284-285
Cylinders, brake	160-161 169 172
Cylinders, engine	8-15 22-23 25 34-35 272 284-285

D

Damper, carburettor	24
Dampers, suspension	118 120-126 129-130 132 134-139
Dashpot	27
Dead beam rear suspension	129
Dealers	236 238-239
Decelerometer	231
Decoke	285
De Dion rear suspension	129 134
Demister	216
Denovo tyres	179
Dents	193 204-205
Diagonal-split braking system	171
Diagrams, wiring	113 250-251
Diaphragm clutch/spring	42
Diesel engine	12-13
Differential	60-63 65 128
Diodes	103 106
Dipped headlamp beam	114 227
Direct-acting overhead camshaft	16-17
Direct drive gearbox	38-41
Direction indicators	114-115 227
Disc brakes	160 162-167 169 174
Disconnecting joint	144
Discount on used car	239
Distributor	18 92-96 98-100 273 276-280 285 301
Dog-clutch	38-39
Doors	194 208-209 290 306-307
Double de-clutch	39

Double-skinned panels 247
Double-wishbone suspension 123
Doughnut joint 57-58
Draining the cooling system 74 283
Drain plugs 32
Drilling holes 247-249
Drive belts 54 101-104 152 285
Driven plate 42-43
Drive shafts 55-57 65 123 156
Drum brakes 160-161 168-170 174
Drum-type starter motor brushes 294-295
Dual-braking 160 170-171
Dunlop Denovo tyres 179
Dwell angle/meter 92 96 98
Dynamic timing 96-99
Dynamo 101-102 104-106 257

E

Earthing 88 246 257 265 284
Economy, fuel 39 48 303
Electrical accessories/components
108-115 246-247 250-259 262-269
Electrics 86-115 273-280 283-284
Electric cars 8
Electric current 250-251
Electric fan 79 84-85 276 283
Electric fuel pump 28 34-35 274 280
282 293
Electric test lamp 96 98 273 278-280 282
Electric wiring 112-113 250-259 262-267
273-274 276-279 282
Electrodes, spark plug 18-21 92-93
100 278
Electrolyte 88-91
Electromagnetically-coupled fan 79
Electronic fuel injection 29
Electronic ignition 94 303
Electronic rectifier 103
Electrophoresis, painting by 196
Emission control 10-11 23 31 289
Emission-type carburettor 25
Emulsion tube 22
Engine 7-35 272-283 307
Engine noises 12 34-35 241 276 284-285
Engine oil 9 30-35 68 285
Engine revolution indicator (tachometer)
96 100 108
Engine temperature 28-29 68 71 77-79
81-85
Epicyclic gears 51-53
Exhaust leaks 33 35 233
Exhaust manifold 16 31 292
Exhaust stroke 10-11 15
Exhaust valves 14-17 31
Externally-adjusted valves (OHC) 17

F

Fail-safe hydraulic braking systems
160-161 170-171
Fail-safe power-assisted steering 151
Fan belt 35 76 78-80 84-85 103-105 276
283-285

Fault finding 64-65 85 136-139 156-157
272-285
Fault finding charts 272-277
Feeler gauge 16 20-21 96-98 100 279
Fibre filler 202-203
Field windings 106-107 257 294
Filter, air 26 28 34 282 291
Filter, fuel 26 29 281
Filter, fuel pump 29 295
Filter, oil 30-34 309
Filter, servo 173
Final drive unit 39 55-57 60 62 65 128-129
Fist-type calipers 166-167
Fixed calipers 162-165
Fixed-jet (fixed-choke) carburettor 22-23
25-27 280-282
Flashing direction indicators 115 227
Flat battery 272 283-284
Flat spot 282 284
Flat tyre 179-181
Float chamber 22 25-26 34 280
Floating calipers 162-164
Flooding, carburettor 34 275 277 280
Fluid, brake 160 164-165 168-170
172-173
Flushing the cooling system 74 283
Flywheel 108-109 283
Fog lights 115 254-256
Footbrake 160-173 230-231
Ford VV carburettor 24-25
Four-piston calipers 171
Four-stroke cycle 10-13 18
Four-wheel drive 48
Franchises 238
Fresh-air heater 214 216
Front/rear split braking system 170
Front suspension system 122-125
130 136
Front-wheel drive 40-41 56 122-123
128-129 154-156 170-171
Front wing, renewing 308-309
Fuel/air mixture 8-10 18-19 22-27 94-95
278 281-282 284-285
Fuel filter 26 29 281
Fuel flooding from carburettor 34 275
277 280
Fuel gauge 34 110 280
Fuel grading 35 276 281 284-285
Fuel injection 29
Fuel leak 34-35 280
Fuel pump 12 28-29 34-35 274 280-282
293 295 312
Fuel savings 39 48 303
Fuel tank 3 28-29 274 280 285
Full-flow oil filter system 30
Full-flow ventilation system 214
Furnishing, interior 241
Fuses 113 255-257

G

Gaiter, steering rack 147-148 302
Gapping tool 20 100
Gaskets 16 19 34 72 80-81 83 276-278
280 282 284-285 292 295 312

Gas springs 130-131
Gearbox 38-65
Gear-type oil pump 30
Gear ratio 40
Generator 91-92 101-106 110 250
258-259 284
Geometry, steering 142 154-155 171
Glass reinforced plastic (GRP)
192-193 202-203
Grease nipples 76 134 148
Grommets 255-257
Guarantees 238

H

Halogen bulbs 114 300
Handbrake 160 174-175 230-231
Header tank 276 283
Headlamps 114 227 300-301
Heating and ventilation 85 210-221 282
314-315
High-tension cables 100-101
High-tension current 94-95 278
Hinged components 208-209
Holes, drilling 246-249
Holes, patching 33 202-203
Home servicing 288-315
Hooke-type universal joint 55-58
Horn 113 233
Hoses 69-77 80 83-85 152-153
216-219 289
Hotchkiss drive 126
HT (high-tension) cables 100-101
HT (high-tension) current 94-95 278
Hubs 62 189
Hydragas suspension system 130-131
137 240
Hydraulic brakes 160-175 230
Hydraulic clutch 42-43 46-47
Hydraulic dampers 121
Hydrolastic suspension system 130
132-133 137 240
Hydrometer 90
Hydropneumatic suspension 131 134
Hypoid gear oil 62-63

I

Ignition-controlled circuit 250 263
311 314
Ignition system 18-21 23 34-35 92-101
268-269 273-280 283-285 303
Ignition warning light 85 283
Impedance 266
Impeller 50-51 79
In-car audio 262-269
Independent suspension 122-125
128-131
Indicators 114-115 227
Indirect drive gearbox 40-41
Indirect overhead camshaft 17
Induction manifold 16 22 24 94-95
172-173 274-275 277 280 282 284
Induction stroke 10-11

Inertia starter motor/pinion 108 293 298
Inertia valve 172
Inhibitors, corrosion 82
Inhibitor switch 52 65 283
Injection, fuel 29
Inlet manifold 16 22 24 94-95 172-173
274-275 277 280 282 284
Inlet valves 10 12 14-17
in-line engine 14 16
Inspecting the underside 3 132-133
Instruments 108-110
Interference, radio 267-269
Interior furnishing 241

J

Jaguar independent rear suspension 129
Joints 55-58 65 123 128-129 142-145
148-149 156-157
Juddering 126 138-139 156 288
Jump leads 272 284

K

Kickdown switch 52
King lead 94-95 278
Kingpin 142-143
Knocking noise 35 276 285
Knock-on nuts 189

L

Laminated windscreen 195
Layshaft 38
Leading-and-trailing shoes 160-161 168
170
Leaf springs 94-95 119 126 132-133
137-139
Leaking coolant 72-73 85 282
Leaking door seals 208 306-307
Leaking exhaust 33 35 292
Leaking fuel 34-35
Leaking gasket 34 72 283-284 292
Leaking oil 44-45 58 62 64 307
Leaking radiator 85
Leaking steering pump reservoir 157
Leaking tyre valve 188
Leaking water pump 80
Legal safeguards on car sales 243
Lever dampers 122-123 136-137
Lighting 114-115 226-227 250 254-256
Limited-slip differential 60-61
Linings, brake 162 164-165 168 230
Linkages, clutch 42-43 45 64
Linkages, handbrake 160-161 174-175
Linkages, steering 142-151 154-157
Linked suspension systems 129-131
Loads and speed 183
Load-sensing valve 172
Locking collar 39
Lock-up, rear wheel 171-172
L-split braking system 171
Lubrication, engine 9 30-35 68

Lubrication, generator 105
Lubrication, hinged components 209
Lubrication, steering 145 148-149 157
Lubrication, suspension 119 134
Lubrication, transmission 44 52-53 64
Lubrication, water pump 76 285

M

MacPherson strut 122 124-125 133 142
Manifolds 16-17 22 24 31 94-95 172-173 274-275 277 280 282 284-285 292
Manual gearbox 38-41 44 48-49 64
Masking paintwork 198-199 304-305
Master cylinder, brake 160 169-170
Master cylinder, hydraulic clutch 43
Mechanical fuel injection 29
Mechanical fuel pump 28-29 280 282 295 312
Mechanical ignition advance 94-95
Mirrors 194 246
Mixing tyres 183 231
Motorways 183
MOT testing 222-233
Mountings 192
Mountings, engine 64 307
Mountings, gearbox 44 64
Mountings, generator 104-105
Mudflaps 315
Mudguards 247
Multi-cylinder engines 9-11 14-15
Multiple-choke carburettors 25
Music on the move 260-269

N

Needle valve 24-26 34 280
Noises 12 34-35 64-65 118 139 157 267-268 276 284-285
Non-sealed cooling system 71

O

Octane rating 35 276 281 284-285
Odometer 108
Ohms 266
Oil, engine 9 30-35 68 285 309
Oil in water 34
Oil, transmission 44 52-53 64
Overdrive 39 48-49
Overhead camshaft 15-17 291
Oversteer 181

P

Pads, disc brake 162-167 174
Paintwork 196-203 240-241 304-305
Panelwork 192-205 208-209
Panhard rod 127
Parking brake 160 174-175 230-231
Park position 52 283
Part exchange 239
Patching holes 33 202-203
Patching underbody sealant 202
Pedal, clutch 42-43 45 64-65
Petrol/air mixture 8-10 18-19 22-27 94-95 278 281-282 284-285
Petrol-burning heater 220
Petrol filter 26 29 281
Petrol flooding from carburettor 34 275 277 280
Petrol gauge 34 110 280
Petrol grading 35 276 281 284-285
Petrol injection 29
Petrol leak 34-35 280
Petrol pump 12 28-29 34-35 274 280-282 293 295 312
Petrol savings 39 48 303
Petrol tank 3 28-29 274 280 285
Pinion, starter motor 108-109 272 283 298
Pinking 35 276 284-285
Pistons, brake 162-163 165 169-174
Piston, carburettor 275 280 282
Pistons, engine 8-15 34-35
Piston rings 8-9 34-35
Piston slap 35 285
Planetary gears 48-49 51
Planet carrier 51-53
Plenum chamber 214-216
Plugs 18-21 34 92-95 100-101 273-275 277-279 285 301
Ply rating 178
Points 18 92-99 273 275 278-279 303
Polarity 88 246 257
Positive crankcase ventilation 31 281-282 289
Power-assisted steering 142 150-152 157 228 285
Power braking 172
Power stroke 10-11
Power and torque 38-39
Pre-engaged starter motor 108-109 293
Pressure cap, radiator 34 71 75 85 282-283
Pressure gauge, oil 34
Pressure-limiting valve 171-172
Pressure plate, clutch 42-43
Pressure-relief valves 31

Pressure, tyre 157 182-183 188 231
Primary windings 92
Primer, paint 196-199 304
Private buying 241
Propeller shaft 48 54-56 58 60 65
Pulleys, generator 101-105
Pulleys, transmission 54
Pump, accelerator 22-23 275 282 284
Pump, oil 30-31 52-53
Pump, petrol 12 28-29 34-35 274 280-282 293 295 312
Pump, power-assisted steering 150-152 157 285
Pump, screenwasher 112 232 299 311
Pump, water 35 69-71 76-77 80 85 283 285
Pushrod and rocker 15-17 31

Q

Quartz-halogen bulbs 114-115 300

R

Rack-and-pinion steering 142-143 145 147-148 150-151 156-157 228 302
Radial-ply tyres 178-183 186 231
Radiator 34 68-85 280 282-283
Radiator, heater 212-214 216-219
Radio fittings 246-249 262-269
Radius arms/rods 127-128
Ratio, compression 12
Ratios, gear 40 48 50 52 60-61
Rear engine 40 56 218
Rear lights 114-115 226 254-256
Rear reflectors 227
Rear suspension system 126-131 138-139
Rear wheel lock-up 171-172
Rear window accessories 112 311 314-315
Recirculating-ball steering 146
Recirculating heater 212
Rectifier, alternator 103 106
Reflectors, rear 227
Regulator, voltage 106
Relay, electrical 106 113 250 253 283 314-315

Remoulds and retreads 180
Rev-counter (tachometer) 96 100 108
Reversing lights 115
Ride height 132 137-139
Road test reports 236 238
Rolling radius 40
Roof-rack 157
Rotoflex doughnut joint 57-58
Rotor, alternator 102
Rotor arm 94-95 98-99 273 276-279
Rotor-type oil pump 30
Rover de Dion suspension 129 134
Rubber mountings 44
Rubber springs 130
Rubbing down 198-199 204
Running-in 186
Running-on 23 276 285
Rust 164-166 192 196-197 200-203 229-230 233 240-241

S

Safety 3 194-195
Safety seat, child 310
Safety tyres 179
Salesmen 236 238-239
Salt on roads 201
Scratched paintwork 197
Screenwasher 111-112 207 232 299 311
Sealants, underbody 56 201-202
Sealed-beam headlamps 114-115 301
Sealed cooling system 71
Seat adjustment 209
Seat belts 194 232
Seat upholstery 296-297
Secondary windings 92-93
Second-hand buying 236-243
Self-adjusting drum brakes 160-161
Self-levelling hydropneumatic suspension 131
Self-servo effect 160-161

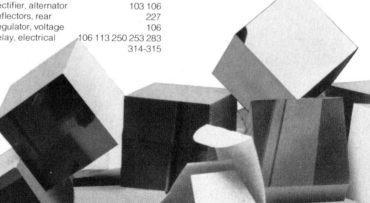

Self-tapping screws 247-249 315
Semi-sealed cooling system 71
Servo 160 172-173 230 282
Shattered windscreen 195
Shims 16-17 104-105 162
Shock absorbers 118 120-126 129-130 132 134-139 194
Shock-absorbing joints 57
Shoes, brake 160-161 168 170
Short-circuit 113 258 273 278-279
Side lights 114-115 226
Silencer 31 35
Single-cylinder calipers 163 166-167
Slave cylinder, hydraulic clutch 43 47
Sliding-caliper disc brakes 163 174
Slip angle 181
Small end 31
Solenoid, electric fuel pump 28
Solenoid, electronic fuel injection 29
Solenoid, starter 107-108 258-259 272 283-284 293
Spark plugs 18-21 34 92-95 100-101 273-275 277-279 285 301
Speakers 262-263 266-267 290
Speedometer 108-109
Speed rating of tyres 186
Spider joint 55 58
Splines 206
Split-circuit braking systems 160 170-171
Spray painting 196 198-199 304-305
Springs 94-95 118-139
Starter motor 107-108 258-259 272-273 283-284 293-296 298
Starting, flat battery 284
Starting from cold 24 28-29 68-69 81
Static timing 96 98-99 279-280
Stator 102
Steady-bar rubber bushes 288
Steering 140-157 228 302 313
Stereo players and speakers 262-263 266-267
Stop lights 227
Stroboscopic timing 96 100
Stromberg-Zenith CD carburettor 24 275 277 280 282 284
Stub axle 123-125 142
Sub-frame 192-193
SU carburettor 24 275 277 280 282 284

Sump 9 30-32 34 283
Sun gear 48-49 51-52
Suppressing radio interference 268-269
Suspension 116-139 142-143 228-229
Swinging-caliper disc brakes 163 174
Switches 84 113 115 194 212 250 253-255 283
Synchromesh 39 64

T

Tachometer 96 100 108
Tailgate 112 208 311
Tail lights 114-115
Tamper-proof carburettor 25-26
Tape player 262-263
Taper-roller bearings 62
Tapley meter 231
Tappets 16-17 276 285
Tapping into wiring 252-253 255
Telescopic dampers 121-126 129 134-135
Temperature, engine 28-29 68 71 77-79 81-85 276 281-285
Temperature gauge 34 70 85 110 282
Tensioning the drive belt 104
'Ten-Twenty' Triplex windscreen 195
Test lamp 96 98 273 278-280 282
Test, MOT 224-233
Thermostat, engine 28 68 71 74 76-77 81 83 85 216 221 283
Thermostatic air intake valve 28
Thinning paint 304
Throttle 22-27 275 281
Throw-out stop 46 64
Timing, ignition 18-19 29 92-93 96-100 275-277 279-280 284-285
Toe-in and toe-out 154-155
Top dead centre 12 92 279
Topping-up automatic gearbox 59
Topping-up battery 90-91
Topping-up brake fluid 170
Topping-up engine oil 32
Topping-up power-assisted steering system 152

Topping-up radiator 75 82
Topping-up transmission oil 44-45 62-63
Torque 38
Torque converter 50 59
Torsion bar 120 137 150-151
Touching-up paintwork 196-197
Toughened glass 195
Towing 52 183
Tow-starting 272 284
Trading-in 239
Trailers 52 256-257
Trailing-arm suspension 128-129
Trailing shoes 160-161 168
Transmission 36-65
Tread, tyre 179-180 182-184 231
Trim 241 290
Triplex windscreen 195
Tubed and tubeless tyres 180-181
Turbine 50
Turret, suspension 124-125 133
Twin-choke carburettor 25-26
Two-leading-shoe drum brakes 160-161 168
Two-stroke engine 10-11 19
Tyres 156-157 176-189 231

U

Underbody sealants 56 201-202
Understeer 181
Universal joints 55-58 65 128-129 142 144 148-149 156-157
Unsprung weight 118 123
Upholstery 296-297
Used car buying 236-243

V

Vacuum ignition advance 94-95 100
Vacuum servo 160 172-173 230 282
Valve clearances 16-17 285 291
Vapour lock 65 285
Variable-jet (variable-choke) carburettor 24-25 27 275 280-282 284
Variable-Venturi carburettor 24-25
Vehicle testing, MOT 224-233
Ventilation, car 212-216 221
Ventilation, crankcase 31 282 289
Venturi 22-25 284
Vibration 12-13 56 64-65 118 151 186

Viscosity, oil 30
Viscosity, paint 304
Viscous-coupled fan 79
Voltage 88 92-95
Voltage regulator 106 284
Voltage stabiliser 110
Voltmeter 110
Volume-control screw 281-282
V-shaped block 14 16
VV carburettor 24-25

W

Wankel engine 13
Warning light, ignition 85 283
Warning light, oil 34
Warning light, rear fog lamp 254-255
Washer, windscreen/rear window 111-112 207 232 299 311
Water cooling system 9 68-85 212 218
Water in cylinders 272 278 284
Water in fuel 273-274 276-278 280
Water in oil 34 283
Water leaks 72-73 80 85 208 282-284 306-307
Water pump 35 69-71 76-77 80 85 283 285
Watts 250
Wax-type thermostat 28 77
Weekend workshop 286-315
Wet-or-dry paper 197-199 204-205 304
Wet roads 182
Wheels 228 247 305
Wheel alignment 154-157
Wheel balancing 156 186
Wheel bearings 62-63 228
Wheel changing 189
Wheel cylinders 170
Windings 92-93 101-102 106-107 253 257 273 294-295
Wind noise 208
Windscreen and windows 195 290 306-307 311 314-315
Windscreen wipers and washer 111-112 206-207 232 299
Wing mirrors 246
Wing renewal 308-309
Winter tyres 178 181
Wiring 112-113 250-259 262-267 273-274 276-279 282
Wishbone suspension 123-125 129 132
Worm-and-nut steering 146-147 157

Z

Zenith carburettor 24 275 277 280 282 284
Zone-toughened windscreen 195

The AA is grateful to the following for their help and advice, and in many cases, for supplying material and illustrations for this book:

Associated Tyre Specialists (Southern) Ltd, Borg-Warner Ltd, Champion Sparking Plug Co Ltd, Citroen Cars Ltd, Dunlop Ltd (UK Tyre Group), FD Graphics, Firestone Tyre and Rubber Co (Great Britain) Ltd, Ford Motor Co Ltd, Goodyear Tyre and Rubber Co (Great Britain) Ltd, Lucas Girling Parts and Service, Michelin Tyre Co Ltd, Pirelli Ltd, Outline Arts, SU-Butec Sales and Marketing Centre, Talbot Motor Co Ltd, Triplex Safety Glass Co Ltd, Zenith Carburettor Co Ltd